*Ex libris:* _____

*Date:* _____

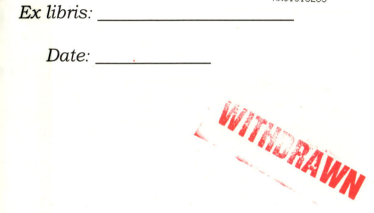

HACKLEY PUBLIC LIBRARY
MUSKEGON, MICHIGAN

# The Road to the Big's

"Baseball is for every boy a good, wholesome sport. It brings him out of the close confinement of the schoolroom. It takes the stoop from his shoulders and puts hard, honest muscle all over his frame. It rests his eyes, strengthens his lungs, and teaches him self-reliance and courage. Every mother ought to rejoice when her boy says he is on the school or college nine."

—Walter Camp, 1889

# The Road to the Big's

An American Journey

By

Gerald A. Barnes

Grateful Acknowledgements

| | |
|---|---|
| Editor: | Susan Whalen |
| Consultants: | John Lockwood |
| | Chris Screen |
| | Mary Alice Wolf |
| Cover Design: | Crissy Will |
| Artwork: | Elizabeth Barnes |
| | Emily Whalen |

# The Road to the Big's

Copyright © 2007 by Gerald A. Barnes

All rights reserved. No part of this publication may be reproduced or transmitted in any form or by any means, electronic or mechanical, including photocopy, recording, or any information storage and retrieval system, without permission in writing from the author and the Norcross Baseball Club, Inc.

ISBN: 1-4196-5938-3

To order additional copies, please contact:
BookSurge, LLC
telephone: 1-866-308-6235
e-mail: orders@booksurge.com

or visit either internet websites:
www.booksurge.com
www.amazon.com

Published in the United States of America

Norcross Baseball Club, Inc.
*"Town Team of Historic Norcross"* [SM]

# Contents

Preface ................................................................. 1

Introduction ........................................................... 2

1. The National Pastime ................................. 5
2. A Historical Bridge ..................................... 21
3. The Hammer and the Southpaw ................ 60
4. Baseball: The Choice is Clear ................... 79
5. Little League – First Year ........................... 92
6. Little League – Second Year ..................... 106
7. Little League – Third Year ........................ 121
8. Pony League Makes a Man ....................... 131
9. Coach Ro .................................................. 138
10. High School Baseball ............................... 151
11. The Game ................................................. 165
12. Junior Varsity ........................................... 183
13. Varsity ...................................................... 197
14. Major League Tryouts .............................. 221
15. Valdosta State University ........................ 248
16. Major League Fields ................................ 262
17. Summer Baseball and Surfing .................. 293
18. College Baseball ...................................... 306
19. It Takes Heart .......................................... 315
20. The Big Leagues of Life .......................... 325

Epilogue ............................................................. 347

# Preface

"My Sword I give to him that shall succeed me in my Pilgrimage, and my Courage and Skill to him that can get it. My marks and scars I carry with me . . ."  John Bunyan

On August 17, 2005, the Dodgers played the Braves at Turner Field in Atlanta, Odalis Perez against Tim Hudson. Braves won 10-2. Good game, good seat, Section 108L, Row 14, Seat 102. Good folks all around. Who's this? Arthur Blanc, one row down and a couple of seats over across the aisle, probably wishing the Falcons were as successful as the Braves. Another beautiful night for baseball.

An hour before game time it was easy to locate a clubhouse attendant near the visitors' dugout. Would the attendant please give this game program to Odalis? Sure. Thanks.

Mr. Perez's brother, Carlos, (we call him Jimmy) had pitched for the Norcross Baseball Club semi-pro team in a special game against the Georgia Cherokees on July 4 in Duluth. With a few leftover programs in the car, it seemed like a good idea to bring one in for Odalis, so he could see what his brother had been up to. The Norcross team was formed to draw public attention to the plight of historic Wingo-Carlyle Field. Many of us had an interest in preserving this particular baseball park.

I had not spoken with Odalis since Thanksgiving, actually the Sunday afterwards. As a healthy, left-handed pitcher, he was once more in the enviable position of being a major league free agent. The difficult part was choosing where to work while deciphering inquiries from eighteen major league teams. For personal reasons, he had hopes of re-signing with the Braves. In fact, he had just bought a new home here, near Atlanta. Before long, the Dodgers grabbed him for a second year.

A few minutes into the game, going to the bottom of the first inning, Odalis came out of the visitors' dugout below and strolled to the mound. From the home dugout on the other side came Rafael Furcal, Atlanta's lead off man. Well, now, this was more than a little bit interesting.

The warm-up tosses over, the throw down and around, the spit, the cap adjustment, the toe on the rubber, Furcal digging in.

"Play!" commands the umpire.

Into his wind-up, I muttered to myself,

"Odalis, if anyone ought to know how to pitch to Furcal . . ."

# Introduction

To say a certain story practically writes itself is an obviation of the creative writing skills ordinarily associated with professional authorship since the lone ability to take notes would suffice. Well, truth be known, the book that writes itself is yet to be written. Truth be served, what is a man to do when imbued with a sense of obligation to take on the task of a scribe and relate a story that has gathered his attention during the simple act of living life? Just do it and not quibble over details, certainly. The office of manhood demands nothing less. Discharge of duty is a compulsion not to be ignored. Otherwise, honor is forfeited, leaving an eternal void, a fate worse than Purgatory.

By even serious reckoning, the telling of a truly compelling story would need only to be orderly and sequential. Here the theme is quite elementary. Every notion is natural. The plot unfurls serenely with an outcome no more surprising than that which follows the four balls of an intentional walk. Yet, unlike the free pass, it contains many more intricacies to excite the imagination. If it were food, it would be palatable and easily digested; if a dream, enchanting; if a heart, completely full; if a soul, simply complete. Of course, in all of God's creation, such a story could only be about one thing: the great game of baseball.

Baseball stories entertain and inspire. For this one in particular, clever writing skills would only be superfluous. As such and so, it shall be written. If this story had been invented, it is doubtful anyone would ever think it could be true. Even knowing it is true, to accept it as such requires a reader to discard logic and deny the intellect. Nevertheless, this journey to the major leagues of baseball yields a story that seems to possess of itself an instinct for self-preservation; a story that seems not to diminish with the passage of time; indeed, a story that seems to have a life of its own. It is a story that could even inspire an ordinary man to write as if he were gifted while not possessing even one drop of artistic ink in his pen.

This story, though less likely than an unassisted triple play, is true. Depicted here are actual events. The source material is mostly contemporaneous notes and records, printed, jotted down, or recorded over many years, left to be rediscovered in scorebooks and yearbooks, league records and association bylaws, newspaper articles and photographs, letters and memos, encyclopedias and films, county deed books and battlefield reports, birth records and headstone inscriptions. This story certainly did not and could not write itself. In fact, it took a small army of contributors over the course of many years. Consequently, it ought to be considered more an assemblage than a creation, having been banded together from many sources, written, spoken, and remembered. Altogether, it makes a story as enjoyable to tell, as it will be to hear.

Many stories from the baseball diamond are similar to this one. They beg words to be recorded for posterity, so that they will live on and never die, all with good reason. Stories about baseball tell of the extraordinary exploits of otherwise ordinary men. Because they may have played some baseball in their youth, men who never earned a footnote in history or ever received their rightful prerogative of fifteen minutes of fame, will have experienced at least a few glorious, self-adulating moments full of human drama. To ask any grown-up American man about his best baseball playing memory as a youngster is to discover how true this can be. Yes, baseball affords the opportunity for every man to be someone special, which, in turn, helps to give the game its universal appeal. The stories about baseball players and their exploits are about who almost every American man is or was or ever could have been. For the very few others, baseball stories can be about someone they have known at one time or another.

The thought of baseball stories having a life of their own may seem a bit peculiar to some. However, this totally valid notion arises from the very nature of the game, the drama and the action, the history and the analysis, the elation and the misery, the hope and the despair. Can these elements be found elsewhere in the human experience? Yes, but not all together in the same splendid way, nor in sufficient quantity, to effect results as grand as in baseball. Add to this the proclivity of baseball fans to devour anything and everything recorded about the game. Whether told in prose or poetry, pictures or paintings, statistics or box scores, without doubt, whatever happens in baseball is always noticed, recorded, remembered, and maybe even embellished a bit when retold, all for good reasons.

Is another book about baseball what the world really needs or wants? The answer to this question is always "yes." Thousands have been written and thousands more are to come. Baseball fans wanting to fill the time between innings and between games can do so by keeping scorecards and reading the sports section of the newspaper. But how about the extended void during the off-season, from the last out of the World Series in late October to the first catch of spring training in early February, when nothing much happens . . . or does it? Never mind that, for now. Many fill this time void by reading books about baseball, therefore, somebody has to write them.

*Chapter One*

# The National Pastime

Baseball is an inextricable part of American life. It is a sporting activity, an entertainment spectacle, and the national pastime. Approaching two hundred years of existence, baseball is the Definitive Symphony of American Culture to which another stirring movement is added each season. It has no peer, no worthy competitor, and no moral equivalent. It transcends all human sporting endeavors. It is the masterpiece of human thought and action combined. Baseball is the greatest game ever conceived by man.

So special is this game, so important, so necessary, that imagining how one could have lived his life before baseball is all but impossible. Thankfully, we do not have to try. For most of us non-professional ballplayers, and for the duration of our earthly existence, our calling as spectators and fans is merely to enjoy the game at whatever level suits us best while exploring its meaning so far as it soothes our perplexed souls.

To begin, consider this metaphysical question: Does baseball contain the essence of the American Spirit or does the American Spirit contain the essence of baseball? The answers are yes and yes. Here is why, as each supposition is a corollary of the other.

The game of baseball began upon the same stage as the formation of the American Republic. If America had not been discovered, would baseball ever have been invented? Probably not. Europeans in Europe, Brits included, would not have done it. However, Europeans transplanted in America were different. In leaving the Old World for the New, most sought a clean slate with which to work. Being less encumbered socially and culturally, they were free to think differently, to form different mindsets. They developed different attitudes and values about virtually everything, not the least of which was the important virtue called self-reliance. To those in the Old World, these migrants may have been seen as foolish or even socially deficient, but, in due course, the new culture they created easily surpassed the one they left behind. A look back at the line-ups and a check of the scouting reports show that those who remained in the Old World never had a chance in this contest. In the heart of their batting order were Rousseau, Voltaire, and Diderot. We had Paine, Jefferson, and Madison. Argument concluded.

Can the differences in thought, in attitude, and in ethical values of American colonists be accounted for by New World circumstances and the accompanying opportunities? Well, yes, they can be. Thomas Jefferson captured the intellectual and motivational essence of this new and expanding culture very well in the *Declaration of Independence*. Every man, not just a privileged few, was endowed with very definable "unalienable rights." Further, these rights were granted by the Creator not to be capriciously tempered by other men.

If a man would have taken leave of the thirteen colonies to tour the entire civilized world during the middle to latter part of the Eighteenth Century, he would have found one nation after another ruled by divinely appointed (or self-appointed) Emperors, Czars, Kings, Queens, Princes, Sultans, Shoguns, etc., where governance proceeded from tribal patterns of human relationships. Jefferson elegantly promulgated the New World idea that legitimate governance only proceeds from notions about human relationships in which each and every man was his own sovereign, an individual first. This was a rather bold contention, directly confrontational to the social and political norms of the Old World, even though in hindsight it seems to have been only the next logical step to follow under the English Common Law. Thus the social and political concepts which the early American colonists, most of whom were English, Scotch-Irish, and German, came to understand by the way they lived their everyday lives, had to have been startling to the Europeans in Europe.

"What! No king? Who will care for us?"

"How about this second baseman-size fellow? What's his name? Bonaparte?"

"But can he hit?"

It certainly seems to be the case that Europe and America experienced two altogether separate effects from the very same Enlightenment. Within the Old World, following the reasoned strains of Thomas Hobbes in the Seventeenth Century unto the dissolute Eighteenth Century French philosophers, there grew the deification of thought. The complete disregard of Pascal, the lack of comprehension or acceptance of the relationship between the finite and the infinite, expanded the frontiers of sophistry as in no other time throughout history. Man's reason, it was presumed, could supersede all things. For many, this included God's enduring creation. Even if God did create the universe, it could now be considered irrelevant. Human intellect had advanced to the point where man could take over for himself. In practice, this meant a few self-selected men should take over the task of providential oversight for the benefit of everyone else. The motivational force provoking this arrogance was a belief that a social contract could be devised solely by the use of human reason, absent Faith, which would create for the individual a man-made commonwealth with a temporal, thus artificial, soul. Whither God?

America's Founding Fathers, conversely, recognized the elevated status of the individual human being precisely because man was God's favorably endowed creation. He must never be a forced subject to the arbitrariness of another. Each man was by right his own sovereign, able to worship his Creator, or not, as he saw fit. Within this American social contract was presupposed a genuine soul, divinely created and eternal, one that man could *not* replicate or displace.

So what does this have to do with baseball? Understanding motivation is to make sense of what a man does or does not do. Consider how the same idea can lead to different actions in different men. Americans took the concept of liberty and pursued private business, formed a republic, and invented baseball. It is also instructive to note that the end of the Revolutionary War in America did not mark the commencement of summary executions of suspected Tories.

On the other hand, we have the French, who when confronted by liberty, quickly sought the comfort of guillotines, along with the wholesale desecration of religious articles, in order to confirm their political resolve. Henceforth, Nineteenth and Twentieth Century Europeans, fortified with this same sort of enlightened determination, pursued multiple forms of nihilistic totalitarianism including imperialism, socialism, fascism, and communism, each one in turn becoming the most infamous of the final social solutions. Their game of choice? Soccer. Indeed, one shudders to think what would have become of Europe and all of Western Civilization had America not been discovered.

America was discovered, thankfully, and so was baseball. The game of baseball reflected a noble American mindset including an optimistic attitude, a desire for a healthy way of life, and the means to understand oneself better. For these and other reasons, baseball became the most prominent, spectacular way Americans found to interact, a way to be entertained while passing their precious leisure time.

In order to develop a more complete understanding of the game, it helps to start by delineating some of the major differences between baseball and other team sports. A good place to begin is the application of rules. Judgments in baseball are rendered for everything. An umpire determines ball or strike, fair or foul, safe or out, making his call for every pitch thrown and nearly every subsequent movement made by the players. There are more official incremental judgments in baseball than in any other game. However, for such an orderly game so thoroughly officiated, it is probably the least predictable.

Baseball is astonishingly different from other sporting games in its design and purpose. There is no acquisition of territory and there is no placement of a ball over a specific line or into a specific goal. Rather, baseball is a game of progression carried on during discreet periods of changing risk and opportunity. The length of the game is measured in innings and outs (i.e., accomplishments) rather than minutes and seconds (i.e., time spent or wasted). Baseball strategy, at its highest level, is constructed from a comprehensive knowledge of situations and tendencies gained by paying mind-numbing attention to minutiae, which are analyzed with exactitude. The carefully crafted strategy is then thrown out upon the field of play where it is subjected to the mercurial whims of statistical aberrations.

Baseball is fundamentally different from other team sports in its execution. In games other than baseball, there may be man-to-man or double-team or triple-team defense. In baseball, there are nine fielders poised in opposition to one batter. In some other games, one man tries to outrun another. In baseball, the man endeavors to outrun the thrown or batted ball. In other games, the player can run in many different directions. In baseball, the nine fielders know exactly where the runner is going, usually without even having to look. In some games, a player gets help from a teammate who blocks or sets a pick or body checks. In baseball, he runs alone. In other games, the entire defense is in jeopardy when the offense goes in motion. In baseball, the defense puts the ball in play. In so doing, the offensive players are placed in jeopardy, one man at a time.

In other games, the movement of the ball causes a score. In baseball, the movement of a man causes a score. Even a home run is not counted when the ball goes over the fence, only when the man touches home plate unassisted. In other games, the clock is an important part of the contest. In baseball, each team is entitled to twenty-seven outs, unless it rains, no matter how long it takes. The amount of action in baseball determines the length of the game rather than a clock determining the amount of action. If a basketball player inbounds a basketball to begin play and the referee notices the clock has not started, he will halt play. Nothing has happened. Play can only be resumed after the clock malfunction has been corrected. However, in baseball, when a pitch is thrown, it has an eternal existence, part of the official scorebook, never to be altered by man. Only God, or a commissioner assuming His role, can negate an occurrence in baseball. One example is a premature rainout.

Finally, baseball is the only team game where the individual always stands entirely alone, whether in the field or at the bat. Does this not closely mimic the authentic American ideal of the individual as sovereign of his own destiny? By contrast, every other significant team sport is, at its essence, a tribal enterprise, a community project as it were, with the possible exception of the wonderful, albeit sleep-inducing, game of cricket. However, our poor British brothers would be far better served if their game of choice were baseball.

What is definitely true is that no other team sport better illustrates the American ideal of individualism than baseball. It is a natural desire of men to participate in contests that simultaneously challenge the mind and the body. No other game does this as satisfactorily as baseball. No other game demands such high levels of intellectual deftness and physical skill. Baseball is the one game that most nobly displays individual excellence within the conceptual framework of a team. It is the game of opportunity founded in the land of opportunity.

Largely due to the simplicity of its basic rules, baseball has a great appeal to youngsters. These rules are a natural outgrowth of ordered and logical behavior making them very easy to understand. They are almost intuitively obvious to even a casual observer, especially children. Without doubt, it was true to us as young boys, mostly regular, though occasionally a tom or two, in the middle-to-late 1950's living in a new era of peace. World War II had ended several years earlier. Now the rest of our service dads were back from the Korean War. All were busy starting out in their briefly delayed young civilian lives, finishing school, beginning careers, getting married, and making babies. We had the hydrogen bomb as we kept a close eye on the Russians. And we played baseball. Life was good. As kids, we had no problem playing the game without specific instructions. Here is why a formal baseball tutorial would have been unnecessary.

When batting, the player gets three chances to swing at the ball, unless he fouls on the third, which is very good and proper. Four strikes would be way too many while two are just not quite enough. Three is obviously the perfect number.

If the ball is fairly hit, the batter leaves home and runs to first base. Well, of course he does! Where else is he going to go? As new opportunities arise, he can dart off to second, may try for third, and, if enabled, will finally come back home. A good man always leaves home for adventure with the intent to return. No further explanation is needed here, either.

While away from home, safety is found when standing on a base. There a runner cannot be molested, even if he is a little kid with the proximate fielder being none other than the neighborhood bully. The quality of the game does not depend upon the size of the players.

After three outs, the teams change sides. Again, two outs are not enough; four outs are way too many. Three outs is obviously the right number. Maybe grown-ups from another world, who have never heard of baseball before, would have to be taught these things. But no American kid needs formal instruction on these basic rules. They simply pick them up.

Certainly, this was the case for the kids in my neighborhood playing summertime backyard baseball on Berkley Road in the Millcreek section of Erie, Pennsylvania. We somehow just knew all these things, just like we knew how to speak English. Perhaps we could not have explained the basic rules of baseball very well even if we wanted to, but we knew them well enough to play the game, which was what we did in the summer during the weekdays by ourselves, after supper when our fathers were home to watch, and on Saturdays. We played on Sundays, too, if we could sneak it in when our mothers were otherwise occupied or distracted.

"Stay clean, Witty Uncle Somebody and Ample Aunt What's-Her-Name are coming over!"

To be sure, America held no monopoly on the love for baseball. The game flourished throughout many parts of Asia, in places like Japan, Taiwan, and South Korea. The capitalist economies of these democratic countries grew very nicely, quickly repairing the devastation caused by world war. The same cannot be said for some other Asian places like communist Mainland China, North Korea, and French Indochina where baseball was not played. Coincidence? Perhaps. Perhaps not.

Just because we all knew how to play the game, it did not mean our games were argument-free. Arguments are a very important part of baseball. When disagreements occurred, they were solved quickly by the older boys. For example, if a nine-year-old said you were out, and you were six, then you were out. Just be glad he let you play at all. The worst situations were sometimes the simplest or most obvious ones. Imagine a player who hit a pop-up and, after it was caught, declared,
"I'm not out, it's a foul ball."
There would have been an awkward momentary silence. Is he kidding? Who is this kid? Where did he come from? With a ball hit in the air being caught before hitting the ground, the batter is out, fair or foul.
"Everybody knows that. Let's play!"
"Yeah, let's play, before it gets dark."
In this manner, some of the finer points of the game were learned. The more complicated arguments required temporary agreements that would be authoritatively settled later when a father could be consulted, things such as, does a tie go to the runner or does a foul tip become a foul ball when the ball goes higher than the batter's head. Thus, the game was passed along, father to son, older brother to younger brother, big kid to little kid, Joe D. to Mickey M.
When it grew dark the game had to stop, but there was always tomorrow. Looking back after a half-century marked by incredible social, political, and technological changes in this great country, baseball has remained the same old brand new game. Yes, indeed, but could not this be said of every period since baseball was invented? It could, without any doubt.

The philosophical construct of baseball is different from other games, too. For instance, there could never be a book written about baseball entitled *The Future is Now,* which was a 1970's favorite around Washington, D.C. about George Allen's Redskins. It would not make any sense. Football, like other team games, does not have to make sense. Baseball does. The reason is this. Baseball is not properly witnessed as an event. If an event turns out to be nonsensical, it was probably not worth seeing. Baseball is not an event. One does not go to "see" a baseball game; rather, one goes to "take in" a baseball game. The single game, by itself, is only a discreet part of a continuum, regardless of what any calculus teacher may say to the contrary. Without a doubt, the main objective is to win a particular game; however, win or lose, the analysis of situations and tendencies are of the utmost importance. Otherwise, the context of the next day's game cannot be properly understood. Therefore, in baseball, the experience normally supersedes the result. When tomorrow does come, it will comfortably merge with the past to produce the new and updated present, thus making the game as ageless as it is timeless. Baseball produces a lifetime of tomorrows, as if defying the passage of time, allowing its adherents to remain youngsters throughout their lives.

One of the many illustrative examples of the philosophical differences between baseball and other team sports can be seen in the treatment of errors. An unplanned or unintentional happenstance in baseball may be considered a statistical inevitability. For instance, if the shortstop boots the ball, well, he should have made the play; however, a certain number of errors at this position will happen. A normal distribution curve can be formulated to determine whether the frequency falls within the standard deviation. It is not so much that errors are acceptable in baseball; it is just that they are understood to be contained within the nature of the game, so long as they occur infrequently. Not knowing when they will happen adds a bit more suspense to the action. By comparison, if a running back fumbles the football, well, there is no excuse. It is entirely his fault. He should have done a better job holding on to the ball. There is no reasonable or acceptable number of fumbles in football.

One final, unique, and very satisfying feature of the game of baseball is the manner in which it distracts one's attention. The baseball game is where to go to get away from the real world, which is to say, from work and responsibilities. The game provides a respite from political and social issues, too. Does baseball do this better than other team games? Indeed, it does, because baseball has no clock. Therefore, within the world that the game creates, no time will pass from the first pitch to the last out. This is not a trivial or inconsequential point. Both in theory and in practice, if time does not pass, what can be missed when taking in a baseball game? Nothing at all. With this comforting thought, all of one's attention can be directed to the field of play since the world, as has been left, will be there upon return, for better or for worse.

"Wait!" Some would say time does pass during a baseball game. "Notice the 'time of game' entry in the scorebook."

True. However, that which is not relevant can be disregarded. If the world of baseball creates a sort of psychosis, and it may, it has to be a healthful one. It is a fact: no time passes during a baseball game. A willingness to accept this concept contains the greater measure of wisdom.

Understanding and appreciating the game of baseball can only lead to this most truthful and palpable of conclusions: There are many other sports and pastimes in the world. Some of them are very fine; however, they all have at least one common deficiency. They are something other than baseball.

One theory holds that the game of baseball evolved. It is an alluring theory that, if true, eventually will hold up under scrutiny. Mankind possesses wonderful capacities in the areas of reason, discernment, art, and mathematics. Evidence of magnificent creative abilities and limitless imaginations occur in every generation. Men also have a very competitive nature. In spite of this, a case could be made that baseball was not a product of the human mind.

Perhaps, a long time ago, following a random mutation from inside a swirling, bubbling pool of amino acids, lower forms of games with rocks and sticks and white base lines came crawling out of some sort of primordial fen. Maybe it was in a prehistoric swamp turned landfill like the Flushing Meadows Park in Queens whereupon now is built Shea Stadium. Then, through many epochs and eons, following the laws of natural selection along with the Number Seven train, the gene pool became such that a physical specimen like Babe Ruth could be born. Simultaneously, and by total coincidence, man's mental capacity leapt forward. Soon thereafter, he recognized that lights should be added to Wrigley Field before the sun entered into its supernova, putting an end to day games forever. This theory is viable though not provable until baseball paleontologists unearth the missing financial link to connect the reserve clause with free agency. Until then, we could call this hypothesis, *The Theory of Evolution*.

On the other hand, there are some who believe that human intelligence designed, invented, created, etc., the game of baseball. Perhaps this supposition could be termed, *Intelligent Design*. Here is what *these* people *think* they know.

No one man invented baseball, not Abner Doubleday, not William Hulbert, not even Hermann Haupt. Rather it originated from a very identifiable source. An early game of ball, brought from the Old World and played in Colonial America, was called "rounders." This game was of English origin. Its early popularity was limited mostly to children and young adolescents since adults of this era tended to eschew recreational activities as being foolish.

Following the American Revolutionary War, the number of industrial and service occupations began to increase dramatically. Working men, especially city dwellers, gradually learned to appreciate outdoor sport for its social and healthful benefits. Additionally, they sought a means of relief from their daily indoor toils. Rounders developed into several different versions all generally referred to as "town ball." Identification of a particular version of town ball depended on the geographical location in which it was played, for example, the "Massachusetts Game" or the "Philadelphia Game." Although similar in nature with common accoutrements of bat, ball, and bases, each had its own peculiarities.

The game we know today as baseball is a direct descendent of the New York version of town ball. By 1846, the town ball players of Manhattan were forced to abandon their original playing fields, the first of which were vacant lots at Madison Square (Madison Avenue and 27$^{th}$ Street) and then at Murray Hill, due to urban sprawl. Undeterred, these ball-playing quality gentlemen of New York City, organized by one Alexander Cartright, began to ferry across the Hudson River after work in order to continue playing their summer evening games. The site they found available was in a New Jersey park called the Elysian Fields near the town of Hoboken. At this point in the game's development, the basic field dimensions and parameters of play were first written down, probably by Cartright himself. During the next few years, codification of the rules of play took a form that would be familiar today. The base paths were set down, nine men fielded the usual positions, and three outs changed the side. The greater significance of establishing universal rules was that it enabled casual games to be treated as legitimate competitive sporting events.

The next important improvement in the development of baseball was the creation of a system by which comparisons between games and players could be made. This came about in the late 1850's due to the efforts of one of the game's earliest and most fervent promoters, an English-born cricket reporter named Henry Chadwick. In his tireless pursuit of making baseball the equal of cricket, Mr. Chadwick developed methods for scorekeeping and for compiling statistics.

Thus, the foundation was complete. Baseball had rules, records, and organized contests. The formation of one hundred or more amateur clubs, involving thousands of participants, all engaged in enthusiastic intra-city competitions, created an aspect of permanence for the sport. By the time of the first battle of Manassas in July of 1861, baseball was an established, sophisticated game that was field tested, in every way ready to be presented to all the young fighting men of the conflicted American Nation. One might even say that baseball had been on a collision course with history.

As New York City was baseball's incubator, the War Between the States became baseball's inculcator. Soldiers played the game during the long periods between battles and marches. They played during lulls in artillery assaults, on the battlefields between entrenchments, in prisoner-of-war camps, even between opposing soldiers. What was probably the largest crowd for a sporting event in the Nineteenth Century was a Union all-star game on Christmas Day 1862 witnessed by forty thousand Union soldiers.

The winter of 1863 was, perhaps, the darkest period for the Union and its incompetently led Army of the Potomac. Shortly following the horrendous disaster of the battle at Fredericksburg came the famous "Mud March" near the Rappahannock River. However, during the few weeks between these two calamitous events, the central Virginia weather was unusually warm and dry. This allowed the troops to play baseball even as preparations were being made to cross the river. While the officers and engineers hoped the favorable weather would hold long enough for their campaign plans to be executed, the regular soldiers hoped to be able to play more baseball games. As fair weather continued until the twentieth day of January, they played upon the open drill fields near Falmouth creating the first ever season of winter baseball. The climactic contest was a game between the 19$^{th}$ Massachusetts and the 7$^{th}$ Michigan for a sixty-dollar side bet. The 19$^{th}$ Massachusetts won by a score never recorded.

If General Burnside's order to move out had not ended the season, the weather soon would have. If only the general officers of the two sides had known better, and had they been able to convince their respective commanders-in-chief to begin peace negotiations, they could have stopped the fighting right there, packed up their best players, and headed south to organize the first spring training in Florida. The others could have been sent home to await the start of the regular season. Instead, we are left with a legacy that includes Gettysburg, Antietam, Second Manassas, Wilderness, Chancellorsville, Chickamauga, Vicksburg, Atlanta, and more, each a name, when spoken or heard, even to this day, sends a winter's chill through the nervous system. If ever there was a nation in need of a pastime, this divided American nation was it. However, Hell's Hole had to be fully explored first, and it took two very long additional years to complete the effort.

Finally, in April of 1865, this period of unpleasantness was brought to a close. The baseball-enlightened soldiers who had remained faithful unto the bitter end were free to return to their homes. The game then spread like a wildfire. It is difficult to exaggerate how quickly baseball grew in popularity. In short order, it became a national passion.

The very first professional baseball team was the Cincinnati Red Stockings. During their first season in 1869, they won sixty-five straight games and were the pride of their town. They also turned a profit of $1.39. In 1870, after winning twenty-seven games in a row, they came to Brooklyn to play the Atlantics. In a dramatic, extra-inning game, the Cincinnati team lost by a score of eight to seven. The astonishing news flashed with electronic speed through the telegraph wires. When the team returned home, fans stopped going to games while investors complained the players' salaries were too high. The Cincinnati Gazette wrote, "The baseball mania has run its course. It has no future as a professional endeavor." The team disbanded, for a while. Amazingly, all this was caused by one loss!

The prediction of the demise of baseball as a viable business was premature. The potential for profit was recognized by many groups of businessmen, as they wasted no time attempting to establish team franchises along with some player associations. One by one, they failed. The first substantial professional league of baseball players, the National Association, was founded six years after Appomattox. Although this league did not last very long, some men who closely observed its performance became convinced that the game of baseball could exist as a business. Five years later, in 1876, *The National League of Professional Base Ball Clubs*, formed by eight clubs, replaced the National Association. As originally recorded, the members were:

> Athletic B. B. Club of Philadelphia, Pa.
> Boston B. B. Club of Boston, Mass.
> Chicago B. B. Club of Chicago, Ills.
> Cincinnati B. B. Club of Cincinnati, Ohio
> Hartford B. B. Club of Hartford, Conn.
> Mutual B. B. Club of Brooklyn, N.Y.
> Louisville B. B. Club of Louisville, Ky.,
> St. Louis B. B. Club of St. Louis, Mo.

These cities shared one very important trait: they were all served by rail lines. It was not an accident. Transportation has influenced the curves and ripples of history as much as anything else has. It may be mere supposition, however, without Hermann Haupt's railroads, one must wonder if General Grant with his Army of the Potomac ever could have triumphed over Lee's Army of Northern Virginia. Without railroads, the war may well have ended in stalemate, or it may never have been fought at all. Businessmen of the day very well understood the value of railroads. They viewed the game of baseball as another way to exploit this modern mode of travel. Likewise, three-fourths of a century later, during the 1950's, Major League Baseball's expansion to the West Coast was enabled by the development of air transportation.

During the thirty-year period between 1846 and 1876, before baseball founded a permanent professional major league, the game planted roots that grew very deep. The document establishing the National League in 1876 revealed that this original group of club owners was not comprised of what could be considered modest men. Coal magnate, William Hulbert, along with all the others, designed a very precise and thorough plan to organize professional baseball as a business.

Their intent was to maintain absolute control over every aspect of the professional game, while avoiding the mistakes that doomed previous attempts to form workable baseball organizations. The simple concept of playing complete schedules had to be addressed not to mention player drunkenness, fighting, gambling, team bankruptcies, etc. Perhaps the most important item with which these men dealt, one that they realized to be essential, was the need for an independent umpire organization. After much thoughtful planning, their focus turned to making competitions between clubs a legitimate form of entertainment. Entertainment, by itself, was the marketable product. However, wherever people could be drawn, an advertising venue was created thus expanding the opportunity to produce revenue.

The players who would turn out this product were to be employees at will, held fast as if under an indenture. The Emancipation Proclamation was not considered applicable to baseball players. At the same time, the club owners wanted to preclude the establishment of any other professional major league in baseball. All in all, the formation of the National League truly was a well-considered exploitation of the public's passion for the game, a passion the owners very well understood because they possessed it themselves.

The plan was successful. For about twenty-five years, their control of professional baseball was hegemonic. Eventually, when the nascent American Association was established, it first was considered a rival to be vanquished. However, it turned out that the ever-increasing demand for baseball was, indeed, sufficient to support two separate major leagues. The National Agreement of 1903, which established the National and American Leagues as the two major leagues, stabilized the professional game.

As successful American businessmen commonly do, these baseball team owners turned a problem into more profit. That which had been deemed a threat soon became another business opportunity. Having two leagues inspired the creation of another unique and extravagant entertainment product, the season ending and immodestly named, World Series. The professional game, firmly established, built upon a sturdy foundation of free enterprise, has continued to thrive ever since.

The typical roster in the early years of the National League listed less than twenty men on each of the eight teams indicating that approximately one hundred fifty players were deemed qualified to play in the majors at any particular time. Today, the rules allow a twenty-five man roster, which means seven hundred fifty major league players are used to man thirty teams. Even though there are about six times as many job positions for players today at the top, the population, along with the demand for the game, has increased many times more. Therefore, the pyramid from the little leagues to the big leagues is a more difficult statistical climb now than at any time in the past, not that it has ever been anything other than an extremely difficult uphill road to travel.

Just how difficult it is to reach the major leagues is a matter of perspective. Whatever the point of view, one thing is certain. Many unlikely events have to occur during the few years that are available to the prospect. Metaphorically, traveling along the road to the big leagues constitutes a journey for which there are no accurate maps, no exact distances, no posted speed limits, no decipherable road signs, and no definitive traffic signals. Just in case this would be an insufficient challenge, there is no certainty the journey will not be delayed, detoured, or halted abruptly, temporarily or permanently, for any number of reasons and without any forewarning. Life is sort of similar to this except when a dead-end or detour is encountered elsewhere, there is not always a need to move beyond it. In baseball, you are either going up or you are going out.

The title of this story contains the grammatical contraction, "Big's." The apostrophe indicates letters omitted from the term "Big Leagues." Lessons in deportment notwithstanding, it is used with sincere apologies to Sister Maria Louise, as her sixth grade grammar lessons granted no license for such a dubious use of the language, hence, she is not to be faulted.

Continuing with deference to our esteemed Sister, the road to the big leagues is only for those men who possess three things: an intense love for the game, an unrelenting desire to play the game, and a fanatical work ethic to develop the required knowledge and skills. It is, in a symbolic way, evocatively analogous to the *Pilgrim's Progress*, often a seemingly endless journey, exhausting and improbable. Likewise, on the road to the big leagues, there is little solace to be found for the self-doubting.

Furthermore, a multitude of individuals is positioned along the way to deflect and dishearten the traveler from his ultimate destination. Appearing to be knowledgeable and well intentioned, these detractors, at different times, can be disguised as coaches, scouts, teammates, relatives, friends, and neighbors. They often act as if they are being helpful when, in truth, they solicit for the Slough of Despond, the place where those wanting commitment retreat in despair to hang up their cleats prematurely. Not so for the traveler who keeps his eyes focused upon the major leagues, the allegorical Celestial City on the Hill, and who is persistent in his single-minded purpose, and who never doubts the destination someday will be reached, hope springs eternal, and success is anticipated as a certainty, attainable, if not within the realm of present reality then, surely, on some future field of dreams yet to be carved out of a patch of earth somewhere between Iowa and Heaven.

Reaching the major leagues is no small feat. It is accomplished by a distinguished group of men rightfully admired as much for their tenacious spirit and devotion to the game as for their refined physical talents. In the face of extreme odds, they devote the years of their youth to developing their baseball playing skills while learning how and when to apply those skills. The major league career, if it comes at all, may last a couple of days or a couple of decades; playing time may constitute half an inning or twenty thousand innings; the player's name may be Archibald Graham or Stan Musial. Those who assemble the baseball encyclopedias, as well as those of us who study the history of the game, will continue to take note of all these baseball facts, examine every figure, and calculate each statistic.

Our chief concern here is something different. It is of the journey. It begins, by necessity, with an acknowledgement that in America, baseball is an inheritance, a birthright. All are invited to come along this road, as many others have done, to follow a boy who was given to learn and love the game at a very young age. He is one man's son and he is every man's son. He is one American boy and he is every American boy. His American history constitutes everyone's American history. As he advances from one level of the game to the next, this young man becomes the beneficiary of a multitude of unlikely events. All can watch his world of baseball unfold as it has for millions of others. All who read this story will learn, or perhaps will be reminded, what it means to become, once and forever, a major league baseball player.

## Chapter Two
# A Historical Bridge

The year 1959 was one of great change for Springfield, Virginia. Indeed, the entire Washington, D.C. area was in the early stages of a phenomenal growth period that began in earnest during, and because of, World War II. Other wars spurred growth in and around Washington, D.C., but not to the same extent as this one. The Capital City was rapidly being transformed from a moderately sized town of mostly southern-style manners, a town socially maintained by cave dwellers and tolerant of governmental transients, into a heterogeneous major metropolitan area with a true cosmopolitan flavor. World war and the worldwide threat of communism were forcing this city, a relic of the Nineteenth Century, and one with sedentary propensities, to become a modern, international city of the Twentieth Century. The words "hustle" and "bustle," heretofore obscure, alien nouns within the vernacular of the District of Columbia, were coming into common usage.

It may have taken two world wars to convince many American isolationists, but, finally, there was nearly universal acknowledgement that the Atlantic and Pacific Oceans were no longer large enough to avoid serious and continuous involvement in international affairs. While the world had changed dramatically, we Americans had changed as well.

Anthropologists would tell us that to adapt is to survive, and Americans know how to adapt. Congruent with this virtue is the tendency to be mostly forward-looking. This, after all, is the one very common virtue attributable to the earliest settlers as well as to those constituting all the subsequent waves of immigrants up to the present time.

Lest we forget whence we came, a sizeable array of symbolic milestones marking the progress of civilization was there to ponder. One distinguishing characteristic of 1959 was that in this year the last surviving veteran of the Rebellion died. He was Confederate soldier Walter Williams. It goes without saying that there was no possibility for the Capital City or for America to remain in the past. The past no longer existed, but who, other than history professors and Foggy Bottom analysts, had the time to stop and think about forming a historical perspective in such a dramatically changing world? What was a Sputnik supposed to do, anyway?

Unbeknownst to most people in 1959, there was another interesting historical fact that tied together the entire history of the United States, a fact that could be relished for just one additional year, assuming anyone living at the time was even aware of it. The Republic was accustomed to marking its time by presidential administrations. A most significant one was about to end, that of Dwight D. Eisenhower. Eisenhower's was the last presidency during which it could be said that a significant number of Americans lived lifetimes that overlapped the lifetimes of every American president. In other words, persons who were born before George Washington died in 1799 and continued to live until after Dwight Eisenhower was born in 1890. At Eisenhower's birth, these old-timers would have been at least ninety-one years old. Most medium size towns in 1890 probably had at least one such qualifying senior resident.

For presidents after January of 1961, this peculiar historical bridge did not exist. Kennedy, who was born in 1917 and even Reagan, who was born in 1911, were too far removed historically from George Washington for there to have been any noteworthy personal connection. Why is this idea worth mentioning? Personal historical bridges are consequential because the significance of any historical event diminishes for most people as their personal contact with it is lost. The same can be said of societies. After 1960, the founding of our Republic ceased to be personal for anyone. It became completely historical.

One of the many suburban, unincorporated communities surrounding the City of Washington was called Springfield. It was in Northern Virginia, situated in the Eastern part of Fairfax County about ten miles southwest from the 14$^{th}$ Street Bridge. The name of Springfield came from the farm of Henry Daingerfield, which he acquired in January of 1851. It was also the name given to the train station built on his property in July of that year, along the Orange and Alexandria Railroad. This road, which traversed what had been the historic twenty-two thousand acre Ravensworth Farm, connected the port of Alexandria with Gordonsville in Orange County. Local legend has it that the Fitzhugh family refused to give permission for the railroad to lay track through their adjoining plantation unless a convenient depot was built so that Mrs. Anna Maria Fitzhugh could go shopping in Alexandria whenever she wanted. The Springfield Station was deferentially built to abide the modest needs of this most notable constituent.

Traveling southwest from Washington, D.C., Springfield was most easily accessible via Virginia State Route 350, officially named the Henry G. Shirley Memorial Highway. It held a very prominent place among the many modern American thoroughfares that "no one would ever use," a list including the Pennsylvania Turnpike before and the Capital Beltway afterwards. Shirley Highway also possessed the most common feature of the many "unneeded" roads that were built in that it was inadequate and obsolete on the day the first section opened to traffic in 1951. Planning for the expansion of Shirley Highway, indeed, continued for decades. As it was in January of 1959, this four-lane divided concrete slab, which began at the Potomac River, continued for about fifteen miles almost to U.S. Route 1 near Fort Belvoir, about a mile shy of Woodbridge. Shirley Highway predated the Interstate system initiated by President Eisenhower. It became a part of Interstate 95 (later I-395) the following year.

For an awestruck seven year old second grader from Western Pennsylvania who had seen no better thoroughfares than the Buffalo Road, along with U.S. 19 outside of Erie, and had only heard of the Pennsylvania Turnpike, this road was quite the marvel. Captured by a child's mind, one of the more memorable traits of this extraordinary limited access expressway was the thumping sound created by bias-ply tires passing over expansion joints every thirty or forty feet at sixty miles per hour.

It was a comparatively warm and brilliantly sunny January morning in the Nation's Capital when we arrived at Union Station. In fact, it was a glorious day, so vastly different from the snow squalls we had braved the night before in mid-winter Erie. In many other ways, there were stark contrasts between the two environments. Even so, the differences did not become apparent all at once.

The overnight train ride had some slumber-interrupting stops along the way, all occurring before daybreak. Often an early riser, my final awakening came happily before the first morning light, just in time to witness an end to this night's final hour of darkness. The emergence of a winter's dawn, quiet and unhurried, exposed the Maryland countryside of undulating farm fields and forests. Here was a landscape accented with only a few intermittent patches of snow, a condition never to be seen on the near leeward side of the Great Lakes at this time of the year. Snow covered every baseball field in Erie, usually from All Saints Day to Easter.

Dad was there to greet us at the station. Besides me, our party included my mother, one brother, and three sisters. Dad had already begun work some months earlier, having gone about the business of buying a house for us while mother executed the sale of our Erie home. The furniture and other goods, including ball gloves, had been delivered the day before by the shipping company called Mayflower. This fact confused me since I knew the Mayflower was a ship, the ship the Pilgrims used, and, at the same time, was unaware that there was a way to sail from Erie to nearby Alexandria. Knowing differently, that is, knowing the truth, would have been even more confusing. Then the intellectual challenge would have been to figure out why our stuff was not shipped by truck (which it was), instead of by such a circuitous route, through canals into Lake Ontario and up the St. Lawrence Seaway, around and down the ocean coast, and up the Chesapeake Bay and the Potomac River (which it was not).

Some little comfort was found in being absolutely sure of one thing. The Mayflower was not a truck; it was a ship. The problem for kids is that they often have too little information. The problem for grownups is that they often have too much. Consequently, being absolutely sure of anything is always a tricky business.

Upon stepping outside of Union Station my immediate attention was gathered by the imposing sight of the U.S. Capitol building to the south. If ever there was a total triumph of design and placement, this was it. The dome rose above in titanic majesty close beyond deciduous treetops bare of leaves. I may not have known how to interpret the meaning of the words "titanic majesty" in the second grade, but a grade school vocabulary does not prevent a kid from knowing when he sees something pretty big and special. This magnificent structure, gleaming in the radiant light of the morning sun, dominated the bottom of a crystal clear blue sky. For the City of Washington, it was just one of a plethora of mesmerizing scenes. From this one I was finally distracted by the clanging wheels of streetcars rumbling along down the middle of Massachusetts Avenue upon recessed rails.

A tall, assiduous porter, uncommonly respectful, yet with no time to tarry, ambitiously tended to the suitcases and bundles amidst a flurry of

"Sirs" and "Ma'ams." How unusual to be polite and in a hurry at the same time. People in Erie had to be moving slowly to be polite. Within this strange environment we soon came upon an island of comforting familiarity, our family car, a 1951 two-tone, two-door Ford sedan, parked along the curb in the circular drive out in front of the station. The front and back seats were couch-like. Admittance to the back seat was gained by pushing the back of the front seat forward, easily accomplished in those days without so-called safety latches or catches. No seat belts or other restraints, either, except for dad's extended right arm during sudden stops. Even though the National Transportation Safety Board was not there to protect us yet, we somehow did not all die from the lack of child seats and other safety devices.

We progressed along Constitution Avenue, a street lined by Federal buildings built of steel, granite, and marble. The intersections were punctuated by the odd placement of traffic lights on corner posts instead of being hung above on wire cables, as they were in Erie. Soon we came to $14^{th}$ Street and, while turning left, confronted the tallest building in town. The Washington Monument was so tall I can remember trying in vain to see the top of it. God could see the top of it, which was a good thing since someone had thoughtfully left a metal plate up there inscribed with the words, "Laus Deo." Next, the passing of the Tidal Basin, which so gracefully framed the Jefferson Memorial, and from every viewing angle made one think of postcards, actually, three-dimensional postcards.

While crossing the Potomac River on the single-span $14^{th}$ Street Bridge, a parallel railroad bridge ran close by over which could be seen the National Airport on the southwest bank, now called *Reagan National*. The new road surface past the bridge was the beginning of Shirley Highway. Soon on the right sat the Pentagon building, just fifteen years old, built with five sides one could not count from ground level without walking the entire circumference, decidedly a frustrating aspect not knowing why anyone would build a five-sided building in the first place, unless the architect foresaw that it would provide an opportunity for a youngster's first lesson in both the Greek language and geometry.

Of more immediate concern was that of now being inside the Commonwealth of Virginia, Rebel Country. My grandfather had warned us,

"Watch out for those Rebels!"

He may have been kidding. Being unsure, however, it seemed prudent to scan the shrubs and trees lining the riverbank for evidence of troop placements with soldiers dressed in grey uniforms. Although this reconnaissance provided no useful military intelligence, there came about another wonderfully vainglorious realization. During this one day, even before lunchtime, I already had been in three of the forty-eight states plus the District of Columbia.

On the left side of the highway was the huge Marriott Motel, which had to be the largest in the world. The Army-Navy Country Club Golf Course appeared on the right. A lot of new names on road signs such as Arlington, Alexandria, George Washington Parkway (I knew who he was), Ridge Road, Columbia Pike, Glebe Road, Shirlington, Bailey's Crossroads, Leesburg Pike, King Street, Seminary Road, Fairfax, Little River Turnpike, Duke Street, Edsall Road. It seemed there were so many places here for someone new to learn. In Erie, there was just Erie, and no signs were necessary to tell you where you were. Finally, or rather, in minutes, we reached Springfield.

The Springfield exit ramp ended at Franconia Road. Turning to the right meant turning onto Old Keene Mill Road Franconia Road to the left was the more useful of the two because it went somewhere, to the east, namely to Franconia, afterwards intersecting with Telegraph Road which, in turn, led to Alexandria. Old Keene Mill Road, to the right, just passed through the main part of Springfield for less than a mile, and then into the hinterland where there was nothing much more than forest, Accotink Creek, some farms, and a few hunting lodges. If a man were fortunate to find his way to Burke Road or Sydenstricker Road, he would eventually reach Ox Road, which would lead to either Fairfax or Occoquan depending on whether he turned to the right or to the left. However, before getting to Ox Road, a turn down the single-wagon-wide Hooes Road provided an almost death-defying, adventurous roller-coaster type ride through the woods ending in a residential subdivision called Beverly Forest, which was situated along Backlick Road, right next to Shirley Highway, a couple of miles south of Springfield.

Those sparsely populated areas of rolling hills, thick forests, verdant meadows, and meandering streams were not yet a part of suburban Washington, D.C. Unlike Springfield, the hamlets of Burke, Fairfax Station, and Clifton were still not untied to their heritage most noteworthy as stops along the Orange & Alexandria Railroad, nor were the residents unaware of what their strategic importance had been during the Rebellion. Lorton and Occoquan, on the other hand, existed for their proximity to the Occoquan River just below the fall line, which gave navigable access to the Virginia tidewater region, the upper and lower necks, and the Chesapeake Bay. These folks who resided past Springfield, past Accotink Creek, and past Fairfax City were not generally of a mindset that included identification with Washington, D.C., at least not yet. For a few more years, they would not distinguish their geographical proximity by saying something like,

"We live in the Washington Area."

They lived where they lived and it had nothing to do with Washington, D.C. Within several years, however, most of the residents out as far as Manassas lived where they lived and it had everything to do with Washington, D.C.

The name of this main east-west road through Springfield changes from Franconia to Old Keene Mill somewhere within, or immediately west of, the Shirley Highway cloverleaf interchange. It does not matter where because highway interchanges, practical and useful as they may be, are really no more than geographic dead-zones. Comprising several acres of land that accommodate thousands of temporary visitors every day, they are the most highly frequented, most strategically located pieces of real estate within any community, yet within these zones no one lives or conducts business, nor does anyone meet or recreate. No address, no mail, nary a single hospitable item is to be found. No one even wants to be there more than necessary, which is fine because this land of the highway cloverleaf, by design, serves no purpose other than to keep people moving along. Yes, the super-highway interchange is a new and mysterious contrivance of modernity. Thus, along with the accompanying increase in motorcar travel on limited access highways, it is a cause of one profound cultural change, replacing the travel notion of "passing through" with "passing by."

A right turn onto Old Keene Mill Road at the end of the exit ramp meant entering the intersection with Backlick Road right away. On the right-hand side stood a single-story, red-brick shopping area. The two wings of the building formed a right angle, the corner store being the Springfield Pharmacy. Within this drug store were several spacious private telephone booths made of paneled hardwood for people without a home telephone, or for those who wished to conduct a telephone conversation without party line interruptions. Not many homes were connected with private telephone lines. The other mercantile partitions included Fischer Hardware, a barbershop, a real estate office, a Western Auto store, and a few other typical small-town businesses. The most important business in the line was the Springfield Sports Center, supplier of baseball uniforms and equipment.

On the immediate left was a gasoline filling station. Across the intersection on the left was a pony ring that offered twenty-five cent rides, but not in the winter. The far right corner was still an empty lot soon to be the home of a Hot Shoppes restaurant. This crossroads formed by Backlick and Old Keene Mill Roads was destined to attain historical importance by becoming the first intersection in Springfield to have a traffic light, but that day had not yet arrived. By the end of the century, Springfield's first traffic light was long gone due to an elevated roadway lifting Backlick Road over Old Keene Mill Road, eliminating this central intersection altogether in order to facilitate the movement of motorcars into and out of the much enlarged Shirley Highway cloverleaf interchange.

Turning left onto Backlick Road, a short distance away, were the bus station on the left and the Post Office on the right. A quick right turn onto Amherst Drive led immediately to the front of the American Legion Post. Behind it, a baseball field was going to be built later that year. It would be a good one, too, lasting about thirty years and hosting thousands of baseball games. Finally, it was paved over and made a parking lot in the late 1980's. The expansion of Amherst Drive, meant to facilitate traffic flow over and around the Backlick Road overpass due to the Shirley Highway cloverleaf interchange, caused the old post building to be torn down. A new structure was built farther back from the street. There just was not enough room to keep the baseball field. Land use restrictions eventually caused most legion teams in Northern Virginia to play their games on local high school fields.

A right turn onto Backlick Road from Springfield's main intersection led to the Springfield Little League fields just one block up at Bland Street, across from the Springfield Shopping Center. Going one block farther east on Bland Street and across Brandon Avenue was the Howard Johnson's Motor Lodge, immediately north of which was the Babe Ruth League's "Lynch Field." By the date of our arrival this January of 1959, if there was anything well established in this unincorporated country village turned suburbia, it was youth baseball.

Springfield, even then, was tethered to Washington, D.C. being a part of the metropolitan area in fact and in perception. It was truly a suburb. Most of the residents were there because of the military and the civil service. A majority of the workingmen commuted to the District, the Pentagon, or to another one of the numerous military bases in the area, such as Fort Belvoir and Quantico. Nearby, old farms and plantations were rapidly being converted into subdivisions and shopping centers. The community grew faster than it knew how to do, maybe not haphazardly, but not unlike the builder who delayed fortifying the foundation in order to finish with the roofing tiles because the new residents had to move in and it looked like rain was coming. Whatever planning there was, it had to be done quickly.

Being just seven years of age when we arrived, there was no awareness of the socio-economics of the area. I also did not see anything of Springfield youth baseball because, besides being in the middle of winter, we did not turn right back at the end of the exit ramp. We turned left onto Franconia Road and headed east back over Shirley Highway. On the other side of the highway overpass, just before Loisdale Road and to the right, was the Sealcraft lumber yard. On the left was an empty lot soon to be the site of a 7-Eleven store, the place where paper route earnings would go to buy candy bars, bottles of pop, and lots of Topps bubble gum baseball cards. Thanks to the Northern Virginia Sun and Washington's Daily News, Evening Star, and Post, my brother and I put together quite a collection. On this day, the first mercantile establishment to be passed on the left was Carl Derryberry's Mobile service station, which had opened the previous May.

Continuing down Franconia Road there was a relatively new subdivision of mostly single-story, three-bedroom, one-bathroom homes called Springfield Estates. It, too, was on the left. The homes were relatively small, most being less than a thousand square feet, some with carports, and some without. In these modern times, thriving middle-class families had homes with a master bedroom, a girls' room, and a boys' room. When the numbers of boys and girls were roughly equal, everything was fine. Situations such as five boys and one girl presented a challenge because two bunk beds and a single could barely fit into one small room. Even then, furniture had to be moved to open or close the door. Space was so limited, all fights had to go outside, or at least into the living room. The bathroom situation need not be explicitly addressed except to say some families, the ones better off, enjoyed the luxury of having one-and-a-half baths.

Adjacent to the far end row of homes on Frontier Drive was the brand new high school, which just opened the previous fall. The school was set back from Franconia Road far enough to allow sufficient room for baseball and football fields that had not yet been completed. On the day of our arrival this school, which later acquired the name Robert E. Lee High School, had no name.

When still in the planning stages two years earlier, the new high school was referred to locally as Springfield High School because the overwhelming majority of students, then attending Annandale and Groveton High Schools, were to come from Springfield with only a very few from Franconia. However, the school board customarily allowed each member to name new schools within his district. In this case, the board member was Hollis Lory, a resident of Franconia, who haughtily named the new school "Franconia High School."

Springfielders petitioned the Fairfax County School Board requesting the name of a famous deceased American be used instead. Superintendent W. T. Woodson sided with the petitioners and, over the strenuous objection of Mr. Lory, it was agreed that "Franconia" would be dropped in favor of a new name to be selected at a later time. By the school's opening in the fall of 1958, the unofficial name "Lee" was being used by default. It derived from the fact that the new school was within the Lee Magisterial District. It was not until August 1963 that the school board granted the request of the Lee High School PTA to name the school for the famous and esteemed Virginian, Robert E. Lee. Truly, a more appropriate name could not have been found.

The land upon which the school was built was once a part of the Ravensworth Plantation, that of the Fitzhugh family. The Fitzhugh's, who were very close friends of Thomas Jefferson, were relatives of the Lee's. Therefore, it was fitting that the school's dedication be something special. It was very special, certainly equaling the dignified heritage of the land upon which it was built. A quite extraordinary inaugural ceremony was held at 3:00 p.m. on Saturday, April 26, 1959. The main speaker was the President of the University of Virginia and former Virginia Governor, Colgate W. Darden. These proceedings could only have been enhanced by the presence of the Sage of Monticello himself. As it was, the dedication of our to-be-named-later local high school was the most significant event to occur in the Springfield area since the waning days of the Rebellion.

Because the entire Washington area was growing rapidly, so was the need for new schools. Often they were hastily built with less than coordinated construction plans. When the classrooms at Lee were ready, the school opened even though many of the facilities, including the athletic fields, were not ready for use. The football team was both winless and fieldless for its first season in the fall of 1958. All games were played away. During 1959 and 1960, home games were played on a new, though lightless, field in the daytime. Football players were dismissed from classes early to prepare for their mid-afternoon Friday games.

The first night football game at Lee was not played until September 22, 1961 during the school's fourth season. Even that special event was in doubt until the last. Finally, local businessmen, not Fairfax County, were the ones who provided most of the funding for the lights. As if it had been scripted, in their very first at-home nighttime football game, Lee beat Groveton 20-0 and, oh, what a crowd they had. It seemed everyone was there.

The installation of football lights means much more than the mere capacity to have a nighttime football game. Friday night high school football is not just an ordinary community spectacle. It is an important cultural event. The home team sends its young men to the field of battle against other young men from elsewhere to determine which the better are, to measure their talents, their dedication, their perseverance, and their preparedness. The football game is an occasion to measure the coaches as well, to determine whether they have the knowledge, the experience, the cunning, and the rectitude to inspire and lead our young men. High school football stadium lights are a beacon in the night drawing attention to an event by which we glimpse the progress of our future generation of adults.

There were many other noteworthy moments in the early sports history of Lee High School. One occurred on November 19, 1959 when a new electronic scoreboard was installed so Coach Tom Hyer and his cagers could begin their second season in modern style. Another took place on April 7, 1959 when Coach Jim England held tryouts for the varsity baseball team. One hundred hopefuls came and nineteen were selected. That is, more than one out of every six boys enrolled in Lee High School tried out for the baseball team.

Lee was built for a capacity of 1,400 students. The first school year, 1958-59, enrollment was already 1,130, even though most seniors elected not to transfer to the new school. The next year enrollment shot up to 1,650. Before the fall semester of 1961, with enrollment approaching 2,000, Lee High School made plans for a staggered school day. At the same time, construction of the new Edison High School was begun about a mile to the east on Franconia Road. But staggered school days at Lee did not end until 1966, when West Springfield High School was opened about four miles west down Old Keene Mill Road and a bit north on Rolling Road. By this time, the hinterland beyond the old part of

Springfield had become numerous subdivisions, the central feature of which was the new West Springfield Golf and Country Club.

In January 1959, Lee was not the only new school in our neighborhood. Beyond the backside of the Lee High School property, there sat the new Springfield Estates Elementary School, which had opened ten months earlier in March of 1958. My brother and I were enrolled there because no convenient Catholic school existed.

Springfield was then in the Richmond Diocese. Growth had obviously overtaken planning and maybe the Bishop, John J. Russell, had not been as concerned with the northern section of his diocese. The nearest parish schools to us were St. Michael's in Annandale and St. Leo's in Fairfax. The logistical problems of transportation along with waiting lists made the public elementary school the only practical alternative.

Before long, a new parish was created in Springfield, adopting as its patroness, St. Bernadette. The pastor, Francis L. Bradican, was already going about the business of purchasing a hunting lodge on a piece of land nestled within a meander of Accotink Creek along Old Keene Mill Road about a mile west of Shirley Highway. Soon the new parishioners were attending Mass in the Lee High School auditorium while construction began on a classroom building and gymnasium behind the old house. Father Bradican was determined to build the school and convent first, and the church and rectory afterwards.

St. Bernadette's new property happened to be the forty-acre Preston Estate. This parcel of land was once owned by the family of Robert E. Lee and it, too, was originally a part of the Ravensworth Farm plantation. Commonly referred to as a hunting lodge, the house of the manor, an older wood-frame structure, was plainly built though handsome in its simplicity and sturdiness. City dwelling hunters had heretofore frequented this expansive area that extended all the way to Burke and Lorton, as it was known for its abundant game.

The Preston lodge stood upon a bluff perhaps thirty to forty feet above the flood zone of Accotink Creek and about two hundred fifty yards away from the original Old Keene Mill Road. The road today is about one hundred feet north of its former location. No real threat of flood existed because in 1943 the Springfield Dam was rebuilt about a mile and a half upstream. The original dam, built in 1918, was dismantled in 1922 because it threatened the railroad bridge on the old O&A. The purpose of the dam was to create a water supply, now called Lake

Accotink, for the Army's Camp A. A. Humphrey's, which was later named, Fort Belvoir.

In 1960, St. Bernadette's school opened for business with grades one through four, under the tutelage of nuns from the Daughters of Wisdom, a French order, led by the school's headmistress, the Reverend Mother Mary Daniel. The first classes were held in vacant U.S. Army barracks on the base at Fort Belvoir less than five miles away. This went on for a few months until the classroom building was ready for occupancy. Those of us making up that first fourth grade class were destined to be in the first graduating class in 1965, as the school added one grade each year as it went along. My brother, being in the fifth grade at the time, remained at the public school.

Immediately past the athletic fields of Lee High and across Franconia Road was Elder Avenue, exactly seven tenths of a mile from Shirley Highway. On the SE corner of this intersection stood an older brick home where the Talbert family lived. Mr. Talbert owned the land that lay between Franconia Road and the new subdivision called Springfield Forest. His land consisted of several cleared acres, followed by a bit of forested land along the left-hand side of Elder Avenue.

One third of a mile down Elder Avenue from Franconia Road, past the edge of the forest and two recently built new houses was Kalmia Street. Turning left, the first house on the right, number 5802 (later changed to 6505) was our new home. From the gravel-paved road, we turned into our loose-gravel driveway. It was a brand-new, two-story, custom built structure made of pinkish color brick featuring a full basement, two large masonry fireplaces, and three dormer windows protruding from the tall roof line above. Sitting several feet above street level made it look even statelier. Our new house was beautiful, deserving of a deeply appreciative first look. This initial sighting of the place where we would live surpassed every sight of every building seen earlier in the day. In fact, the bright and clear Northern Virginia January morning sunshine made our home look like something that belonged in a large Easter basket. This was much better than anything in Erie had been. We ran inside for the first time without knocking. Unpacked boxes were everywhere.

Not quite twelve hours earlier our grandparents stood on the trestle at the Erie train station waving good-bye, Busia standing still and Grandpa walking along the station platform trying to keep pace as long as he could, waving vigorously, as the train slowly pulled away, until his foot speed could no longer maintain the close separation. The distance between us grew, as did the increasing realization that loss of eye contact was imminent. An unconscious slowing of the hand waving signaled the parting was complete. Suddenly, there was just the desolate rumbling of steel wheels thumping along iron rails, a muffled sort of loudness somehow quieted even more by the silent falling snow outside. I was passing through my hometown, leaving. The horn kept sounding, formidable and haunting, to announce our approach at every road crossing, until there were long distances between road crossings. Then the horn blew very infrequently. The diesel locomotives dragging us forth probably were built right there in Erie at the General Electric plant where my dad until recently had worked as an accountant.

Erie grew up to become a manufacturing town, as did many cities and towns along the Great Lakes. The lakes provided the means of transportation necessary to move raw materials and finished goods. However, the original European settlers-turned-entrepreneurs were not initially attracted by the region's timber, minerals, oil, and grain. Throughout most of the 1700's, Erie was an outpost for French-Canadian fur traders who traded mostly in beavers pelts. Industrialization in the late Eighteenth and early Nineteenth Centuries changed all that. Facilitated by an extensive network of canals, the Great Lakes eventually became heavily trafficked waterways with heavy-laden ships.

Now, through the night, we were going to the capital city of the United States and my perceptions of what lay ahead were mostly from photographs, though not entirely. There were also some first-hand remembrances from the age of two. The family had been in Washington in 1953. Dad was a commissioned officer with the Army's Military Police recalled to active duty during the Korean War. He was stationed for a year at Fort Gordon, near Augusta, Georgia where we lived together in base housing, that is, dad, mom, older brother, and me. Traveling back to Erie at the end of this tour of duty, we passed through Washington, D.C. not failing to visit some sights. Photographs my dad had taken were a part of the memories, but there remained a few vague personal recollections. One was being able to run around on the grounds of the White House. What exactly we were doing there, I do not recall.

In broader terms, no one could possibly know where this overnight train ride would lead. Certainly, a child has not the presence of mind to be cognizant that such things have life changing implications. A seven-year old is barely aware of his own existence. Erie as a hometown would henceforth be little more than a frozen memory, a place to visit our beloved grandparents and some other relatives once or twice a year; to go fishing in the bay; to swim and picnic on the Peninsula that is Presque Isle State Park. Washington, D.C., rather Northern Virginia, would now stake a claim to our residency. Our new lives would be as Virginians instead of Pennsylvanians, Rebels instead of Yankees. Oh, boy, what to do about that!

The profundity of a migration only becomes evident with the passage of time, being understood within the context of life experiences. We tend not to notice much of what affects us distracted as we are by the exigencies of everyday life. Therefore, when reading the editorial page of the Wall Street Journal on the Wednesday morning before Thanksgiving, there comes a wish to know who to call at Dow Jones & Co. to thank for their poignant reminder. Every year in this edition, the Journal publishes an account of the Pilgrims' departure from Leiden and arrival in the New World. These passages are significant on many levels. Each passing year they are understood differently, conveying a new meaning, as life experiences change a man's perceptions. They are never redundant.

The call to come aboard accompanied with the admonition, "the tide waits for no man," can be two things at once, disconcerting as well as comforting, until such time that one effect overrules the other. A man can go when and where he chooses or he can remain until the decision is made on his behalf. Is this the meaning or the consequence of true freedom? Knowledge of the Pilgrims and their circumstances creates a craving to understand though not necessarily a desire for further explanations, as a cause is without need of a purpose, a point without need of a reason. While being neither fair nor predictable, life is best lived as it is understood rather than how it is explained. Failure to accept this often seems to culminate in one or another form of anguish.

The greater significance of the Pilgrims' story is not found in terms of their tribulation; rather it is found in their equanimity born of optimism. Departure from Delfs-Haven is a similitude of everyman's departure from the past to an arrival in the future. Erie was now past and Springfield was to be future, at least until taken hence by life's next ebb or flow. The Journal does a great service to its readers with this annual reminder as it prompts a thoughtful reflection of who we are and, even more importantly, why we are here.

Dad moved us to Northern Virginia because, like many men who took seriously their role as head of family, he sought and found a more promising career opportunity within a growing business and economic environment. It was no more complicated than that. After Korea, he had remained in the Army reserves spending some time at Fort Belvoir. As a young, college educated man with a growing family, he developed an attraction for the area while recognizing its great potential. Washington, D.C. was an important and exciting place even for those not employed by the government or involved with politics, as was his case.

The growing family included five of us children in 1959, boys ages eight and seven, and girls ages four, three, and one. Number six came later. Though it was unnecessary, Dad thought he had to ease this life-changing transformation for my brother and me by giving us some valid reasons why this was going to be a better place to live. The fact that my dad wanted to move was sufficient reason to be totally accepting of the situation. However, among the many good reasons to move, the most prominent one, always topping the list, was Washington, D.C. had a major league baseball team, as well as other professional sport teams. True, the Senators were in the junior circuit, but still it was major league.

The very idea of living in a major league city created a sense of awe in a boy. In my mind, major league baseball players did not seem quite real. Minor leaguers like the Erie Sailors seemed sort of real. However, major leaguers lived in another world that was beyond my world or any world I could possibly know how to attain. It seemed that when a man made it to the major leagues he left "here" and went "there." "There" was a special place where not just anyone could go.

All of us kids had already heard of the older greats like Ruth, Gehrig, Hornsby, and Cobb. The grown-ups talked about them. The new greats of our time were Mantle, Musial, Spahn, and Williams. These were real men, they had to be, but never having met any of them, without any kind of personal contact, made it very hard to imagine them as real. None of them lived in our neighborhood. We never saw any of them in church or at the grocery store. If they had kids, they did not attend our school. No one around the neighborhood ever met any of them. I vaguely recall one kid saying his uncle once saw Babe Ruth play and got his autograph. I did not believe it. So where were these major leaguers? They had to be somewhere when they were not at the ballpark. They did leave the ballpark after the game, didn't they?

Now that we lived near Washington, D.C., the idea that we would get to see a major league baseball game was a cause of great excitement.

Unfortunately, Clark Griffith was already trying to move the team to Minneapolis. Things were changing rapidly in professional baseball, more so than anyone could possibly have guessed just a few years earlier. Several baseball teams moved during the 1950's. The Braves had moved to Milwaukee, the Athletics to Kansas City, and the Giants to San Francisco. President Eisenhower, not acquiescing to this trend, said the Senators should stay in Washington and try to improve. Who, at this time and in this town, would defy a proposition of the Commander-In-Chief? Impossible! There was a time, was there not, when a suggestion by the President was regarded as an order. Or was this more imagined than real?

Be that as it may, immediately after the 1960 season, the team moved to Minnesota. Improve the Senators did, as the Twins, that is. They could not have gotten worse, becoming a first division team in their second year, 1962, then going on to win the pennant in 1965. Meanwhile, the new expansion Senators continued the traditional battle for last place in the American League with the New York Yankees farm team known as the Kansas City Athletics. This new Senators team continued in Washington through the 1971 season when they moved to Texas becoming the Rangers. Washington went without a major league team for the next thirty-three years. It turned out, sort of ironically, that the next time a major league team moved from one city to another was when the Montreal Expos of the National League moved to Washington, D.C. for the 2005 season, changing their name to the more traditional "Nationals." Luckily, this time around Washington joined the senior circuit.

Bitter for forty-five years? Oh, no. Wanting to spit on the ground every time the thought of the Senators leaving comes to mind is not bitterness. It is just an appropriate amount of gratitude. Recognizing that living in the past is not a healthy thing, a treasured authentic 1965 expansion Senators solid-red home cap has been kept wrapped in a plastic bag atop the hall closet, only to be worn on special occasions. One such special occasion was an inter-league game between the Rangers and the Braves in Atlanta in 2003. Take that, Mr. Griffith, along with your Twin Cities Twinkies!

New Senators or old Senators, it did not change our dislike for the Damn Yankees. We disliked them so much that we could not pass up going to see Mantle and Maris and Ford and Kubek and Richardson and Boyer whenever they came to town. By this time, Elston Howard was catching, Yogi Berra was wandering around in left field, and Casey Stengle had been replaced by Ralph Houk. Personnel changes did not matter to us, though. We always had plenty to hate on any Yankees team. Our new Senators had a few bright spots such as slugger Frank Howard, but we no longer had Harmon Killebrew.

In addition to the Yankees, we made the effort to go see the Twins when they returned in 1961 to play the Senators. If memory serves, the last game we saw in Griffith Stadium was between the Twins and Senators. It was during one of those meetings that I managed to scramble successfully after a Bobby Allison foul ball hit into the upper deck grandstands on the third base side. Holding on to that souvenir was short lived because, at the suggestion of my mother, it was sent to my cousin, Emilio, in Italy, whom I never met. Whatever happened to that baseball remained a mystery. I kind of wish I had it back.

A sentiment that is often heard and fun to believe is the one that says everyone remembers his first major league baseball game. I saw the Yankees, but forgot the score. It is certain that the Senators won because, after seeing two games between the Senators and Yankees, the Senators having won both, dad suggested,

"Since the Senators win every time we go to the game," his rhetorical question continued, "do you think Mr. Griffith should give us season tickets?"

What a great idea! It made perfect sense to me. What are a few free tickets compared to winning the pennant?

"Would they be box seats?"

The part of my first major league game that is remembered vividly was that of walking through a portal into the stands and looking down upon green grass, so magnificent in color, so perfectly manicured; and the whiteness of the lines, bases, home plate, and the pitching rubber. What a beautiful sight it was. Was it possible that this was real grass? We had very nice grass in our yard at home, but it did not look like this.

Two structural features stood out prominently in Griffith Stadium. One was the square black-and-white center field clock under which was written "Longines" and the other was a huge bottle of National Bohemian Beer. This raised two questions. What did "Longines" mean and did it have anything to do with the clock? The beer bottle was easy to figure out. Kohler Beer was in Erie, but here in Washington, D.C., there was National Beer. An advertising jingle went,

"National Beer, National Beer,
brewed on the shores,
of the Chesapeake Bay."

It was comforting to know where it came from. Kohler Beer did not have its own song, though it may have caused much ethnic singing in local saloons. The Longines clock followed the team to D.C. Stadium (later named RFK) when Griffith Stadium was abandoned, but the fate of the big beer bottle remained unknown.

Those were the more memorable sights of Griffith. The characteristic smells of the place came from brief aromatic wafts of buttered popcorn, and, even more so, from the ever-present tobacco smoke, the latter being sorely missing from today's public ballparks. In particular, there was the cigar smoke. It seemed cigar smokers always made the best comments during the game. Cigarette smoke was there, too, but it was everywhere in those days, not at all unusual, not enough to be very noticeable. Dad smoked cigarettes back then, usually Pall Malls, sometimes Luckies (i.e., Lucky Strikes), occasionally Camels, but never Chesterfields, regulars or kings.

Our pre-occupation with major league baseball was not limited to bemoaning the Senators and hating the Yankees. We also nurtured favor for a National League team, the St. Louis Cardinals, and not because it was another former trading post for French-Canadian fur traders. It was because of one particular player, Stan Musial. My dad knew everything about Stan Musial. He was the Polish kid from Denora, Pa., near Pittsburgh, who played for the Cardinals his entire career. He could also play the harmonica and, I am sure, played it better than Bob Dylan did, although no one yet knew who Bob Dylan was. In fact, at that time, Bob Dylan did not even know who Bob Dylan was.

Dad could, and would, recite any or all of Musial's statistics at any time with little or no prompting: this season, last season, career, anecdotes from All Star games and World Series games. I distinctly remember how my dad first told me he was called, "Stan the Man." How imposing this title sounded, so difficult to imagine the magnitude, the power, the supremacy that could be contained in the one man who was "*The* Man" amongst all the baseball-playing men.

Pitchers knew what it meant. They pretty much agreed on how to pitch to Musial in order to obtain the most favorable result:

"Throw your very best pitch and then hurry over to back up third base!"

Catcher Joe Garagiola, who had been a teammate of Musial, suggested a different tactic:

"What's the best way to pitch to Stan Musial? That's easy. Walk him and then try to pick him off first base."

Without a doubt, Stan Musial had to be the best baseball player who ever lived. Ty Cobb had more hits. So what? Musial hit for more bases and did it in two fewer seasons. Ruth had more homers. So what? Half of Musial's doubles off the thirty-six foot high fence in right field at Sportsman's Park would have been homers in Yankee Stadium. Let the two change teams and Aaron would have been chasing Musial instead of Ruth. Did I mention he had one hundred seventy-seven triples and more extra-base hits than Ruth?

Musial, more so than any other player, found the closest-to-perfect balance in hitting for both power and average. He hardly ever struck out, could hit the ball to any part of the field, and had just tremendous bat control. Musial was awarded three MVP's compared to one apiece for Cobb and Ruth. However, aside from twenty-two memorable seasons in the majors, his greatness as a ballplayer was equaled by his greatness of character and dignity. My dad knew boys looked up to baseball players, so he knew which one to encourage as a role model for his sons. As much as he talked about Musial and the Cardinals, though, he never said much about the "Gashouse Gang." Learning about that crew came later in life. Regardless of anything else, what was true then remains unaltered today. If asked to pick just one player from the whole group of Hall of Famers, forget about *Ty the Peach* and *Herman the Babe*, give me *Stan the Man*. To complete the outfield, how about the "Splinter" and the "Say Hey, Kid?" That should do it.

"On second thought, let's put Clemente in right and move Musial over to first base . . . gimme back that line-up card."

The best Christmas present ever came in 1961. To replace yards of copper wire hung from the rafters in the attic attached to a crystal diode and a wire coil meticulously wrapped around an empty toilet paper roll, Santa brought a plug-in General Electric AM radio. After turning it on, and marking the time, it took about twenty seconds for the vacuum tubes to warm up. During the day it was mostly tuned to WPGC-1580 ("home of the goodest guys in town") and WEAM-1400 (answer your telephone "listen to WEAM" and win $100) because these two stations played the latest top-forty rock-and-roll hit songs. At night, my radio became a connection to a wide swath of the country. Even though station transmitters had to power-down after sunset, the AM signal, especially those of the clear channel stations, carried farther without the electro-magnetic interference from the sun's rays. Hence, stations such as WABC in New York, WOWO in Fort Wayne, WLS in Chicago, WBZ in Boston, and countless others were clearly received. As local stations, they gave the local news and weather from which could be derived large amounts of demographical and geographical information. Exposed in commercial advertising were many of the local merchants and something of the nature of commerce in each area. Some stations also carried baseball games. My AM radio, positioned in historic Northern Virginia, became sort of a window on the entire eastern half of the country. By listening in, up and down the dial, faraway places became close, as places never visited became familiar.

Searching the dial, it did not take long to find a couple of men named Jack Buck and Harry Caray broadcasting the play-by-play of the Cardinals on KMOX-1120 in St. Louis. I listened to many of the night games during Musial's last two seasons of 1962 and 1963, usually only missing the first few innings depending on the time of the season and where the games were being played. Sunset between April and September varies with daylight savings time and the length of the day. If the Cardinals were playing the Dodgers or Giants on the West Coast, the games began after sundown, but staying awake became the problem.

If only I had had a better appreciation of what was going on in baseball in 1963, as memorable as that season was, but being only twelve made for a severely limited perspective. Musial appeared in his twenty-fourth All Star game, and then he hit a home run on September 10 during his first at bat as a grandfather. Warren Spahn became the most winning left-hander ever and, at the age of forty-two, completed his thirteenth twenty-win season. Sandy Koufax won the Cy Young Award and the MVP. The icing on the 1963 baseball cake was the Dodgers sweep of the Damn Yankees in the World Series. It was such a long time ago, long before "I don't believe what I just saw!" and "Holy Cow!" Important historical moments, they were.

Northern Virginia was well on the way to becoming a hotbed for youth baseball. When we arrived, some youth leagues were already well established though many were still relatively new. The very first little league in Fairfax County was formed not quite ten years earlier in 1949 in Falls Church. By 1953, there were additional little leagues in Vienna, Fairfax City, Annandale, and near the general aviation airport in Bailey's Crossroads. Peeking ahead, to 1970, Northern Virginia youth baseball had grown to thirty-seven leagues with twenty-five thousand players.

Springfield was not left behind. In 1956, not only was there a little league established in Springfield, but a Babe Ruth league for older boys, as well. They grew rapidly. The Springfield Little League, which included North Springfield, formed twelve teams in 1958, engaging one hundred eighty boys with an operating budget of $3,500. An extra clinic for the boys who were not quite good enough to make a team was established for instructional purposes. Local business support was tremendous. Even the Washington Senators contributed $125. Meanwhile, the Babe Ruth League formed six teams with ninety boys. The following year, 1959, the little league about quadrupled in size to seven hundred players while the budget tripled to $10,000 ($14.29 per player). By 1960, the Springfield Babe Ruth league had joined the Northern Virginia League with two divisions; six teams each, with one hundred eighty players.

The Springfield American Legion Post jumped into action in 1958. Tryouts for their new team were held at Annandale High School on June 1 & 2. Manager Frank Hammond was assisted by former college and minor league center fielder, James W. Allen. Mr. Allen, who had been signed by the Red Sox and played briefly for Scranton of the Eastern League, helped to establish the Springfield Babe Ruth League. In his chosen profession, he was a leading scientist in the field of data transmitting weather balloons.

All of the growth around Springfield put enormous pressure on the availability and use of fields. Baseball was not to be shortchanged, however. Springfield businessmen demonstrated time and time again that they were about as dedicated to baseball as they were to their businesses. After all, they had kids, too. Even with the growing challenge of obtaining available space amid rapidly rising land values, they always managed to find what was needed.

In addition to league support, most of the individual teams had their own sponsors or benefactors, along with the usual volunteer coaches and managers. Support through the early years and beyond was extensive and persistent. Old records and local newspaper accounts show clearly that the creation and operation of these leagues amounted to second full-time jobs for scores of men.

Of the many instances of dedicated support for Springfield youth baseball, one occurred after the 1959 season. The Springfield Little League was finding itself a victim of its own success. Expanding as rapidly as the Springfield community, the league soon had outgrown its fields along with extra commercial land lent to them. Moreover, this land had become so valuable it had to be put to better economic use. Even the area around the fields no longer afforded places to park cars.

With little fanfare, Edward R. Carr, the leading land developer in Springfield at the time, stepped in and gave thirty-six acres to the Springfield Youth Athletic Association. As a result, the kids never went without baseball. Mr. Carr, in a press interview, explained he gave the land directly to the youth association, not to the county parks authority for fear that "it would be years before the county would do anything with it." The kids needed ball fields immediately. He also promised more parkland if the association showed it could handle the development of the first parcel.

While little league baseball on the Springfield side of Shirley Highway was well established, youth baseball on the Franconia side was just beginning. In 1960, another league formed about a mile east of Springfield Forest with ball fields across Franconia Road from the construction site of the new Edison High School. It was called the Greater Franconia Athletic Association. The difference in this league was the way the teams were formed. In the Springfield Little League, boys attended tryouts and were selected by team managers in a draft. The Franconia League had no draft. Boys tried out for the team within their own subdivision. To begin the new league's first year, there were five teams, each one representing a subdivision located off of Franconia Road between Beulah Drive and Telegraph Road. They were Rose Hill, Winslow Hills, Ridgeview Estates, Franconia Estates, and Burgundy Farms.

Before 1960, Springfield Forest did not have its own team so boys old enough to play organized baseball went to Springfield. This was soon to change, however. A few exceptional men took measure of a most improbable confluence of unlikely events, applied their tenacious will, and, for a brief few years, Springfield Forest baseball came into existence.

In those days, baseball on black-and-white television was infrequent and the visual quality of the broadcasts was far less satisfying than what the imagination could provide while listening to a game on the radio. In fact, tied for second place on my favorite things-to-do list were listening to baseball on the radio and watching baseball games in person. All alone in first place, naturally, was playing baseball. We, i.e., the boys in Springfield Forest, found a place nearby where we could play baseball every day, whenever we wanted to. Walking northward along Elder Avenue, just beyond the forested area on the right, a little more than halfway between Kalmia Street and Franconia Road (two tenths of a mile from our house, to be exact), lay a vacant and fallow bit of land still owned by Mr. Talbert. We quickly put it to good use. Wayne and Jimmy Talbert played there, too.

Directly across the street, a mere couple of hundred feet away from our home plate, sat the old graveyard of the Broders family. This cemetery plot was a square measuring not more than about thirty feet on a side enclosed by a chest-high whitewashed wall made of cement blocks with a single black iron gate. The Broders lived on this land from 1825 to 1911, a fact I did not know then. Nor did I know for sure, then or now, that there was no such thing as ghosts. Before long, a moderate amount of trepidation gave way to a very substantial curiosity, which led, in turn, to a close inspection of the Broders' graveyard one day, alone. Some company would have been welcomed; however, being a susceptible ten years old at the time, there was a disinclination to reveal my desire to inspect grave markers to anyone else, even though this effort in historical research was being done for a completely noble purpose.

Entertaining the desire to peruse headstones did not materialize out of thin air. It was prompted upon hearing an astonishing tale that some of these people were buried more than a hundred years earlier, that several of the graves were unknown because there were no inscriptions, or had inscriptions so weatherworn they could not be deciphered. It was not the idea people had died a hundred years ago that most concerned me; it was that they had been right there living in my neighborhood, my brand new neighborhood, over a hundred years ago. They had been living in the old house behind the grove of trees. Already being in the fourth grade, my educational background was sufficient to know about the major historical landmarks and personages of American history, enough so to relate these things to the point where some definite conclusions could be drawn. The first conclusion was if these Broders had been dying here over a hundred years ago, then they must have been living here for even longer. Realizing that if they started dying before the Rebellion, maybe they were living almost back to the Revolution. Since Mount Vernon was a mere seven miles away, could any of these people who once lived in my neighborhood have known George Washington? By a close inspection of these headstones, reading the dates of birth and death thereon, much more would surely be learned.

Plans made without prior study often end up being inexplicable later. Entering the graveyard by crawling over the block wall instead of using the iron gate made no sense. Once inside, though, an immediacy of purpose took over. The first graves to be examined were the small ones. Nothing at all was written on some of them, while others had inscribed a date without a name, or something inscribed that could not be deciphered. Most of the larger markers had complete information, more information than could be comprehended, and more information than needed. Only dates were of interest, particularly those before 1800. Alas, there was none. The earliest readable dates of birth were in the early 1800's. Still, there remained the possibility a few of the severely weatherworn stone slabs had people beneath born before 1800.

After reluctantly entering, there seemed to be an even greater reluctance to leave, so inured I had become while facing the grave markers. Just because nothing had happened so far, more moving around inside of this final resting place might wake somebody up. On the other hand, by seeing everything there was to see, all curiosity was satisfied, leaving behind only a growing apprehension. It was time to go. The better time to ponder this newly acquired information would be after an escape.

To leave this enclosed place in a direction other than straight up or straight down involved turning around, walking away without seeing what was behind, hoping to make it out of the compound and into the street before whatever might be behind could catch up. Another thought was to walk backward, keeping an eye on the graves, thereby watching out for whatever fiendish article might appear. Well, this would be too stupid and cowardly. Then there was the gate. It was closed because it had not been opened. An attempt could be made to exit using the gate, but what if it did not open? There would be a delay, wondering, alarmed, why it would not open. The more difficult alternative was to escape in the same manner of entry, to scale the block wall, though it now appeared higher from the inside. During a struggle to gain this height, a slip backwards might provide enough time for the something that might be following to foil a second try. The memory from that point has failed, meaning the unconscious decision had to have been to turn away and run as fast as if stealing home. My guess is that I climbed over the wall in a hurry.

The English speaking history of Springfield Forest began in the Year of Our Lord One Thousand Four Hundred and Ninety-Six when King Henry VII of England commissioned John Cabot to go out and discover countries then unknown to Christian people and to take possession of them in the name of the English King. Cabot performed his office, which led eventually to the establishment of Jamestown in 1607, etc.

The more immediate, more germane part of the history of the Springfield Forest neighborhood began in the year 1714 A.D., when Catherine Culpepper, wife of Thomas, the fifth Lord Fairfax, sold three hundred and eighty-four acres to a couple of speculators named Watts and Harrison. The land became forfeit soon thereafter, reverting ownership, and in 1730, Catherine's son, Thomas, sixth Lord Fairfax, granted one thousand acres, including the Watts and Harrison tract, to John Warner. Adam Crump bought the land five years later from Warner and it passed on to his sons, who eventually sold it to Robert J. Taylor.

The story of the Broders family in America is estimated to have begun in 1777 when legend has it that Joseph Broders came to Alexandria from London to work as a cabinet maker and carpenter for George Washington at his nearby Mount Vernon plantation. Records do show he worked at Mount Vernon around 1779 and nothing more. Mr. Broders died in 1831.

In 1825, Joseph's son, John H. Broders, an Alexandria grocer, purchased seven hundred acres from Taylor, which included the original Watts and Harrison tract. John Broders then built a brick house sometime between 1825 and 1830 on his newly acquired property. The house sat near the colonial thoroughfare called Rolling Road, directly across from where the future Robert E. Lee High School baseball field would be. The name of this road changed to Old Fairfax Road during the Rebellion and then to Franconia Road afterwards. The Broders homestead, somewhere along the way, acquired the name "Oak Grove."

Broders eventually increased his land holdings to about one thousand acres by purchasing another three hundred fifteen acres from Anna Maria Fitzhugh between 1847 and 1853. The whole of this particular tract of land lay between what is today Frontier Drive and Beulah Drive. When the Springfield Forest subdivision was developed in the 1950's, the placement of the Broders' house, along with a reduced amount of acreage, fell between Frontier Drive and Elder Avenue.

John H. Broders died in 1860 at age sixty-two, almost a year before South Carolina seceded from the Union. His wife, Elizabeth, was left to run the farm with two sons, five daughters, a tenant farmer, and fourteen Negro slaves. A very tense period followed as the Rebellion ensued. Old Fairfax Road (i.e., Franconia Road) right away became a main artery to the front, just as was the Orange & Alexandria Railroad running through present-day North Springfield and over Accotink Creek. Early one morning in mid-July 1861, Brigadier General Samuel Heintzelman's Third Division departed Alexandria for the first infantry battle of the war using the Old Fairfax Road. He was headed in the general direction of a town called Manassas, to a farm owned by Wilbur McLean through which trickled a lick of a stream known as Bull Run. The spectacle was almost certainly witnessed from the parlor window in the north side of Oak Grove by the anxious widow and her hapless brood.

Many legends and stories from the Rebellion years persisted in this neighborhood, though few can be substantiated. Whether true or not, most are plausible. One such tale worth mentioning relates the plunder by Union troops early in the war of the house at Rose Hill a few miles away towards Alexandria. On September 27 and 28, 1863, Ranger John S. Mosby raided and briefly held Rose Hill to the surprise and consternation of the Federals. Finally, the last review of Sherman's travel-weary troops took place on the grounds of this same plantation a month after the final capitulation of the Confederacy. Military movements and activities occurred throughout the immediate area for the duration of the war, although no major battles were fought nearby. Skirmishes, on the other hand, did take place.

Within the immediate Springfield Forest neighborhood, another such story survives mostly as Broders family lore, but not entirely. Col. Mosby's men attacked a Union encampment commanded by Lieutenant Colonel H. H. Wells on the land in front of the Oak Grove house and adjacent to the graveyard. Said to have occurred about July 30, 1864, a perfunctory account of this attack was recorded. Further corroboration was secured in the 1970's by local relic hunter, John Berfield, who found period bullets on both sides of Elder Avenue. Something of the war, indeed, did happen on this property where our future little league baseball field was built. In fact, the diamond sat exactly in the midst of this battle site.

Probably not much fighting went on here because if it had, there would be greater documentation in the historical record. Mosby's Raiders or not, there is no doubt the residents of the neighborhood, with all the troops coming and going for the duration, experienced much stress during those years. The Union troops, however, lacking much opportunity to shoot at Rebels, most likely played a lot of baseball; therefore, the game in Springfield Forest had preceded our arrival by about a hundred years.

Following the passing of Elizabeth Broders in 1872, the farm was parceled out to the five daughters. Oak Grove and forty-four acres passed to Rebecca and her husband William G. Moore. Moore fought for the Confederate Cause and spent a year-and-a-half imprisoned at Fort Delaware from December 1863 until June 1865. Oak Grove passed to Moore's son, Dr. Samuel B. Moore, in 1909. After two years, he sold it to Walter Dornin who farmed it for twelve years until his death in 1922. With a loan in default, the property was sold and resold, ending up in the hands of James W. Talbert, for which he paid $5,000. Mr. Talbert sold ten acres, including the old house, to Harold A. O'Connell in May 1937. This parcel included the land between Frontier Drive and Elder Avenue, extending south of Franconia Road a short ways past the graveyard.

Mr. O'Connell was a lawyer, having graduated from Georgetown Law School in 1920. He joined the Roosevelt Administration in 1932 working for the National Recovery Administration, one of many New Deal programs. This new owner of Oak Grove, a Yankee, came from Westfield, New York, a small township about twenty-five miles up the Lake Erie shoreline from the town of Erie. Westfield had only one significant characteristic of interest to Erie's older teenagers: it was the first town across the state line made attractive by the fact that the legal age for consuming alcoholic beverages was eighteen in New York and twenty-one in Pennsylvania. For those thirsty traveling Pennsylvanians under the legal age, counterfeit identification cards were readily accepted at most establishments when proprietors bothered to ask.

The house at Oak Grove was modified several times through the years. The original two-story brick structure was built in the colonial tradition, a typical two-on-two floor plan, although architecturally it more properly belonged in the federal period. It stood out nicely. Old and stately in appearance, set back from the road amidst a luxuriant grove of large trees and well-trimmed shrubs, the grounds bore evidence of an owner with much pride in his property. At first glance, it seemed a bit unusual that the front of the house was facing the wrong way, as it were, towards Elder Avenue to the east, that it more properly should be facing the main road on the north side. The house was situated as it was for a practical reason, to receive the warmth of the morning sun in the winter. The mailbox was out beside Franconia Road, upon which the name "O'Connell" was printed in easily seen large white block letters. It was a very large receptacle so, perhaps, Mr. and Mrs. O'Connell received a lot of mail.

Fairfax County eventually condemned more than six acres of Oak Grove's ten-acre tract in 1964 to build Forestdale Elementary School. Hence, all that remained of a thousand-acre Broders estate was a bit more than three acres and the house. The graveyard became a separate island beyond the school, left as if an orphan in the middle of a parking lot. The rest of the original Oak Grove plantation had become both residential subdivisions, like Springfield Estates and Springfield Forest, and commercial areas, like the Springfield Mall. Even our little league field was to be gone by 1965.

Mr. O'Connell died in 1979. His son finally sold the remains of Oak Grove to Lynch Properties in April 1988 for over one million dollars. Mr. Lynch, along with several preservationists, tried to do something with the Oak Grove house, but, in the end, economic practicalities won the day. On the seventh day of June 1996, at 5:40 a.m., the house at Oak Grove was bulldozed, twenty-five years on the Historic American Building Survey Inventory for Fairfax County notwithstanding. It took exactly one hour to tear it down.

Examination of the historical record, newspaper accounts, and especially the comments of many individuals closely associated with the matter, leads one to conclude that there is no villain here. Not every termite eaten structure can be saved, or should be saved, just because it is old. This house served its purpose well for over a century-and-a-half until it could economically serve its purpose no more. The finite is, after all, just that. As in the entire material world, change becomes necessary when the amount of effort required to resist it surpasses available resources.

Getting back to the future in 1959, we the boys of Springfield Forest had made out of an unused plot of land, close to where we lived, a makeshift baseball field, which was isolated by woods, farm fields, and nineteenth century grave markers. The Talbert house was the nearest structure, just a few hundred yards away. The position of home plate was approximately in the same spot as the front stoop of the house now located at 6525 Elder Avenue. To the far right, near the SE corner of the Talbert property was another house where a young couple lived with their two little kids. The husband was a drunkard, a loud one at that. Instead of going to work every day, as the rest of our dads did, he often drank whiskey. This young family may have been somehow related to the Talberts. It was very sad. However, since we went there to play baseball, we ignored things like that.

As with most boys of our day, we faced three major challenges in our pursuit of the game: gnats, thirst, and equipment failure. Gnats tended to hover around the highest part of the anatomy, that being the head while standing up, which made these insects a major annoyance especially when they flew into the eyes, ears, and mouth. To alleviate this problem we held our glove hand above the head and induced the swarm to move upward or, while batting, we would hold the bat straight up. The strategy did not work very well. The gnat problem was not solvable, but our efforts made the most of an aggravating situation.

Thirst presented another predicament altogether. It was much more complex. First, the game was halted, followed by verbal agreements to return by a certain time. If necessary, provisions for personnel changes and equipment needs would have been made at this time, too. The natural instinct would have been to make our ways back home. This, however, took more time than desirable and, worst of all, there was a substantial risk of being noticed by our mothers who might saddle us with chores before we could return. The best alternative was to drink out of the backyard hose of a house where there was good reason to believe no one was at home, or would not take exception to a bunch of thirsty boys if they were at home.

Equipment failure required repairs. Replacement was far too expensive and usually out of the question. The notion of asking our dads to run out to buy us balls, bats, bases, and catcher's equipment never crossed our minds. A cloth sack filled with small rocks or just a flat stone or piece of lumber made a base. We used black electrical tape for torn baseball covers. Wood screws for cracked bats usually kept the game going, too. We also shared mitts and gloves, practicing the quaint old tradition of leaving ball gloves on the field when coming in to bat. Not every kid had a baseball glove. Some had gloves so worn out that they sought to borrow another one.

My brother and I had fielder's gloves. Dad bought them for us years before at the Post Exchange in Fort Belvoir during one of his summer camps for reserve officers while we were still living in Erie. They were made of leather so he showed us how to keep them oiled. He also told us how important it was to keep them dry.

Occasionally, someone would get a baseball for his birthday or a bat for Christmas. One of our crew caught a ball at a Senator's game, an official American League Rawlings ball, so we played with it. Surprisingly, he did not want to put it away as a souvenir. No one offered that suggestion, either. When the need for a new baseball became desperate, that is, when our last ball was damaged beyond use or hit foul into the woods and lost, a collection of coins was gathered to make about a dollar and fifty cents. Someone with a bike, someone trustworthy, would be sent on the mile long ride over Shirley Highway to the Springfield Sports Center to make the purchase while the rest of us waited at the field.

We spent many summer days playing baseball on Mr. Talbert's field. A field was about all it was that first summer, an otherwise unused parcel of land. Finally, later on during 1959, Louis Lorenson and Willard Johnson, two of the dads in the neighborhood, joined later by Robert Pedigo, decided it was time to organize our sandlot band of ballplayers into a real little league baseball team. The Springfield Independent newspaper picked up the story with this report in the April 14, 1960 edition:

> "Through the combined efforts of the Springfield Forest Citizens Association, the Springfield Forest Women's Club, the Gibson-Lloyd Construction Co., Coaches Louis Lorenson and Willard Johnson, and the generosity of C. P. Talbert, the boys of Springfield Forest will have the opportunity to play baseball this spring and summer."

Mr. Talbert permitted free use of his land. The Gibson-Lloyd Construction Co. provided a bulldozer and operator for a day. The Springfield Forest Citizens Association bought the grass seed while the Springfield Forest Women's Club raised funds to buy baseball equipment. Tryouts were scheduled for Saturday April 16 at 10:00 a.m. at the field. My brother and I were there.

Coca Cola gave us a manually operated scoreboard bearing the title "Talbert Field." Our dads, with our help, worked the field into shape during several Saturday workdays using no more than our own shovels and rakes. Still the bad bounces were as abundant as the gnats, or so we thought. It was possible we were trying to excuse suspect fielding abilities. Fencing, benches, and spectator seating were installed, too. There was no electricity, which meant no lights, water-coolers, concession stand, or sound amplification. There was no running water at all. The Franconia Fire Department sent a pumper truck to water the field until the grass seed started to grow. Otherwise, water was brought to the field in those very common dark-green rectangular U.S. Army metal containers in the back of station wagons. Fortunately, we did not appreciate the extent of our deprivations; it allowed us to go ahead and play baseball anyway.

The Springfield Forest team was made up solely of boys from the Springfield Forest subdivision. This was one of the smallest residential subdivisions in the area. Consequently, our talent pool was very limited. We had no access to any sort of league tryouts or player drafts, either.

What we did have was a heightened curiosity of the make-up of any new family moving into the neighborhood. Immediately upon the arrival of newcomers, we would go up to their house, knock on the front door, and ask if they had any boys our age. If they did, we never asked if they played baseball, it was assumed.

"Grab your glove. Let's go! Do you have a bat? What's your name?"

To complete the geographical record of our brand new historical neighborhood, the Springfield Forest subdivision was bounded by Franconia Road on the North; the Southern Railway tracks that ran from Franconia Road, just beyond Roso Street on the East, to the General Services Administration main depot off Loisdale Road on the South; and Elder Avenue on the West. An appendage of homes along Frontier Drive south of Franconia Road was also included. The O'Connell's would have been included, too, if they had had a ballplayer, but their kids were already grown up. The outer side of Elder Avenue to the west below Oak Grove was all forest from the graveyard going south to the train tracks. Today, a brick wall stands next to Elder Avenue beyond which is a Home Depot parking lot. Beyond Home Depot a street called Frontier Drive remains although it bears no resemblance to what was once a dirt and gravel road cut through to a gravel pit with a few small houses alongside. The gravel pit, fully operational in 1959, later became the site for the Springfield Mall, proving once again that not all change is progress.

Our Springfield Forest baseball team was real. We had our own field, coaches, and uniforms. The uniforms were a medium light gray flannel-type cotton material, perhaps a wool blend, with forest-green lettering. We wore green fitted caps with the two white letters "SF" sewn on above the bill, sewn on by our mothers who knew how to do that sort of thing. Adjustable baseball caps were unheard of at the time. The stirrups were also green. Best of all, we did not adopt a name of a major league team, as was common in most other leagues. Our team's name was "Springfield Forest," nothing more.

For the first two years, Springfield Forest was an independent little league team. We invited teams to come play on our field, or we traveled to other places to play. We went to Springfield, Franconia, Fort Belvoir, Fort Hunt, Falls Church, Fairfax, and even to Arlington to play baseball. One time we crossed the Potomac River and entered Union territory to take on a team in Maryland. The fascinating aspect of playing all these different teams was that, most of the time, we had no idea what to expect. Some games were close in score; others were lopsided, as the quality of our opponents varied greatly. The first couple of innings of every game were spent figuring out the abilities of the other team, particularly those of their pitcher. The rest of the game was spent trying to do what we figured out we had to do to beat them.

In January of 1962, it was decided that we would join the Greater Franconia Athletic Association with a team in both the minor and major categories. I have no idea why we joined the little league in Franconia instead of Springfield. We were a little closer to Springfield than Franconia. Maybe the well-established Springfield league did not need or want another team. Besides, their system of drafting players would have effectively dissolved our neighborhood team. Maybe it was because the Springfield league fees were too high. There is no telling why and no way to find out anymore. Looking back, it was best that things worked out the way they did. We stayed together and we had our own home field right in our own neighborhood. Besides, how can one improve upon an ideal situation?

Springfield Forest became the sixth team in the league, the other five being the original members in 1960. The largest of the subdivisions in the GFAA was Rose Hill, named after the plantation land upon which it was built. Since they had more boys from which to choose, their team was usually the best one of all. The other teams were also good. Enough balance existed within the league so that no team during these years experienced either an undefeated or a winless season.

By representing a subdivision, each of the teams had an extra dimension of support that did not exist in leagues with open drafts. Furthermore, each subdivision had a particular history emanating from a colonial land grant or plantation. Franconia Estates, as just one example, happened to be the first subdivision to be developed on land that was once part of the original thousand-acre Oak Grove Farm. Although this suburban area was filling fast with foreigners, i.e., non-Virginians, the history of the land could not be bulldozed away or hidden under pavement, not as long as baseball teams continued to represent each of these historic tracts.

All of the Springfield Forest home games continued to be played at Talbert Field. The intra-league away games were played on fields across from Edison High School on Franconia Road, near Franconia and Rose Hill. Springfield Forest was unique because it was the only little league team anywhere in the area with its very own little league baseball field, always available for our exclusive use, just like the Washington Senators had their Griffith Stadium and then, afterwards, D.C. Stadium. We knew nothing of time limits for home games. There was no sharing of practice time, either. We could play everyday until dark.

In addition to the league schedule, we continued to play some out-of-league games, traveling to different places like before, or hosting teams who wished to come visit us. Only a very few games were scheduled against Springfield teams. Wherever we played, two things were certain, unless it rained. First, we always had a great time. Second, dad was there for the first and the last pitch, including all the ones in between. I do not remember that he ever missed a single ball game. My mom was at most of the games, too, but she did not understand baseball as well. This was due to the fact she was born and raised in Italy, where boys did not play baseball. She disliked my spitting all the time and issued rebukes whenever she heard utterances disrespectful of an umpire.

At one time or another, I was assigned to play every defensive position except first base. My brother, Don, played mostly third base and right field. He had a much stronger arm. In fact, mine was weak. To become a decent little leaguer, the first challenge was to compensate by acquiring good fielding techniques such as not letting ground balls roll between the legs. Next, much diligent effort was expended learning to get rid of the ball quickly while still making accurate throws. Developing a good bat came easier, although good hitting when compared to most of the other kids who could not hit at all constituted a relative judgment of what was good.

In our defense, unlike subsequent generations, we played genuine baseball using real wooden bats. Mine was a thirty-two inch long, two-tone Hillerick & Bradsby "130S Special *Safe-Hit* Yogi Berra" model. My last year playing little league, 1964, age twelve, three homers (over the fence) came from this bat. The first one was to the opposite field in right. The pitch was just above the belt over the outer half of the plate. My mind took a photograph at the very instant the ball hit the bat, never to be forgotten. Then, while rounding first base, Mr. Lorenson called out the three most exquisite, most delightful, most eloquent English words that could ever be spoken or heard,

"Touch 'em all!"

Nearly tripping over the bag, I turned to acknowledge his directive,

"Yes, Sir."

My other two homers went directly over the center field fence. One hit the scoreboard and bounced back into the playing field. A discussion ensued whether it was a home run. It was. The only other homer hit by anyone on our team was by our next-door neighbor, Johnny Iaderosa. Sadly, he moved away during the season because his father, who was an Army Major at the time, was being transferred. They were set to leave on a Saturday in June. We had a game that day and the Iaderosa's moving van was packed and ready to go. Johnny, his elder sister, Jan, and his parents were driving up Elder Avenue in their packed car heading out of town. To everyone's surprise, their car stopped at the field. Out comes Johnny wearing his uniform ready to play. He played the entire game. He hit a home run. The game ended. He got back into the car and off they went, leaving a big hole in our line-up for the rest of the season. Transfers were routine in the Washington area since there were so many military men. Johnny Iaderosa was never seen or heard from around Springfield Forest again. The Suttons moved into the Iaderosa house, nice people, but no little league age boys.

In one respect, our team was no different from every other team in the history of baseball; we needed more pitching. One day Mr. Johnson decided to try me out on the practice mound. Playing about half the season at shortstop without a throwing error was probably the main reason he had me play shortstop, that is, when not playing center field. Never in my life has shortstop been a comfortable position. The ability to make straight A's in geometry in high school did not help maybe because angles on paper stay still. Balls hit to shortstop have an infinite number of angles that are constantly moving. They never stay still. Having asked many shortstops, including some major and minor leaguers, to explain how they manage to adjust and adapt to these changing angles, has not solved the mystery. No one has yet been able to explain it satisfactorily. They might just do it naturally which means they may not perceive the problem in the first place, which also means it may very well be a knack. As far as preferences for playing positions went, it was second, third, or the outfield, or even catching. However, playing preferences were not solicited, not once. I played when and where my manager dictated, always elated to be able to play at all.

Fortunately, playing shortstop was about the only thing in sports that ever felt uncomfortable. Even seeing a shark or a large Florida tarpon swim by while sitting on a surfboard never had such an unnerving effect. In fact, the most comfortable place on the infield, rarely made available, was in on the grass at third base. The ball gets there quick, no time to think, just block, pick, and throw. The opportunity to pitch would be fine; anything other than shortstop was fine. The minor issue of not knowing how to pitch could have been an obstacle, but it was not. How can a player be bothered by something he does not know? Besides, trying to convert infielders into pitchers has always been as common in baseball as spitting.

"Just throw the ball into the catcher's mitt," Mr. Johnson advised, "some faster, some slower."

"Anybody can do that," I thought.

Since most little leaguers cannot hit, not walking batters is a sure road to success, and that was easy to do, too.

Actually, this was not the first lesson in pitching. A couple of years earlier one of the neighborhood boys tried to teach me how to throw a curveball. Buddy Fultz was a year older, my brother's age, and lived over at the end of Roso Street. His older brother, Ray, played football at Lee High School. Buddy's technique was to grip the ball along the two narrow seams with the thumb centered underneath, like a two-seam fastball. From there he had two releases. First, with an overhand delivery, he would throw and then turn the wrist while bringing the forearm inward toward the stomach. Years later, this type of breaking ball was taught by Leo Mazzone as pitching coach of the Atlanta Braves. He called it the "throw and turn" breaking ball.

The second release, with the same grip, came from a more side-arm type delivery. The snap of the wrist turns the ball with more of an equatorial spin nearly parallel to the ground. It tends to float like a Frisbee for a while, and then breaks across and down a little, like a slow slider, but without the elbow strain. In spite of practicing these pitches incessantly, they never broke. Now was the time to try them again. And again. And again. They still did not break. Over forty years later, still trying, still unable to get them to break.

Unlike Johnny Iaderosa, Buddy was heard from again. In 1967, we moved to a new house about four miles away built within the former hinterland, now called West Springfield. This caused a transfer from Lee High to the brand new high school called West Springfield. Apparently, the school board must have concluded all the worthy names of great Virginians and Confederate Generals were used up. Had the board disregarded rank and deferred to local history, the name of Colonel Mosby could have been considered. A large measure of inspiration was there to be gained for the athletic teams by calling themselves "The Raiders," especially when playing Lee High School or Edison High School over in Franconia! Instead, the choice of mascot boiled down to Spartans or Indians. In an act quite disrespectful of the earlier inhabitants of this fair land, the West Springfield students voted to pay homage to the Peloponnesians.

Nonetheless, the opening of a new high school was exciting for many students who eagerly pitched in to help move during the Christmas break. One Saturday morning, while working in the computer room sorting IBM computer punch cards, along with S. John Davis, the Principal, a sad news report was delivered over the radio about a police shooting during an attempted robbery the night before. Buddy and an accomplice had broken into the Springfield bus station on Backlick Road. The Fairfax County police, having been tipped off in advance, decided to wait inside. Buddy entered holding a tire iron, which he had used to pry the door open. The police said afterwards that he did not drop the tire iron when told to do so. Instead, he allegedly made a move towards the officer who promptly shot him dead. The accomplice took off running. When this event became a topic for conversation, Mr. Davis said Buddy got what he deserved. I did not agree, nor did I argue.

When my dad got home from the office later that evening, he asked me if I had heard about Buddy Fultz. It was reassuring to hear him say that the police could have done something to avoid the whole sorry incident because they knew about the burglary in advance. Instead, they staked out the place to guard the coins in the vending machines. The result, a sixteen-year-old kid was shot down. Some police work. How much change could there have been? Pop was a dime. A pack of cigarettes was a quarter. But, then, this was the same police force that, a few years later, started ticketing rush-hour motorists for driving one mile-an-hour over the posted limit when county representatives did not grant them the pay raise they demanded.

As for the principal, well, he did not know Buddy so he was talking about a stranger from the other high school, a statistic, a presumably bad young man, and a felon. For me, it was about a real guy. He had a father and mother, several brothers and sisters, and he was a founding member of our sandlot baseball team, a member of our regular travel team, the only one of us who could throw a real curveball. These things made all the difference to me. Admittedly, there may have been some agreement with Mr. Davis if Buddy had been a stranger. It was not a tough call for either one of us. As for this being considered an important life lesson, had a choice been offered, it would have been postponed.

A great desire to play baseball notwithstanding, figuring out that making the American Legion team or the high school team were very unlikely was a gradual revelation. One day in 1961, while playing a pick-up game on Mr. Talbert's field, we could hear the Lee High School baseball team practicing. So we walked the short distance up to Franconia Road and stood outside the fence to watch. To a ten year old, these guys looked and played as if they were almost grown-up baseball players. We wondered if maybe they were good enough to play in the major leagues someday. After all, they were good enough to play on the high school team. The infielders seemed to catch everything, moving every which way, staying real low to the ground, throwing the ball fast and straight across the diamond. All of them looked very good.

Another easily remembered incident occurred one Saturday morning in 1962, going to see a game at Legion Field, the first time being so close to older baseball players. Two things were most noticeable; they were tall and they wore real baseball shoes with steel cleats. To a boy age eleven, these older teenagers looked big. They went on to the field and they played baseball well, extremely well.

While still in little league, seeing these older boys play made me aware of the existence of standards by which real baseball skills were evaluated. Being a little league all-star, hitting home runs, batting cleanup, stealing bases, playing every position, etc. did not mean so much. To play the game as well as the older boys played it required real skills, advanced skills. In my estimation, there was no amount of practice that could have earned for me a starting position on the high school or American Legion teams. Springfield was loaded with baseball talent. Even some players cut from these teams were very good. Maybe with a great effort, a spot on the roster was possible, but being a first rate starter was out of the question. The arm was too weak and the wrists lacked the quickness needed to hit good pitching. So who would want a second baseman with holes in his bat? The fact was that Northern Virginia baseball was very competitive. Throwing out slow runners on a small diamond from third or short and hitting balls thrown by pitchers who could not pitch did not quite make the grade.

Late in 1964, just after turning thirteen, it was time to hang 'em up. This was not a deliberate decision at all. In fact, there is no memory of having made it. The sign-ups for the next Babe Ruth league season in Springfield were ignored. Perhaps it would have been better to continue playing baseball; still, there are no regrets. As it turned out, the West Springfield High School team did very well, indeed, without my assistance. During the team's first thirty-three seasons, they won the district twelve times, the region six times, and the state three times.

There was a similar situation while attending The University down in Charlottesville. The Cavaliers' baseball team did quite well from 1970-73 aided by a terrific second baseman from St. Louis named Duval White. It did not take long sitting at a particular game in 1972, relaxing in the warm spring sunshine (the chemistry lab must have been cancelled that day), to erase any doubts that may have been left.

On May 7, 1964, just before finishing the final season of little league, a special event was held in Springfield Forest called "Talbert Day." After several years, it had become a custom for our neighborhood to hold a springtime "Funerama," as it was called. The festivities began on a Saturday morning with a parade that included the baseball and girls' softball teams, a fire truck, and any other groups who wanted to join in. The parade wound its way through most of the streets until it reached the ballpark on Elder Avenue. Then there was a mother/daughter softball game followed by a father/son baseball game. There were pony rides and lots of food, too. It lasted all day. On this particular day, Mr. Talbert was presented with a plaque and a scroll commending his generosity to the neighborhood, specifically for the baseball field. Many plaques and scrolls should have been given out that day. Without these men, maybe we would not have been able to play organized little league baseball at all. An American boy not given a chance to play baseball would have been the tragedy of a lifetime.

The teen years had arrived so it was time to branch out. This meant playing the guitar and piano, participating in high school wrestling, cross-country, and tennis, surfing whenever it was possible to get to the shore, and thinking a lot about going to college. What was not realized back then and for some years to come was how intimately engaged I had become with the game of baseball in just those few years of playing in the little league. The love of the game always was there, held to the side maybe, perhaps in the subconscious, not forgotten, rather, more like a cask of vintage wine aging in the cellar waiting for the right occasion to be poured. One popular bit of wisdom declares that you do not appreciate what you have until it is gone. Here is another two bits worth of insight: you do not appreciate what you throw away, or leave behind, or set aside, until it comes back around again. When my son was born seventeen years after my last little league season I was struck down with a seriously contagious disease called nostalgia. The cure for it was, yes, of course, what else? Baseball.

*Chapter Three*

# The Hammer and the Southpaw

Graduation from the University of Virginia in 1973, armed with a Bachelor of Science degree in Chemistry, secured a move to LaGrange, Georgia, to begin a job as quality control supervisor in the new Manhattan Rubber bowling ball factory. The degree and the job responsibilities were vaguely related as The University taught theory rather than practical application, as it should be. To one who retains a more traditional sense of things, college should be a place to go for an education, not a vocation; to learn to think, not do; to quench a thirst for knowledge, not satiate a lust for salary.

The company's old factory in Passaic, New Jersey had been recently closed. The more profitable product lines were disbursed to new manufacturing plants, mostly around the labor friendly South. Fortunately, daily sessions spent in the school laboratories, learning to test chemicals and evaluate chemical reactions, to conduct experimentation, were of some value. What seemed at the time mostly academic drudgery, on this job proved advantageous. Compiling results into lab reports was excellent training, to describe what happened and to explain why it happened. For one who might be truly inspired, this was a golden opportunity to opine about the greater significance of the effort, how it applied elsewhere, where it might lead in further experimentation, the key watchwords being interpolation and extrapolation.

Within the laboratory of a manufacturing plant, the results gathered from testing materials were essential in making useful things, to make them correctly, and to make them better. For instance, the frontiers of industrial science were visited when the surface tension of a hard rubber or polyester bowling ball could be adjusted to make it grip the lane better as it rolled, allowing for a greater curve angle into the pins.

LaGrange, following some not inconsiderable adaptations, proved to be a more than tolerable place to live. Located about sixty miles southwest of the Atlanta-Fulton County Stadium, this small, textile producing West Georgia mill town presented a completely new cultural experience. The job was mostly satisfactory, too, even though the company president, who was otherwise a decent man, thought Ted Williams had been a better ballplayer than Musial.

After arriving in this unassuming relic of the Jim Crow era and beginning a working career, a larger issue persisted; that of having a mostly vacant view of major league baseball. The expansion Senators had left Washington, D.C. almost two years earlier following the 1971 season to become the Texas Rangers, an event barely noticed although it made me a man without a team. A nativistic case could have been made to follow the Pittsburgh Pirates, an especially attractive idea after their pennant-winning year, but that thought did not stir a passion. Likewise, the thought of going for the Orioles was awkward, sort of like a Catholic turning Protestant, or maybe vice versa. Besides, picking up a team on the junior circuit meant having to hate the Yankees full-time again, not an enticing prospect. Maybe, if forced to choose a favorite team, it would have been the Cardinals, although since Musial retired, not much interest remained there, either.

The month was July. Upon renting one-half of an unfurnished house located at 608 Hill Street while owning not a single stick of furniture, my first evening home after work was memorable nonetheless. Without a television, the old AM tube radio would have to do. Of the two local stations, one broadcasted the Braves game with Milo Hamilton and former Braves pitcher Ernie Johnson describing the play-by-play action. The Braves led the major leagues in runs that year (799) and homers (206). Three players hit forty or more homers: Hank Aaron (40), Darrell Evans (41), and Davey Johnson (43). With the highest team earned run average (4.25) in the National League, all this bunch needed was a little more pitching. The first night listening to Braves baseball was all it took. I had found my team, in the National League no less, the senior circuit.

Even the pre-game song was a rousing ditty played in the background while Mr. Johnson announced the sponsors and invited everyone to listen to their broadcast of Atlanta Braves baseball, "with all the excitement of Major League Baseball."

"It's a brand new game, good to have you along,
Hope you're ready chief ...
Batter up, let's go
'Cause they're startin' to throw
And we're all so glad that we came,
'Cause it's a brand new game."

The "chief" referred to in the song was the famous Chief Noc-a-homa. The game could not begin until His Royal Tomahawkness did a dance on the mound and returned to his teepee in the left field bleachers. This brought good luck. I wondered if anyone ever thought of asking the chief to dance around the home team's bull pen mound before each game where the luck was most needed.

The Braves landed in the Western Division of the National League because of a choice made when still in Milwaukee, based on the relative strengths of the other teams. Now in Atlanta, in the Eastern Time Zone, West Coast night games began rather late. Being young, it was not too much a problem, even on work nights. Staying up was just about mandatory, too, because anything could happen. No lead was safe in those days. The Braves could go into the eighth inning with a seven-run lead and, still, sometimes it was not enough, not even against a team like the Padres, and often not against the Giants or Dodgers.

My intention all summer long was to get to at least one game before the season ended. Always something got in the way. Finally, the trip was made on the last day of the 1973 season to see the Braves play the Astros. The drive was only about an hour even though Interstate 85 was not yet finished between LaGrange and Newnan. Hank Aaron was sitting on seven hundred and thirteen home runs. The distinct possibility that he would break Ruth's record of seven hundred and fourteen that day permeated the entire ballpark. Naturally, the game was well attended, but it did not appear to be quite a sell-out, although it may have been.

As a bonus, this was "fan appreciation day." Before the game, fans were permitted to walk out on the warning track to greet the players and take photographs. Aaron did not make himself available because, they said, he needed to conserve his energy. A concern over death threats probably had more to do with his being absent. However, the rest of the players were there and, while enjoying themselves, actually seemed to be a little bit embarrassed by all of the attention. How surprising that they were bashful about being in front of a crowd of baseball fans, something they did every day. Maybe this was different. In this setting, they were just standing around responding to quips and queries, chatting with fans, and not playing baseball.

The Braves lost 5-3 and Aaron did not hit any homers. A minimal effort to walk down the aisle by the field level seats, combined with just a bit of audaciousness, yielded one good photograph of the Hammer from right behind the home dugout as he came in from the field between innings. Over in the other dugout was another sight to behold, the one and only Leo Durocher, the manager of the Astros. Seeing him was a thrill, more so because it prompted thoughts of the well-known company he had kept over the years, first as a player with St. Louis, then as manager with Brooklyn. Could there ever be another bunch like the 1934 Cardinals, better known as the "Gashouse Gang," with guys like Dizzy Dean, Ducky Medwick, Wild Bill Hallahan, Ripper Collins, and Pepper Martin? Well, how about the 1941 Dodgers, also called "Da Bums," with Pee Wee Reese, Mickey Owen, Dixie Walker, Pistol Pete Reiser, and, again, Ducky Medwick? This was one of those occasions, being alone in a crowd of 50,000, during which private thoughts that cause chuckles and laughs had to be subdued, otherwise people nearby may have wondered.

As a player, Durocher had a good glove, though not much of a bat. He could not run very fast, either. But, he was always entertaining. As a manager, he was more than capable of becoming the whole show at the drop of a hat and was totally deserving of the nickname "Leo the lip," having been ejected from more games than anyone else except John McGraw, at least for the time being, until future Braves' skipper Bobby Cox eventually surpassed him in 2006. Baseball during the era of Leo Durocher was very colorful.

Being at the ballpark on this crisp and clear early fall afternoon in Georgia, recalling personal baseball memories while taking in a game, made one afraid to think that the trip might have been forgone, so good it was to be there. Everything was right with the world. Could there ever have been a better day than this for Aaron to overtake Ruth's career home run record? No, there could not be, and there would not be. A certain thought did not even occur during the game (it should have because it became so obvious later) that Durocher never would have let Aaron pass Ruth at his expense. Never.

When Aaron broke Ruth's record the following April, I saw it on television, with no regrets for not being at the ballpark in person, either. The game was a sellout because of the publicity buildup over the winter.

This was arguably the most important accomplishment in all of sports. The one troubling aspect was how Major League Baseball, the Atlanta Braves, and Television tried to take control of the event, ignoring the proper requisites of the game, instead giving favor to crass and self-serving publicity.

The Braves 1974 season schedule was set to begin with a three game weekend series in Cincinnati, the first game to be played on Thursday, April 4, with single games to follow on Saturday and Sunday. After this opening series, the team was to return home to face the Dodgers on Monday night, the eighth. The Braves certainly preferred that Aaron hit number seven hundred and fifteen in front of the home crowd in Atlanta. To make sure, he would have to be kept out of the lineup until the team returned home. Commissioner Bowie Kuhn, not favorably disposed to this plan, ordered Aaron to go ahead and play in Cincinnati. As it turned out, he played in two of the three games.

Mr. Kuhn and the Braves' team management, assuming they were being realistic, must have figured that Aaron would tie and/or beat Ruth against the Dodgers in Atlanta at the earliest. What were the odds of hitting two home runs in any three games, assuming a dozen plate appearances? Good question. If a man were to hit two home runs every three games, he would collect one hundred and eight dingers during the season. Aaron's best year was forty-five. His career average was thirty-three. The odds of hitting two home runs during the Cincinnati series were not very good for anyone, even for an accomplished home run hitter, and especially when starting a season in the cold dense April air of the upper Ohio River valley.

Still, the exact odds would have been worth a close examination. During his major league career through the 1973 season, Mr. Aaron averaged one home run every 4.15 games, or one home run for every 15.81 times at bat. Based on this data, utilizing a binomial distribution, we would find that the probability he would hit two home runs during the three games in Cincinnati, assuming twelve official times at bat, was 0.1735. Stated more directly, there was approximately a seventeen percent chance he would do it, or an eighty-three percent chance he would not.

Well, as Benjamin Disraeli once smartly observed,

"There are three kinds of lies: lies, damn lies, and statistics."

Genuine baseball folks know how to deal with this. They tend to rush through the lies and the damn lies in order to get quickly to the statistics, which forms their zone of comfort, where they experience an ambiance as if at home, where they are confident and secure. The world of statistics is a wonderful place in which to be. Any point of view can be argued for as long as one can present numbers, which means for a long time. Since numbers are, by their very nature, equal until given a dimensional value and pressed into service, an argument depending solely upon presentation and interpretation is mostly pointless. The winner of an argument, therefore, is usually the man with the most numbers, and not necessarily the best numbers.

Sometimes arguments degenerate beyond the use of numbers. When such a moment of desperation occurs within our world of baseball statistics, we can assuage any surprise or disappointment by simply adjusting the old numbers, by finding new numbers, or by reinterpreting all of the numbers. Since we cannot play the game, we can play with the numbers, still a very satisfying pursuit. Turning a double play on the field cannot possibly be any more rewarding than turning a slugging and on-base distribution on its head with a pencil and piece of paper.

Very well, as the First Earl of Beaconsfield is not available for consultation, it could be accepted as given that statistics are useful most of the time. Or are they? There was not even a fifty-fifty chance that Henry Aaron, soon to be the greatest home run hitter of all time, would hit one homer in Cincinnati, forget about two. So, going back to the opening day game on April 4, 1974, what consolation could be found by Atlanta Braves management when the very first pitch thrown to Mr. Aaron in the first inning of the first game of the season became number seven hundred and fourteen? Actually, there was some consolation in knowing he had not yet figured out how to hit two home runs during one at bat. In any case, this probably was the only home run in the history of baseball regarded as a problem by the team for which it was hit. The problem was if Aaron hit another home run in Cincinnati, the Braves would lose the once-in-a-lifetime chance to host the most important event in baseball during the Twentieth Century. He did not hit another that weekend.

Feigning normalcy sometimes does have its virtues. Aaron ranks high amongst the all-time greatest ballplayers. Everyone knows this. However, the game of baseball is far greater than any individual player, manager, owner, commissioner, or record. In fact, it is greater than the whole lot of them put together. The game itself is supreme. Unfortunately, to those who make a living out of trying to control the game, not all of the elements of baseball put together are greater than money, or the opportunity to make more of it. Would it be that it was not true. Since it is largely true, professional baseball is a business in foresight, and a game mostly in hindsight.

To authentic fans, where the record-setting home run happened did not matter. Unsullied by coarse commercialism, the true and pure followers of baseball just wanted it to happen as a normal part of a game, any game, just as long as it was random. Unfortunately, this desire was not realistic, simply too much to expect. Setting the new all-time home run record could not ever be a normal part of any baseball game. Where it happened did matter greatly. It mattered because unforgettable events matter more than forgettable ones, especially when they are known to be unforgettable before they happen. Maybe it would be better to say that real baseball fans would have preferred that everyone behave as if it happened as a normal part of a game. Whatever the case and however it was perceived, it was going to happen.

Many important people wanted to witness this historic event, or be seen witnessing this historic event. A large national network television audience tuned in, in addition to an enthusiastic hometown crowd at the stadium. The principals involved anticipated this spectacle would reap substantial benefits. What these men, event creators and event seekers that they were, absolutely did not want was to remain in Atlanta for days, or maybe even weeks, watching the Braves play baseball games. One easily drawn conclusion was that this event might have become much too important to be random. That was not all. What consideration had been given to the death threats directed at Mr. Aaron? Did they enter into the equation, too? Would not setting the new record put an end to them? Probably everyone hoped so. Logically, it would be best for Major League Baseball, the Braves, television, and, most especially, Aaron himself, to get it done in Atlanta as soon as possible.

Well, as we all know now, they did not have to wait very long. Aaron drilled number seven hundred fifteen off the "Bank Americard" sign into the bull pen in left-center field during the fourth inning of the first home game against the Dodgers on April 8, to the delight of the spectators who could then leave early, and to the dismay of the television network which preferred a later inning to keep viewers. Not surprisingly, the place was packed when he hit it. The sale of standing room tickets must have been an all-time record, too, because the number of people who said they were there was about ten times the seating capacity of the old Fulton County Stadium.

Even at such an event as this, fans can be fickle. By the end of the fifth inning, the ballpark was mostly empty, like on a normal April night.

It was a disgrace. For those who may have missed it, Ron Reed pitched for the Braves as they beat the Dodgers 7-4 to even their record at 2-2 on the season. Now, with Aaron's home run record business over, we could get back to baseball. Still, the event had secondary benefits as it attracted some big time attention for Atlanta, the up-and-coming metropolis of the New South.

The question remains whether this was a legitimate baseball game. One commentator at the time evaluated the situation with a great deal of wisdom and diplomacy by simply saying that trying to sneak a fastball past Henry Aaron was like trying to sneak the sunrise past a rooster. He did not have to mention that every pitcher in baseball knew this, including Al Downing. A middle-in, belt-high fastball would have been a meatball for minor leaguers. It was no surprise that Aaron crushed it. In truth, that 1-0 pitch was the equivalent of batting practice. To start this great slugger with an off-speed breaking ball into the dirt suggested nothing more than a lame attempt at a purposeful set-up pitch. After the game, Mr. Downing offered that he was trying to throw his second pitch, the fastball, away. Sure he was, and he missed by two feet. Perhaps what he meant to say was,

"Mr. Aaron, sir, excuse me. Where would you prefer the next ball to be pitched?"

The important thing was that Aaron did become the new home run champion of all time. But in my opinion, again for what it is worth, the home run that actually beat Ruth happened on Thursday evening, April 11, against the Dodgers' Charlie Hough. Hough came into the game in relief in the seventh inning. First, he gave up a leadoff home run to Mike Lum. Two at bats later Aaron hit a solo home run, officially number seven hundred sixteen, in front of 5,114 devoted fans, helping future Hall of Fame pitcher Phil Niekro record another win. Aaron's two home runs during the week did have one thing in common, though. Dusty Baker watched both of them from the on-deck circle.

The bowling ball factory in LaGrange closed in September 1974 because of economic factors emanating from the Arab oil embargo, higher than expected start-up costs, and lower than expected product sales. The only thing left to do was pack up, move to Atlanta, and find another less than satisfactory job while trying to survive a worsening economy aggravated by three consecutive presidents whose leadership consisted of wage and price controls, WIN buttons, and a general malaise.

The Braves finished the season in third place, fourteen games behind the Dodgers. Ralph Garr had a terrific year batting .353 while hustling out seventeen triples. Bench, Morgan, Rose, Schmidt, and Stargell all had excellent years, too, but Steve Garvey inexplicably won the National League MVP. Finally, Hank Aaron left the Braves. He found a new home by returning to his old home in Milwaukee, which afforded designated hitter opportunities with the American League Brewers.

It would be a while before the Braves had another good season, namely 1982. Announcer Milo Hamilton left after the 1975 season, but Ernie Johnson stayed. Why Mr. Hamilton left may not be a mystery. During the late innings of a radio broadcast near the end of the season, he mildly berated the fans for not supporting the team. Everything he said was true even if surprisingly tactless. The next four years found the Braves at season's end in last place while attendance numbers remained anemic. The team needed more than fan support, however, to improve the situation.

In 1976, the Braves hired two additional broadcasters. One was Skip Caray, the son of Harry Caray. He had grown up in St. Louis and, from time to time, would make an extraneous trifling remark that seemed to indicate he might have been a Cardinals and a Musial fan from his boyhood days. In fact, Mr. Caray's manner of expression, choice of words, opinions, and evaluations relating to baseball were markedly similar to those of my father, so much so, they almost could have been brothers. The other new voice of the Braves was Pete van Weiren, "the Professor." Mr. van Weiren was practically a walking baseball encyclopedia.

About that time, Mr. Johnson gave an interview to the *Georgia Bulletin*, the Atlanta Catholic Archdiocesan newspaper, during which he was asked about the toughest batter he ever faced. Without hesitation, he declared it was Stan Musial. These gentlemen, informative, clever, and optimistic, were always enjoyable to hear. Oh, and the Braves picked up a new owner along the way; some guy who owned a TV station on West Peachtree Street, a billboard company, and a very fast sailboat, a ten-meter one at that. After all was said and done, even when the home team was in last place, living in a major league city again was very good.

The 1981 season started with the hope that the Braves would get out of the basement of the Western Division. April 15, 1981 was a typical Georgia spring day. The azaleas and dogwoods were in bloom, the recent winter chills barely a memory. On the Wednesday before Easter, the Braves were playing their sixth game of the season against the Astros in Houston, Tommy Boggs against Nolan Ryan. During supper, before the game started, the wife went into labor. In anticipation of my first-born, we departed for Piedmont Hospital a very few minutes away. Once situated in a room near the delivery room to wait it out, whatever "it" was, there was little for the expectant father to do. The dramatic interlude passed easily while paying attention to a television on the wall tuned to Turner's WTCG-Channel 17 beginning with the bottom half of the first inning.

The evening was very fortunate except for one thing. The Braves lost 2-0. Boggs went the distance giving up two hits, two runs, one earned, while striking out four and walking one. Ryan went seven innings with three hits and nine strikeouts. LaCorte got the save. The Braves had chances in the fourth and sixth innings with men in scoring position and Dale Murphy up to bat, but he struck out each time. Murph went 0-4 on the night. Chris Chambliss produced most of the offensive punch by hitting safely three times. Not much else was forthcoming from the Braves' bats. Good news, the time of game was a short two hours, which allowed plenty of time to see the post game show and still be in the delivery room for the blessed event occurring shortly after midnight. Maybe the pitcher's duel enticed the little one to get outta there.

The presentation to a father of a healthy baby is always a wonderful occasion or, at least, it ought to be a wonderful occasion. This one was wonderful. A baby boy, born on Holy Thursday, marked the start of a new family. He looked remarkably like his great-grandfather; therefore, it was fitting to give him the same name, Alexander, but not entirely for this reason. I loved my grandfather and my middle name is Alexander, but in truth, when choosing a boy's name, the two main considerations are how it will look in a box score and how it will sound over a stadium's public address system. He would be called "Alec" as in:

"Now pitching for Mudville, number six, Alec Barnes."

The father has the general task of choosing one of the many good Christian names that he has determined meets the above criteria. By no coincidence, my grandfather was called Alec, too.

Choosing a girl's name is a completely different matter. Here one must first consider how it will look when engraved on a wedding invitation and then, just as importantly, how it will sound during formal introductions. Precisely for these reasons, girls should be named

Jacqueline or Michaela while boys do better with Jack or Mike, and not the other way around. Likewise, on less than formal occasions, the same theory works well for Allie and Alec.

A quick count of the toes and fingers, and a survey of other crucial body parts, yielded the preliminary conclusion there were no apparent physical abnormalities, a very happy occasion, indeed. When a baby is born the parents are always concerned first with health matters. Once this hurdle is cleared, if the parents are normal, they immediately return to making plans for the kid's future, a task that usually begins around the time of conception.

The "baby-boomer" generation, those born mostly between the late 1940's and early 1960's, was the first in history to be thoroughly admonished by child psychologists not to plan their children's lives, so loathed and feared parental guidance had become. Therefore, the newly minted parents of the day, having perfected the "hippie" mantra of "do your own thing" during the late 1960's and 1970's, faced a discomfiting quandary. Should they follow the worthy inclinations endowed by nature or, with a sycophantic recalcitrance, continue to pay homage to the most profound philosophical inanity of their generation? For many, the mantra provided the most appealing alternative. They would continue doing their own thing while the raising of children would pass largely into the hands of day-care providers, schoolteachers, and counselors, who would in turn be counseled by (whom else?) child psychologists. Validation as parents would then be attained by unremittingly hovering above their surrogates. Naturally, these parents were wrong. The American Culture has always paid a dear price for applying socialistic thought. Good parents generally provide the best guidance as well as make the best plans from which their children deviate at their own risk.

My plan did not presuppose having children with above average athletic abilities. The first hope was that they would be good students, and, secondarily, they would be willing and able to participate in some sporting activities. Boys, out of necessity, would have to become adept at digesting the sports page every morning. The only specific athletic skill that would be mandatory was swimming, this being in deference to the fact that most of the earth is covered by water. The issue here was safety.

The plan for a boy's team sport included a choice limited to the big four: baseball, football, basketball, and ice hockey. Lacrosse may have been acceptable, too. A personal bias naturally put baseball first. Granted, if the family's genes indicated more height and size the choice might have been different, but being average or below in both those capacities created a practical limitation. Even if the possibility of meeting the physical requirements of football or basketball existed, passing up little league baseball would have occurred sometime after an ice storm in Hell.

Most gainfully employed parents of the boys who began grammar school during the 1950's considered participation in team sports important as healthful avocations while growing up, but not as a realistic career choice, particularly not a way to earn a decent living. A few athletes made a lot of money in those days, but most earned less pay than the typical automobile assembly line worker did. The economics of playing sports professionally made such aspirations dubious, at best. Even Mickey Mantle worked a second job during the off-season after his first year with the Yankees. The same was true for most football and basketball players. Dad would sometimes point out particular players for the Redskins and Senators who had to work when they were not playing football or baseball. The kinds of jobs they did were not very exciting, either. More likely, they worked as barkeepers rather than bankers. Even most of the college baseball players in those days did not play with hopes of being drafted into the minor leagues upon graduation. Their role model was more likely to be Frank Merriwell of Yale, rather than Christy Mathewson of the Giants.

Even though player salaries had risen drastically since those days, preconceived notions tend to linger. Therefore, in my mind, participation in team sports had to be secondary to academic achievement, never a substitute for it. Another factor that may have induced some bias was the fact that, as a family, we had produced only one professional athlete. He was an uncle-in-law, Wade Herren, a locally well-known tennis player from Birmingham who was an NCAA southeast champion somewhere back in the late 1940's or early 1950's. My grandfather was also a fairly good gymnast while a student at Alliance College in Pennsylvania around 1920. Otherwise, there was no legitimate role model to follow into professional sports from our family. In any case, it was a truly great surprise years later when all three of my kids earned high school varsity letters, Alec in baseball and the girls, Pam and Elizabeth, in basketball. "Proud father" summed it up pretty well, but mostly because all of them proceeded to attend and graduate from four-year universities solely on their academic merits. Even so, just because a father does not consciously plan for his son to become a major league ballplayer, the subconscious can contain many more notions and expectations, which, even when well hidden, can reveal themselves readily, often with little prompting.

Alec's first significant baseball moment took place in 1982 before his first birthday while we were visiting relatives in Mountain Brook, Alabama. One Sunday afternoon he was playing with some empty wooden thread spools on the floor in Aunt Harriet's parlor when suddenly she exclaimed,
"He's a southpaw!"
I turned to see him throw a spool with his left hand and my mind immediately conjured up thoughts of Spahn, Koufax, Ford, and Musial! It is funny, sometimes, how the mind works on its own. What would be the psychoanalysis of this pattern of association? Now, before the kid could even walk, he just happened to pick up a spool and throw it with his left hand. The immediate thoughts were pitcher, first base, or outfield. Granted, this may have been jumping the gun a bit even for a father. Besides, we could have been mistaken, or maybe it was a decoy. You know, baseball players do that sort of thing. Not to worry, though, because as it turned out, our first impression was, indeed, the correct one. He did not inherit his father's physical handicap. He was, by God's Grace, left-handed.

Nothing much related to baseball happened to the lefty for the next two years until, for the first time, he met a catcher, not just any catcher, but the Atlanta Braves' Bruce Benedict. Mr. Benedict helped us put on a Christmas Party for underprivileged inner-city kids at our Cross Creek Clubhouse in Buckhead. The Braves were cruising, one might say, during the early 1980's. They were fun to watch. Dale Murphy and Phil Niekro were the toasts of the team. Unfortunately, opportunities to attend games were very limited. The combination of time, money, young kids, work, MBA School, etc., just did not allow it.

About first grade the time was right to introduce the boy to some actual baseball, i.e., throwing, catching, and hitting with a real hard ball. There was quite a bit of impatience in wanting to pass on everything I knew about the game as the memories of playing baseball as a kid were furiously returning. They were good memories, not just good, out-of-this-world great. Those days back in Springfield Forest were the best ones. Even after all the years that had passed, after not setting foot on a baseball field for two decades, I could still recall every impression of the game, along with all its physical accoutrements, with the greatest of ease. The full range of sensations came alive, from the ethereal pleasure of catching a high fly ball to the augmented tension of an 0-2 count; the intoxicating triumphant rush of solid contact as the sweet spot of a wood bat connects with the ball; the smell of glove leather; the inspiring sights and sounds of the little league ballpark; the constant din of taunting chatter; the thirst, the dirt, the spit, the bubblegum, the neighbors watching from the stands. An American father does the right thing when he introduces his son to baseball, in teaching him love and respect for the greatest American game.

Normally, there are only a few years time during which a boy gets to play baseball just for fun. This carefree endeavor often ends abruptly with junior high school since most players do not advance to the high school level, the time when play becomes more serious. Though brief, this period before high school may contain the most important baseball years of all. Boys acquire their practical understanding of the game during this time. Even for those who go on to play at higher levels, most of the skills that a player ever develops, including major leaguers, are acquired before entering high school. Not only skills, but also most tendencies and attitudes are acquired at a young age. This makes the proper instruction of youngsters a serious business. Since baseball is the national pastime, teaching it should be considered a sacred trust, not to be taken lightly.

Every boy who can run and throw can play baseball regardless of size, shape, quickness, agility, strength, mental acuity, or personality. No matter if the boy is weak or strong, tall or short, thin or plump, fast or slow, aggressive or shy, there is a place waiting for him on a little league baseball team. Baseball is the perfect game for boys, perfect in every sense a sport can be. He will be made a member of a team, challenged, and given opportunities to perform. Most importantly, he will succeed in his efforts. Every boy who plays little league baseball plays it with success.

It is often said that baseball is a game of failure. Plenty of false examples are then used to fortify this argument. Home run king Henry Aaron failed to hit a home run ninety-five percent of the time. The all-time game winning pitcher, Cy Young, is also the all-time loser of three hundred sixteen games. Even the best hitters fail to hit safely seventy percent of the time. One could go on and on like this, making what seem to be legitimate statistical arguments. Every point, however, can be disputed by its own inverse. Consequently, any such proposition that baseball is a game of failure should be dispatched with vehemence. Baseball is a game where every single action can be evaluated simultaneously in terms of both success and failure. For example, a strikeout is a failure for the batter as it is a success for the pitcher. In a 6-inning little league game each team gets eighteen outs, meaning each team will succeed and fail at least eighteen times at the bat and in the field. However, in reality, many more successes and failures will occur. There will never be a game with only the minimum number of successes and failures, just as no golfer will ever shoot a round with only eighteen strokes.

The greater point is that successes abound within every baseball game. Therefore, it is virtually always true that every player in any given game will participate in at least one very meaningful success during that game. Rather than being a game of failures, baseball is a game in which every player succeeds, even those on the losing team.

The absolute worst part of living through the baby-boomer parenting culture, full of parents who so fervently worshiped the false god of an ill-defined self-esteem, has been enduring the unfortunate misconception that European football should be the game of choice for boys, instead of baseball, or real football. If there is any game where failure is the rule and success is the rare exception, it is soccer. The difference between the two sports is very conspicuous in this regard. In baseball, self-worth is achieved through individual success, even if the team loses. Soccer is richly characterized by the sharing of group failure, even when the team wins. Running after a ball may be a good form of exercise, but hardly a good way to build confidence.

The point is better made by considering some of the more positive aspects of playing baseball. During a game, there are many opportunities to succeed. When a player bats, he could get a hit, a walk, a sacrifice, or he could reach base by an error or by being hit by a pitch. He could also make a productive out by moving base runners. Later on, after little league, it is even possible to reach base after striking out. As a base runner, he can steal a base, score a run, or break up a double play with a good slide. On the other side, a fielder succeeds any time he has a putout, an assist, or prevents a runner from advancing an extra base. The pitcher and catcher experience success and failure with each sign given and pitch thrown.

The worst little league game for my son that I can remember (I remember most of them quite well) was at Murphey-Candler Park in DeKalb County one Saturday afternoon in March of 1991. My nine-year-old had struck out every time up and not a single ball had been hit his way into center field until the last inning. His team was getting clobbered. Finally, the ball was hit into the gap and rolled past him all the way to the fence. He and the left fielder ran after it. Alec won the race to the ball, turned, and threw it directly to the cut-off man, well enough to prevent another run from scoring. After this miserable game ended, we talked on the way home about his good effort to get to the ball, his good throw, and the importance of both. The next day, in deference to practicality, we went back out to the field for more batting practice.

Sure, they lost and everything seemed to go wrong that day, except that he executed one play very well. Under other circumstances, such a play could have saved a game. Emphasizing the highlights, based on a well-considered analysis, is what every kid needs to hear, win or lose, good or bad. Understanding the game, executing the plays, and analyzing the results build true self-esteem. It is self-esteem based on knowledge and use of skills, attained by preparation through drills and practice. It comes from understanding more and more about the intricacies of the game. Most of all, it is the self-esteem that comes when an individual's performance helps the team, not when the team's performance helps the individual. Winning is only a consequence in baseball, not a measure. If a pitcher gives up ten earned runs, is he any better if his team scores eleven; or worse if they score nine? In truth, he pitched badly that day under both scenarios. Conversely, if he pitches a no-hitter and loses due to an unearned run is he any worse than if his team had scored two runs and won?

The reasons for which a team wins or loses a baseball game are not always as obvious or as simple as sometimes reported. We often hear that a game was won by a "walk-off" home run in the ninth inning or by a hit that produced the game winning run. Maybe the win was credited to the pitcher who threw the shutout, without mention of any defensive plays or of the fact that someone had to score a run; otherwise the game would never have ended. Fortunately, a more complete and faithful report can usually be found in the newspapers where sportswriters take the time and space to cover all relevant details.

The search for answers, the quest for a greater understanding of the game, is a peculiarly varied undertaking. Some are more inclined to study statistical descriptions of situations. Others tend to focus on behavioral tendencies. It turns out that both approaches are vitally important.

It also turns out that more happens in baseball when the ball is not in play than when it is. The period following the conclusion of one play and before the next pitch is thrown, is bursting with mental activity. While defensive positioning and pitch selection are being considered, each team is trying to second-guess the other. It is amusing to hear some people say that baseball is boring because everyone is just standing around waiting for something to happen. Preparation is the greater part of the game while execution is assumed.

There are times when intuition plays a crucial role, too. It does in the sense that baseball intuition requires the use of perception and insight that comes from knowledge, not in the sense of using feminine-type feelings. Why did Lasorda send Kirk Gibson in to pinch hit in the ninth inning with the first game of the 1988 World Series on the line? The easy answer is that he put in a left-handed hitter to face the right-handed Eckersley. In addition, Gibson led the team in home runs that year. No doubt, a home run was what the Dodgers needed. However, the injured Gibson, still suffering from an old hamstring problem, could barely climb the steps of the dugout. If he had hit the ball between the third baseman and the shortstop, the left fielder might have been able to throw him out before he reached first base!

Sometimes baseball managers seem to act on a hunch, or on intuition. In reality, their success is ultimately determined by a superior understanding of both situations and tendencies. Lasorda's intuition was based on something very substantial. A scouting report indicated Oakland A's pitcher Dennis Eckersley tended to throw a backdoor slider on full counts. Gibson, the veteran, knew this, too. Moreover, Gibson was very adept at fouling off two-strike pitches, which he did during this at bat. When Gibson had two strikes he started looking down and away, and when he got the pitch he sought, he knocked it out of the park. This pitch may not have even been called a strike, but it was very close, almost a perfect pitch, nearly impossible to hit for most batters in most situations, though not if the batter was looking for it. Lasorda guessed that an experienced player, one who had the right skills, even though crippled, would have the best chance to work the count, know what was coming, and then know what to do with it when it got there.

In baseball, there seems to be a natural craving for statistics, almost to the point of overwhelming even the statistician. Statistics do go a long way in explaining the rational part of the game. However, if knowledge of numbers was all that was needed to understand the game, a computer program could be written that would enable everyone, or anyone, to manage. In truth, very few can successfully manage a baseball team, with or without computers, something worth remembering when calling a sports radio talk show after a game to criticize managers and coaches.

Baseball statistics, as comprehensive and complex as they may be, do not tell the whole story. Very often, something more subtle, such as defensive positioning or a set-up pitch, is the key that determines the outcome of a game. Furthermore, good players regularly do odd things that help their team, some of which do not turn up in box scores. Those that do may even look bad in the box score, such as a ground out to the right side that advances runners into scoring position. Nor do statistics reflect some well-executed efforts that end up having severely negative consequences. How many perfectly thrown pitches are hit out of the park? Many more than the one Eckersley threw to Gibson.

The reasons why any one particular game is won or lost could fill a decent size book. Chapter one would contain the scouting reports and chapter twenty-something or thirty-something would analyze why the pitcher shook off the first two signs for the last pitch of the game. Those who think baseball games move too slowly and take too long should ask any manager how much free time he has to goof-off between innings or between pitches. Moreover, when was the last time an NFL game took less than two-and-a-half hours? Or three hours? There have been double-headers completed in less time than some Super Bowls.

Finally, to instill in youngsters a more enduring appreciation for the game, a youth coach or parent should never hesitate to show a proper amount of respect for their intelligence. When teaching baseball, how to do things is no more important than the philosophy and the logic that constitute the reasons for doing things. Kids enjoy being challenged to figure out numbers and theories. One could start by asking little leaguers to explain the "Mendoza Line." Baseball is unequalled in its algebraic and geometric complexity. A profound mathematical elegance attaches to the game not to be found in any other team sport. In fact, baseball is as intellectually compelling as chess. Leading off with a drag bunt is a strategy just as exquisite as, say, opening with a King's Gambit, as if the second baseman and first baseman were the opponent's King's pawn and King's Bishop's pawn, respectively. When the ball is finally "live," that is, moving within the field of play, baseball suddenly becomes artful. It is ballet; it is poetry; it is living sculpture. Imagine the combination of Ballenshine, of Shakespeare, and of Michelangelo, accompanied by the commentary of Bobby Fischer. There is a lot to teach kids about the game, and very little time in which to do it.

Every American boy benefits from being introduced to baseball. More than just playing a game, it means participating in a cultural heritage. Other sports can be very useful and satisfying, too; however, learning and playing the game of baseball will lead a youngster into a uniquely American social peerage as a man. For this, there is no substitute. Diminished is the value of a man who does not know how to take a lead or hit behind a runner or, Heaven forbid, back up a play. Diminished is the value of his intellect if it is bereft of this game's universal and always appropriate metaphors. An American boy who is kept from playing youth baseball, who is denied the chance to play in an organized league, is a casualty of child neglect.

By playing baseball, a boy learns many things about life as well as about work. He learns the value of perseverance, of individual effort, and of teamwork. He learns to appreciate the tools of a trade. Baseball has implements and materials with which players forge a close and lasting relationship. They become much more than mere inanimate objects. The dirt and grass, the wood and leather, the steel cleats and favorite chew, the dugout walls and the chalk lines. Many things physiologically bind the player to the game. This connection is cemented by sight, feel, smell, and sound, sensations that are warmly remembered for a lifetime. Mark these words: a man is much more likely to remember, and to have kept, his first ball glove and his first bat than his first girlfriend.

*Chapter Four*

# Baseball: The Choice is Clear

The early European settlers to America, by necessity, traveled light, leaving behind those tangible possessions not deemed essential, and even some that were deemed essential, due to cargo limitations aboard ships. Not so for intangibles. Seeing how courage and devotion did not occupy space in the hold of any ship, their most valuable baggage had no size or weight restrictions at all. By and large, the men came with mountains of courage, daring to escape the stifling societies of the Old World, willing to seize the opportunity to begin anew. The women were devoted to their families, keen to bringing forth and nurturing a subsequent generation. That which was not vital to the cause of starting a new life was better left behind or thrown overboard. In truth, greater security was to be gotten from noble character traits than from material possessions.

Deciding what to bring to the New World was an exercise similar to selecting the necessary props for a theatrical play. Found within this playhouse of their own choosing was the stage upon which they had to perform or perish. Already products of an advanced civilization, each of these self-motivated, thoroughly challenged newcomers was set to author an original real life drama. History has shown that their subsequent cultural designs, including the creation of new sports, oftentimes proved utterly brilliant.

Regrettably, through the passage of time, some detrimental parts of the European cultures crept into America, things like socialist theories, the United Nations, the Mafia, Sauerkraut, Bohemian Existentialism, etc., along with an entirely meager form of team sport, a distinctly inferior brand of football. Not to be daunted, the great integrity and character of the early settlers survived enabling an authentic American Culture to endure in spite of repeated attempts by some Europhiles to inflict fraudulent Old World affectations. Even so, the one such contrivance, namely soccer, continued to pose a credible threat to the character of American boys.

I was not unaware of European football as a child, recalling how it was played by some young adults near the ellipse behind the White House when we passed by on the way to visit museums after church. Staying at home to play baseball would have been preferred, except we were not allowed to play baseball on Sunday. We had to stay clean and spend time with the family, as if we did not see enough of each other all week long.

Here was the first exposure to the spectacle of this odd, seemingly pointless game, taking place virtually in the back yard of the White House. Often we parked the car nearby and walked past, though never stopped to watch. The players spoke a foreign language that sounded like they were Europeans, although they may have been from Central or South America. My mother, having been born in Italy and raised in Porto Albona, Trieste, and Venice, told us that all the Italian boys played this game. How they should be pitied. Italian boys here in America were the lucky ones. The thought of, say, Joe DiMaggio wearing those silly-looking short pants and running around aimlessly like a sissy created a very frightful image. Besides, what possible concern should any American boy have had for whatever games the Italian boys played over in Italy? Joltin' Joe and his brothers played baseball. No doubt, the rest of the Italian boys would play baseball, too, if they were lucky enough to live in America.

Soccer in the backyard of the President's house was a sacrilege, an outrage. Less than a hundred years earlier, the ellipse was the sight of daily baseball games. President Grant routinely walked down to the field in the afternoon to get in a few swings with the boys who regularly played there. Now this sacred baseball land was being desecrated by a fatuous European game. We strolled along paying it little heed for it was no more than a minimal distraction. The main objective was to get through those cavernous museum buildings on the mall and back home as soon as possible to start playing catch. Admittedly, even with the mind oriented towards baseball, some elements of American history and culture presented inside the Smithsonian were absorbed, to be appreciated more so in later years.

Between Pennsylvania Avenue and Franconia Road is an area that has witnessed an immense portion of American history. The United States is now united though the view of our nation, and more specifically of the Rebellion, from either side of the Potomac River, from every Yankeetown and from every Rebelville, has varied quite a lot over the years, and continues to do so even to this day. General Lee, unquestionably, was a far better military man than the entire sequence of Union commanders. However, General Grant won. Both sides, while seeking to preserve the integrity of the principles contained within the Constitution, were in conflict with it as well as with each other. In the end, what mattered was the way the nation healed its wounds and reunited. Similarly, the major leagues consist of two circuits, each producing a worthy contestant for the final championship. Thus, the World Series is not played to see who is best; it is not played to see who is right; it is played to see who wins. Then everyone takes a short break before reporting for spring training in order to prepare for a new campaign.

As we came to know them, the traditions and tales associated with the White House, along with the surrounding neighborhood, were very significant, very much connected to Springfield, going beyond even former presidents, famous generals, civil rebellions, and baseball. This area was the geographic centerpiece of the nation's soul, of its executive power and governmental functions. As older teenagers, we came to understand this place better, to visit this neighborhood frequently, and to appreciate its existence, though not always for edifying purposes.

Emblematic of the ties forming an indissoluble connection between presidents, generals, White House grounds, Springfield, and baseball was a modest neighborhood saloon called the Old Ebbitt Grill. Grant was known to frequent the place, along with many other famous personages. Lee, as far as anyone knows, never did. Ebbitt's was contained in a very narrow building, sandwiched between two other taller buildings on the north side of E Street just a few paces to the east down from 15$^{th}$ Street, about a block from the White House. Ebbitt's survived all the significant events befalling the executive mansion throughout the many years. That is, it survived everything except the young urban professionals, the so-called "yuppies" of the 1980's.

During the 1960's, before the Aquarian Age and before Our Lord was awarded a rock and roll "superstar" status, the Old Ebbitt Grill was the preferred gathering place in the District of Columbia for the more socially adept young men of Springfield's Robert E. Lee High School. Some of the West Springfield High School students became a part of the tradition, too. Many of these early, and sometimes first, saloon visits were made when the revelers were still somewhere on the shy side of the legal drinking age, which was eighteen years in those days inside the

District of Columbia. Within the Commonwealth of Virginia, it was twenty-one. Had the driving age been eighteen, too, instead of sixteen, visiting Ebbitt's would have been far more difficult.

Ebbitt's was a place of true historic charm. Everything wooden creaked with an audible oaken splendor, not annoyingly, not any more so than the squeaking of finger movements on a six-string guitar. The floor, the chairs, the tables, even the bar when leaned upon, all creaked. The interior was long and narrow. The hardwood bar ran almost the entire depth with an appearance of sloping from back to front. Actually, it was built level. The floor did most of the sloping, or so it seemed. It felt like going uphill coming in and downhill leaving.

Above the entrance on the inside, way up near the top of the entirely too high ceiling was a large clock, large enough to discern the correct time from across the room even through the thick haze of tobacco smoke. Around on the walls, various stuffed animal trophies were mounted. They were hung so high one could not see to read the accompanying plaques, which were engraved with details of the hunter and quarry. All were the just rewards of gallant trips by hunters unknown. It was said Teddy Roosevelt bagged some of them. Maybe he did. Maybe he did not. An evening spent inside the Old Ebbitt Grill was more enjoyable when the legends were simply believed as one could imagine them to be. No more charm would have accrued with further evidence on any topic of observation, one way, or the other.

On the wall behind the bar were numerous glass and wooden shelves adorned with fancy beer steins adding a bit of German ambiance to the place. The tables and chairs, positioned along the western wall opposite the bar, were smaller than what would be considered the proper size today. When full of patrons, Ebbitt's was truly close quarters. In short, here was an authentic American classic city saloon, a place fit to refresh all of Washington, D.C. occupiers, from the famous to the infamous, from presidents to presidential assassins, from generals to spies, from government transients to the (always incognito) high-society cave dwellers.

For those of us young visitors coming from the Confederate side of the Potomac, Ebbitt's was a genial place to meet with buddies or even to bring a young lady. A small glass of draught beer was fifteen cents in 1966 and fresh baked bread rolls were a dime if they did not forget to charge you. Sandwiches were hearty and delectable. There was no television set and no amplified music, no music at all unless revelers decided to sing. Making up some loosely enticing conversation was never a problem, either, since stories here were easy to invent.

"John Wilkes Booth was sitting over at that bar stool second from the door with his hat drooped down and drinking whiskey when he spied Lincoln's body guard stroll in on the evening of April 14, 1865. They say the guard sat down at *this* table in *your* chair, ordered a shot, while Booth slipped out the back, got on his horse, and rode over to Ford's Theatre."

"You're kidding me, aren't you?"

"That's what I've been told. Too bad Lincoln didn't think to slip out the back of Ford's Theatre about that time and ride over here for a drink. Things could have turned out different."

The Old Ebbitt Grill on E Street would be considered a curiosity today because, in this meeting place suitable for young and old people alike, there was productive and mostly civil conversation with no need to raise voices to be heard and understood. Dress was informal which, in this era, meant a blazer or tweed jacket, with a white shirt and tie. Each young lady, each one escorted, of course, wore a dress, or a skirt and blouse. The waiters were a sight from a better time, too. They wore pale yellowish evening jackets, white shirts, and black bow ties while maintaining a high tone and an elegant demeanor.

Occasionally, a meddlesome Springfield parent, wise to these illicit gatherings, would make an informing call to the D.C. Police, yes, the very same D.C. Police charged with guarding Lincoln. The officer sent to investigate would politely pause at the front door just long enough to allow anyone who may be under eighteen years of age, and finding they had immediate business elsewhere, to retreat towards the lavatories in the rear, continuing out the back entrance to the alley and be on their way. No underage drinking was to be found here.

Ebbitt's in the 1960's provided an enchanting travel through time. With a little imagination, one could actually be transported in thought back to the latter half of the 1800's. If U. S. Grant had walked through the door, he would not have seen anything startlingly different within the establishment he knew other than the electric light fixtures. This was soon to change. Sometime before the end of the Twentieth Century, the Old Ebbitt Grill became just a part of a chain of trendy Washington, D.C. area watering holes located in a fancy, upscale place around the corner on $15^{th}$ Street having about as much true American character as a European football game on the ellipse.

As for baseball on the White House lawn, thankfully, President Bush (#43) made an effort to initiate some positive change in this regard when he brought a group of little leaguers to play in his back yard once again. As for the new Ebbitt's, it drew different patrons, a breed far different from the ones who visited around the corner in years past. The old crowd, the one that would have continued to appreciate the old E Street Ebbitt's the way it was before, had been dispersed, but hopefully not forever.

Between the conclusion of my little league career in 1964 and the beginning of playing catch with my seven-year-old son in 1988, youth sports underwent some significant changes, not the least of which was the increased popularity of the aforementioned European brand of football. Having had no more than an ancient youthful glance at the game, I was caught totally unawares at how widespread it had become. Somewhere along the way, the more common name of "soccer" emerged. For me, the first indication of the spread of this contagion was seeing the many strategically placed roadway signs around our Atlanta suburb of Norcross advertising soccer sign-ups for kids. While not giving it much of a second thought at the time, my vague assumption was that these leagues attracted no more than a minor subset of the youth in the area, probably mostly girls, and maybe some of the foreign boys.

Unbeknownst to me, the growth of soccer had been going on for a long time. In fact, it had begun at least as far back as the formation of the Franconia Little League. While playing baseball in the early 1960's, along with tens of thousands of other typical American boys in Northern Virginia, there appeared an announcement in the local newspaper for a soccer tryout at Annandale High School. This particular advertisement marked the beginning of recreational league soccer in the Northern Virginia area. The boys of Springfield Forest, and their parents, had failed to notice.

In those days, most soccer people called their game "football," usually with a foreign enunciation of the vowels unless spoken with one of the several types of British accents. One might conclude this would have caused some confusion with the American sport of the same name. Maybe the word "soccer" was adopted to avoid this supposed confusion. If so, the confusion belonged to them, not to us. When it came to football, Americans did not become confused. If someone with a foreign accent and a proclivity to mispronounce vowels said, "Fūtbōl," it was, assuredly, the foreign game of which they were speaking. Even if one did not know this, there was probably no opportunity for confusion anyway because most regular American folks did not know anyone who talked about European football.

In the workplace, men mostly talk about the major sports. The one they discuss generally depends on the season of the year. For example, in my dad's office, after the World Series was over, the talk was one hundred percent Redskins. In Washington, D.C., Redskins football was about all that mattered, especially after the Senators left. Now a new Nationals team is back and baseball talk will increase. The way it was forty years ago, is similar to the way it is today. The interesting thing is that even after a full generation of their kids playing soccer, office talk about sports is still the same: football, baseball, basketball, and ice hockey as the major team sports with a bit of golf and tennis thrown in when appropriate. Do men gather around the coffee pot and discuss a match between Liverpool and Everton, or Manchester Union and Chelsea? Not likely. Maybe women's soccer can get some honorable mention when they win an important world championship game, rip off their shirts, and then run around in their branded underwear while celebrating. There is no other way they can get any noteworthy attention. Even then, it only works if they are attractive gals. The sport they play, in and of itself, is immaterial.

So why in the world, during the 1980's and 1990's, did parents become so enamored by a sport for their kids to play when they had little or no interest in its entertainment value when played professionally? Was there anything intrinsically and uniquely beneficial about soccer? No, there does not appear to be any kind of intelligent reason for substituting soccer in place of any other major or minor team sport. There may not have been anything wrong with soccer, other than being European and boring, but this was true with many other sports. What exactly was making soccer so popular? Soccer for European kids was understandable because their parents had not yet adopted superior alternatives for sports, such as we had in America. In other words, they did not know any better. Moreover, the game was already long established as a major part of their culture.

Maybe a certain level of affinity for the game is understandable in some first-generation American boys who had soccer in their immediate heritage, especially when there is a lack of any other significant athletic inclinations. Without any doubt, it provides good exercise. Maybe girls, for whom the purpose of sport is far different than it is for boys, find something uniquely satisfying in this game since they cannot play real football, lacking the size, strength, and dexterity it requires. Besides, for girls, one form of sporting exercise is about as good as another one since professional aspirations that are economically feasible are essentially non-existent.

How could one understand the parents who were going soccer crazy; who were out there coaching, cheering, and driving everywhere, hither and yon, to get their kids on more teams than time permitted. They were of my generation, presumably raised in a similar way, so how did they all of a sudden become so enamored with a game very few of them ever played. The struggle in trying to understand how this soccer fad came about reached no end as no one could be found who could provide a rational explanation for it. This left only speculation.

One seemingly logical conclusion was that this attraction to European football had to be a part of the feminism, and maybe even the socialism, being promoted in our society. For a large part of the Caucasian, suburban, born after WWII generation of mendacious and narcissistic baby-boomers, perhaps this was a way to reject the sports passed down to them by the previous generation. Soccer presented an opportunity to adopt something new while simultaneously rejecting many cultural and family traditions that served this nation quite well for a long time. Since unconventional wisdom defies worthwhile traditions, this way of thinking could have been a part of it.

Soccer's popularity may also have been a sympathetic response to the way the family structure had so dramatically changed. By the 1980's, most kids were being raised by minimum wage hirelings in day care institutions because first-person parenting was deemed to be a denigrating occupation by many women. Similarly, fatherhood after conception was increasingly considered optional, and in some arenas, even undesirable.

Fathers are essential in teaching the logic, the strategy, and the discipline required in baseball and real football. A boy does not need a man to teach him how to follow the crowd around a field, as one more sheep in a herd, waiting for a random accidental scoring opportunity to appear. When a boy cleverly runs around the bases, he scores a run. When he courageously runs down the gridiron breaking tackles, he scores a touchdown. Running aimlessly around a soccer field accomplishes absolutely nothing.

Many in the baby boom generation who found fault with the Vietnam War went on to formulate a countercultural attitude that opposed all war, all capitalism, and, by association, all that was good about the United States of America. Many sought to define moral equivalencies with opposing political ideologies. Who is to say what is right or wrong? Courage for some meant criticizing the strong and the successful, i.e., the United States. Every war was horrible when committed by America. When committed by another less capitalistic nation, however, America should somehow be blamed. Is it mere coincidence that support for these contentions can be found in most of the soccer-playing world?

For anyone seeking a way to attack the American Culture, showing disregard for baseball and real football should be the first item on the list. Both are serious capitalist enterprises. Both are intimately related to America's glorious military history. Both contribute significantly to American cultural superiority, especially baseball.

That war and worthwhile team sports are related to each other should be assumed. War is divided into two types of activity. One is the time spent engaging in battle. The other is the time spent preparing for battle. Football simulates the battle very accurately while baseball provides the pastime getting ready for the battle. Football mimics two opposing armies killing each other attempting to gain territory. Baseball fills the time during the lulls in the killing, something to pass the time while keeping the mind agile, the will strong, and the competitive edge sharp. Baseball keeps the competitive juices flowing, as the mind ruminates. Soccer, on the other hand, mimics the United Nations: a lot of running around in circles, wasted energy, without ever a single worthwhile achievement.

At the time of the Rebellion, baseball already was in full use as such a pastime. Football was invented soon thereafter. Fortunately, for the good of civilization, both great American sports were in full bloom before a soccer playing Europe invented worldwide conflagration.

After attacking America's strength as a free and capitalist nation, and before discovering the thoughtless joys of avariciousness, some baby-boomers proceeded to malign the social mores that made this country morally superior. Paternalism and masculinity had to be deposed as well. How wonderfully curious it is that soccer teams in the younger age groups were of mixed sex. Until the age of eleven or twelve, little girls are often equal to or more advanced than little boys are in terms of maturity, coordination, and size. This fits perfectly into the misguided feminist ambition of promoting the self-esteem of young girls at the expense of the young boys, especially if one subscribes to the modern convoluted definition of the term, "self-esteem." However, hardly anyone does anything measurable while playing soccer so no one can fail, relatively speaking. Whether or not everyone who plays soccer is a loser or a winner does not matter just as long as everyone is the same. Some might ask how this can be true in light of parents' spirited sideline behavior. Perhaps there is a coherent explanation. Perhaps not. More than likely, there is not.

In a different vein, it may also be that soccer is perceived to be a physically safer and psychologically healthier game, neither of which is true. Soccer has many serious injuries. Furthermore, what kind of psychology promotes personal failure as beneficial? How many kids score a goal all season long in soccer? Answer: almost no one. How many boys score at least one run in a little league baseball season? Answer: everyone, or just about everyone.

Many parents in my neighborhood would proclaim how much their pre-school and early grammar school children loved playing soccer. Kids love playing with other kids no matter what they are doing. A child just goes where his parents take him. That he is going to have a lot of fun can be assumed because others his own age will be there. They could be climbing trees, eating cupcakes, splashing in mud puddles, or playing kick-the-can. They do not know any difference at this age nor do they care. The fact that some soccer kids continue to play the game into junior high school and beyond is simply a matter of inertia combined with personal enjoyment, as any form of physical activity can be enjoyable. Some kids would learn to enjoy curling and bochi ball, too. Where do you sign up for those?

Most times when a father declines to enroll his son for an athletic activity there is no consequential societal reaction. Not so with soccer. Upon rejecting this game for my kids, insinuations were issued that befitted a subversive, one challenging a movement, as if committing an anti-group crime, something on the order that assailing Berkeley Free Speech after 1965 would have been. Could it be that such irrational reactions to this rejection indicated my choice might have hurled an affront at a seminal social change in parenting? More than a few people nearby who chose soccer for their kids took this rejection personally. It was even nastily remarked once that my kids would feel "left out." Was this supposed to make a man tremble? The not very subtle implication was that a judgment had been passed to indict an unfit parent. Would that I be shunned, too!

Soccer, in short order, came to typify the fully developed upper middle-class baby-boomer mindset with its penchant to control everything in their own lives, and even to extend this control over others, if necessary. Not only did the non-conformist baby-boomers adopt soccer in droves, many did not tolerate anyone who resisted conforming to this non-conforming choice. Not to champion soccer as the equal or the better of the authentic major sports was decidedly insulting to those who promoted it. Maybe soccer had become an alternate religion for some of these people. They seemed to think anything less than 100% participation was anti-social, or even counter-revolutionary, Heaven forbid, akin to United Way campaigns in large corporations and their fixation on 100% participation. After all, as many of them learned within their place of employment, blatant intimidation is the customary way to garner support for an unworthy cause.

Complete bafflement over the popularity of soccer, however, did not occur until the unspeakable hit home. Finding out some of my very own siblings were signing up their kids for soccer could have infused some self-doubt, maybe even caused a review of thought processes and a re-evaluation of my analysis. It did not. There was no need. The non-liberal boomers had now been compromised, nothing more, nothing less. A well-organized and militant group, perhaps even an insurgency, had to be faced down. Most likely, it was no more than a minority faction that seemed enormous only because it had created such a presence in white suburbia. Who would have thought that the hordes of 1960's non-conforming, middle and upper middle-class, S-2 deferment individuals that they were, comfortably living in homogeneous suburban residential neighborhoods, would so eagerly create such a herd then allow themselves to be led by it, especially one established for the sole purpose of promoting a culturally debasing European game?

Well, what good is a movement without a stern assertion? To augment the soccer cause and further intimidate even a suffocated and waning opposition, some of these soccer parents began to openly and confidently declare that, in a short time, soccer would become enormously popular in America, just like it was in much of the rest of the world; that baseball was losing its popularity and, they said, soon would no longer be the American pastime. Many further proclaimed that when this new generation of pampered kids became adults no one would watch baseball anymore. Presumably, they would all go to watch soccer games, just like in Europe. How incredible such drivel became so widespread, that so many people could be so wrong, especially when the reason they were so wrong was so easy to discern.

An element of respectability and personal pride should exist within the parental task of choosing the sports for which their kids are best suited. Of the many relevant considerations, fealty and respect for family traditions and American values should matter greatly. Had I been so rakish to choose soccer for my son, a very uncomfortable telephone conversation with my dad would have ensued.

"Hello, dad. Remember your first born grandson who is left-handed like Stan Musial? Yea, well, I signed him up for soccer instead of little league. That's right. You know, that thing they call 'football' over in Europe, except they can't use their hands. I'll send you the schedule because I'm sure you wouldn't want to miss any of his games. Oh, I guess he won't need that baseball you got him last Christmas. Aren't you excited?"

How much easier it would have been to explain many other choices some people have been known to make, such as a Christian becoming a Mohammedan, or an American joining the Communist Party, or a man choosing to adopt some form of shamefully deviant behavior. It makes one wonder, what ever happened to metaphorical closets? There was a reason we had those closets, to place within a hidden realm those things that need not be revealed in order that they might be politely ignored. Closets are a good place to hide soccer balls.

Games, all games, ultimately rise and fall on their merits. The main reason soccer is, and always will be, an inferior game is because it does not have the distinguishing characteristics that, one should say, separate the men from the boys. It has no batting averages or shooting percentages, no yardages gained or quarterback sacks, no blocked shots or stolen bases. Soccer is a sport that provides little or no statistical evidence of individual excellence.

When all was said and done, soccer people were living in a fantasyland. In reality, baseball adherents had no need for consternation under any circumstances. American Culture, as in the past, would continue to survive any onslaught, particularly such a feeble one as this. The proponents of soccer were suffering mighty illusions. The most logical approach was to acknowledge it for the little game it was. Eventually it would decline, as it had in England, into a rowdy tribal affair espoused mostly by Pikeys. Let soccer and its disciples follow their own course until they burned themselves out. Soccer would replace baseball, indeed! As the sun continued to rise every morning, there was no need to despair in the face of substantial soccer sign-ups. In truth, these people, and their view of youth sports, was and will continue to be, irrelevant. Prudence suggested forgetting about this soccer nonsense to be the better course to follow. That which is irrelevant can safely be ignored. The fact is soccer will never be a major sport in America.

In many parts of the country, certainly in the South, and very much in Georgia, football is considered to be like a religion by many. Yet never had anyone even hinted that it was a mistake not to sign up my boy for football. He liked baseball and he was probably not going to be big enough or fast enough to play football. This was perfectly fine because baseball people and football people like each other. Because of the nature of these two sports, they are related, like cousins. Some boys play both sports. In high school, those who do not play both, regularly attend the others' games, sharing much camaraderie. The same is often true of basketball players.

To set the table of why and how family choices are made, an important principle should be stated first. There are two types of kids in this world: mine and everyone else's. Such a constructive premise allows for clear thinking. Before encouraging a kid to play a particular sport, especially a boy, a father should suggest one with lasting social and cultural value. He should pick a sport that will make the effort worthwhile, a sport well-known and understood, a sport that would be enjoyable to watch, or even coach. Possibly, the youngster will become very good at it, good enough to play in high school, or college, or maybe even professionally. One never knows. Why not pick a sport that can lead somewhere instead of choosing one that goes down a dead end road? Why not spend time playing a sport that has high commercial regard in America? Why not choose a sport that has stood the test of time, one that has lasting social and cultural benefits?

Fortunately, even amidst my generation's habitual ardor for creating cultural tumult and confusion, baseball actually was still alive and well in the hearts and minds of many parents. Not every boomer was an ill-formed remnant of People's Park and Kent State, or an unrelenting disciple of the late Reverend William Sloane Coffin, Jr. Nor did every boomer succumb to those who were. Without much effort, the others, the sensible and true, were found. When this happened, it felt like going home again to Springfield Forest, as if nothing had changed, as if my personal connection to George Washington remained intact, as if the year was 1959.

*Chapter Five*

# Little League - First Year

An American boy at the youthful age of seven, or even younger, should be having a daily game of catch if he is capable. Much evidence indicates that the simple act of throwing a baseball over a long period increases the durability of the throwing arm, so there is no reason to wait to get started. Many parents seem to agree. They are the ones seen throwing the ball around with their kids in the yard on evenings and weekends. Some go further and enroll their kindergarten and first grade sons in something called T-ball.

Any notions that my obliviousness to the growth of soccer was not to be outdone were short lived. When it came to T-ball awareness, I must have been in a coma, thinking at first the "T" stood for toddler. The kids who played it were not much older than toddlers were. But, no, this was not it. The name came from the way the game was played. The ball, after being placed upon a tee positioned directly atop of home plate, was hit with a bat, sort of like in golf, hence the name, "T-ball." Or was it "Tee-Ball?" Whatever the precise name, one question loomed. If they were going to use tees, why not just play golf? Each game was good by itself. What purpose was served in trying to combine them? Was the game of golf better learned by having someone pitch a golf ball to a kid swinging a 3-iron?

The idea that there was any practical athletic value for a kid to play T-ball was quickly rejected, especially when he was just learning to throw and catch. Nevertheless, these leagues did attract many participants. Perhaps, some dads wanted their sons to get an early start on their baseball careers. Maybe it would enhance their chances for a college scholarship or a higher draft pick, the theory being,

"Start 'em young; the sooner the better."

Maybe some of the moms thought the kids needed the additional socialization, since day care and grade school combined only provided about fifty hours a week of this suffusion. Or maybe there was a little bit of keeping up with the soccer kids who also started playing in organized leagues this young. Finally, there was the old and very useful standby reason that needs no justification:

"Everyone else is doing it."

Well, not quite everyone. As implied, one dad and his seven-year-old took a pass on Palmer peg-ball. We would join a baseball league when the kids could pitch and hit for real, otherwise it was not very close to real baseball. Rather, it seemed to be more like a babysitting cooperative on a nice grassy field with neat white lines, done more for the entertainment of over-caffeinated spectator parents than for the kids. Do kids have fun playing T-ball? Surely they do, as they have fun playing soccer or eating mud pies. A convincing reason to enroll in this activity could not be found. Besides, little girls were playing T-ball with the boys and this would not do. Boys do well enough playing baseball by themselves. Adding girls to a boy's team does not increase the value of the game, nor does it enhance the boys' experience in playing it.

Instead, we began baseball home-schooling with the game's basic skills, which, in short order, attracted the participation of some other neighborhood kids. Alec had an accurate arm from the start and was able to throw the ball back right away. Catching the ball took some extra time and effort. The drill used to teach him how to catch was simple. He placed his glove in four different spots: up, down, left, and right. He would put his glove at the first spot then I would throw the ball at the glove. Not having to move the glove very far made it much easier to catch the ball. After several catches in a row at one spot, we went on to the second spot, and so forth.

In the next drill, he caught miniature fly balls thrown underhand and not very high at first. After a couple of weeks of practice for about thirty to forty-five minutes a day, he was able to catch almost everything. To add pressure, throws and catches were counted to see how many times the ball could go back and forth without an error by either one of us. Sometimes it would become aggravating, but the added challenge made playing catch a great deal more entertaining. When the size of the yard at home became somewhat limiting, trips to the athletic field behind nearby Peachtree Elementary School were mixed in. The added room and backstop made it easier to practice some real hitting and fielding. Before long, he was going after batted balls and making catches on the run. The pursuit of excellence continued like this almost every evening all year long.

The first episode of batting practice was one for the books. Alec took the bat while I prepared to make a pitch until he turned and stood in the right hand side of the batter's box. Figuring it was his first time and he did not know which way to face, he was instructed to turn around into the left hand batter's box. After all, he was left-handed. The results were dismal. It looked like hitting was going to take much more work than catching and throwing. Every time, after we paused to pick up the baseballs, he would stand back in the batter's box as if he were a right-handed batter, and every time he had to be turned around. At one point, I said to him that he would have to learn to hit from his normal side, the left side, before trying to become a switch hitter! This was not working so finally, out of frustration, he was left to his own devices. Swinging from the right side, he immediately started to hit the ball. Obviously, he was a throw left, bat right player, a combination that for some inexplicable reason had not immediately occurred to an imperceptive hitting instructor.

For the next two years, we played catch almost daily, along with going to the nearby schoolyard whenever possible to hit and field. He was still small in stature, but he could throw and hit the ball well, just not very far. We kept playing and he kept slowly improving. Every opportunity to advance the cause of baseball, to see more, to learn more, was exploited. Eventually we reached the point where it was time to think about playing little league baseball. At the age of nine, the kids would pitch instead of the coaches. The year before, Alec had a classmate playing in the coach-pitch little league at Murphey-Candler Park so, one afternoon, off we went to see him play.

The boy's father and I met while watching the game. He eagerly explained how the league was organized and how it operated. It turned out that several of the boys from their school, Our Lady of the Assumption in Atlanta, played baseball at Murphey-Candler. This created a dilemma. Norcross Dixie Youth baseball was closer to us since we had recently moved into the Peachtree Corners area, which bordered the old town of Norcross. On the other hand, it seemed Alec knew more boys at Murphey-Candler so, naturally, this was where he wanted to play. His choice was fine with me. We kept practicing the rest of the year until the following February when sign-ups and tryouts were held. He did well at the tryouts, obviously very excited about being able to show his ability to field grounders and catch fly balls. We practiced specially for that day so Alec knew exactly what to expect and was well prepared, better than most it seemed, even though most of the other boys had played in the league previously.

It was drearily obvious that nearly every boy came to the tryouts not having touched a baseball since the previous season ended. Also on display was a surprisingly lackadaisical attitude. Everyone would make a team, this was true, but a boy coming to the first day of baseball tryouts unprepared to do his best showed a total lack of respect for the game. Again, by relating to my own experiences, there was a need to be reminded the year was not 1959. Our tryouts in Springfield Forest determined which players would even make the team. Next, we had to play well to keep our positions. I broke into the line-up for the first time when an older boy made a couple of errors one day. Not so here. The parent pays money; the kid gets to play. All the kids understand how it works.

Every youth league nowadays has a draft. The team that drafted Alec was called the Dodgers and managed by Larry Hight. The second order of business was to attend a team parents' meeting. Arriving with personal age-old biases, the foundation of my understanding of little league baseball was already well formed. Right away, it became apparent that this league had been around for a long time and these folks had a well-established plan for running things. Murphey-Candler Little League was an impressive organization. One surprise was finding out they had officers designated as player agents. The Franconia Little League did not have this sort of thing. Either a player made the team in his subdivision or he did not. Here, everyone was taken by a team. The player agent was available to make adjustments in rosters for special circumstances, a very useful function when dealing with hundreds of kids having widely varying skill levels.

Another surprise was the existence of the time clock. In Springfield Forest we played six-inning games and, if needed, extra innings. Games were shortened only for inclement weather or darkness because we had our own field, a luxury we surely took for granted. Even at the Franconia Little League field, no more than three games were ever scheduled on a Saturday, and only one on weekday evenings. At the time, we did not fully appreciate the benefit of having two fields for six teams. Here at Murphey-Candler, as in most leagues, many more teams used the same fields so severe time restrictions had to be imposed. As a result, many games did not last a full six innings, thus the kids were often cheated.

The last major change during these intervening years, one that caused much dismay, was the use of metal bats. Sometime between 1964 and 1991, wood was replaced by metal. Reporting some exact dates and circumstances would not do any good. Of what utility is evidence when the crime will never be prosecuted? The arguments in favor of metal bats are well known and universally unpersuasive. There is no place in baseball for any kind of non-wooden bat. Too many people refuse to recognize metal bats as a problem and, therefore, it remains uncorrected. Imperfect as it was, this was little league and the boy came to play. The player agents were fine, but the time clock and metal bats were no less than abominations one had to accept for the time being.

To a casual adult observer, there is nothing particularly dramatic or noteworthy about a boy being given his first baseball uniform. Yet it is one of the most significant and memorable events in his life. Grown-ups characteristically become less insightful, not so much in the sense of remembering, rather in the sense of understanding. Their ability to become excited over childhood triumphs lessens as their universe of the mundane expands. What causes these cataracts to form in the mind's eye of adulthood, the shroud that conceals many of the joys of youth? A convincing argument could be made that they are the found fruits of an increasingly problematical search for material security fueled by irrational fears.

However, there can be exceptions. Even when a former little leaguer is made insipid by maturity, the receipt of his first little league baseball uniform is something he is likely to remember fondly forever. The moment he puts it on is precisely the moment when he realizes he has become an official member of a real baseball team. Now he will play in real baseball games against other real baseball teams in which there will be real umpires. If he scores a run, a new number will appear on the scoreboard. Everyone will see it.

The wearing of his uniform gives him a new identity that is better than before. It creates in him the sensation that he is someone truly special. His uniform distinguishes him from those who are on other teams, and from those who are not baseball players at all. Clad in his team's uniform, he is one with his teammates in opposition to any other uniform they encounter. The uniform serves as his passport into the physical baseball world. Certainly, he could go walk onto a baseball field any day when no one is around. However, when a game is scheduled and people come, only those who wear the correct uniforms are permitted to set foot inside the fence and to cross the white lines. Others who have the wrong uniform, or no uniform at all, must remain outside.

When a boy puts on his baseball uniform for the very first time, it is not a simple thing as if getting dressed with everyday clothes, not at all. This outfit causes a transformation. It makes him aware of larger circumstances. He is changed forever. He may not understand it all right away, but this is the very first meaningful step on the road to the major leagues, the importance of which he can sense. Everything he does from this point on will be seen, judged, recorded, and remembered. I had played for just one team, Springfield Forest, unless the Franconia League All Star teams count, too. Alec would eventually play for many teams, but this first one was exceedingly special. In future years, he would again encounter his first coach along with some of these same players, being reminded of the fun and camaraderie they shared. In fact, three of the players on that first team went on to play high school varsity baseball, beating all the odds.

Murphey-Candler has an impressive opening day festival. All of the kids from all of the age groups, including the girl's softball leagues, are brought together and introduced, team by team. Each manager gathers his team together and waits for the announcement calling them forth. Parents wait patiently nearby, many with cameras. Some of the kids do as they are told and others, semi-oblivious to their responsibilities, carry on with playful mischievousness. If the manager is fortunate, his entire team arrives on time at the appointed place, each player wearing the complete uniform. The more experienced managers know to bring a couple of extra caps and maybe a team jersey for the forgetful. How could any boy go to the opening day of the baseball season without his baseball cap? As difficult as it may be to imagine, it does happen.

Alec was one of a few boys totally focused on his manager, looking more like a soldier awaiting field orders than a distracted nine year old. When the Dodgers were called out, they entered the park by running through a gate wide enough for almost two at a time, bumping shoulders like marbles through a funnel. Alec came through and turned the corner with the look of a second lieutenant with his first battle commission: total confidence, total commitment, and total focus. Quickly, at a glance, one could tell which of the boys were ready to play baseball, the few having a look of purpose and intensity. Others had facial expressions that varied between timidity and obliviousness. Mannerisms aside, all seemed content to be there, or, at the least, none seemed anxious to go someplace else.

Gradually the park turned into a colorful menagerie as the groups of different colored uniforms gathered. Finally, the entire field was covered with baseball teams, truly a wonderful sight to behold. It made for a marvelous photograph. A brief program was presented. First, the obligatory introductions of a few unmentionable and shameless politicians who all but took credit for causing the sun to shine and the grass to grow in DeKalb County. Then the previous year's championship team was introduced giving everyone the chance to see the best of last year's players from this league. Also mentioned were the particular high schools where these boys were planning to continue their baseball careers. I looked closely at these very good young players, the all-stars from the previous year, wondering if they were as good as the boys who went on to play at Lee High School in the early 1960's. After a few remarks, there was the singing of the National Anthem and, lastly, the commissioner ceremoniously called out,

"Let's play ball!"

The first baseball season for my son was underway.

Most of the time, Alec played an outfield position, batting towards the bottom of the lineup. He could hit the ball in practice, but in the games, he would not swing. Some of the other players came up to bat eager to swing at anything. A few had already learned to be selective. A few just did not swing at all. Mine was one of the latter. I detected early that he was maybe begging for a walk, not an uncommon malady at that age. Kids like to be up at bat. They wait a long time to take their turn. If the batter swings and hits the first pitch, his turn is quickly over. This is all right if he hits safely and ends up on base. However, it is more likely that he will make an out, being left to endure another long wait before coming up again. Recalling how the physics of time dilation works in the mind of a boy, all this waiting for just one pitch is not worth it.

While he stands in the batter's box, he might make an out without swinging, too, but at least he gets to stay up there longer. With a little luck, he may just draw a walk. So while trying to figure out these things some kids stand there doing nothing encouraged by the fact that sometime, somewhere they heard someone say it is a good thing to work the count. The trouble is that umpires also notice when a kid does not seem to want to swing and, consequently, the strike zone tends to expand.

Usually being called out on strikes a few times cures this ailment. It made sense to wait a while for Alec to start swinging, but waiting proved not to be the remedy. Soon the paternal patience was exhausted.

Everything was tried. He was given extra batting practice every day, and before games, along with every kind of verbal encouragement. When his games continued to be swing-less, they were followed by pleading, bribing, yelling, and threats. Nothing worked. He would not swing the bat in a game. Finally, the inevitable disaster happened. He actually drew a walk. Witnessing this base-on-balls from behind the backstop was like having a prolonged parenting effort instantly negated. Ball four created a sickening feeling as Alec confidently started toward first base, but an annoyed umpire, declaring it was only ball three, called him back. In truth, it was ball four. The ump had lost count. When the next pitch was called a ball, Alec looked back at the ump as if waiting for permission to go to first base, just too good a moment to let pass, and out came a tactful comment.

"Ball five! You can go to first now!"

The ump turned around. I smiled. He just shook his head.

Sometimes it is good for parents to say stupid things at little league games if for no other reason than to enhance the entertainment value. Still, the problem remained. Beyond the verbalized frustrations and ump-baiting, not swinging the bat was now a serious matter turned desperate. After the game, there was no choice but to let Alec have "it" with one of the most comprehensive ravings of all time. First, he was treated to an indignant review of the fundamental requirements of the game that a ball must be pitched by a pitcher, hit by a batter, and fielded by a fielder. Second, a pointed query that had better not be answered lest it interrupts this infuriated flow: what if the pitcher did not pitch the ball or the fielders let the batted balls go by? Or what if no one ever swung the bat? What would happen then? Well, obviously, there would be no game.

"*No baseball game! Do you understand what that means?*"

Nothing could conclude such a tirade short of an ardent declaration that left no room for negotiation, invited no alternate opinion, sought no consensus, entertained no excuses, and allowed no appeal. Very simply, if he wanted to be a baseball player on a baseball team, he had to play baseball. Playing baseball meant fielding, throwing, running, *and* hitting. If he did not swing his bat, he was not playing the game. Lastly, the Final Judgment, if he did not swing the bat in the next game then that game would be the last baseball game in which he would ever play. His father would yank him off the team and out of the league right there in mid-season.

This particular boy knew the sentence for this crime would be carried out. The necessary parenting groundwork had been well laid during the course of his upbringing, part of the family foundation. There were no doubts, just as there was no power above or below this earth that could or would intervene. His father had spoken. That was "it."

I grew up knowing what "it" was and made sure my son knew, too. Many boys in this latest generation were not taught the concept of "it." "It" assumed its most consequential meaning when used in the exclamation:

"You're going to get 'it' when your father comes home!"

Many kids of the day never heard such a warning because they had stay-away-from-home moms who were not around during the day to threaten "it." Some moms could never threaten "it" because there was no father coming home to administer "it." One further convolution in parenting that helped eradicate the use of "it" occurred when the father played the role of housewife allowing the mother to go to work. Presumably, such a father could threaten the kids with,

"You're going to get 'it' when your mother comes home!"

Perhaps, stay-at-home dads would not see anything askew with this reproach.

In my home, "it" was alive and well, and utilized. The best way that "it" works is for the mother and father to work as a team. To administer "it" successfully, to make the concept fearfully comprehensible, the proper arrival sequence is crucial. If the kids and mom are gone when the father arrives at home, "it" does not work, not after dad has already started to relax. Discipline is best when he walks through the door after having finished a long day at work and sat in traffic for an hour.

The judicious use of threats by the mother, followed by the proper administration of discipline by the father, serves a very useful purpose in reinforcing family cohesion because it teaches the child a healthy fear of retribution for misbehavior. Without a father and mother faithfully filling their traditional roles, kids are left to wander, or maybe wallow, as they search for a suitable anchorage in which to place their loyalties. Many times, they are led astray, eventually having to face miserable conditions. A child upon whom strict limits are imposed is far more likely to be a secure and happy child.

Child-rearing theories aside, failure to swing a baseball bat at good pitches during a game, absent a "take" sign, constituted a behavioral emergency under any circumstances. However, this one particular base-on-balls, if ignored, would have tolerated the reward for taking pitches, and further aggravated the problem. Immediate action was required. "It" could not wait until after another long day at the office or a rush hour wreck. There was not even time for a matriarchal threat.

Proof of the value of "it" as a child-rearing tool came during the next game. The result was overwhelming. Every time Alec came up to bat, he swung at almost every pitch. If the ball was anywhere between the on-deck circles, he swung. He looked like Ralph Garr. Well, sort of. Not only was the problem solved, it made me realize just how important playing baseball had become for him. The threat of not being allowed to play baseball was very persuasive. To my relief, my son's baseball career did not end in the middle of his first little league season.

Perhaps the most important lesson to be learned from team sports is the one that teaches a player the value of a two-way commitment. The team has obligations to each member and each member has an obligation to the team. When a youngster agrees to join a baseball team, or any other team for that matter, he enters into a tacit agreement to go to every practice and every game, being on time, every time. In addition to the scheduled games and practices, he should work on his own to supplement what he learns in practice. In short, he has an obligation to the team to do everything he can to improve his own skills in order to help the team.

Faithfulness to team commitments was mandatory in my house. Whether or not the other players on the team fulfilled their commitment was worth noting though it remained entirely irrelevant. One afternoon, the Dodgers had a scheduled practice on the field behind Kingsley Elementary in Dunwoody, about twenty minutes away. Alec returned home late with his sisters and mother from a trip to the mall. Being on time for practice was defined by me as arriving early enough to get completely warmed-up and ready to play *before* practice started. On this occasion, we had barely enough time to get there for the start of practice.

The drive to practice was just long enough for a comprehensive lecture on the importance of fulfilling obligations to the team. The practice was typical. About seven or eight of the thirteen boys on the roster showed up, while only two were warming up when we arrived. The others came later. But it did not matter. An obligation to the team had to be fulfilled even if no one else showed for practice.

In leagues such as Murphey-Candler, everyone who signs up is placed on a team and everyone on a team gets to play. Since there is a draft, the talent should be more or less evenly distributed. It is a good system. The important thing is all the boys get to play. This arrangement to provide approximately equal playing time can lead to quite an interesting dynamic. In a league where the talent is mostly evenly dispersed, a team's success will usually be determined more by the extent to which the worst players improve than by how well the best players perform. The coaches who understand this have the most team success. Rather than bemoan those of lesser ability, the key is to work to improve the ones who need it most. To accomplish this, it helps to challenge the better players to tutor their teammates of lesser skill. The more they help each other, the better for everyone, and the better the team. Therefore, well-attended and well-ordered practices are essential for team success.

Some parents held an alternate view of team sports. They considered recreational sports to be just that, recreational, with the mistaken belief that recreation and amusement were synonymous. Their kids joined sport leagues for recreation, to be amused, not necessarily to learn anything, and certainly not for the benefit of anyone else. Commitment was a simple one-way street with all traffic going in the same direction as their child. Their methodology worked this way: the parents paid a fee for their kid to be on the team, thus, the kid got to do whatever he wanted to do whenever he happened to show up.

Parents who adopted this point of view tended to put their kids on several sports teams at the same time. They made their own schedule according to their own priorities, which were directed by their own self-interest. Based on an understanding that the team and the league existed to serve the interests of their kid, he had no reciprocal obligation to serve the interest of the team. Scheduling conflicts were typically resolved with a pecking order starting with the games of the most favored team, followed by the games of the less favored teams. Afterwards came any other preferred activity, followed by loafing, and, lastly, practice. Team practices were routinely missed. These sorts of people apparently believed games were more important than practice. However, as their kids grew older and the teams became more competitive, they found practices to be mandatory. Kids who were not taught the importance of practice had to learn it late. Some could not. Then the alternatives narrowed. They could quit the team, sit on the bench, or maybe be cut.

Two other important lessons little leaguers should learn right from the start which are actually mutually inclusive are found within the ability to control their emotions and the development of good attitudes. Since the kids see professional athletes behave badly all too frequently, they need to be told what is acceptable and what is not. To aggravate the situation, video clips of bad behavior seem to be re-played, the number of times being directly proportional to the level of depravity. For instance, a player signing an autograph before a game will usually not be shown as a highlight on ESPN *SportsCenter*. However, a player punching a drunk and rowdy fan in the nose will be shown a hundred times from each of several different camera angles.

One of the most important unspoken rules in baseball is never taunt your opponents publicly. Let it come from the dugout anonymously, if at all. There is absolutely no value in excessive field celebrations either. Baseball is not like football. Getting pumped-up with uncontrolled emotions does not help to play better. Baseball requires a clear head, controlled emotions, and a rational perspective from every player on the team. The competitive spirit in baseball is best displayed by preparation, focus, and execution. Frustration, anger, jubilation, haughtiness, etc. are very distracting emotions, which often result in diminished performance. Winning the game is infinitely more satisfying than losing. Winning is also much more likely when employing skill and cunning rather than a disagreeable temperament. The sooner that a youngster learns this, the better he will play.

It is most unfortunate that many professional athletes, especially in football, are so quick to display a grossly overconfident demeanor and braggadocio, often punctuated with silly or vulgar jeers, profanity, insults, or adolescent-like showmanship, often just for doing what they are expected to do, and paid well enough to do. Seeing such infantile behavior could easily lead a rational man to assume it was the first time the player ever caught a pass or scored a touchdown or recovered a fumble or made a tackle, or that these were extremely rare occurrences in their playing careers. Is this not what they are supposed to do? Thank God, this nonsense has not become prevalent in baseball. Imagine if a baseball player hit an RBI double and then started jumping up and down on top of second base, removing his cap, waving the index finger, declaring,

"We're number one," while pointing at the pitcher and yelling, "who da man?"

An answer to that question would come exactly nine batters later in the form of a ninety-five mph fastball in his ear or ribs, and deservedly so. His own pitcher would not bother to retaliate, either.

The Murphey-Candler Dodgers missed the playoffs, ending up with a few more losses than wins. Still, it was a completely successful season for more reasons than need be mentioned. Just the experience of playing the first year of little league surpassed anything imaginable. Mr. Hight was one of many dedicated baseball fathers who did a very good job coaching. His son, Justin, did much of the pitching and played well at several positions. He eventually played center field for Chamblee High School before going on to play baseball in college, too.

Three players from other Murphey-Candler teams this season, unbeknownst to us, would become Alec's high school teammates six years later at Norcross. They were Inman Dubberly, Chris Horwath, and Andrew Dodson. Important baseball relationships had begun already.

To end the season, the team held a picnic. Teams in all the leagues did this sort of thing, usually organized by the team moms. Each of the parents was asked to contribute money for a manager's gift and for the kids' trophies. This year and in future years, I asked for a breakdown between the two, contributing for the gift, but not for the trophies, further insisting that my son not be given a trophy when the team had not earned one. For some reason, other parents thought kids should be given awards for failure.

"Oh, no! There are no failures here. Everyone is a winner!"

When confronted with senselessness, when the language spoken is unintelligible, there is no way to explain the point of view that when a team wins less than half its games and ends up in the lower half of its division, the players do not deserve a trophy. Trophies are for champions, for those who win, for those who beat everyone else. Losers do not deserve trophies.

"Oh, easy for you to say, the kids think getting a trophy is important."

"If it was so important, why did they not practice harder and try to play better?"

"You mean, earn it? How insensitive can you be!"

The fact is many parents simply refuse to show respect for the decisions and the achievements of their own children. While winning is an important goal in sports, it is important in reality, not in make believe. Giving a trophy to a loser in an effort to make him feel like a winner is a highpoint of stupidity. It insults the child by disparaging his effort, particularly if it was an honest effort. It is more important for a boy in the little league to learn the game, how to play it and how to be a member of a team. They win as a team and they lose as a team. Phony trophies do not change the outcome, nor do they add to the experience. If anything, they distract from it. My son was initially disappointed when finding out he alone would not get a trophy, so I tried to explain. He was not moved. Then I said,

"Okay, would you rather have the trophy or ten bucks?"

He took the cash without hesitation, the first indication that he had a clear business sense about him. When given a rational choice, most boys quickly recognize the difference between real and bogus. If only every important childhood lesson could be taught so cheaply, parenting would be a breeze.

The year 1991 was a memorable one for the Atlanta Braves, too. They won the Western Division of the National League after finishing in last place the previous year. The excitement of having a successful major league home team was contagious around every little league park in the Atlanta metropolitan area. While being enthralled with the Braves during the rest of the summer and autumn, our baseball practice continued, this time with the immediate purpose to improve for the next spring season. Watching the Braves was definitely a source of motivation as they finally ended their season with an extraordinarily captivating World Series against the Minnesota Senators . . . I mean, Twins.

For nearly three years, baseball had been a continuous activity around the house. Indeed, it was virtually everyday, meaning seven days a week including holidays. We threw the ball in every kind of weather and everywhere we went, never being without a ball, a bat, and ball gloves. We played catch everywhere including the beach, while visiting the homes of relatives and friends, even at interstate rest stops while traveling. One day it rained hard without letting up so our only choice was to play catch inside, which we did. The result was a broken window. It was my fault, too, for missing a catch, as there is a first time for everything, including the breaking of a window with a baseball from the inside. The lesson learned was simple. Rainy days are made for visits to baseball card shops.

*Chapter Six*

# Little League – Second Year

Murphey-Candler Park, with its unified complex of baseball fields, was located about a dozen miles or so away. Norcross Dixie Youth had four separate field locations, all within close proximity of each other, all within the city limits of Norcross, and all within four miles from home. The difference in travel time to the two league locations, however, was far more significant than the distances in miles would indicate because during the late afternoons and early evenings on weekdays, traffic was awful around Atlanta. Besides the travel problems, other shortcomings with Murphey-Candler were bothersome enough to consider moving to the Norcross league right away. One of the more egregious faults was just another inanity stemming from the lapsed side of baby-boomer culture so contemptuously inattentive to cogent thought. The issue: a girl was allowed to sign up and play little league baseball with the boys during the next season.

An aspiring young lady has no place on a boys' baseball team. If some parents desire their daughter not to be a proper young lady, fine for them, but they should not be granted license to afflict the dignity of boys' baseball leagues with their tasteless standards. A girl on a boy's baseball team is a needless distraction that does absolutely no good for the boys in their endeavor to learn the game.

Little league for boys exists for good reasons. Mainly it furthers the healthy development of male adolescents by constructively channeling their energies while, at the same time, promoting the game. Boys' youth baseball leagues thrive because the founding concepts continue to be deemed beneficial. If a girl is desirous of playing baseball, she should find other girls of like mind and form a girls' little league. If she prefers to play with boys, then she should find others of like mind and form a co-ed little league. She should not be allowed entrance to a league designed for boys, just as a boy should not be allowed to join a girls' softball league. If girls' baseball and co-ed baseball are valid concepts, each will succeed separately.

Instead of respecting tradition and the rights of others, a lonely self-indulgent crank of a parent can devalue a wonderfully successful organization. These sorts of oddballs, however, are not the ones to blame. Rather, those who tolerate them, who acquiesce to their bizarre whims, who dispense with propriety in order to travel the path of least resistance, should be held responsible. The idea of a girl in a boy's baseball league is an intellectual convulsion that would otherwise be laughed out of the park if not buttressed by the obtuse rules of "political correctness." So aggravating it is to live in a place and at a time where the overriding consensus opinion is not to speak up or stand up for anything that may offend anyone, except when insults are directed at those advancing the traditional causes of normal decency. If any of the other dads at Murphey-Candler agreed with this assessment, one could not be sure. Even though placing a girl on a boys' baseball team shows an obvious lack of respectability along with a failure of parental authority, no one else within earshot dared to voice an objection. I asked for, and received, an immediate refund of fees.

All things considered, it seemed Norcross would be a better place for my son to play ball. There was still another reason that made Norcross preferable, namely the baseball past of this historic small town. The tales were such they could hardly be believed, until taking the time to conduct a thorough study of the matter at the Norcross Baseball Hall of Fame. The stories told by the locals turned out to be modest when compared to the documented history found within the clippings and records that some of the older Norcross baseball-playing gentlemen managed to preserve.

The City of Norcross indeed had a fascinating history, which included a rich baseball tradition. Incorporated in 1870, Norcross was established as a resort for wealthy Atlantans, situated about twenty miles northeast of Georgia's capital city along the railway line built by the Danville and Piedmont Airline, now the Norfolk Southern Railroad. Norcross grew quickly to a population of about eight hundred and remained this size for nearly a century. It was regarded as a leafy island amid small farms, secluded by tall oaks and magnolias, projecting the very essence of bucolic simplicity. Once referred to as a "town of houses," Norcross had but a small commercial district with no meaningful or lasting manufacturing enterprises. Not much changed here until the inexorable onslaught of urban sprawl arrived in the 1970's.

The baseball story began in 1874 when three of the town's prominent citizens, Milton Lively, Stephen McElroy, and John Thrasher, sold a four-acre parcel of land to the Norcross High School for three hundred and fifty dollars. It sat at the bottom of a steep ridge, about one block southeast of the train station. This piece of land, now adjacent to the current downtown historic district and named for the two pairs of brothers from Norcross who played in the major leagues, came to be the town's baseball field. When baseball was first played here, no one knows for sure. However, Carl Garner, former baseball player and former mayor, was sure his father played on this field as a youngster, approximately 1900-1910.

At least three good reasons exist to suppose that baseball was played on this site much earlier than the senior Mr. Garner's era. First, the popularity of baseball exploded after 1865. The game almost certainly was played in this area before 1870 as it was in most small towns. Second, since this field was sold for the specific purpose of making a schoolyard in 1874, it is easy to imagine young men were already gathering here to play baseball. Third, the records show that by 1908 Norcross began producing a long list of professional players. The game must have been played in Norcross for more than just a few years prior to this time or the development of such good players would have been very unlikely.

From about 1908 until the 1950's Norcross produced more professional baseball players per capita than any other town in America. The best of these players may have been the freckle-faced, red-haired catcher named Ivey Wingo. After playing two years for Greenville of the Carolina League, Wingo was signed by the St. Louis Cardinals in 1911. He began playing in the majors that same year at the age of twenty. Four years later, he was traded to the Cincinnati Reds where he played until 1926. In 1913, he made a world tour with a team picked by John McGraw, traveling to China, Japan, Australia, England, and France.

Ivey Wingo was given major credit for the Reds' 1919 championship over the Chicago White Sox (a.k.a. Black Sox) because of his extraordinary ability to call a game and handle pitchers. He also had the arm most feared by base runners of his day. Even more remarkable for a catcher, Ivey Wingo had the foot speed of a center fielder, stretching doubles into triples as if he did not know that catchers were not supposed to run so fast. During his career, he legged out eighty-one triples, eight more than Bench and Berra combined, and he stole eighty-seven bases. Also worth mentioning is that Ivey Wingo caught the last game pitched by Christy Mathewson in which the Reds beat Mordecai "Three Finger" Brown and the Cubs. This was the only major league game Mathewson pitched for a team other than the Giants. Although he had already become manager of the Reds, he and Brown arranged their final dual on September 4, 1916 as a publicity stunt to help draw a larger crowd. The very fortunate attendees witnessed the conclusion of two marvelous baseball careers.

Ivey's brother, Absalom H. Wingo, was also red haired and freckled. He was called "Red" back home in Norcross though in the majors he went by "Al." Red Wingo played one season for Connie Mack's Philadelphia Athletics, followed by five more for Detroit where he became part of a record that will very likely never be broken. In 1925, the Tigers featured a starting outfield all of whom batted .370 or higher. It consisted of Red Wingo in left, player-manager Ty Cobb in center, and Harry Heilmann in right. The trio batted .370, .378, and .393, respectively, with Heilmann winning the batting title in the American League. (Hornsby hit .403 for St. Louis to lead the National League that year.) Red Wingo's .370 batting average in 1925 came in the only year he had enough plate appearances to qualify for the batting title, which created a rather curious anomaly in itself. For a player to attain this high of a batting average, and not be given enough at-bats to qualify for the batting title again, is difficult to imagine.

Another pair of Norcross brothers, Roy and Cleo Carlyle, both outfielders, made it to the big leagues in the 1920's. Roy played with Washington, the Red Sox, and the Yankees. Cleo played for the Red Sox.

The most memorable moment associated with Norcross baseball history was when Roy Carlyle hit the longest home run ever. The date was July 4, 1929. Roy was a big kid in his time, tall and lean, he stood six feet, three inches in height and weighed one hundred ninety-five pounds. People of the time said he could hit a baseball with such force it was frightening. On this day, he was playing for Oakland of the Pacific Coast League in a game against the San Francisco Mission team in San Francisco. It was customary back then to play two games on holidays, one in the morning, and one in the afternoon. During the afternoon game, Roy clobbered a fastball thrown by Ernie Nevers, the former Stanford All-American fullback. (Nevers had an unspectacular and brief career in the big leagues for St. Louis, 1926-28.) The baseball hit by

Roy Carlyle left the park and landed on the roof of a house. Witnesses marked the spot made visible by the impact of the ball on a rainspout and the next day it was carefully measured to be six hundred and eighteen feet.

Through the years, claims of longer home runs being hit by Babe Ruth, Mickey Mantle, and others have been made, but they involve conjecture or estimates of trajectories, not to mention Yankee exaggeration, and, therefore, are neither precise nor reliable. Carlyle's homer was measured by tape and not even at his team's home ballpark. Babe hit some good ones, that is for certain, and he hit many more of them, but Roy Carlyle of Norcross hit the longest home run in the recorded history of professional baseball.

At least sixteen other identifiable professional ballplayers grew up learning to play baseball in Norcross during this period, including two more Carlyle brothers, making for some astonishing statistics. While there were about five hundred major league players out of a total United States population of one hundred twenty-five million, about one in every two hundred and fifty thousand (0.0004%), the town of Norcross by itself had an incredible 0.5% of its population in the majors, one in every two hundred. If every town in America had produced ballplayers like Norcross, there would have been six hundred and twenty-five thousand major leaguers between the world wars and it would have taken twenty thousand teams for all of them to be properly employed. The minor leagues would have required a proportionate expansion to accommodate two-and-a-half million players! That was a lot of baseball talent to come out of one diminutive Georgia town remotely situated at the southernmost tip of Appalachia.

The loss of all these players to professional teams did not mean the absence of quality local baseball in Norcross, however. Semi-professional independent Norcross teams won many championships in the Granite and Chattahoochee Leagues. Local high school, American Legion, and Dixie Youth teams were legendary as well through the first six decades of the Twentieth Century.

Having learned about the history of Norcross baseball, there seemed to be no reason to search elsewhere. Here was a rare opportunity to be part of a very special tradition, to play on fields close to home, fields haunted by the propitious specters of great ballplayers now departed. The entire town was thick with tradition and Wingo-Carlyle Field, the full regulation-size field, was the centerpiece of this tradition. Although not well kept in recent years, the town's historic baseball field had an aura better to experience than attempt to explain, an aura that made one think this piece of property could never be anything other than a baseball field, and a special one at that.

An old granite stone wall, several feet high, borders the right field foul line. In another ballpark, such a structure might appear peculiar. Not here. At Wingo-Carlyle Field, it serves a useful, necessary purpose as the perfect perch for any of those old troubled baseball ghosts to find consolation while seeing to it that legends of the past continue to inspire each new generation of players. In places like this, when great moments occur they cause no surprise, as if they are expected. Within such a ballpark, the exceptional is normal. Within such a ballpark, every game is exceptional. Why, indeed, go play baseball in DeKalb County when already living near a true baseball town like Norcross?

All it took was a telephone call to a good friend who had a son playing in the Norcross Dixie Youth (NDY) league. He referred me to the league president, whom I called immediately and, within minutes, arrangements were made for Alec to be included in their program. He had to attend a tryout the following Saturday morning, a make-up date from an earlier rainout. The manner in which this league operated, in addition to the more convenient location, proved to be more than satisfactory. The coaches and other parents were a motivated group who ran the league calmly and efficiently, striking a good balance between structure, flexibility, and economy. Every boy in town had the opportunity to learn the game, play well, and have fun.

Parents' involvement in a youth sport league can be good or bad depending on their motivation. The fact is that if these adults did not have children in the league they would not be there in the first place. Without them, there would be no league at all. However, if a parent's prime motivation is to promote his own child before the interests of the team and the league, problems can arise. One can never be sure of another's motivation, so it is speculative to say that some parents get involved primarily to push their own kids onto a tournament team. Even though putting personal advancement first defies logic, it happens, and maybe it happens quite often.

It could be that some parents falsely think a good little league record, especially playing on all-star teams, will enhance the odds of making a high school team, perhaps leading to a college scholarship or something else. On the other hand, there may not be any reason beyond the natural urge to promote one's progeny. These urges should be reined in. Constructive support in a general sense is the best way for parents to show they possess a wise outlook of the purpose for having little league. If needed, they can help the coach conduct extra practices and run drills. If not needed for these purposes, unless the league or team is entirely mismanaged, most parents would do well just to sit back and enjoy watching while the boys play.

Parents sometimes have unrealistic expectations of coaches. A good youth coach is one who directs his players' focus towards the two things that contribute most to the success of the team. First, he encourages each boy to do his best, and, second, he asks that all the boys encourage each other to do their best. By advocating this type of constructive attitude, the boys will have the best conditions in which to learn skills and perform to the highest level of their abilities, while enjoying themselves.

The world of kids and sports is fortified by wonderful intentions, motivational metaphors, and thoughtful proscriptions, the more ambiguous, the more fun they are to say and hear. What we get from them is a never-ending stream of hackneyed phrases the meanings of which are mostly indeterminable. They mean whatever the speaker wants them to mean. One such overused term that cannot be overlooked because of its essential importance in any discussion of baseball is "respect for the game." For present purposes, to make the term useful, there is just one acceptable definition: One who has Respect for Baseball Subordinates his Will to the Exigencies of the Game.

Kids should be taught to respect the game right away so they do not ever think that the game exists only for their personal benefit or that it revolves around them. We teach our boys to remove their caps while the National Anthem is played as a show of respect. Though baseball may not be quite the national treasure as Old Glory, it is an extremely close second and it, too, deserves respect. Besides, if a player does not respect the game, why does he even bother to play it?

Disrespect for the game is shown in two general ways. One is poor behavior and the other is poor play. Behavior is a matter of self-control while quality of play is determined by practice and motivation. Talent, by itself, is of minimal value. Very talented players can be the most tiresome to watch when they do not give one hundred percent effort or if they misuse their skills. Less talented players can be very enjoyable to watch when they give it their all. Joyful enthusiasm is definitely transmittable to spectators.

Kids who learn to play with respect generally learn to love the game at the same time. Without a love for the game, the desire to play becomes tenuous. Two years of little league for a boy is more than enough to instill a love and respect for baseball. After that, he can decide for himself to keep playing or not. However, as long as he wants to play, as long as he is enthusiastic about playing, he will want to do it with dedication and daily practice. If this is not the case, his interest in the game is passive and he is probably getting ready to quit.

From the opening day of my son's first little league season, I was mindful of the end that would come, the last day, the day on which he would play his final baseball game. The prime objective was to make sure when that day came, when his playing days were over, his memory of playing baseball would be only sweet, just like my own, and not the least bit acrimonious. When he decided the time had come to hang up the cleats, he would think it had been all worthwhile.

During his three little league years I had absolutely no thought of Alec making a tournament team, much less making the high school team later on, and did not even dream of reaching higher levels beyond that. There were no objections to any of these things if they were to happen, however, a plan for something beyond little league simply did not exist. My own experiences largely caused this sentiment. Besides, he was not an outstanding player starting out, in fact, he was probably considered only average for his little league age group. There was nothing wrong with being an average player on his baseball team, or even a below average player. Some of the boys experienced physical maturity early. He was not one of them. In spite of physical stature, his interest in the game grew and he kept working to improve his skills. In fact, no one around worked harder. No one. Although his improvement seemed slow, it was steady.

Aside from all the meaningless comparisons one could draw with his peers, there was a very stark statistical reality to consider as well. High school baseball would be very selective. The way it actually turned out confirmed this assertion. In 1992, Norcross Dixie Youth Majors, including all boys age eleven and twelve, had enrolled one hundred and sixty-seven players on fourteen teams. Out of this group, sixteen went on to play high school varsity baseball. Only three of them would actually experience the delight of being a starting pitcher in a varsity game.

Had I been asked to speculate about the ninety percent of these little leaguers who would not be playing for their high school team, logically I would have assumed my son would be in that large majority. Such a conclusion was not a product of defeatist thinking, not at all, because who got to play in high school was not the point. The most important point was to realize not playing beyond little league would be no reason to consider that a boy's baseball career had ended in failure. The correct view would be that any boy's baseball career would end during the normal process of choosing to pursue vocations for which he has talent and motivation, while choosing to abandon those for which talent does not exist and desire has faded away. No matter when my son stopped playing, for whatever reason, it was important for him to have been enriched by the baseball playing experience. The two-year plan or three-year plan in little league could accomplish this.

The first year in Norcross, Alec was drafted by Kenny Hawk, the manager of the NDY Majors Orioles. Mr. Hawk was one of the few managers who knew someone with a vacant lot where the team could practice anytime. He was willing to have practice everyday except Sunday if anyone wanted to come. This arrangement was very fortunate because practice fields were hard to come by and most teams were able to practice only a couple of times a week. The kids on the Orioles team, having their own practice field, received much more baseball than most of the other kids.

Attendance at the Orioles' practices was also very good. Mr. Hawk had coached before and the experience taught him to draft players as much for their attitudes as their playing ability. As a result, his team exhibited a most agreeable attitude. They played well together and their season ended near the .500 mark after playing seventeen games.

My son, as one of the smallest members of the team, having turned eleven years of age at mid-season, stood only four feet, six inches tall and weighed sixty-five pounds. Anticipating a growth spurt is the phrase most used to describe this predicament. While waiting for biochemical reactions to occur, Alec mostly played the outfield, but occasionally he played first base, too. The Oriole's scorebook showed the little lefty had thirty-one official turns at bat with nine hits, two doubles, five walks, and thirteen strikeouts. He also scored four runs and managed a couple of stolen bases. I do not specifically recall the stolen bases, but they were in the scorebook. Many things appear in little league scorebooks, or not. Best of all, when it came to swinging the bat this season, he did not vacilatte, making it a good time to introduce the concept of being a little more selective in choosing which pitches to try to hit. How odd things can be sometimes. The year before, he would not swing at anything. Now he swung at everything. Most times the game is simple, but rarely is it easy.

In the very beginning, even before his first tryout at Murphey-Candler, Alec had to be told that right-handers could play any position, but, as a left-hander, he would be limited to play outfield, first base, or pitcher. Catcher, third base, second base, and shortstop were not open to him, not now and not ever. At the start of his second year, I had to reiterate these limitations because he expressed interest in playing other positions. Another point to be made, peering into the future, it was genetically unlikely he would be tall enough to play first base (yes, I know about Kruk) or fast enough to play the outfield (yes, I know Yogi played some left field) at the higher levels of the game, even though he was becoming a very good outfielder. I knew it was far more reasonable to expect him to fit the physical description of Rudy Ruettiger, the Notre Dame football taxi squad walk-on once sardonically described as "five foot nothing and a hundred and nothing."

Telling him all of the things he could not do seemed to depress his spirits, thinking his future in baseball would be confined to playing the outfield. His outlook completely changed when it was suggested that he learn to pitch. He eagerly agreed. We constructed a pitching area by the side of the house and he started to pitch. Everyday, in addition to team practices and games, he pitched. Everyday, his dad crouched down to catch. Thank God for sturdy knees.

Most little leaguers are never taught how to pitch correctly. The ones with the strong arms and the most athletic ability are just put on the mound following a brief lesson in windups, and then told to give it a try. If they can throw the ball near the strike zone with any velocity, most of the batters cannot hit it. Therefore, the objective is to throw the fastball trying to avoid walks and hit batsmen. The boys who do this successfully are given a few more pointers along the way, maybe a few lessons from a paid pitching instructor, after which they become pitchers, or think they become pitchers.

This mode of developing pitchers has many problems. The first one is that through this method boys do not become pitchers first, they become throwers. Eventually, the time does come when batters can handle their best fastball, recognize the spin of their curveball, and are no longer being deceived by off-speed pitches thrown with a slower arm motion. This usually happens in high school. If the high school pitcher has never learned to pitch before, he has to do so in a hurry unless his fastball is in the mid-eighties mph or higher range. If this is the case, he can get by without pitching skills a little longer, maybe until college or the minor leagues. However, the longer he goes without learning real pitching skills, or the good mechanics that should go with them, the harder it gets. The reason is not so much physical as it is mental. A pitcher who has confidence in what has worked in the past tends to revert to his former way of throwing at the first sign of trouble. In other words, he loses confidence in what he has learned he must do to succeed in the future.

Alec was not endowed with a high-velocity throwing arm, so he never could have been just a thrower even if he wanted to be one. If he was to pitch effectively, he first had to master good pitching mechanics with a proper throwing technique. His velocity would naturally increase over time as his body grew and his strength increased. In an ideal world, every kid who pitches would be taught proper pitching mechanics from the start. Alec was convinced from the very beginning that the only way to get batters out was to make good pitches. Anyone close to baseball has heard it said a hundred times,

"If you can locate and change speeds, you can pitch."

Never does anyone say that if a player can throw a baseball X-mph, he can pitch. Nobody ever says that because almost everyone knows, or should know, speed by itself, uncontrolled, is useless. Rather than apply what they know to be true, many coaches pay lip service to good control and good mechanics while looking for more and more velocity. Doing so makes the evaluation of pitchers sound more complex as the evaluators aim their radar guns during every wind-up. Far too many baseball managers, coaches, and scouts live and die by the speed of the fastball. What good fortune it was for us to be living near Atlanta where we had professional pitchers like Tom Glavine and Greg Maddux who based their hall-of-fame careers on the correct philosophy of pitching, being masters of control and speed change. Neither one had a blazing fastball. Both practiced their trade as if it were an art form, a matter of great skill, setting a useful example for youngsters.

Before pitching in an actual game, even though this was just the little league, it was important for him to be able to throw a fastball and change-up with the same delivery motion and arm speed. The only change in the delivery was to be an undetectable grip on the ball. Right away, it was apparent that my left-handed student had an uncanny ability to repeat his windup and delivery motion with the consistency of a machine. Within a few weeks, he was able to locate pitches very well horizontally. Mastering the vertical location took a bit longer, until he learned to release the ball consistently from the same point. This essential skill was gained only after much repetition and the establishment of a timing mechanism for the release.

Many youngsters are endowed with the physical ability to become good pitchers. Unfortunately, very few of them do, usually for three general reasons. First, they do not receive the proper instruction. Second, they suffer injuries. Third, even if they receive proper instruction and avoid injuries, they are too lazy or disinterested to practice. Why a particular young boy is lazy about working to improve his baseball skills is more of a personal choice issue.

The causes of arm injuries in baseball are not a mystery. Most often, they are due to improper mechanics, lack of adequate conditioning, and over-use. Over-use and conditioning are related through physical training. The right amount builds endurance. Pitching mechanics are taught. A youngster who is left to employ poor mechanics is heading for double trouble. First, it is almost impossible to pitch consistently with bad mechanics. Second, bad mechanics places too much unnecessary strain on the arm.

When beginning to teach pitching mechanics to an eleven-year-old little leaguer, one must realize he is not yet physically capable of performing the complete motion one would see in an adult. Because of this, it would be a big mistake to demand of a youngster to perform any physical mechanic before he is physically able to do it. No eleven-year old boy I have ever seen can perform a windup and delivery identical to Sandy Koufax or Tom Seaver. Trying to force it can only lead to needless frustration and, sometimes, an injury. Instead, there are drills that can be done at an early age to help the young pitcher develop the strength and coordination he will need to pitch like a man when he becomes a man. Drills are time consuming and boring, this is true, but they are necessary. Besides, what is the hurry? If the kid wants to learn, and is a good sport about it, he should not mind doing drills. Alec was told at age eleven he was not going to be ready to pitch in a game until the next year, so in the meantime he may as well just keep plugging away trying to learn his new trade. He had no problem with this.

To start, the young pitcher should learn the proper grip on the fastball. There are only two grips on a fastball, the two-seam and the four-seam. If his hand is too small to hold the ball with just the index and middle fingers on or across the seams, then he should use three fingers. The early change-up is done very easily by moving the ball in closer towards the palm of the hand. The thumb should always be directly underneath the ball. Nothing more about the grip is important at this stage. Nearly all of the training should be devoted to the wind-up motion and delivery motion, while the pitches thrown should be either the fastball or change-up, mostly fastballs.

Although mastering a fastball and change-up are quite enough for any little leaguer, it is impossible to teach a boy to pitch without showing him how to throw a breaking ball, or curveball. Every kid wants to know how to make a baseball curve. They will niggle you to death until you show them how to do it. The greatest amount of glee a young pitcher can have is to see a batter swing at a ball that bounces in the dirt after it drops twelve inches out of the air. Equally gratifying is to throw a baseball that is aimed at the batter's head, causing him to jump back out of the batter's box, as it breaks down into the strike zone, and then to see the umpire raise the fist and yell,

"Steee-rike!"

To be sure, many youth coaches object to youngsters throwing curveballs, as they are concerned that the throwing of any kind of a breaking ball by a youngster can lead to an arm injury. It certainly can, but it does not have to. The kind of breaking ball that should not be thrown by a youngster is the one usually called a slider. This pitch is thrown with the middle finger pressuring the inside of a seam one hundred eighty degrees apart from the thumb following a severe tomahawk arm motion. The delivery is accompanied by a full arm extension and much stress on the elbow. The slider is also the breaking ball a younger boy will learn from an older boy if his father or his coach does not teach him differently. Instead of leaving the health of Alec's arm to chance, his attention was directed to two kinds of curveballs, the throw-and-turn and the Frisbee-style toss, the same ones that Buddy Fultz had shown to me. Since I never could get those two pitches to break, there was minimal expectation of seeing much of a break when Alec threw them, either. I nearly expired when he threw both with immediate success.

"How did you do that?"

"You showed me," he answered in bewilderment.

After entreating him to show me how he threw the ball, I tried again and again to copy him, but still could not get the brainless ball to curve. The important thing to note about these breaking balls is that they are thrown without a full extension of the arm during the release so there is no significant risk of injury to the elbow. To clarify a bit, there is another name for the throw-and-turn breaking ball, at least when thrown slowly with an overhand motion and a large arc. Some call it the old-fashioned, country curveball.

As mentioned, our baseball efforts included two separate programs complimentary of each other, one at home, and one with the team. It seemed we were becoming almost all baseball all the time, after church, school, and homework, of course. Not only were his skills now beginning to increase more rapidly, there was also a marked increase in his understanding of the game. It was a good year for Norcross Dixie Youth, as well. Many of the boys playing in the majors were good ballplayers being coached by dedicated fathers and roundly encouraged by supportive mothers. Alec did not know these boys from school since most of them went to the public school. As teammates, though, acquaintances were quickly made. He had a good observation once, suggesting that he thought the Norcross boys were more interested in playing baseball than the boys at Murphey-Candler. Several of them would go out to the fields to play ball on their own, more like my mates back in Springfield Forest. It was enormously satisfying to watch all of them as they progressed.

American boys of the 1980's and 1990's were living in an era of expanding indoor activities abetted by the proliferation of electronic games, television channels, and computers. More and more, kids were being distracted away from outdoor activities, becoming increasingly sedentary while staying mindlessly engaged in an electronic wasteland. Many parents allowed it and many actually encouraged it. Some went so far as to wait in crowded, contentious lines for hours to purchase at full retail the latest costly device. I experienced no wait when purchasing an A-2000 Wilson ball glove on sale at Sports Authority, nor was the episode of executing this incredible bargain captured for the local evening news broadcast.

If a boy wants to stay indoors, better to let him do chores, read books, or work math problems. When he is ready to go outdoors, take him out for some fielding and batting practice. During the early 1960's, those exact alternatives kept us at the ball field all day long until dark. Few parents today have the foresight or the courage to cancel the cable or satellite television, to throw away the electronic games, to stop buying snacks, and to turn off the air conditioner during the day. After being worn out by baseball, when the heat of a Georgia summer afternoon becomes oppressive, swimming pools offer ample relief.

By the following autumn, anticipation for the next baseball season had already taken over. Generally speaking, life in America in 1992 was as good as any other time in memory. One Monday morning in early November, I left the office to go down to the Norcross train station to await the arrival of President Bush (#41). He was making a series of campaign whistle stops the day before Election Day following an early morning television appearance in Atlanta. Here was a truly fine gentleman of great character. He was also the first presidential candidate I took time to go see. The country made a grievous error not re-electing him. It seemed one of the main reasons was the so-called "soccer moms" who rushed out to polling places to vote for the lesser man because he was, presumably, the lesser of a man. Upon arriving home after work, no doubt projecting a bit of parental smugness, I informed Alec of having seen the President earlier in the day and, by the way, he was a left-hander, too, and he played baseball for Yale!

"Have you ever heard of Frank Merriwell?" I asked.

*Chapter Seven*

# Little League – Third Year

The 1993 spring baseball season opened with Alec on the roster of the NDY Majors Blue Jays, managed by Charles Williams. This third year of little league was going to be the year for his star to shine. He expected to play the outfield as before, but, mostly, he hoped to have a chance to pitch. Practicing everyday throughout the past year built the strength and confidence needed along with the most important pitching skill one could ever have, namely the ability to locate pitches while changing speed. Also contained in his repertoire was a serviceable breaking ball. He was as ready as he could possibly be to pitch a baseball in a game against real batters for the first time.

During the initial team meeting, Mr. Williams asked the boys to let him know which positions they wanted to play. Some hands went up for every position as he announced them and as he dutifully jotted down the names. Outfield counted as one position. The very last one called out was for pitcher. For this position, it appeared every hand went up. Apparently, my kid would get his chance at center stage even if it meant waiting in line for a while. Just the thought of him pitching made me nervous. We were both very excited in separate ways. Even though he had practiced pitching every day for a year, practice is not quite the same as a real game with real batters. In a real game, an umpire is calling the balls and strikes. Would the batters murder his fastball, which was not very fast? Would he be able to keep his focus, to throw strikes and avoid walks? For the next couple of weeks before the season opener, pitching practice continued with a heightened sense of purpose. The day of reckoning was now close at hand.

The season opened on a Tuesday evening at 6:00 o'clock against Ryan Doering's White Sox. The Blue Jays won 11-1. Then, on Thursday evening, they played their second game losing to Russ Hunt's A's by the score of 8-5.  We figured the A's to be one of the better teams mainly because they had Jeff Hunt, a tall left-hander with a good fastball few could hit.  Every team hoped to play the A's when Jeff was not pitching so they could make a game out of it.  He was not pitching that day, which was why the Blue Jays were able to score five runs, though it was still not quite enough.

Two games into the season the Blue Jays' record was one win and one loss.  Still waiting to make his pitching debut was the novice left-hander.  The third game was scheduled on the following Wednesday against the Mariners, managed by Brian Haggard.  For Alec, waiting to pitch was not a bad thing at all.  In fact, the postponement was probably fortunate because it gave him the opportunity to observe the other pitchers and batters from his new perspective as a potential pitcher.  With plenty to analyze, we had long discussions after each of the first two games, making our next few practice sessions more meaningful.  No longer was pitching practice just the act of throwing baseballs to a mitt.  We began to talk about real "what if" scenarios to figure out the best pitch to throw in different situations, and about anything else that might help in being prepared.

Mr. Williams probably viewed Alec as not being the best pitching prospect on his team, not only because he did not have much velocity on his fastball, but because he had never pitched in a game before.  It would be understandable if his intention was to put Alec on the mound when there would still be time, in case he got into trouble, to pull him out before maybe losing the game.

In game three, the Blue Jays jumped out to an early lead giving the manager a perfect opportunity to get his last aspiring hurler in there to show his stuff.  Alec was pulled from his outfield position during the top of the fifth inning and told to warm up.  There were no spare bull pen catchers available, but there was a spare catcher's mitt.  We started to throw.  My anxiety level was high to say the least, but he seemed cool as a cucumber, however cool that may be.  I wondered if he was ready, if he had been taught enough.  I wondered if he would be able to field the position, suddenly realizing we had not gone over backing up bases and coverages.  What was I thinking?  There are no coverages in little league, just tell the third baseman to watch for a bunt.  Getting on to the more horrible concerns, would he be able to react to a come-backer and, then, would he throw to the right base?  He was an outfielder.  He did not have very much infield experience.  So, I wondered, could he field a bunt?  Did he know to turn to his right (since he was left-handed), away from the runner, before throwing to first base? Would he know when to cover first and back-up home? It was about then the cold sweat of reality struck.

"He is not ready!"

Too late, now, to do anything about it, as the sides changed. He was almost loose. He kept throwing through the bottom of the fifth inning, which went quickly for the Blue Jays. The score was 6-0 going to the top of the sixth. It was time. Mr. Williams peered around the side of the dugout.

"You want to pitch, Alec? Here's the ball. You warm?"

"Good luck, Alec, you'll do fine."

Was that a send-off to pitch baseballs or to swim with sharks? Whatever, the game must take care of itself. All that remained for a spectator, personal interest aside, was to go directly to the seating area immediately behind the backstop, just slightly to the right of center, so that the view of home plate was not obscured by the catcher. With a notepad and pencil in hand, the need to do something could be fulfilled by charting pitches.

"Chart pitches? What in the world for?"

This was not the time to debate that issue with myself. My kid was warming up on the mound. The batters were lining up in the on-deck area adjusting their batting helmets and swinging those loathsome metal bats. Actually, it was good not to be needed.

Remembering what it was like to be called upon to pitch in a little league game for the first time gave this occasion a much more appealing air. It was different then, I thought. Well, maybe it was not. No. Not really. It was not very different and surely could not have been thirty years ago. It was not. It was thirty-one. Thirty-one years sounded like a long time. Something about it must be different. It was during an afternoon game, we had no lights at Talbert Field. There was no warming up in the bull pen. We had no bull pen. It was during an inning, between batters, called in from playing center field. The Springfield Forest team was getting beat badly. First, our pitcher gave up a bunch of hits and runs. Then he started walking batters. It was no surprise when Mr. Lorenson came out to the mound. He had to change pitchers, but it was obvious he had not figured out whom to put in. So there he stood, holding the baseball, looking around the field, as the removed pitcher hovered on the infield grass inside the first base foul line wondering if he would be sent to the dugout or to some other position. First, the new pitcher had to be determined. Who would it be? A few head swings around the diamond between the foul lines . . . him? . . . no . . . him? . . . no . . . him? . . . no. Somehow, the manager's stare became fixed on me. I think I turned to see if there was anyone behind me. No, nobody there. The finger pointed (who, me?) with a silent summoning gesture. I jogged up to the mound to find myself surrounded by the other infielders and the catcher. Our skipper was too disgusted to say too many words when he dropped the ball in my glove.

"Throw strikes."

As primers go, this was brief. In those days, that was how a kid had his self-esteem built up. He was gone before I could say,

"Yes, Sir."

In this earlier era, there was no limit to the number of warm-up tosses or the number of manager visits. We did not know about those things because they had never existed. I threw two or three warm-ups before the umpire gruffly asked how many more I needed.

"I guess I'm ready."

Having never pitched in a game before, how could I know if I was ready? Besides, ready for what? Was I supposed to know what was going on here? All I knew was that Mr. Lorenson told me to do something and I could not disobey a grownup. That would be a sin. I threw strikes. I do not remember how many. My one very clear and lasting remembrance of this occasion was that almost every pitch was a strike and almost every strike was either a called strike or a swing and a miss, except for one foul ball. For the few pitches that were called balls, I confidently assumed the umpire was wrong. The side was retired very quickly. No one walked because I was told to throw strikes. The inning ended without further damage. The only ball hit into fair territory was a big-hop come-backer to the mound, easily snagged and tossed to the first baseman in time for the out. Enough of the past, that was then, this was now. Would Mr. Williams remember to tell Alec to throw strikes?

The NDY major field was located adjacent to the (old) Norcross High School football stadium, one block from Buford Highway, and about three blocks from Wingo-Carlyle Field. The property was owned by Norcross Dixie Youth, Inc., bequeathed to the organization by a local estate so long as it was used for youth baseball. The miniature stadium was a classic style little league field in its simple design and dimensions. It had bull pens and batting cages, a concession stand, equipment shed, and a press box. The turf was always well maintained and consisted of

Bermuda grass with rye over-seed in the cold months. The nighttime lighting gave brightness to the grass-green hues while it enlivening the deep reddish tint of brick dust in the cutout areas of the infield. The field looked good, day or night, but in the evening twilight with the halogen lamps burning, it exuded an otherworldly kind of aura, the magnificent other world of nighttime little league baseball.

An electronic Coca-Cola scoreboard stood high on stilts just beyond the center field fence, very much like the one we had at Talbert Field, though ours was manually operated. Spectator seating was created by terraced, smoothed-over poured concrete, which curved around behind the backstop from dugout to dugout giving every spectator easy access and a good elevated view. Good standing room positions were available along the fence lines, too. The first base side of the park was bounded by Price Place, a street that ran parallel to the first base line about one hundred feet away. It was a rare and joyous moment for the boys when a foul ball hit a moving vehicle that happened to be passing by. When else could a boy cause damage to property under the full protection of their parents and the Norcross Police Department? Beyond the outfield fence, from left to right, was the girl's softball field, Summerour Middle School, and an open athletic practice field. Now was the time to sit down and watch the warm-up tosses.

Alec was coming into a game where he had a six-run lead, so the odds of getting through this half-inning without losing the game were very good. All he had to do was pitch it in there and make the batters put the ball in play. The outs would come. Baseball works in this manner. The only way to blow this lead was to start walking batters.

Some moments during our lives, we are destined to forget. Some moments we try to forget and cannot. Some moments we try not to forget, but still cannot remember. The following moment has yet to fade even the smallest degree over the many years since it occurred. The recollection of this moment never has required even the least bit of effort, the moment my son threw his first pitch in a baseball game.

Without doubt, every father would like to be able to say his son's first pitch was a called strike fastball nailing the outside corner at the knees. This one was not. Alec's first pitch was a ball, way outside and in the dirt. Furthermore, he walked the first batter on five pitches. In less than two minutes, my analytical confidence in baseball statistics became an irrational panic. My mouth was so dry the chewing gum turned into a hard lump.

Alec caught the ball when it was thrown back to him by the catcher. As the next batter stepped into the batter's box, he turned, spit like a real ballplayer, adjusted his cap, and assumed a tall, deliberate stance atop the rubber. Spitting is important in baseball. Maybe some would say it is a kind of masculine territorial marking, a challenge of superiority furthering the display of a foul attitude. That is not it. If a player does not spit while playing baseball, he will end up swallowing a lot of diamond dust during the season. So, unless the boys like eating dirt, it is a good thing to keep the juices flowing while continuing to spit them out. Chewing tobacco and bubble gum work real well for this, gum being the healthier choice for little leaguers, better make that sugarless gum.

Continuing to fret over the situation was a completely mindless and involuntary reaction, accompanied by a deepening anxiety. The main cause of this exaggerated concern was the thought that he might keep walking batters until the manager had to go get him. Then what? Will he ever want to pitch again? Will he ever play baseball again? What will become of us? The sheer terror produced by just this one base-on-balls was almost unbearable. Thankfully, the uneasiness lasted only a little while, only until he calmly and efficiently struck out the next three batters with a paltry thirteen additional pitches. The most contact any batter managed to do was a foul tip. The base runner was stranded at first base. The game was over. The team was all excited about the shutout and the excitement centered around the mound and the little boy with the big smile on his face. Yes, some things are easy to remember.

The rest of the season went by fast. Too fast. Alec pitched five complete innings over five different games. He gave up some runs, some hits, even a few walks. He also struck out seven batters. Brett Moon tagged him for a home run, a solo shot, the first and only one he yielded until his high school junior year six years and hundreds of batters later. The team did pretty well, but the single most important aspect of the season was the opportunity every boy was given to try any position he desired. This simple accommodation by a very considerate youth baseball manager established an inimitable and long-lasting legacy in each of these youngsters' lives.

After Dixie Youth Majors, ages eleven and twelve, comes Pony, ages thirteen and fourteen. Approximately one-half of the little leaguers keep playing and make a successful transition to the higher league. Those who do, find the game is played on a noticeably more challenging level where each player is normally consigned to a more specific role.

Therefore, the little league is the last realistic chance for many of them to play certain key positions, like pitching and middle infield. When a boy pitches in the little league, he will never forget it no matter what else happens in his baseball career. If he only pitches one inning and gives up five runs, he will remember each of the three outs he got and forget the runs he gave up.

Every coach should want the boys at this age to think winning is very important, that winning the game is the main goal. At the same time, the grown-ups, the coaches and parents, should know better. When the years go by, unless they win a state championship or some other big tournament, these kids will have forgotten their team's win/lose record, but they will remember their own particular successes, instances when they stole a base, or hit a home run, or struck out the side.

After each succeeding game during the season, we had more to discuss, delving more deeply into game situations and into the tendencies of batters. It is never too early to teach the strategy of the game or for a boy to learn the lessons that game situations provide, especially if the little leaguer wants to become a competent pony leaguer. For a pitcher, these lessons are essential.

A young pitcher must come to understand that the characteristics of a batted ball have more to do with the way the pitch is thrown than with the way the bat is swung. In other words, most of the time, when a ball is well hit, it is because the pitcher has made a mistake. Each batter has his zone where he can hit the ball with the most authority; however, this zone is always well less than half the area (volume) of the strike zone. All the pitcher has to do is determine where the preferred hitting zone is for a particular batter. Then he can pitch outside of it while still throwing the ball inside, or close to, the rest of the strike zone. If the pitcher can locate pitches like this, changing speeds while he is doing it, he is going to get most of the batters out while making it look easy.

"How hard can it be? Glavine and Maddux do it all the time! Why not you?"

A large part of understanding the hitting zone comes from being aware of the rebound characteristics of the bat. Only about five or six inches of the thirty to thirty-four inch bat can normally account for effective contact with the ball. To demonstrate, hold a bat in one hand while bouncing a baseball on it sequentially with the other hand starting at the trademark and proceeding to the outer end. The bounce-back qualities change drastically from inside and outside of the "fat part" of the bat.

The pitcher can control the ball, but not the swing; therefore, his primary objective cannot be to prevent the batter from hitting the ball. Rather, the pitcher must try to make the batter hit the ball on the end of the bat or near to the handle, that is, outside of the "sweet spot." This result is most easily achieved by properly locating pitches and changing speeds. Thus, the batter will not get the ball in his most favorable hitting zone and he has the further difficulty of timing his swing. Leo Mazzone, perhaps the finest pitching coach in baseball, made an outstanding instructional film called *The Four Aces*, in which he makes the point as well as it can be made that hitting is timing; therefore, the pitcher should focus on throwing off the batters' timing. A pitcher should never allow his actions to be directed by a fear of contact. If the batter's timing is off and he makes contact, he will most likely make an out. It sounds simple, but it is true.

The point of teaching this theory of pitching is to emphasize the greater importance of skill and knowledge in besting batters. This approach gets more sophisticated in its detail as the level of play increases, but the validity of the underlying principle stays exactly the same from little league all the way up to the majors. The overpowering fastball is a great tool, but it is only one tool, and one tool is never enough. Moreover, the adjective "overpowering" has more than one application. If overpowering means velocity in the mid to upper ninety's, very few major league pitchers have it. Fewer still are able to use it effectively and consistently over extended periods. In reality, eighty-five mph can be overpowering if it follows a properly thrown seventy-three mph change-of-pace. Similarly, a seventy-three mph change-up can be an overpowering pitch following a perfectly located eighty-five mph fastball.

Finally, the pitcher must know how to act and think when he is in the game. Some call it "mound presence." It is the way a pitcher displays his confidence and goes about his business. The best condition under which a pitcher can display these characteristics is when he controls his emotions. At no other time is self-control more important than when things are going badly. Whether the batters are hitting every ball thrown or whether the fielders are booting every ball hit, a pitcher should never lose his composure, particularly while in the view of others. The past cannot be changed. Of greater importance is the rest of the game, and the rest of the game always depends upon only one thing, the next pitch. The way a pitcher feels about what has already happened is irrelevant. Therefore, he has no reason to feel anything. Feelings never help to get a batter out.

While a game is in progress, a pitcher should never listen to anyone who is trying to tell him how to pitch, particularly if it involves his delivery. When a game starts, the pitcher cannot improve his pitching ability. He has what he brought to the game and nothing more. If anything needs improvement or adjustment, it should be done in a practice session the next day. This goes for all players whether they are pitching, fielding, or batting. One of the more silly occurrences in youth baseball is when coaches yell out instructions about how to hit or to pitch or to field. To watch a middle-age, big-bellied coach with bad knees trying to demonstrate how to get down and field a grounder after his shortstop let one go between his legs, is very comical. Or the customary refrain after the batter has watched two fastball strikes go by with the bat never leaving the shoulder:

"Now you're ready!" accompanied by a pantomime of swinging the bat, pointing a finger to center field, followed by the boisterous command, "Drive the ball!"

"Sure, coach."

Better yet is this familiar instruction to the pitcher about to face the best batter on the opposing team, immediately after walking the bases loaded,

"Now, throw strikes, Joey, but don't give him anything he can hit!"

The fact of the matter is that learning and improving skills is done in practice, not in games. Games are for showing what you have learned. The best time to improve skills is actually during off-season practices, while in-season practices are more for maintaining skills.

But kids are kids and theory, even when it is correct, is not always easy to apply. When a pitcher is on the mound, he can find it very difficult to keep his composure, especially when everything is caving in all around. Whether he is not pitching well or his teammates are making errors and misplays, disasters are very distracting. Nor is it easy to ignore the catcalls and ridicule coming from the opposing dugout. It does not take much for frustration or anger to misdirect his focus, or to cause him to burn up emotional energy needlessly. Even so, he should resolve that no energy at all should be expended that does not contribute to his pitching. Everything should be done for the good of the team in its effort to win the game. Moreover, a pitcher should never show displeasure with a fielder's errant play, rather he should be the first to offer encouragement.

"Shake it off. We'll get two on the next one. Let's turn it, guys."

To get Alec to stay calm and focused was easy. He wanted to pitch more than anything but in those early years he did not get to pitch very often. What did it mean when an error was made? Every error meant he would pitch to one more batter and he would do so in a more challenging situation. Errors may not have been desirable; however, they were not to be dreaded, either. What he wanted to do, more than anything else, was to pitch.

"Five unearned runs? So, what's the problem? Keep pitching!"

At the time little league was ending, thoughts about the next step up along baseball's dusty trail began. Before the last weekend of the Blue Jays' season, a visit to Best Friend Park was in order to watch a NDY Pony League game, to see what was coming next. It made sense to gauge his reaction when seeing a higher level of baseball, to make sure he understood that continuing to play would involve a lot of work, more work than his current level required.

The pony league players looked much bigger and seemed to play much better than in the little league. The game was faster, stronger, more like the real game, on a bigger field, too. The distance between bases was seventy-five feet instead of just sixty feet. After watching for a while, maybe a couple of innings, I asked him if he was sure he wanted to play in pony league. He said he did. Did he think he could play with these guys? Again, the same affirmative response, while exuding that supreme confidence so very often found in adolescent males. There were no more questions. At this point, my son had been given everything he needed to become a baseball playing man. When we got home, the home plate was moved two paces farther away from the pitching rubber. Life on the diamond was moving on.

*Chapter Eight*

# Pony League Makes a Man

"Show me a boy that doesn't participate in baseball, and I will show you a weak, sickly, hot-house plant, who will feel sorry, as he grows older, that he was ever born."     Michael J. "King" Kelly, c. 1890

The development of a baseball player must not be separated from the development of a man. All good parents want their sons to grow up to be good men. However, what constitutes a good man is open to intelligent discussions, which are often followed by irrational arguments. No matter. The more opinions exchanged in the marketplace of ideas, where corrections are best made, the stronger the culture will be. This is true precisely because not all thoughts and prejudices have equal validity. If they did, the tenets fashioned out of "political correctness" would be morally and intellectually equivalent to the tenets fashioned out of the Ten Commandments. The Ten Commandments are unquestionably superior, just as the Creator is unquestionably superior to His Creation. Of this, there can be no doubt within a properly formed conscience. Those who do not agree and who choose to ignore the better inferences offered them, must live burdened with the spoiled fruits of false intelligence.

Since we live in a free society, any and all points of view can be freely expressed. Consequently, a never-ending flow of unreasoned notions come about, many of which gain credence. Jefferson was one who never worried about anybody's ideas, even bad ones, as long as others were free to dispute them. False intelligence is rather easy to countermand, in most cases. As a particularly humorous example, the term "girly man" came into common use in recent years to counteract the trend of societal feminization. Girly men do not usually make good baseball players, so a full description of that species can be omitted.

What makes any man a good man is of great interest in baseball. Those characteristics should be clearly defined. With the use of a little deductive reasoning and, without being capricious, the following serves this objective:

A man is not a woman.
A man is not a sissy.
A man does not wear his emotions on his sleeve.
A man never cries in public.
A man pays his debts in full, those incurred by gambling first.
A man never shirks his responsibilities and obligations.
A man initially assumes a woman is a lady, unless she holds elected office.
A man understands he is created in the image and likeness of God.
A man understands he is not God.

Now that the constitution of a man is clearly defined, the next task is to give a general description of the parameters by which he conducts himself. Thus, a man would prefer to lose all his material possessions, be stripped of all his titles, be denied all his perquisites, and even lose his life, rather than bring dishonor to his family, his country, or himself.

Finally, a good man displays the noblest virtues of his manhood while playing baseball when he:

allows himself to be hit by a pitch,
hits an opposing batter to protect his own,
sacrifices his at bat to move runners,
assumes personal responsibility for failure, and,
gives credit to his teammates for success.

Baseball does not replace, nor does it diminish, other important elements of a boy's life. It enhances them, especially during adolescence, by adding structure and meaning to his life. Baseball is an activity with an immediate and serious purpose, one in which relationships are formed, confidence is built, and the importance of teamwork is taught. The perseverance required to play baseball creates authentic self-esteem. Baseball builds character. In short, baseball supplements the development of a boy into a man, particularly when the game is properly taught by good men.

The two-year period of pony league baseball falls between little league and high school. It is transitional in terms of both playing skills and strategic thinking. During this brief segment of the journey to the big leagues, if properly instructed, the youngster will acquire knowledge of the game as it is played by men. He will learn signs and indicators. He will learn to which base the ball should be thrown and which base to cover. He will learn the lineup during a rundown. He will learn how to execute a double relay. He will learn when and how to trade outs for runs. He will learn how to sacrifice. In short, he will learn much of the inside game. If the coaches do their jobs correctly, by the time a boy finishes pony league and starts high school he should already be a grizzled veteran of the game.

The boys in the upcoming group of Pony players in the 1994 spring drafts were well known by the veteran managers. Thad Joiner drafted Alec onto his team, the NDY Pony Braves. Now he could wear the uniform of his favorite team, the Atlanta Braves. I had known Thad for five years by then, first as a business acquaintance and then as a very good friend. Like many of the other men involved in youth baseball, he was a good coach who volunteered his time year after year, doing so with a true sense of devotion. Thad had two older boys with whom he had experienced youth sports before, both good athletes in their own right. Now his youngest was playing pony league baseball, following the same path as his brothers. Thad's three sons kept him busy coaching for a long time and, at this point, he was doing it with a verve and levelheadedness that comes only after years of experience.

The best way to observe the various cultures in a community is to go to the places kids congregate, like schools, playgrounds, and sports leagues. Norcross, as it was in the rest of Gwinnett County and throughout the greater Atlanta metropolitan area, was fast becoming a cultural mixing bowl of which the Pony Braves were a representative sample. The challenge of coaching a diverse group of adolescent boys goes far beyond just teaching the game of baseball. This particular team was about as disparate as eleven boys could possibly be.

Men who wish to do a good job of coaching this age group must remain mindful of the many special challenges with which each boy has to deal, both on and off the field. As far as the sport goes, a boy's skills can vary from very good to almost never played in the past. On this team, two of the players had parents from India or Pakistan, or some such place, who did not understand how unusual it was for a boy to start playing baseball at this late age. It would not have mattered had they been told. Baseball was the great American pastime and these foreign parents wanted to have their sons normalized in a cultural sense. They signed up for baseball and, like everyone else, got to play.

The baseball part of the job was difficult enough by itself. What was a little more challenging came when facing the reality that some of the boys had home and family situations not at all conducive to happy childhoods. Some had problems with school, or social problems with peers. Perhaps worst of all, the occasional use of alcohol and even illegal drugs occurred. Unfortunate as some of their personal lives may have been, the baseball park provided one positive, safe, and enjoyable place to be. While on this properly coached Norcross Pony Braves team, every player found that he was important and wanted.

Randy Lambert, Tom Harris, and I did our best to help Thad with coaching and practices. My primary function during games was to keep the scorebook making sure the updated statistic sheets were available within twenty-four hours after every game. It was not too early for these players to begin to understand the value of statistics in baseball.

The Pony Braves team was remarkable in many ways and imperfect in a few other ways. Most of the players accepted our guidance and encouragement very well, two essentials in the development of young athletes. Most, but not all. Sorry to say we had a few boys with enough natural talent to become good high school varsity players, but they never made it. They did not make it because they had already begun to engage in self-destructive behavior, and did not have a father, an older brother, or some other good man in their lives interested enough to provide guidance away from the bad behavior. It was regrettable, but try as we might, thirteen years of neglect is not easily overcome by a couple of months of coaching. We did what we could and hoped something made a positive difference in the longer run.

The NDY Pony Braves record was eight wins and eleven losses. The team had decent pitching. The main problem was they batted only .203. A.J. Lambert, Sage Joiner, and Alec were the three boys out of this group who went on to play baseball for Norcross High School. Inexplicably, these same three ranked seventh, eighth, and ninth in batting average on the team. The tenth and eleventh place batters were the two who had never played baseball before. A.J., Sage, and Alec became much better baseball players later suggesting it may have been our coaching that was deficient. Maybe it was too many first-pitch take signs. Maybe not enough batting practice. Who knows? We tried.

The starting pitching was done mostly by David Vanderboom, Sage, and A.J. The main relievers, Charlie Stoeckert and Adam Herron, contributed eight more innings combined. The pitching staff altogether had a respectable pony league ERA of 4.12. Alec did not pitch at all because Thad was unaware that Alec had ever pitched before and we did not bother to mention it. Besides, the judgment was that, realistically, he was not quite ready to pitch in pony league, so maybe it would be better to wait until the next year. The pitchers we had were more than adequate. If the pitching had turned out to be inadequate, we could have used him. Instead, Alec played the outfield as we continued to work on his pitching at home.

Pony league baseball is different than little league in a couple of significant ways. The runners can take a lead from their base, and this induces pitchers to go to the stretch position while being careful not to commit a balk. These things, combined with bigger and faster players who have higher skill levels and wear metal cleats, make the pony league seem like the first level of real, grown-up baseball. The Pony game is quicker and more serious. Just about all the boys thrived on it, especially Alec, who was getting more excited about the game every time he played. He would eventually get to pitch again, this he knew. First, there were other baseball lessons to learn.

After the season ended, we continued to practice on our own every day in lieu of playing in a fall baseball league. A typical practice session was about an hour to an hour-and-a-half. First, we played catch to warm up. Then it was fly balls and batting practice. Finally, he pitched. The sequence generally stayed the same, but we used various drills to make each part more interesting, trying to avoid tedium. Occasionally, another kid would join us, and then each one would take his turn hitting the cut-off man, or batting.

When just the anticipation of being called upon to perform in baseball motivates a young player to improve his skills, it is certain that he loves to play, and has a healthy respect for the game. With the next season would come another opportunity to pitch. Meanwhile, there was enough time and plenty of motivation to prepare, focusing primarily on mechanics, and on the two simple elements of location and change of speed. However, a pitcher does more than just throw a baseball. He also occupies a defensive infield position. We now included drills on fielding, covering first base, and backing up plays during most practices, as well as talking about game situations. The differences between little league and pony league are more than a little bit noticeable from the vantage point of the mound, and this point cannot be overemphasized.

February of 1995 finally came and Alec was drafted by Larry Lancaster to play on a team called the Pirates for his second year of pony baseball. Arriving about forty-five minutes early to the first practice at Best Friend Park allowed Alec some time to become familiar with the mound. Though he knew the field very well, he had never thrown pitches from this mound. As he was throwing, another father-son pair showed up. The dad came behind me in the catcher's box to watch the pitches. The throws were not very fast, but the movement and location were excellent. Thus, the word got out that the team had a left-handed pitcher.

By an odd circumstance, the lefty got to pitch in the Pirates' first pre-season scrimmage game. Mr. Lancaster had not known that Alec could pitch when he drafted him so it was a pleasant surprise when he did well. After the long wait and all the practice, it was a great encouragement to be considered qualified to pitch in the pony league by his new manager. Without a doubt, great excitement was there. He had worked very hard, practiced diligently for almost two years, just hoping to get another chance to pitch, knowing that if his chance came he had to do well. The season was going to start the next week. Everything was going so right, until everything went so wrong.

What was perhaps the greatest amount of joy and anticipation in his young life vanished the next day when he was intentionally blind-sided in the locker room at school after gym class by a fellow classmate. Boys do scuffle, usually in a way that attempts to assert their burgeoning masculinity. It was not so in this case. This attack was a cowardly, pernicious act, intended not to challenge, but to injure. It was not a fair fight in a gentlemanly sense; rather it was an act of total dishonor. In my time, a boy like this would have been called a punk. Unfortunately, whatever they are called these days, this type of boy exists in every age. They can be found in almost every caste and circumstance, even in an expensive private Catholic school.

The school nurse called my office about 9:30 a.m. indicating that my son was hurt and it might be a broken arm. I called our family physician to let him know we would be there shortly, and then headed for the school. Alec was sitting in the office entrance area holding his left arm that had been immobilized from above the wrist by a temporary splint. He just said,

"I don't think I can pitch."

It was a pretty clean and typical break of both bones in the wrist. It happens to kids all the time. They heal quickly. The doctor said the cast would come off,

"Let's see . . . that cast is coming off . . . (the day after the last game of the season)."

"Not surprising."

Attending the Pirate's games while on the disabled list meant just having to watch, which he did with a keen interest. Watching the others play also meant wondering. A great opportunity to pitch was lost, and never to be retrieved. Some satisfaction was to be had in knowing he was good enough to pitch, that he certainly would have pitched this spring. As soon as the cast came off, the workouts resumed. Slowly the strength in the weakened arm returned. Pony league was over, but before too long, another new baseball season would begin. Meanwhile, it was summertime.

*Chapter Nine*

# Coach Ro

Following pony league, Dixie Youth baseball has two more levels for boys, ages fifteen to sixteen and seventeen to eighteen. Actually, when they pass their fourteenth birthday they can sign up for the age fifteen to sixteen teams, having something to do with the age turned in the year in which something or another happens. Whatever the rule, after spending two years in the Norcross Pony League, Wingo-Carlyle Field is the place to go. Age sixteen is sort of a swing year, too. A kid could play up or down depending on the circumstances and his abilities. This level of ball has an equivalent in Northern Virginia and some other places where it is called the Babe Ruth League. The game is played on a full regulation-size field. Many of the boys in this league, but not all, play for their high school teams. For those who do not play at school, this is an opportunity to continue playing a good competitive level of baseball.

There are several reasons a young baseball player might not play for his school team. The first and most obvious one is that he is not selected from the tryouts. Some players do make the initial roster only to be subsequently cut. Some choose not to try out for their high school team for personal or social reasons. Finally, some are prevented from playing in school because of a poor academic record. Leagues such as Dixie Youth and Babe Ruth baseball give each of these boys another place to play. In many cases, these recreational leagues provide a better place to play than the high school team. All in all, the level of competition is comparable.

The fact that an otherwise qualified boy would have negative perceptions so strong that he does not even try out for his high school baseball team is terrible. However, feelings of alienation, whether warranted or not, are not as regrettable as a school unilaterally denying a student his chance to play sports due to academic performance. Of the many dim-witted regulations school boards and school administrators continually adopt, this one policy, commonly referred to as "no pass/no play," deserves the highest disdain. The policy, in its simplest form, states that if a student fails more than one class he cannot play sports or participate in any other extracurricular activities. Georgia is not alone in this regard; many other states have similar policies, as does the National Collegiate Athletic Association (NCAA).

The authors of no pass/no play and their supporters usurp a basic child-rearing privilege that should be reserved for parents. On its face, the policy seems proper because of the reasonableness contained in its stated purpose, which is to make sure school is primarily for learning. Fair enough. Objectively, this is the primary function of a school. The logic of this argument becomes extraneous, however, when attempting to discern the proximate cause of scholarship. Exactly how does the establishment of academic standards for participating in extracurricular activities help to further learning? Can scholarship be induced by punishment and reward? Can it be educed by manipulations of students' interests through threats?

Grades are supposed to be the measure of academic achievement, motivating those students who choose to take heed. If grades are not sufficient motivators, no denial of extracurricular activity will be either. It would be illogical to assume otherwise.

What can be made of the other implied assumption, that the cause of poor grades is participation in sports, i.e., that there exists a cause and effect relationship? If this were so, then grades and sports must be inextricably linked in some inversely proportional way so that a student failing in the classroom will somehow receive academic benefits from being kicked off the team. This, too, is absurd, as numerous studies have shown. For instance, a report by Parents United for the D.C. Public Schools in June 2001, after doing a comparative study of athletic programs in the District of Columbia and suburban public school districts, offered these comments:

> "The benefits of a strong athletic program are extensive and widely regarded. Playing in sports can help keep young people motivated to stay in school and to continue on to higher education."

> "Though unproven, it seems obvious that strong athletic and extracurricular programs could help to reduce the system's extremely high drop-out rate. The drop-out rate for D.C. senior high school students

exceeds one-third, with a disproportionate number ... being boys. A student's difficulty with academic studies is often a motivating factor to leave school. However, for many students, it is clear that a strong athletics and student activities program can combat disillusionment and provide an opportunity to excel and feel a valued part of the student body."

A September 1995 report by the U.S. Department of Health and Human Services found that students who spend no time in extracurricular activities are 57% more likely to have dropped out of school by the time they would have been seniors, 49% more likely to have used drugs, 37% more likely to have become teen parents, 35% more likely to have smoked cigarettes, and 27% more likely to have been arrested, than those who spend one to four hours per week in extracurricular activities. A Fairfax County Public Schools study found ninety-six percent of school dropouts did not participate in extracurricular activities while they were in school and, furthermore, participation in extracurricular activities was one of the best predictors of future success in college.

In America, at the dawn of the Twenty-first Century, thirty percent of high school students never graduate. The number of studies done on this topic is staggering, more so because they all say the same thing: extracurricular activities are very helpful in reversing tendencies towards underachievement. Therefore, no pass/no play policies cannot be helpful. Rather, they appear to be just another aggravating factor further impairing the progress of marginal students.

Not allowing a student to participate in an extracurricular activity does not motivate him to learn. How is it sensible, therefore, to argue that such a denial to the failing student of the opportunity to participate in sports is a useful way for the school to demonstrate that learning is more important than playing? It is not. Such an argument is entirely disingenuous. In reality, students kicked off of high school teams for failing grades more often show an increase in dropout rate, drug usage, and the number of arrests than an increase in academic performance.

Any legitimate relationship is a two-way street and can be tested as such. Suppose the tables are turned. Suppose a policy is adopted that calls for suspending a student ballplayer from attending class lectures if he strikes out more than once during a game. Could we assume that this threat of suspension would motivate a boy to keep his eye on the ball when swinging the bat? Not likely. How preposterous to think it would.

However, it is preposterous not because batting average is more or less important than grade point average.

The naturally occurring symbiotic relationship between academic and other school-related activities is a positive one, which is one of the main reasons extracurricular activities exist in the first place. They are not inversely related, neither are they directly related to each other in a strict sense. Playing clarinet in the concert band does not create confusion between sines and cosines in trigonometry class, nor would such confusion, if it existed, be resolved by quitting the band or by switching to the tenor saxophone. Success within any area of endeavor comes to the student who is generally motivated to do good and constructive things, who possesses a willing spirit, an active mind, a healthy body, and an optimistic outlook. In other words, the positive relationship between different areas of endeavor derives from the idea that success in one area tends to spill enthusiasm over into other areas. Alternatively, failure spills poison from its guts. If a boy is successful playing second base and is failing chemistry, taking away baseball means taking away his success and retaining his failure. He would do better to quit chemistry and keep baseball. However, the best strategy would be to keep both.

When academic performance is sub-par, the appropriate course is for parents to intervene as they see fit. Not surprisingly, restrictions enforced by parents generally have very good results, usually better than those set by institutions. For parents to keep their child off the team, for whatever reason, is perfectly fine. Everyone is different, and so is every family, so the best assumption to make is that each child's parents know better than institutions or other children's parents what motivation or punishment, aside from grades, is appropriate. The obligation of a school is to provide opportunities, academic and otherwise, and to evaluate the students' efforts. Parents should be left to do the parenting. Otherwise, both school and parents are doomed to perform their duties poorly.

Unfortunately, rather than admit the issue addressed in no pass/no play is far beyond their competence, school board members acquiesce, or pander, to the demands of publicity-seeking politicians or self-serving teachers' unions or small vocal groups of activist parents. The result is predictable. One unfortunate characteristic of group dynamics is that the so-called "common ground" most often is found by a very few instigators employing false logic rather than rigorous, principled thought. The others, normally constituting a majority, do not have an opinion, do not care, or are cowed into going along. It is telling that the few who most vehemently advocate no pass/no play policies seem to be parents who have kids to which this sanction does not apply. Is it because they have a genuine concern for the underachieving children of other parents? Not likely. Then what is their motivation? Could it be the reasons are somewhat less than altruistic, perhaps even self-serving, or bigoted? The importance of extracurricular activities is such that they should not be bureaucratically subordinated to academic achievement. This is not to say one is more or less important than the other, or that they are of equal importance. Both are very important each by itself and in conjunction with the other.

If it is true that academics and extracurricular activities are mutually beneficial, no pass/no play must be an a priori failure. This assertion can be easily proven by a test of logic, by proposing an opposite policy while considering the likely outcome. Specifically, boys failing a course should be *required* to participate in an after-school athletic activity. The best place for underachieving male students after school is on a sports team where they are not left to idleness, rather, they can be subjected to the pervasive force of peer pressure. If already on a team, class-failing starters can be made to ride the pine for a while with extra running after practice. How enjoyable would it be for the entire basketball team to run an extra twenty-five full-court suicides every time one player misses his homework assignment? Baseball players are always in need of extra conditioning and would not they be most grateful for the opportunity to run an extra ten poles after practice when one of their teammates is tardy for class. These age-old techniques, to be sure, are still in use by savvy coaches because they have always been successful.

When a recalcitrant student is kicked off a team, he is given an escape through alienation. While on a team, there is no escape. He has nowhere to hide. He can be made to account for his actions, as classroom indolence can draw definite consequences. Off the team, he is left to suffer abandonment, not the ideal situation for an adolescent boy susceptible to tomfoolery.

The repeal of no pass/no play policies would have a secondary benefit, namely the elimination, or at least the curtailment, of some of the hypocrisy that derives from inconsistent treatment of student athletes. Even under no pass/no play policies, some students remain on teams because of their superior athletic talents in spite of failing classes and worse. Somehow, grades and bad behavior do not prevent star players from playing unless their misdeeds just cannot be kept secret.

The most positive comment that can be made about broad administrative policies such as no pass/no play is that they may be the lesser of evils, in some cases. They are not intelligent, not thoughtful, and not proper. They are mindless. One-size-fits-all, zero-tolerance, and any other ephemeral prattle are all very predictably poor substitutes for brains. No pass/no play purports to serve the best interests of students when, in fact, it does more harm than good. Granted that being allowed to remain on a sports team may not turn a failing student into a Rhodes Scholar; however, more often than not, it will increase his chances of leaving school with a diploma, along with much happier memories.

In anticipation of proceeding to the next level, we went to see the older boys play a ball game at the historic Wingo-Carlyle baseball field. Sitting in the stands above first base, we looked down at players nearly the size of men playing baseball on a full regulation-size field. Unperturbed by this sight, Alec proclaimed his readiness to run down and join them right away, if he could. I had watched my son play for five years now. At this point, he had already surpassed the level of my own baseball achievements, limited as they were. The matter of whether to continue to play or not was settled instantly. The next league sign-up in this age group was at the end of summer for the fall season, plenty of time to get ready.

First order of business was to move the pitching rubber at home back to sixty feet, six inches. Workouts went slowly for the first couple of weeks because the cast had just come off the throwing arm. Kids mend quickly, though, and soon we started to go to the big field every available chance to pitch, field, and hit. This could have been a decent field if it had not been long neglected by the city. Currently, it was in a run down, dilapidated condition. How shameful given what the history of baseball had been in this town.

In the 1960's, after the Glory Days of Norcross Baseball had passed, the town baseball field received some attention, but gradually became little more than a sandlot type of ball field. In the early 1990's, a local Norcross politician "resigned" her post as chairman of the county commission over "discrepancies" on expense accounts. She then successfully won election to her old job as the mayor of Norcross. Years earlier, she managed to get the Norcross City Council to lease the park to the county parks and recreation department for a nominal amount. The purported benefit to Norcross was that responsibility for maintenance of the facility would shift from the city to the county. Actually, it was an act of abandonment obscured by labeling the nefarious deed with the political aphorism, "a community benefit." Somewhere during all this shenanigans, the field received a plaque dedicating it in her name, Lillian Webb.

Politicians tend to be shameless just as bureaucrats tend to be incompetent, unless public pressure is brought to bear. Gwinnett County Parks & Recreation was supposed to maintain the field and improve the facility. The construction effort proved to be atrocious. They built ugly, but functional, institutional-style cement block dugouts, restrooms, and a concession building. They also installed lights, drains, seating, and fencing. The result was visually hideous, sickening really, since the same amount of taxpayer money, prudently spent, could have made the ballpark very useful and attractive.

The county parks department, stubborn and incompetent, had maintained for some time a policy that all county baseball fields would have dirt infields. Any of the local youth baseball associations wanting to plant infield grass had to do it at their own expense while assuming the responsibility for maintenance. The county would no longer maintain any baseball field with a grass infield. So it was with this historic Norcross field. The grass on the infield was immediately skinned.

During the succeeding years, the infield lost about twelve inches of topsoil to erosion. In some areas, the granite bedrock was exposed. The drains became clogged with the dirt that washed away during downpours. Slowly the infield became a bowl that held water like a lake following every hard rain. By 2003, an inch of rain would make the field unusable for forty-eight hours even under the hot Georgia sun.

To add to the difficulty, someone at the county decided that dumping tons of sand on the infield would help. This made the infield not unlike an ocean beach. To make it somewhat playable, the leagues had to bring in more dirt and hope it did not rain too much before the season was over. Rain tended to wash away the dirt and leave the sand.

The county also installed seating for about two hundred on the first base side of the field. Because of the poor positioning of the first base dugout, the height of the roof, and the unnecessary fencing behind the dugout, spectators could not see the batters' box or home plate from about eighty percent of the seating area even though it was a good twenty to thirty feet higher than the surface of the field. They also built a bull pen that was about five feet too short. Attempts to correct these problems and save the field came several years later, along with the new name.

The Norcross Baseball Club, the *Town Team of Historic Norcross*, was formed in 2002 to promote renovation of the field and save the property from development. The Club defiantly informed the press that the field would henceforth be known as Wingo-Carlyle Field, hopeful that a dignified name would gather the attention of the citizens. Madam Mayor was not noticeably amenable to the name change. Everything has a time and place and she failed to recognize her time had long since passed. It was sad for Norcross that such a politician became so entrenched for so long, especially since it was mainly due to voter apathy. Apparently, the only ideas she deemed worthy were her own, or those for which she could take credit, or those coming from her cronies. Not to be dismayed, after all is said and done, the legacy of such a politician ends, rather than begins, with retirement.

During one of our first practice sessions at Wingo-Carlyle Field in early June of 1995, we met some other boys of similar age who also came out to practice. They were Jose Covarrobias, Victor Rodriguez, Bernardo Fulleda, and Kiko Herrera. None of these fellows played for Norcross High School although each of them was good enough to make the team. Quickly this chance gathering turned into a regular baseball practice. These were Spanish-speaking kids, and each of them had good baseball skills. Although not a part of any team or league right then, they would be playing in the Dixie Youth fall league come September. Meanwhile, they were being independently coached by someone. This someone was Rogilio Fitten. He liked to be called "Ro."

Mr. Fitten was the most knowledgeable baseball man I had ever known. He was of Latin American heritage, raised in New York City, and rooted for the Mets. He was also a great admirer of the pitching talents of Tom Seaver. Ro played a lot of baseball in his youth, eventually playing in the minor leagues for the Pittsburgh Pirates organization. Now, as a judicious student of the game, he was trying to pass it on to youngsters. Most importantly, he had the unusual ability to detect a youngster's potential and instruct him accordingly. He was not just another pretty good coach. Ro Fitten was a master of baseball who knew how the game should be played at the highest level, someone you were not likely to find just anywhere, much less run into accidentally during the midday on some dusty, small-town baseball field in Georgia. But we did. After all, this was Norcross, the town that baseball did not pass by. This was also Wingo-Carlyle Field, where the exceptional in baseball can happen at any time.

While busy pitching batting practice to the boys, Ro showed up. He walked around the field giving each of them instructions how to play their positions, calling out pointers to whoever was batting. My arm began to give out after about a couple of hundred pitches, but I dared not stop until everyone had several turns at the bat. A baseball teaching session this extraordinary should not be allowed to end prematurely. Finally, it did end and, fortunately, my arm was still attached to my shoulder. Afterwards, everyone met and found out what every one was doing there. Ro obviously loved baseball and enjoyed teaching it so much that he would spend time with anyone who wanted to learn. Conversely, he had little use for anyone who was not serious about learning the game.

While questioning Alec, Ro found out about his baseball playing history and what position he wanted to play, which he declared was pitcher. The next thing we knew, Ro had taken him on as a student giving him two drills to do on his own. The first was a simple throwing drill. It began by standing straight and squarely facing the target. Alec was directed to raise his throwing hand behind and level with the head, and then step forward onto the ball of the front foot keeping the trailing toe on the ground while throwing the baseball. Throughout the drill, the body had to be maintained square to the target. He was told to repeat the exercise one hundred times each day, until the next session.

The second drill is one better known, one that makes use of an additional prop, a hand towel held by the middle finger of the throwing hand. The pitcher is positioned sideways to the target, steps with the left foot going behind the right foot (for a left-hander), then steps forward with the right foot, turns to square the body to a stationary target, and brings the towel down with an audible "snap." The target here is another player holding out his glove hand. At home, this can be done with a chair or bed. Both drills are designed for the pitcher to become accustomed to aggressively releasing the ball with his body squared up to the target.

These drills were added to our daily routine. After about two weeks, Ro took a greater interest in Alec for two reasons. First, he did everything he was told to do, exactly as he was told to do it. Second, he showed real talent.

The practice sessions went on for the rest of the summer. Ro's lessons were complete in the sense that if a boy learned them properly, he would be able to pitch successfully at successively higher levels. Included were proper pitching mechanics, as well as the approaches of how to use the skills, how to sequence pitches, how to analyze the strengths and weaknesses of batters, how and when to cover bases, what to throw in different situations, and how to work with a catcher.

Ro's approach to pitching was based on what he considered to be the four essential attributes of a pitcher, what he called the four C's: concentration, control, consistency, and confidence. Better pitching lessons could not be had anywhere for any price, at any professional level. Ro treated his students as if they were already playing in the rookie league or instructional ball, well beyond what most high school players were taught. Alec, the rising eighth grader, soaked it up eagerly, like a dry sponge. These things he had only heard about before were now becoming part of his game. This knowledge gave him power that he could use. He realized these were the secrets of the inside game of baseball, those that professional players knew and used. Now, could anything have been better than this?

The first concept Ro taught these young players, a concept very often overlooked by others, was preparation. Preparation is not only the learning of skills. Preparation includes learning how and when to use those skills. Everything Ro taught was designed to make the players ready to play the game, mentally and physically. Baseball is played between the ears as much as it is on the field. Some would argue more so. Yogi Berra supposedly made a comment that went something like this: baseball is fifty percent hitting, fifty percent pitching, and ninety percent mental.

Regardless of improperly applied mathematical laws, the mental preparation has to be at least as rigorous as the physical. Baseball is a game in which there is an indefinite number of situations and tendencies, any one of which can be vitally important at any given time. When a player is not prepared to play, he shows up at the ballgame wondering what is going to happen, hoping he will play his best. By contrast, the well-prepared player shows up knowing what he is going to do, and, if he is surprised, it is usually because he plays better than he thought he could. Ro insisted his players be the latter growing impatient with those boys who chose to be the former. Any indication of laziness produced an obvious displeasure in his demeanor. The decision was theirs to make, but he let them know which decision was correct.

In life, it is very often the case that the most important decisions we make do not seem to be so at the time. This is because not all of the consequences are yet known. Besides, what constitutes an important or difficult decision is certainly a relative matter. For instance, the sailors aboard the H.M.S. Bounty had an extremely important decision to make one particular morning when they were roused from their slumber in the pre-dawn hours on the high seas of the South Pacific. They were required at once to decide between being set adrift with Captain Bligh and face almost certain death in performing an act of loyalty or remaining aboard with the mutinous Fletcher Christian in an act of disloyalty, ultimately punishable by death if caught. This decision, made instantly by sleepy young men in darkness and confusion, eventually turned out to have the gravest of consequences.

Captain Bligh and those loyal, instead of being killed, were given an open hulled sloop measuring twenty feet long and seven feet wide with a shallow draft along with a few days' rations, in other words, a sporting chance. Bligh's nautical skills brought the overloaded sailing rowboat and crew three thousand nine hundred miles in forty-eight days to the Island of Timor. Upon arriving, near death from starvation and dehydration, not to mention being severely sunburned, he stood offshore a few hundred feet in an exhibition of the most proper etiquette, calling out for a government official, of whom he asked permission to come ashore.

The most taxing decision for the mollycoddled suburban Norcross kids to make was whether they wanted to play baseball, assuming they could get out of bed by the afternoon. How difficult can this be? Still some grown-ups were known to say blithely,

"Kids have it tough these days."

Perhaps so, if "having it tough" meant they were being raised by this generation of permissive and overly indulgent parents.

If asked directly by an adult, naturally, all the boys would respectfully say they wanted to work hard at playing baseball. Alas, most did not follow through with the necessary effort. Many of them squandered both their talent and this opportunity. However, several were willing to put forth the great effort it took to learn the game well, giving hope that on this legendary Norcross baseball field, home of over a century of baseball excellence, a knowledgeable baseball man like Ro Fitten offering first-rate professional instruction could somehow keep the tradition alive.

If ever there was a more perfect summer for a left-handed fourteen-year-old boy who was learning much more about pitching, I would like to hear about it so I could say,

"Not so!"

Besides eating and sleeping, all he had to do was play baseball until he was worn out, followed by a refreshing plunge in the swimming pool before eating supper and watching a Braves' game. Alec was understandably excited, caused by a combination of things: the attention he was getting from a real coach, his continual improvement, and the great success of the Atlanta Braves. Had baseball become an obsession? Yes, no doubt it had. One good outcome from all the new baseball excitement was that the memory of his pony league season having been lost to a broken arm earlier in the spring was all but gone and totally irrelevant now.

In early August, we finally went for a week's vacation in Virginia Beach. Every day, between surf sessions, we played catch, keeping the arm in shape. When we returned home, it was time to prepare for school and to sign up for the NDY Fall baseball league.

Autumn baseball leagues give players the chance to close out the year with some fun, maybe to work on some new skills, or to refine some existing skills. The atmosphere is decidedly more casual than the spring version. Extra time is taken for instruction and players are given chances to try different things. The coaches make use of this opportunity to find out about the boys who will be playing in the spring.

Norcross fielded two teams in the fourteen, fifteen, and sixteen-year-old age group. Ro managed one of them. His roster included all of his Spanish speaking kids, Alec, and a few other pick-ups. The team was called the Bees. They played games against the other Norcross team and several other teams from around the area including Lawrenceville, Duluth, Mountain Park, Lucky Shoals, and some others. For the first time, Alec experienced the challenge of playing teams from other towns with players whom he had never seen before.

Ro wanted to work with Alec more in order to get him ready to pitch in the spring. He had a couple of other pitchers, older boys, with whom he had been working for more than a year; consequently, they did most of the pitching. Playing the outfield was fine; playing baseball was fine, always and everywhere. Practice time continued to be mostly devoted to pitching drills. On two or three occasions, he was called on to pitch in relief and did so with surprisingly good results. The scorebook showed two and two-thirds innings pitched, one earned run, and one strike out. Pitching in this fall league, on the large field, against mostly high school age boys, was not only an absolute thrill, it was great experience. Now there would be something tangible to think about during the winter months, about what was required to become a competitive high school pitcher. Could life have been any better than this? Only if the Braves could beat the Indians in the World Series, which they did in six games, due mostly to excellent pitching, Leo Mazzone's four aces, Glavine, Maddux, Smoltz, and Avery. Yes, for all concerned, 1995 was a very good year for baseball in Georgia.

## Chapter Ten

# High School Baseball

Chances to see Braves' games in person were rarely passed, first going to Atlanta-Fulton County stadium, then to Turner Field following the 1996 Olympic Games. When Turner Field was built, it was designed specifically for the Olympics with the intent to turn it over to the Braves as a baseball park, after some modifications, for the 1997 season. Not only did it prove to be a much better stadium for baseball than the old "multi-purpose, cookie-cutter" one, the gates to the plaza area and bleachers opened three hours before game time, affording the opportunity to see most, if not all, of the pre-game warm-ups and batting practice.

If a young, aspiring pitcher arrived two hours before game time, the time when the gates opened at the old Fulton County Stadium, he could still watch the visiting pitchers work on the side mound along the third base side past the dugout. Often during the pre-game period, nearly every member of the visiting pitching staff could be seen from this post. Standing underneath his baseball cap a mere few feet away, never tiring, gazing in rapt attention, ball glove securely positioned on the right hand, always containing an official Rawlings National League baseball, the lefty was ready for anything. The look on his face gave him away. It plainly stated he was ready to take his turn warming up, needing only a single nod from the pitching coach to jump over the rail and onto the pitching rubber. That is how kids think.

"Can I play, too?"

On September 21, 1996, we made our final visit to the old Atlanta ballpark to see the Braves play the Montreal Expos. As luck would have it, the side-session in the visitors' bull pen included Pedro Martinez. The kid was transfixed. When it was over he politely asked for an autograph and Mr. Martinez, having noticed this most earnest of aspirants, graciously obliged. The Braves won 5-4. Denny Nagle beat Omar Daal. Mark Wohlers got the save.

This pitching session gave us a useful tip, too. During part of the exercise, a pitcher threw from just behind the mound. Therefore, the stride towards the catcher was uphill. This caused the pitcher to pull through a bit more to get the ball down to the catcher's mitt. It also caused him to slow down his delivery because of the extra distance through which he had to go before his release. The combination of a slower delivery and more use of the body created an elongated pulling motion to the release point, which also kept the body square to the target a bit longer.

When the 1996 Norcross spring baseball season started, Alec was barely five feet tall and weighed less than a hundred pounds. He had not yet hit his growth spurt and was just about the smallest one out on the field. No matter. Ro had him play the outfield and pitch. The age range of fourteen to sixteen covered eighth graders along with high school freshmen and sophomores.

The best description of the players in the Norcross league here at Wingo-Carlyle Field was old-fashioned. Even at this age, they were already showing the characteristics of real baseball players, the kind that look this way because baseball was just about all they played. As compared to athletes in other team sports, baseball players are more sedate and cerebral, less emotional, but perhaps more intuitive. Their movements are more deliberate and calculated as they anticipate the moment when they must burst into action. Between the seconds of action, they go through minutes of calm and thoughtful focus. Baseball players, by the time they leave junior high school, know all too well that from a single moment of distraction an embarrassing boner can result. A single instant of inattention can create a lifelong humiliation.

A good many of the Norcross Dixie Youth players from the previous year, slightly more than half of them, were not interested in advancing to this next level and had dropped out of baseball altogether. Most of those who did come back for the start of this spring league of 1996 were there because they wanted to play, and most could play well. The dropping out was just the normal attrition to be expected during the junior high school years. Those who kept plugging away did so usually because they enjoyed playing. Some had specific baseball goals left to achieve. A few were there due to the encouragement of their dads, which is not a bad thing, either. Boys in their early teens ought to be doing something athletic. No harm is caused by a father pushing his son a little bit in the right direction if the boy is unsure of which way to go or what to do next.

Baseball skills are noticeably different going from one league to the next. Each time a move is made to a higher level of ball the challenges increase dramatically. Although the players at this age could play more than one position and even play them well, each was becoming known mostly by his best position. Assigned positions were the norm, the position at which the player could best help the team. Players just did not get to play wherever they would like anymore. Consequently, greater proficiency at their best position was expected.

Alec was a pitcher. For the third time in his six-year baseball career, he was considered one of the main pitchers on the team. He viewed himself specifically as a pitcher. When he was called on to play outfield or first base he enjoyed it immensely, but he did not identify with those positions. They were secondary. When he played there, he was just filling in for a real outfielder or first baseman.

A little bit of pitching in the little league and pony league was one thing. Pitching on a full size baseball field to high school batters, some of whom were already man-size, seemed much more like the real thing. At this level, pitching was not just "chuckin' taters," as some in this part of the world, those transplanted from Idaho, I suppose, would describe the lack of real pitching ability. If all a pitcher could do was to throw the ball into the strike zone, he got murdered, fulfilling just another one of those more disagreeable life-changing experiences. Ro had developed Alec thoroughly for a role as a skillful pitcher so when the time came to put him into a game, he not only knew what he was doing, he not only looked like he knew what he was doing, he could actually do it.

When called into a game to pitch, neither was there an introductory discourse with words of encouragement, nor was there a reduction in expectations because he was a novice. Ro never said:

"All right, kid, you're new at this so don't expect too much. Just do your best and don't worry about anything."

Instead, even on the first occasion, he talked to Alec as if he were a veteran pitcher. Being told which pitches to throw to get the next few batters out presupposed an actual ability to throw those pitches correctly. Could this be how true self-esteem is built into a young man?

Ro always operated at a higher level than the other coaches did. Most managers of teams in this age group expected pitchers not to walk batters and to throw strikes. If that was all a pitcher could do, Ro could not use him. Ro never lowered expectations. He expected his pitchers to understand the batters and the situations. Furthermore, he expected them to know what to do about it. He expected every pitch to be located and to be thrown correctly. He expected the right sequence of pitches. When you pitched for Ro, there had to be an intelligent reason for every pitch because every pitch had a purpose.

At first, some of the other players and would-be pitchers wondered why Alec got to pitch right away, his fastball being barely sixty mph. But the results were good. He got most of the batters out. One of the players, Will Ramsey, a middle infielder with tremendously quick hands who could catch and release the ball better than anyone else in the league, also liked to pitch, having done so many times in the past. One day only a few games into the season, Alec was pitching along getting through inning after inning, frustrating batters by changing speeds and locating his pitches. Ro was calling the pitches from the dugout. They had set up a batter for an out pitch that was designed to get a double play and get them out of a little jam. Alec turned, alerting Will at shortstop to expect a grounder coming his way and to turn it. It did and he did. After turning the double play, heading back to the dugout, Will was heard to say,

"Why don't we just let Alec pitch every game?"

Oh, yes, if only things could go so well all the time!

In the middle of May, the team had a double header scheduled on a Saturday beginning at 9:00 am. For the first time ever in his life, Alec would have to miss a baseball game due to another event, other than the broken arm. He was graduating the eighth grade at OLA. The baccalaureate Mass started at the same time as the first game. We hoped it would not take as long so that he could be present for the second game. On the way to graduation, I noticed under his white shirt, tie, blazer, and slacks he was wearing his baseball uniform. His plan was to leave as soon as possible and go straight to the ballpark. Okay with me. After Mass, the graduates were called up in alphabetical order, convenient for the B's, to receive their diplomas, but instead of returning to his seat, he walked back up the aisle towards the exit. We arrived at the ballpark during the last inning of the first game. As planned, the rising high school freshman left-hander started the second game.

The season went by very fast again. When it came time to pick the tournament team he came aboard as a relief pitcher. For the very first time he was selected as an all-star and with it came a new level of self-assurance. Being an all-star afforded the opportunity not only to continue playing baseball for the next six weeks, but also to play with the best players in the league against the best in other leagues. Practice was held every day intermingled with several practice games, all of which led up to the regional tournament at South Gwinnett High School in Snellville.

Norcross had a good team, but they did not play well enough to advance to the state tournament in Valdosta. Their season ended by mid-July at South Gwinnett. Tommy Moon, Brett's father, did a fine job managing the team, a sensible job. He made good use of all his players and everyone got chances to contribute in a significant way. The importance of this experience to Alec was inestimable because he got to pitch quite a lot in practice games, in addition to two appearances in the tournament, both in relief. During the tournament, he gave up some hits, but fortunately only one earned run. He did get a couple of strikeouts. On the one hand, his performance was a bit shaky. On the other hand, it was certain that he had the ability to get some good batters out, not all of them, just some of them.

By being on this all-star team, he became better acquainted with some of the boys who were already on the high school team, such as infielders Brett Moon and Brad Teaver, and pitchers Scott Nielsen and Langston Poole. He already knew who these boys were because they all came up through Norcross Dixie Youth together. They were a year ahead of him so he looked up to them as the best ballplayers of this age group in Norcross. Becoming their teammates would be a fine accomplishment. Now he wanted more than ever to make the Norcross High School freshman team. In the next year, these other boys would be moving up to the junior varsity team, or the varsity team in the case of Moon, but still they would be teammates within the same system, if only he made the high school team.

During the autumn of 1996, workouts continued every weekday in the early evening and in the afternoon on weekends, usually at the nearby baseball field behind Pinckneyville Middle School. The high school tryouts would be in January. Another Norcross freshman named Dallas Austin joined us. Dallas planned to try out for the high school baseball team, too, and thought he could play third base and pitch. The three of us continued to meet regularly through the autumn. Many more drills can be done with three than with two.

Practice in sports causes the mind and body to adjust so that unusual motions become routine. Even accomplished athletes who have not played for some time will appear awkward until their playing movements are repeated many times. A freshman trying out for a high school team may have but a few days, and just a few opportunities, to show his skills to the coaches. Those who have not touched a baseball for several months had better hope that they regain their form quickly or that the others are equally ineffectual. Since the latter is more likely to occur, an excellent opportunity is created for those who come prepared to play. When Dallas and Alec arrived for the first day of tryouts, they were not just ready to try out; they were ready to start the season. The others were not.

During the previous summer, Ro had introduced a more advanced pitching drill meant to improve location delivery. It involved the use of a thirteen-inch automobile tire as a target. Inside the tire was inserted a sawed-off wood bat to divide the tire in half vertically. The tire was hung on a backstop so the bottom was about twelve inches above the ground. The drill began by pitching baseballs from about ten feet away and hitting the bat in the middle of the tire. When this skill was mastered, the ball was thrown to the area within the inside circle of the tire, but alternately hitting to one side of the bat or the other. The challenge was to hit accurately the intended area at least twenty out of twenty-five times. When eighty percent accuracy was surpassed, the distance was increased by five-foot intervals until reaching the full sixty feet, actually sixty feet, six inches. After the drill was mastered for the fastball, the same was done for the change-of-pace and then the breaking ball.

The last stage of the drill called for aiming at each of the four corners of the strike zone by hitting the outer edges of the tire corresponding to up and in, down and in, up and away, and down and away, with both the fast ball and change-of-pace. The breaking balls were thrown to hit just the spots that would be used in a game, for example, throwing the slider to a right-handed batter up and in; the curveball thrown outside to break to the outside corner at the knees; etc. His goal was to master this skill of accuracy before the high school tryouts started in January, which he did. After about three months of doing the drill every day, he was consistently nipping the selected corners of the tire from the full distance. We referred to this exercise as "throw at the tire" and never stopped using it on a regular basis. It is one excellent pitching drill for learning how to locate pitches and then to maintain this skill.

Soon after the fall school term started, Ray Martin, the varsity baseball manager, called a preliminary meeting of players to see who was interested in trying out for the team. Alec went and soon thereafter, I even attended one of the monthly evening meetings of the dugout club. The dugout club, run solely by the parents of players, supported the baseball program. The president was Chip Horwath, someone I had never met and did not know until making a connection with his wife, Maureen. I knew Maureen Horwath because she was the Assistant Principal at Our Lady of the Assumption school, but never knew she had sons who went to Norcross High School.

The Horwath's had two sons who were playing baseball this season, Steven a senior and Chris a freshman. Both had played little league at Murphey-Candler. Steven was already an accomplished high school baseball player. He played shortstop and had been a pitcher. He also had a terrific bat. Since this was his senior year, he decided it would be better to focus on playing his shortstop position and on his hitting rather than do any pitching. Steven was one of very few players in the county who could have been a legitimate varsity starter at any defensive position.

Before attending any more monthly meetings of the dugout club, I first wanted to see if Alec would make the team. In all honesty, hopes exceeded expectations. Remembering the high school baseball tryouts in Springfield during the 1960's left me assuming the odds were low. As for my reluctance to get involved in the dugout club, and being new to the modern world of high school team sports, it seemed far too presumptuous to become active in the baseball booster club before my son had even made the team. Someone did give me a tip that joining the club was considered by many to be a means by which one could increase the odds of his kid making the team. The club had to refund the club dues if the kid was cut. Apparently, the operational theory here was that if your money had already been spent, your kid would get to play. In spite of this good counsel, my mind was not changed about seeking premature membership. Neither was an effort made to speak to any of the coaches or other dads, or even to stop by the field and watch the tryouts after school. Alec's father deliberately stayed completely out of the way so as not to give the appearance of trying to influence the coaches or anyone else. If the kid made the team, it was going to be entirely on his own merit.

The last day of tryouts came. Alec had survived the initial rounds of cuts already. Even so, when going to pick him up after practice, there was the accompanying fear that the elation he experienced from being on the tournament team the previous summer would now become disappointment if he were cut on the final day. Preparation was made to point out that he could still play baseball in the NDY league in the spring as some bit of consolation. Minutes after parking the car in the gravel lot beyond the right field fence underneath the Coca-Cola scoreboard, the first of the boys were exiting the field walking along the path up the first-base side. Dallas Austin was one of them. He walked over to the car and said,

"Hi, Mr. Barnes. Alec made the team."

"How about you?"

They both had made it. I was quite pleased. All those afternoon practices during the past few months with these two boys paid off. When Alec reached the car, he was positively proud of himself, but did a good job of maintaining his composure. He said he was not surprised. I congratulated him with a handshake. Men do not hug each other in my family except when they win the World Series. Since this will likely never happen, there will be no hugging. While remarking how he was now a high school baseball player, even as the words were spoken, the realization of how magnificent it sounded briefly maintained the dream-like nature of the event, until reality arrived sometime later, as it always does.

"How does it feel?"

"Pretty good."

"I bet it does."

Most high school pitchers, including freshmen, have fastballs over seventy mph. A few can throw consistently over eighty mph and, of those, fewer still can do it effectively. The ninety mph high school hurler is extremely rare. For a freshman hoping to make the team only as a pitcher, the fastball should be at least seventy mph, and that is assuming he has the ability to throw other pitches, has decent mechanics, and maintains excellent control. Alec showed up with the quality pitches, good control, and good mechanics, but no velocity, maybe not even sixty-five mph. One other unfavorable factor was the freshman manager, Sean Gilbert, who also helped to coach football and basketball. Only in his second year managing freshman baseball, he had little other baseball experience.

Mr. Gilbert was a 1991 graduate of Norcross H.S. where he played football and was awarded a scholarship to play in college. His baseball playing experience was limited. Ray Martin, the varsity manager, also attended Norcross, graduating in 1975. Unlike Gilbert, Martin actually played baseball in high school earning three varsity letters. After taking in a varsity game the previous season, I thought it obvious that Ray Martin had a good knowledge and understanding of baseball.

As a football oriented coach, Gilbert naturally favored the boys he considered better athletes. I am quite sure he thought that if a kid had good football and basketball abilities then he would probably be good in baseball, too. When it came to pitching, he was more impressed with the velocity of the fastball and the size of the pitcher than with technique and skill. I had further assumed Gilbert would pick his own team, which was another reason for not being too optimistic about my lefty's chances. What actually happened was that Martin gave Gilbert a little help picking his team. Fortunately, Ray Martin knew what he liked in a pitcher and he understood what he saw.

Quite a few freshman boys were cut from the original group who turned out on the first day of tryouts. Various bits of information came my way that, when pieced together, allowed me to figure out how Alec was selected and why. Martin had his hands full with his varsity team. However, when time allowed, he made a point of noticing the junior varsity and freshmen players, too. The freshman players who were finally selected mostly came from the same group of pony leaguers. Their parents had hired a local coach to manage their travel team during the summer and fall. The point of this exercise was to form a group that would play together, go to school together, and then make the freshman team together. Gilbert and Martin were alerted to their existence and given continual updates on their progress, as it were. Alec was not a part of this pony league travel team since he played with older boys under Ro. Neither was Dallas. In fact, Gilbert and Martin probably did not even know who Alec was before the tryouts started.

On the last day, Martin came over to the freshman team's practice and told Gilbert he wanted to see all the pitchers and catchers in the bull pen. He spent a good deal of time watching each of them pitch, one by one. Fastballs were flying everywhere and the curveballs were bouncing everywhere as the neophytes tried to impress the varsity manager by throwing as hard as they could.

Alec was one of the last to throw. He told the catcher to move the mitt back and forth from one side of the plate to the other, to give him a good target, then proceeded to deliver his pitches to the target, fastballs, change-ups, and breaking balls. Martin spent the most time with him, asking for different pitches to be thrown over and over again. He even asked Alec to try some different things. Martin went so far as expressing amazement over the quality of the different breaking balls, something a baseball coach would not normally do under these circumstances. The speed of the fastball apparently did not concern him at all. When the session was concluded, he went to review Gilbert's final roster and added Alec's name to the bottom of the list. The varsity team and the junior varsity team each had seventeen players, as was the predetermined target number. The freshman team now had eighteen players. There was no extra roster slot open before this last bull pen session, so Martin created one, and Alec was in.

Gwinnett County high school students in 1996 began their day at 7:15 a.m. Classes were dismissed at 2:00 p.m. The baseball team reported directly to the field for a daily practice lasting until dark, which came around 6:00 p.m. in this part of Georgia during early February though growing later with each succeeding day. The old Norcross High School baseball field did not have lights so sunset was quittin' time. When the boys finally arrived home and ate supper, there was a little time for homework and not much else.

During practice, the freshman pitchers mostly threw long toss and ran poles, that is, running back and forth on the warning track between the foul poles next to the outfield fence. Actual pitching was very limited. Being accustomed to daily rigorous throwing drills, Alec found this new routine to be entirely inadequate. Therefore, even though the freshman team was usually dismissed early, he normally stayed around to throw batting practice to the varsity and junior varsity players. When the regular season began, he found himself to be physically well prepared to pitch, more so than any of the other pitchers.

The very first regular season high school baseball game in which Alec was called upon to pitch was eerily similar to his first little league appearance. That is, they were similar in the way all ocean waves are similar. They roll in, they build, and they break. However, if little league was summer surf at Panama City Beach, Florida this seemed like winter surf on the North Shores of Oahu, Hawaii. I went behind the backstop with camera and notebook in hand ready to record the event, which looked like it could last for a while because of the circumstances.

Something, an urge, a thought, a compulsion, demanded that there be a photograph of his first high school pitch.

Norcross was playing at home, losing decisively. The lefty was called in during the top of the last inning after a few other relief pitchers failed to staunch the blood flow. No other pitcher was left. Down by many runs already, two outs holding as several opposing batters had avoided making the third, it seemed the bases had been loaded for quite some time. At last, another relief pitcher's final effort abetted the visitors' cause by walking in a run. From a manager's point of view, one shared by nearly everyone else, this game just needed to be over. The game was lost; Norcross blew it, just get an out, take one more turn at the bat, and go home. The lefty jogging in from the bull pen, however, had distinctly different thoughts running through his mind. His first high school appearance was something special. On this occasion, whatever the score happened to be, it did not matter.

The game situation, resulting from a full afternoon of failure, was as bad as one could be. Nothing positive could be done for the team's sake unless one thinks of shooting a lame horse in the head to relieve its misery to be a positive thing. Norcross had the last chance to bat. However, even with metal sticks, they were not going to be able to come back, not with their line-up, but that was another story. Total and complete success meant getting the first batter out so they could go home losers as quickly as possible. Failure meant prolonging the agony, but still they would go home losers. This was not so great a setting for a pitching debut.

His jog in from the bull pen, which was located down at the end of the first base line, ended at the edge of the grass bordering the mound dirt. He got the ball with no conversation from the manager, threw a half dozen warm-ups, adjusted his cap, spit on the ground, assumed the pre-set position on the rubber, and looked in to catcher Inman Dubberly for the sign. After a full stretch, the ball glove settled under the nose momentarily, just long enough to check that no foolish base runner intended to steal home, and then the first pitch was delivered, a four-seam fastball on the outside corner, directly at Dubberly's target. The camera clicked just as the ball left his hand. The over-anxious batter chased it by leaning and reaching. The result was a soft liner hit off the end of the bat right to the second baseman for the third out. What ever happened to taking the first pitch from a new pitcher just called in to get out of a jam? It sure looked easy. Once again, no need to have worried.

The freshman team had a dismal season. Their record was one win and thirteen losses. Alec never got to start a game, but he pitched relief in eight of the fourteen games. In their one victory, he was the pitcher of record, the lone freshman pitcher to record a win all year for Norcross High School. In spite of results, Gilbert apparently never thought Alec could pitch, or at least did not think he was one of the team's better pitchers. It was an unfortunate conclusion, contributing to a persistent problem that lasted all season long. The boys he thought could pitch were always getting into trouble, every game, usually early in the game. He would eventually call on Alec, but more out of frustration than any sense of confidence in his ability. Fortunately, Alec was always prepared to pitch, resulting in good efforts just about every time. Quite appropriately, he pitched in more games than any other pitcher on the team by far.

Many managers at every youth level do not understand the relative value of locating pitches and changes speed. This freshman manager thought the other pitchers were better because they had seventy-plus mph fastballs. When confronted with managers like this there is not a thing that can be done about it. A preconceived notion is always tough to overcome, particularly when it stems from purblind prejudice. Even if a pitcher like Alec has some success, such a manager will think it is due to luck. As soon as the batters figure him out, he will be done in, or so the logic goes. Such a manager believes the pitchers who throw harder are the good pitchers. When they pitch badly it is because of bad luck. Presumably, the bad luck of a hard thrower will change to good as soon as he finds his groove, or some other such nonsense. The interesting thing is that no amount of evidence to the contrary ever seems to change the mind of a manager or coach who thinks this way.

Alec's other great weapon was that he knew how to work with his catcher. This young man happened to be Inman Dubberly, a very smart student bound for a fine academic career at Georgia Tech. One of the many important things Ro taught Alec was the necessity of forming a partnership with his catcher. A pitcher cannot pitch well without a good catcher working with him. One day, while chatting with the father of one of the other pitchers during a game, I pointed out how Inman was calling certain pitch sequences and framing a target for every pitch on the corners of the strike zone, engineering a strategy. The point to be made was that this had a lot to do with Alec's pitching success, would that the other pitchers learn to do the same thing. Left unsaid was all the other pitchers on the team lacked the ability to locate their pitches so any effort by them to develop a strategy of any kind was futile.

High school has many crossover athletes, those who play more than one sport. When a kid is so talented, when he is able to adjust successfully to the demands of different sports, he should be considered exceptional. Some competitive characteristics translate well from one sport to another. However, some may be helpful in one and detrimental in another. One that has a negative effect when applied to baseball is the football mentality.

What forms the football mentality is the notion that athletic success is built upon a foundation of brute strength and high emotions; then, and only then, can skillfulness succeed. To say it another way, if a player is not pumped up, he cannot do his very best. When things are not going well during a game then the solution is to get more emotionally pumped up, get angrier, and hit harder. This approach does not work in baseball. In fact, an uncontrolled emotional outburst is a baseball player's worst enemy. It is a distraction, counterproductive for virtually all baseball situations and all players, most especially for pitchers.

Pitching is about control, along with the other C's, confidence, consistency, and concentration. The baseball must be controlled to pitch effectively; therefore, the body must be controlled. The body is controlled by the mind. Emotional frenzy makes the mind spin out of control. If the mind is muddled, where is the ball going to go? Those who apply football thinking to baseball misunderstand the nature of the game. Football players' numerous ebullient celebrations, conducted with the least amount of provocation for the most evanescent accomplishments, make it appear that every marginally successful deed is both unusual and unexpected, combined with an apparent emotional need for exaggerated adulation. Such effervescence in baseball is properly reserved for the most exceptional of occasions, for instance, when the last out is made in the last game of the World Series, not for any other time.

The Norcross freshman team of 1997 did not have this problem because there were no particularly joyful performances. For one freshman, however, every day was a celebration, a controlled one, that is. Each game was progressively more satisfying no matter what the score. The few games in which Alec did not pitch, he usually was told to warm up at one point or another, making him an active participant all season long. When a pitcher warms up, he is having an impact on the game, though it may be a small one. His presence is felt in that the other team surely has taken note of the activity in the other bull pen.

Near the end of the season, Martin came to address the freshman team after practice, telling them he would attend their last game at Berkmar High School in Lilburn. He wanted to check them out first hand. He also announced that Alec was to be the starting pitcher and Jon Johnson, another lefty, was to be first relief. Gilbert interrupted to say he had already promised the start to one of the other pitchers. Martin was obviously annoyed once again, but what could he say? I would have suggested something like,

"You're fired!"

After a dramatic, momentary pause, Alec was designated as first reliever and that was that. If previous patterns held, first relief would likely come early, maybe real early.

The opportunity to impress the varsity coach made this last game of the season rather more exciting than usual. In the first inning, as luck would have it, the starting pitcher got into a little trouble. Martin had come with a quick hook. The first two batters were walked and Alec was in the bull pen. Another batter, then a hit, and the call went down for the lefty. He had time to throw no more than five warm-up tosses when he was ordered out to the mound. Fortunately, he knew how to get warmed up while pitching. We covered that, too. The game went well as he stayed in to pitch five complete innings, keeping the score close. As it turned out, the runs allowed by, and charged to, the starting pitcher were enough to win the game for Berkmar because the Norcross team just could not score the runs needed to take the lead. A couple of other pitchers finished up the last two innings. Norcross had chances to win the game throughout with plenty of base runners, but, in the end, it was just another loss.

After the game, Martin issued the usual season ending encouragements, about continuing to play during the summer, and to keep practicing. He liked what he saw, looked forward to next year, etc. We drove home terribly excited about the season that had just passed, about this last game in particular, and about the summer baseball coming up. Life at Norcross High School was working out just fine. Being on the school's baseball team, as it turned out, made all the difference.

*Chapter Eleven*

# The Game

    The Norcross Dixie Youth baseball league began during the latter half of March, about the middle of the high school season. Alec eagerly signed up to play, as did several of his high school teammates making the total pool of players large enough to form two teams of mostly fifteen and sixteen-year-old boys. One team was managed by Dan Kinney, the other by Terry Woody. Brent Kinney, Dan's son, had attended OLA with Alec, but he went on to attend Marist High School, a very prestigious Catholic school in Atlanta, excellent in both scholastics and athletics. His father loved baseball, had a superior knowledge of the game, and was a quite capable manager. The other fellow, Terry Woody, a young man I guessed to be still in his twenties, had played college baseball for the University of Maine. He was also a very capable baseball man. Mr. Woody drafted Alec for his team, along with catcher Inman Dubberly and two other school teammates, Dallas Austin and Jon Johnson. They were called the Red team. Mr. Kinney's was the Blue team. The team names were compatible with the distinguishing trim color of their respective uniforms.

    Kinney managed to get several junior varsity players on his roster, making it the better team. The way the teams were drafted and put together gave rise to speculation that the process may not have been entirely equitable. It is also fair to say that this sort of talk happens every year in every league no matter who is involved. I did not know first hand what went on during the draft, nor did I care. As long as every player gets to play, what difference could it possibly make? Playing on a winning team does not automatically produce a superior sporting experience than playing on a losing team. Actually, being on a team with less skilled players presents a valuable challenge, particularly for a pitcher. If approached with the proper attitude, the result can be a better playing experience, one with the potential for even greater personal achievement. Steve Carlton of the Phillies comes to mind. Besides, the fact that a team rates better on paper does not win for it any games.

These were two interesting teams with several very good baseball players. Alec had his catcher from the high school freshman team, an immediate advantage. Most of all, he was excited about a challenge looming on the near horizon. Before very long, these two Norcross teams would play each other thereby presenting him with the opportunity to face batters mostly from the next level of junior varsity. He would be tested to see exactly how much good he could do throwing a baseball. What better way was there to get a glimpse of the future, of the challenges that would come during the next high school season?

Woody's baseball knowledge was substantial and impressive. In short order, he decided that Alec was his number one starter. Even as he was being mostly disregarded by his high school freshmen team manager, being used reluctantly and only out of the bull pen, he became the ace of the Norcross Red team. The other difference between Alec's two teams was that the Red team was actually winning some games while the high school team sputtered along. Whether as a starter or a reliever, Alec only wanted to pitch. In this pursuit, his wishes were completely fulfilled. Since the high school and Dixie Youth seasons overlapped, for a few weeks it seemed he pitched almost every day, an inning or two during high school games, and one or two starting assignments usually lasting five or six innings for the Red team. He was given more than enough chances to pitch.

Anticipation that the Blue and Red teams soon would be playing each other brought the competitive spirit of these boys indoors to the hallways and classrooms, and even into the high school dugouts. Most of the players attended Norcross High School, many being on the freshman and junior varsity teams, where they were united as members of the same program. Outside the school, they were split between the two NDY teams, poised in opposition. There had always been a split, players from the same school playing on different recreational teams, ever since little league. However, this time it was different. This time there were only two teams outside of school, not a dozen, or half-a-dozen. Furthermore, these were the best baseball players of their age group in town; a matter of pride was at stake. Not surprisingly, that which began as a bit of tête-à-tête here and there inexorably escalated to a widely subscribed banter. Soon, the exchange of verbal assaults involved not only the baseball players, but also many of the other athletes and students in the school. From there it spread into the community at large.

Sustained by innuendo and intrigue was a rapidly growing teenage male bravado. The Blue team players made it known that they were the class act of historic Norcross, a boast fortified with tetchy, caustic ridicule of the Red team players, mocking everything from their baseball playing abilities to the quality of their uniforms. The left-handed pitcher on the Red team enjoyed every bit of this prelude with great anticipation. As the presumed starting pitcher, he would be right in the middle of it all when they finally took the field, when the chips were down, when execution would supplant speculation. Who would not look forward to this kind of a showdown?

The day finally arrived, Tuesday, May 13, 1997. Game time was 8:00 p.m., an hour late due to some late arriving coaches which delayed field preparation. It had been scheduled for 7:00 p.m. in deference to the fact this was a school night, though not as if these boys were presently thinking about homework assignments. Wingo-Carlyle Field was the site, as a new episode of history and tradition stood by once again. The Red team pitcher entertained no doubts that he would stifle the Blue team's lineup, that the matter would be settled in his favor; of this, he had complete and unwavering confidence. Although not everyone else was as free of doubts, the one that mattered insisted he knew each of their batters, and knowing individual weaknesses with the ability to exploit them would tell the tale. He and Dubberly had it all worked out, he said.

One preliminary billing of the game was Kinney's "stacked" team versus Woody's "leftovers." In addition to a couple of carefully selected players from other schools, Kinney had Norcross junior varsity pitchers Jeff Hunt and Scott Neilsen, infielders Jesse Erickson and Dan Sineway, and outfielder Troy Fallaw. He also managed to get the best Norcross freshman speedster and outfielder, Kerry Gray, who was good friends with Alec and Inman. Besides the few Norcross freshman players, Woody had an assortment of cut players, poor students, and other stragglers who were just looking for a place to play. On paper, the Red team did not have a prayer. Since they refused to acknowledge the Blue team as superior, the verbal sparring continued unabated. When the time came for these two teams to meet for the contest, there had been built up a great anticipation around Norcross, as much as for any game in recent memory, for what had come to be known as *The Game*.

When on the evening of May 13 all gathered to see this important matter settled, an inauspicious omen appeared. Woody could not be there because, at the last minute, he was held up at work. His assistant, Don Parsons, would manage the team. Woody sent the order to start Alec, not that there was any question about it. Alan Hankins, NDY League Commissioner, arrived and took up a neutral position behind home plate in the scorer's box intending to operate the scoreboard while keeping the scorebook.

The night was clear, the air was cool, as the small town stillness was periodically interrupted by the serenade of locomotives sounding their horns when passing the Norcross train station one block beyond the hill, as they went away with rumbling wheels into the night on a journey to somewhere. A fair crowd of spectators arrived, taking seats in the grand stands. They came to see their sons, brothers, and friends play the important game. Who would be heroes? Who would be vanquished? They had no better place to go, nowhere else they would rather be.

The first impressions of this place returned quickly as I imagined the presence of the many ghosts of Norcross baseball past, not seeing, but sensing their presence, perched along the grey wall constructed a century ago of cut granite and mortar bordering the right field foul line. The stone wall was the last remnant of the terraced hillside backing the original red brick schoolhouse long ago demolished. The schoolyard with all its glory remained, as it should, so succeeding generations of ballplayers could face a test of skill and cunning that only the game of baseball can elicit.

The smell of Georgia clay dirt hung fast whiles the scent of tobacco smoke wafted by. Familiar sounds were to be heard if one would only listen, the sounds of voices from the field and dugouts speaking the language of baseball as the players warmed up. To listeners' ears came the unmistakably unique sounds made by balls being hit and caught, coaches barking out fielding commands, players narrating the good, and the bad, of the abbreviated drills with quips and spurs while pressing themselves and their teammates to reach that comfortable point of readiness. A blind man passing by would have known, without having to be told, that he had come across a baseball park with a game about to begin. It was, as they sometimes say, a beautiful night for baseball. Time to start, so as the managers exchanged lineup cards with each other along with pleasantries, umpires included, along came the customary words used to politely cause action, less than a command, more than an invitation,

"Good evenin', gentlemen. Y'all know the ground rules? Good luck."

The game lived up to its billing as a truly exciting contest. During the first couple of innings, the Blue team could not accomplish anything at the bat. The Red team's left-hander mixed up his pitches, inducing grounders and pop-ups. He was spotting his pitches, changing speeds like never before. Inman was calling their predetermined and brilliant game. Most of the time they pitched away, unless a batter was drawn in close, and then the inside four-seamer or slider produced the needed effect. Not once did it appear that Alec shook off a sign. Dallas Austin played third base, Kam Cheung patrolled the shortstop position, and Jason Tharpe held down second base. All three had chances and made good plays throwing out runners to Jon Johnson, his foot securely finding the bag at first.

Watching the game from behind home plate, the best seats in the house, Mr. Hankins and I had a perfect view along with a very enjoyable chat. Before the Blue team batted in the bottom of the third, the Red team had taken a three-run lead. Since it was a seven-inning game, only fifteen outs remained while at least four runs had to be scored. Being casually confident at this point, even with their superior talent, was not a good battle plan for the Blues. Mr. Kinney, apparently subscribing to this very same sentiment, took the opportunity to proclaim the urgency of this predicament to his players by saying, among other things,

"If you lose to these guys you'll never live it down!"

How true. Even though every man is entitled to his point of view, in this case, there was no other valid opinion on the subject. Maybe a more direct form of this admonition would have been,

"If you lose this game, you are bums. Period."

Fortified with this additional motivation and the score being 3-0, the Blues proceeded to the bat. Scott Neilsen led off determined to reverse their misfortune. He portrayed an image that resembled that of the Mighty Casey, in that "his teeth are clenched with hate." Now, outside of the batter's box when he is not wielding a metallic weapon, Scott is one of the most pleasant and polite young men in the neighborhood. However, being a big kid, strong, and not one who fools around when trying to hit a baseball, if he could get a hold of one he was more than capable of knocking it out of the park. Well, he got his pitch to hit. It was Alec's only very bad mistake of the game. The 1-1 offering was up a little, hanging over the plate. Scott hit it square with all his might.

My greatest fear through all the years of his pitching was the possibility of being hit in the head with a batted ball. These young men were using metal bats, light and easy to swing, with rebound characteristics about twenty percent greater than wood. Self-defense should be part of a pitcher's training, even with wood bats, but with metal, it was crucial. As he was taught to do, Alec's follow-through included the act of keeping the glove at the ready. When I saw this one pitch coming to Scott, I anticipated the consequence and it scared me frigid. A ball thrown up and over the plate is often going directly back whence it came. Thus, I perceived the swing, the contact, and the flight of the ball all in slow motion, combined with a feeling of utter helplessness. My son, a baseball traveling over a hundred miles per hour directly at his face less than fifty-five feet away, and I am sitting only a short distance behind home plate, contained by chain-linked fencing. The ball would have taken Alec's head off if he had not ducked and raised his glove just in the nick of time to catch it for the out. Turning to Hankins, the utterance came out something like,

"L-1?"

"Yep."

What followed was a grounder to third and a strikeout to complete the nine-pitch inning. It went quicker than it seemed.

The frustration continued for the Blues as the next two innings breezed by unproductively and the Reds scored one more run. After five innings, the Red team enjoyed a propitious 4-0 lead. Alec had faced seventeen batters. He struck out three, walked none, and gave up only two singles. Hohenstern was the only man to reach second, and it required a sacrifice bunt in the fourth inning by Kerry Gray to move him over. A scoring disagreement occurred here as I thought Gray, being the fastest runner on their team, was trying to reach. Added to that was the fact he played center field for the freshman team and had watched Alec pitch many times from that excellent viewing angle. He well knew when Alec's pitches were on target no one had an easy time at the bat. The odds of reaching base with a bunt were far greater under these circumstances. At least Kerry advanced the runner to scoring position.

Meager offensive effort that it was, it went for naught. Sineway and Hunt followed with infield pop-ups, both on change-ups. Having gone one man shy of two trips through their lineup, this was the extent of the Blues' metal bat attack against a mid-sixty's mph fastball and other assorted tosses. The Blue team was beginning to look doomed. The Reds, on the other hand, cautiously anticipated pulling off the upset. The commissioner and the father of the pitcher were chatting along when, surprisingly, a new pitcher came out to the mound for the Red team in the bottom of the sixth inning. Hankins wondered if Alec was hurt. A few seconds later, the lefty walked around the back of the dugout towards us looking for ice, shrugged, and just said,

"He took me out."

Before returning to the dugout, Alec confirmed he was not injured or hurting, and obviously not pleased about being pulled, fretting that the game would now be lost. Why the manager decided on making a pitching change was not apparent to us at this time. As it turned out, the reason was extraordinarily simple. Parsons had just decided to let someone else pitch, as is commonly done in recreational league games. It never occurred to me that he was probably completely oblivious to the importance of this game. Parsons did not have a kid on the team and he did not live in Norcross. He had no idea about the rivalry that was going on. He was just making sure everyone got a chance to play. This should always be how it is done in a recreational league, with few rare exceptions. Parsons did not understand this was the rare exception. Kinney, however, understood the importance of this game and his dugout was bustling. Hankins and I were more than a little bit astonished at what we were seeing.

The Blue team wasted little time going to work. After the leadoff man, the ninth batter in their lineup, made an out with a pop-up to the third baseman, the next seven batters reached base starting with a walk, then a double, three singles, an error by the second baseman, and another single. In a matter of minutes, the lead was lost as seven of the first eight batters in the sixth inning scored.

The rules in NDY baseball allow a starting pitcher to re-enter a game. Why it is allowed is anyone's guess. Reinserting a cooled-down starting pitcher is never a good decision; however, in this case, it was no worse a decision than pulling him in the first place. Alec was put back in to try to get out of the inning. His arm had already cooled off in the chill of the evening and he was not as sharp. Still, he turned the side out, but only after a bit of a struggle. First, he got Erickson to pop out to the second baseman for the second out; then came two singles and a walk to load the bases. Fortunately, he was able to induce Scott Neilsen to fly out to right field for the third out. No doubt, Scotty was thinking, "grand slam" while looking for another hanger. Alec was smart enough not to make the same mistake two times in one night. In the inning, the Blues had batted around plus two. The Red team was unable to score again in the top of the seventh inning and the game was lost 7-4.

Neither team had won unquestionable bragging rights. The matter of supremacy remained unresolved. The game, well, it was more remarkable for how it was played than the outcome. The Blues knew the only reason they won was because they received one inning of batting practice against a secondary pitcher who was primarily a position player. He had asked to pitch before and Parsons thought this was as good a time as any other to switch pitchers. Another important element here was that Parsons did not know anything about the Blue team except what he saw that evening. After five innings, he concluded that they stunk, instead of assuming that his pitcher was doing a superlative job of pitching. The truth became apparent only after it was too late. The fact remained that the mostly older junior varsity Blues had been completely stymied by a freshman.

One was left to wonder what, if anything, each of the kids learned from this evening of baseball. The lesson they should have learned was probably entirely overlooked by most of them. This lesson was to recognize the greater relative value of a pitcher who can pitch rather than one who can just throw. The Red team had also played their best defensive game so far. Perhaps the impetus from their field play propelled their offense. They scored runs off of J.V. pitchers Dan Sineway and Scott Neilsen, no small achievement, but they needed more. Jesse Erickson, who came in from shortstop to be the closer, quickly shut the Reds down in the seventh inning with two strikeouts, a walk, and a 4-6 fielder's choice. The Red team was fortunate, I supposed, that Jeff Hunt did not start for the Blue team or the game could have been scoreless after five.

From Alec's point of view, he knew he had pitched the game of his life so far. He had raised his stature as a pitcher. He also knew the next day at school would be immensely gratifying. His pitching was the real story of the game for everyone except me. For me, the real story was catching Scott's line drive before it killed him. This benevolence came courtesy of Ro's tutelage and the Grace of God. Lastly, Alec experienced no arm injury from going back into the game after cooling down. Regardless, it was a mistake to take that risk and should not have been allowed. He dodged a bullet, for sure.

When Woody heard the story the next day at practice, he lowered his head and shook it side to side in disbelief. This he did while smiling, since he understood what it meant. He had to have been proud of his

Red team. They were a good bunch of baseball players who had played up to their full potential. Contests like this one make the game of baseball so incredibly satisfying. Where else can one experience triumph even within the mire of frustration? Well, one such place is Wingo-Carlyle Field in Norcross on any evening a baseball game is being played.

The rest of the season went on without much fanfare. Nothing could have matched the exhilaration of *The Game*. Finally, the time came to pick a tournament team. Kinney was designated to manage this team and Alec was one of the players asked to be on it. They went through the typical practices and games leading up to the statewide competition. Before leaving for the tournament, Alec was told he would not start, nor would he be used except maybe as a fill-in if needed, leaving him no other rational choice except to turn in his uniform. The manager's decision, I thought, would doom the team. Kinney wanted to use his own pitchers, plus one he borrowed from a neighboring team, regardless of their records, presumably because they threw harder. It was good we learned of his intentions beforehand so as not to waste time and money traveling to Augusta. Let it suffice to say that the Norcross all-star team did not do well at the tournament. All that Alec missed was the opportunity to sit in a dugout and watch supposedly better pitchers not able to do their job.

Fortunately, this was not all of the baseball for the boys of Norcross in 1997, not by a long shot. Actually, the best came in another league altogether. While still playing for Woody's Red team, the Gwinnett County high schools were beginning their summer baseball league called the Connie Mack League. This program was divided into two levels, A & B. The A-teams consisted of returning varsity and some rising junior varsity players who were expected to be on the varsity team the following year or as many as it took to complete a roster. The B-teams were mostly players from the previous year's freshmen teams plus a few left over from junior varsity. Alec went to the B-team along with his other freshmen teammates.

Arranging for the summer high school league was normally a simple matter, but not this time. It became complicated at the end of the school year when the decision was made to fire the Norcross High School manager. Some of the parents who were dissatisfied with the baseball program managed to convince the principal and the athletic director to make a change. Ray Martin was out. They later hired Ron

Edwards from a high school in a neighboring county. No one was very satisfied with the performance of the varsity baseball team; however, the greater part of the problem was not with the manager. Rather than blame Ray Martin, a more sensible approach would have been to indict the players who were often guilty of a general lack of dedication abetted by some over-indulgent parents, not all of them, but several. Also indictable, the previous Norcross athletic director who for many years had placed football above all else, treating baseball as a tolerable stepson. Martin's only fault was being too accommodating for too long of too many misdirected people.

When the new manager took over in the autumn, he addressed the particular problem of laziness right away by demanding more effort during expanded workouts. He lasted two years before he was driven out. Perhaps, a better solution straight away would have been to write off the entire varsity and junior varsity teams concentrating entirely on a few of the freshmen who truly wanted to play. Their enthusiasm could have been put to good use. From there he could have begun working with prospective junior high players. This would have resulted in agitated parents, no doubt, causing them to demand the manager be fired right away, instead of later. At the beginning of this summer of 1997, though, the boys were without high school baseball coaches. Fortunately, some of the dads stepped in to manage and coach. Chip Horwath agreed to be the B-team manager.

Chip and I were two of the dozen or so parents of freshman players who attended every game, home and away. I came to find out that he grew up in Springfield, Virginia. To be exact, he lived in the subdivision called Beverly Forest, the one down Backlick Road about a mile or so south of the center of Springfield, on the other side of Shirley Highway from where we had lived in Springfield Forest. Chip attended Lee High School after it opened in 1959. Furthermore, he played for the high school team just as he had played youth ball in the Springfield Little League and Babe Ruth League. Upon learning this, the image of standing outside the baseball field fence on Franconia Road that summer day in 1961, watching the Lee High team practice, came back immediately in my minds eye. Chip was one of those players taking infield grounders, no doubt about it. After thirty-six years, in a place that could not be less likely, both of us, now parents of baseball players, met again, so to speak. His son played shortstop and my son pitched, both on the same high school team.

Mr. Horwath did a superb job of managing this summer team. His substantial reservoir of baseball knowledge combined with much playing experience, enhanced by a very judicious temperament, allowed him to find the right balance between many competing interests. He made it the best summer of baseball most of these boys ever had.

The Norcross High School summer team played teams from the same schools they had played during the spring season. With few exceptions, the players were the same, too. One main difference during the summer season was that Norcross was actually winning some games. Other than having a different manager, everything else was just about the same. Horwath actively managed the team choosing to maximize participation, allowing all the boys substantial playing time. Under such conditions, everyone had the best chance of succeeding. Consequently, because the boys were playing better individually, they became a much better team. The irony was that this approach, not overtly concerned with winning, turned a losing team into a winning team.

Like Woody from the Norcross Red team, Horwath used Alec quite a lot. He started eight games while also providing some relief work. The tables had turned drastically for the left-hander in just a few short months. On the spring freshman team, he was used sparingly, the least of all the pitchers. On the Connie Mack team, he pitched more innings than anyone else did.

For the entire year, including all three teams, Alec worked sixty-two and two-third innings in official games while facing two hundred and seventy-six batters. He threw seventy percent strikes while not surrendering even one home run or triple. Best of all, he only walked fourteen batters, an average of two per nine innings, or about one for every twenty batters faced. This first year of high school pitching revealed quite a lot; mostly it gave a clear picture of what kind of a pitcher he was. Alec was a control pitcher. He kept the ball around the edges of the strike zone, did not give up walks, and did not hit anyone, at least not by accident. His style forced opposing batters to put the ball in play while keeping it inside the park. Pitch selection was very often designed to induce the batter to hit the ball on the ground or in the air as needed. On better days, when everything was working just right, the batters he faced sometimes resembled dangling marionettes. With one of the slower fastballs in all of Gwinnett County, those seeing him for the first time tended to ridicule him out loud, especially for what they saw during pregame warm ups. Then the game would start. Soon after the first few batters were embarrassed at the plate, they could be heard mumbling to themselves, instead.

Sometimes the frustration erupted into such an irrational outburst that the need for some kind of professional counseling was indicated. During the first inning of one particular game, a batter was being taunted by his own teammates for an exceptionally ugly at bat in which he swung mightily, missing a second strike by more than a foot. He turned to his agitators in his own dugout and said,

"We'll see how you do up here when it's your turn!"

Next swing he grounded out to shortstop after trying to pull an outside pitch. There were hits, there were errors, and there were runs scored. When Alec was pitching, however, until he tired, he never gave up many runs, usually keeping his team in a position to win the game, or at least in the position to make winning a realistic possibility.

One of his most important attributes was just being comfortable on the mound as a control pitcher. Alec believed in what he was doing. He understood why locating pitches and changing speeds was a successful combination. A higher velocity fastball would have been helpful, but successful pitching could be achieved without one. There were power pitchers and there were control pitchers. This lefty was successful with control.

Both approaches to pitching, power and control, are legitimate in baseball. Most pitchers, if not all, would love to be both. The control pitchers want a little more velocity while the power pitchers want a little more control. The grass is always greener on the other side of the bull pen, or seems to be.

Regardless of what kind he is, each type of pitcher enjoys natural advantages over the batter. The first and most obvious one is that he knows what pitch he is going to throw while the batter does not, or is not supposed to. In addition to this, when a ball is hit the odds are better than even that it will result in an out. If the batter's timing is off when he hits it, and he hits it fair, the odds of making an out drastically increase.

The control pitcher locates the ball to avoid the fat part of the bat, while changing speed to disrupt the batter's timing. One more element of confusion he can inflict is ball movement. Suppose the batter expects a fastball, which he has timed, and then guesses correctly that it will be on the outer corner of the strike zone. He moves a bit closer to the plate while taking his stance in the batter's box and he prepares to swing. The ball appears to be going where he expects, so he swings aggressively.

However, if the ball moves off its line during the last twenty feet of its flight, the result is often a ball struck off the end of the bat or chopped into the ground. He will be very lucky to get a single. If the pitcher does not get that late movement, the ball will likely be driven into the outfield alleys for extra bases or maybe leave the yard altogether.

The power pitcher relies on speed to limit the amount of time the batter has to see the ball and react. However, a faster thrown ball usually means less movement and a straighter path of flight. Good batters can adjust to almost any ball speed so, to confuse the batter, even a power pitcher has to have a reliable second pitch. Usually it is a breaking ball, typically a slider. The slider has the advantage of looking like a fastball at the point of release, but has less velocity and some good late movement generated by a tight spin. Batters who have trouble distinguishing between the two pitches succumb quickly. Experienced batters, on the other hand, see the spin as a small white circle usually in the upper region of the ball. Those who are able to tell which pitch is which sometimes will let the slider go by, hoping to see a subsequent fastball. When a batter does make solid contact with the fastball, the result is a harder hit ball because of the greater rebound energy.

When the pitcher makes a mistake and leaves the slider up in the strike zone, the result is often an aggressive wallop, especially if the batter suspects it is coming. This pitch is called a "hanger" because it appears to hang up in the batter's power zone instead of breaking across or down. Giving a hanging breaking ball to a proficient batter usually has serious consequences.

The typical scenario and pitch sequence of the power pitcher is to get ahead in the count by throwing fastballs for strikes before the batter has adjusted to the speed. Then he will try to throw the breaking ball at the strike zone intending for it to break outside or down, causing the batter, who does not want to take a third strike, to swing unproductively. Since the batter is not unaware of what the pitcher is attempting to do, he may guess the pitch scenario, hoping he guesses correctly, in order to resist being duped. Thus, the battle goes on between pitchers and batters.

Both types of pitchers work better when they pitch ahead in the count. First pitch strikes are extremely important because they immediately place the batter in a more defensive position. Other than this, there is little similarity between the two pitching approaches. The control pitcher has greater flexibility because he has three separate weapons: location, velocity change, and movement. If one is not working very well on a particular day, he can still pitch effectively with the other two.

If the change-of-pace is not working, he can rely upon location and movement. If he is having trouble locating his fastball, he can rely upon change-of-pace and breaking balls.

The power pitcher faces a greater challenge. He must have both of his weapons working or he is doomed. Once the batter detects a deficiency in one pitch, he will focus on the other. And if the pitcher starts falling behind in the count, the batter may not swing until he is thrown a strike, or maybe even two, while he waits for a mistake, a ball located in his hitting zone. Power pitchers have many more strikeouts than control pitchers. They also have many more walks, wild pitches, hit batsmen, and home runs. Control pitchers give up more base hits, but fewer home runs, along with fewer strikeouts and walks.

During this summer of 1997, Alec took full advantage of the opportunity to establish himself as a decent high school pitcher. Having demonstrated that he could do the job meant he could look forward to being on the junior varsity team for the next season and maybe even the varsity team after that. The remainder of the year, from August until January, was spent working on skills and building strength. The search for more velocity never ended. Fall baseball was omitted because the time commitment was not justified. It was better to spend an hour of focused effort each day in practice than to spend many hours traveling, just to get a bit of sporadic playing time somewhere on the other side of the county where the fall team decided to play. The new manager at Norcross also wanted the boys to spend more time working with weights, which they did two or three times a week after school. Furthermore, if Alec had played in the fall, the extra time commitment would have caused his grades to suffer, something I would not permit.

Without the drawbacks, being on this fall team would have been a good thing. The manager, Joe Testa, had coached in Norcross for years, mostly for the boys who were in the age group just above Alec. When these boys got to high school age, he did most of his coaching in the fall, but was available all year to assist. Testa, who was a major part of Norcross baseball for many years, was widely respected by all for his skill and devotion to the players and to the game.

Alec worked more than ever on conditioning all the way through the Thanksgiving and Christmas holidays. In addition to weight training, he threw long toss, ran, and threw at the tire in some combination just about every day. In fact, he arrived on the first day of team conditioning in late January completely prepared to pitch a ballgame. Most of the fall-ball players had not touched a baseball in almost three months since they played their last game in October.

Every one of Alec's pitching efforts from the beginning, ever since he pitched his first time for the Blue Jays in little league, was recorded. This effort was not premeditated, not a deliberate project, especially when begun that first evening he went to the mound. Pulling out a piece of paper to chart pitches was a semi-conscious, semi-automatic endeavor little different from taking notes in a lecture. Once this undertaking was set in motion, momentum, more than diligence, I should think, helped to carry it through.

Starting with the summer of 1997 Connie Mack season, the written record of each appearance was replaced by recordings with a video camcorder. Prior to this, just a few games were filmed. Upon failing to capture on film *The Game*, the one between the Blue and Red teams at Wingo-Carlyle Field, it seemed best not to miss filming anything again. Filming baseball games served mostly a personal interest, though it also managed to squelch argumentative proclivities. Being occupied with a camera makes one less inclined to notify the umpires of all their many crimes against the home team. Besides, everything said while the camera is turned on is recorded, preserving all blurted comments, be they clever or idiotic, forever.

Reviewing film served a couple of very useful baseball purposes, too. We could evaluate the pitching effort against each batter and we could generate good statistics. Combining all the high school, recreational, and Connie Mack games that were recorded, virtually every Gwinnett County high school batter was captured on our film. As much as Alec was called on to pitch, many of these batters appeared on tape several times. Starting in his sophomore year, he would go to a game after having reviewed the at bats of every player on the opposing team, further enabling him to detect their weaknesses.

The most astonishing part of this was that he also remembered what these batters did against him in the years before we started filming. There were instances after games when I questioned his sequence of pitches to a particular batter based on what was on the film. Then he would justify what he did by pointing out the particulars of an at bat this player had against him two or three years before. He had a phenomenal memory for games, players, pitches, situations, and results. More than phenomenal, it was unbelievable. He remembered everything, about baseball, that is.

Alec's unusually good memory did not work all the time. When it came to school or other things, he was as forgetful as anyone else could be, maybe more so. One of his teachers telephoned to report that he had not turned in an important homework assignment, which would result in his grade in the class being lowered quite a bit. Having stayed up late to finish the work, he took it to school, and even heard the teacher say to turn it in on the way out of class. So what happened? He "forgot" to turn it in on his way out of class! To which I said,

"You can remember every pitch you've thrown to every batter of every game you've ever played, but you can't remember to turn in your finished homework?"

The rest was unprintable dugout kind of talk.

Starting at the age of seven until entering high school, Alec had thrown a baseball virtually every day, except during the period from around Thanksgiving through New Years Day. If he played anything else during this time, it was basketball in a recreational league. Georgia's relatively mild weather allowed us to go outside just about every day, though we were never dissuaded from playing catch even with snow on the ground or a light rain falling. Conveniently, our basement was slightly over sixty feet long. Just enough room to establish a bull pen area for the few awful weather days and for after-dark throwing sessions. The hot water tank stood in as a surrogate right-handed batter.

This much baseball would have been much too much to expect from any boy except for two things. First, most days the effort lasted for no more than an hour. Second, he never minded doing it. The time investment was not huge, less than that of playing on teams all year, especially travel teams. The only fall team he had played on was the year in which he could not play in the spring due to a broken arm. Only twice was he chosen for all-star teams, which just extended his spring season into the early part of summer. What he did do was what every youngster ought to do, which is some sort of physical activity every day. His choice of physical activity happened to be throwing and hitting the baseball. Many of the other boys who continually played travel teams during every season became weary of playing baseball. Some even sustained injuries from overuse. A brief daily catch during the off-season before dinner to loosen the arm usually does not cause burnout or injury.

The result of doing a little every day over a long period is to do quite a lot. Using reasonable estimates, through 1997 he had thrown a baseball nearly half a million times, in practice and in games. Most of it was done while warming up and playing catch. The simple act of throwing a baseball with a fifty to sixty percent effort almost everyday from the age of seven was the reason he had developed great strength and durability in his legs and his throwing arm. Most importantly, this was probably the main reason he never experienced arm problems.

Young pitchers have to be taught how to take good care of their arms. The first rule is to have good mechanics. After that, it is always good to wear sleeves to keep the arm warm while pitching and between innings. Some pitchers do not like to pitch with long sleeves or even with three-quarter sleeves. If this is the case, they should wear a jacket between innings in the dugout. Alec was required to wear a thermal polypropylene long sleeve undershirt when the temperature was under fifty degrees and a regular cotton long sleeve mock turtleneck for higher temperatures. When the temperature was expected to be above eighty-five degrees, he could wear a three-quarter sleeve baseball undershirt. Never did I allow him to go to a game in short sleeves no matter what the temperature, even on the hottest Georgia summer afternoon.

The reason for covering the arm is mostly to protect it from evaporative cooling between pitches and between innings when sitting in the shade of the dugout. The surface temperature of the skin can drop significantly when even a slight breeze blows over an exposed sweat-covered arm. If the arm cools too much, it can cause warm-up problems when going out to pitch the next inning. A much too common sight is high school pitchers with sore arms after just a few innings, having thrown only forty or fifty pitches. Also common is to see high school pitchers wearing just a short sleeve uniform shirt when the temperature is in the forties or even lower. Some may think they are being real tough guys. Actually, they are just exposing their arms to needless risk. With the combination of sporadic and overdone throwing regimens along with generally neglectful treatment of their arms, it is no wonder there is always a critical shortage of injury-free pitchers.

Before the start of his 1998 junior varsity season during the sophomore year, Alec had faced a total of three hundred fifty batters during eighty innings of pitching going all the way back to little league. The development of a pitcher is terribly interesting to watch. The experience gained by being on the mound causes a gradual increase in the level of self-confidence. The transformation is visible in terms of both mechanical execution and level of comfort. At the point of junior varsity baseball, around age fifteen and sixteen, many of the boys start taking on the characteristics of grown-up pitchers and players, meaning they begin to look more like men rather than boys. They also start to play more like real grown-up baseball players. Consequently, their ability to accomplish workouts that are more demanding also increases. Those who continue to play from this point better decide to do so as men, because there is no place for boys anymore.

## Chapter Twelve
# Junior Varsity

    Being assigned to the junior varsity team to start the 1998 season was exciting, a tremendous opportunity to continue a pitching career, not to be taken for granted or begrudged. Never one to lack confidence, Alec's firm and unabashed judgment was that he was ready to pitch for the varsity. He was not. Better to demonstrate more success in real games against junior varsity teams, which would, in due course, confirm or deny his claims of a greater potential. Besides that, the varsity team already had a hopeful and hearty group of junior and senior pitchers, each with a compelling story, each deserving of a chance to succeed.

    The junior varsity coach was also a newcomer to Norcross. People were saying that he had played some baseball at a small college, a third baseman first, before being converted to a relief pitcher. Both stints were brief. His coaching experience amounted to a couple of years as an assistant at another high school. Now a schoolteacher for Norcross, he took on the additional assignments of junior varsity manager and varsity pitching coach. One of his first projects was to try to change Alec's mechanics in order to generate more velocity. His proposed means to this end employed the method of delivery known as the "power-position." A couple of very good examples of pitchers who used this technique were Braves' left-hander Steve Avery and right-hander Jack Morris. Morris spent most of his career with the Tigers, but he was best known around Georgia for having pitched the seventh game of the 1991 World Series for the Minnesota Twins, a splendid pitching effort that earned for him some renown in these parts, though not quite on the same par with General Sherman.

    The most prominent characteristic of power-position pitching is the elevation of the throwing hand above and behind the head from where a strong pulling down motion is made to deliver the pitch. While bringing the ball to the release point, the pitcher has the feeling of an exaggerated downhill throwing motion. The J.V. coach also wanted to end Alec's toe drag, which many pitchers use to stabilize themselves at the point of their delivery for greater control. He preferred allowing the back foot to fly up upon release thereby allowing for a less restricted body turn.

These instructions were not amusing to me, nor were they to Ro when he heard about them. Ro did not want some apprentice high school baseball coach "fixing" his student's pitching mechanics. It made no sense whatsoever to try to convert Alec into a fast ball/breaking ball power pitcher even if it was possible to do so, which it was not. The coach's desire for more velocity with the fastball was not even the issue. The disagreement came from sacrificing control to achieve it. Moreover, such a change in mechanics would quite likely have increased the possibly of arm injury.

Alec was one of only two pitchers in his school with excellent mechanics and control, the other being senior right-hander Joe Gullett. At his age, the last thing he needed to do was change his fundamental delivery in the hope of achieving a little more velocity. Even if this result were realized, the new fastball would still not have been fast enough to intimidate anyone. Eventually, Alec would need more velocity, especially if he hoped to keep pitching at higher levels. Meanwhile, his method of pitching was fundamentally sound, yielding good results. The best course was to leave it alone for the time being.

The coach's motives, without doubt, were good. Both he and Edwards had to know that if Alec could continue throwing the same quality pitches, but with an additional ten to fifteen mph on his fastball, he would become one of the top pitchers in the region, enhancing the possibility of their team going to the state tournament the next year. The trouble was that the power pitching technique would add maybe a few miles per hour at most, not enough to make a substantial difference. Therefore, the loss of precision and a higher likelihood of arm injury would have made the exchange a bad deal particularly when made for the ancillary purpose of pitching junior varsity high school baseball. This was not at all intended to belittle JV baseball, just meant to keep an intelligent perspective of the relative value of things. Had nothing been said, had the coach been allowed to introduce the power pitching technique into his mechanics, Alec would have ended up pitching like most of the other unsuccessful pitchers on the roster, just a little slower. Nothing of value would have been achieved.

Only this one pitching direction given my son during his entire baseball career caused enough concern for me to express a contrary opinion to one of his coaches about the way he was being coached. After identifying the appropriate level within the chain of command, a single call was made to the varsity manager. More than enough opinion was exchanged during this one conversation to learn Mr. Edwards knew his business when it came to baseball. About the power position pitching, he had no choice but to respect my wishes although he gave no indication of disagreeing with my point of view, anyway. So, this misguided attempt by a moderately qualified subordinate to teach Alec how to pitch came to a quick end. I chose to consider the matter settled and forgotten. Later on, it became apparent the junior varsity coach did not.

More velocity would come from increased body size and strength. The problem was in having to wait because it could take a long time. At this point, he was about five-feet six-inches tall with about four or five inches to go, and weighed about one hundred ten pounds. The coaches' next plan figured him to be a perfect candidate for chemical enhancement. Not surprisingly, the subject of taking Creatin, hormonal supplements, etc., came up in the weight room. Having previously discussed the subject with our family physician, this suggestion was disregarded as well. He was going to have to rely on eating more and throwing more. No telephone calls from the father were necessary here. The kid handled this one on his own.

Otherwise, preparations for the new season went very well, so did the humorous stories and anecdotes which are so much a part of baseball. One afternoon, before the season got under way, the varsity team went to play a preseason game leaving behind the junior varsity and freshmen teams to practice. The newly minted freshman coach who replaced Gilbert remained in charge of the whole group. He decided to have the two teams play each other in a scrimmage game. Alec got the start for the junior varsity team maybe because the freshman coach thought his freshmen players would have an easier time hitting the smaller kid with the slower pitches. An easier time for the freshmen was not exactly what happened. This coach most likely had not seen or heard of the Red/Blue game, so he can be forgiven his ignorance. He soon learned. In four innings, all twelve batters who came up to the bat were sent away empty-handed with several strikeouts. Not one batter managed to hit a ball as far as the outfield grass.

Like the incoming group before them, most of these freshmen played together as a special team of Dixie Youth pony league all-stars during the previous summer, and then on a fall travel team, for which their parents hired a well-known local coach. In other words, this was, allegedly, an elite travel team comprised of the very best baseball players, and designed purposefully to be the pre-selected high school freshman team. Elite or not, after four innings the junior varsity led 5-0. The coach then decided to let someone else pitch for the older boys. On came the other junior varsity pitchers along with their faster fastballs and power-position deliveries. After three more pitchers took a turn during the last three innings, the freshmen won the game by a lopsided score, something like 13-5, if memory serves correctly. Alec reported after the game that these batters on the freshman team "could not hit any ball that moved," declaring that this was the easiest lineup he had ever encountered. So what happened to the other pitchers?

"Well, they couldn't get anybody out. It was like batting practice."

What did this suggest about the future of Norcross baseball? The outlook was in serious doubt.

Alec's team did better in junior varsity competition than they had done as freshmen. They actually came close to winning half their games, seven to be exact. The starting assignments were spread around more than Gilbert had done allowing Edwards to evaluate fairly each of the pitchers. Alec started three games during the regular season winning all of them, making him the most successful pitcher on the team. Two of the games he started were complete seven-inning affairs. Danny McGee won two games while two other starters won one game apiece. Alec also did relief work in six additional games giving him the most appearances of any junior varsity pitcher, that is, he pitched in nine games out of fifteen. When the junior varsity played a game and he did not pitch, it was unusual.

This vigorous routine bore good fruit. Every time he went to the ballpark, he had to be mentally and physically prepared, and he was. His managers, and everyone else associated with any team on which he played, came to know that Alec Barnes was always ready to pitch; that he could go out to the mound any time, under any circumstances; that there were no physical ailments, and that he possessed the most endurance on the staff. Twice he threw over ninety pitches in a game. Near the end of the season, in a game against Duluth High School, he went the distance earning a 6-3 win. During this contest, he threw ninety-seven pitches of which sixty-three were strikes, gave up only five hits, all singles, struck out four, and walked two. Only one of the three runs was earned. Just four days earlier, he had thrown ninety-four pitches, sixty-three strikes again, during six and two-thirds innings in a game against Collins Hill. Three runs came quickly in the first inning before he settled down and pitched well, taking his team into the sixth inning ahead by the score of 10-3, only being pulled when getting into some two out trouble. The final score was 11-7. All seven runs were earned, a performance mostly good, but shaky at the beginning and at the very end.

The junior varsity coach did not hesitate to make his starting pitchers stay in a game when they got into jams, even when things were rough. More than a few times, a struggling pitcher would look into the dugout hoping to be pulled, that is, other pitchers, never Alec. Then the coach could be heard calling out something like,

"I'm not coming out there. This is your mess. You clean it up!"

Being forced to continue pitching under trying circumstances is good training for young pitchers, when not overdone. Only one way remains to get relief, which is to complain their arms are too sore to continue. Some of them did exactly that. For a high school coach to leave a pitcher out there when the kid says his arm hurts and while his parents are sitting in the stands can be dicey, even if the coach is sure the kid is lying.

In a few instances, pitchers tried to get out of a starting assignment when scheduled to go against a very good team. How very disconcerting that some players were afraid of a challenge. Perhaps they knew they were ill prepared, but were they also that much afraid of failure? Not only did Alec want to pitch everyday, he preferred going against the better teams. Given the chance, he would have pitched against the Atlanta Braves. Knowing him, he would have taken the mound expecting to win the game. He would not have won. He would have gotten his brains beat out. Then, without a doubt, after the game, he would have insisted that he had figured out his mistakes, deciphered each batter's weakness, and would be ready to face them again in a few days confident of better results. His mental approach and attitude towards baseball and pitching simply could not have been better.

During every season, there are certain games that stand out in a way that just capture the imagination. Which game will become so memorable, no one can know beforehand. For this reason, it is best to attend all of them. The second game of the 1998 Norcross junior varsity season was just such a game, as captivating at the time it was played, as it was memorable later on. Alec was given his first regular season starting assignment as a high school pitcher against neighboring Meadowcreek High School, just five miles away. Norcross expected to win the game because Meadowcreek was assumed to have another weak team that year. Even so, weak is a relative term. They were a regional opponent in the top region in Georgia and, like any other team, would not be beat by playing badly, this being a lesson in sport taught more often than it is learned.

After school on the day of the game, Alec moved his car from the student parking lot over to the gravel parking area down below the back of the school by the baseball field. He changed into his uniform and, one might guess, amidst all the excitement in anticipation of his first important high school starting assignment, along with the intense anxiety of getting mentally prepared, he fell asleep. Half an hour later the team was getting ready to leave when someone noticed the starting pitcher was not aboard the bus. Dallas Austin, rightly deducing he was most likely napping in his car, made a dash to retrieve him. The respite must have served him well because the game turned out to be a pitching jewel, a real masterpiece.

Alec pitched a complete game, seven innings, throwing only sixty-three pitches of which fifty-three were strikes. While giving up only three hits and one earned run, the lefty struck out three and walked none. Of the twenty-seven Meadowcreek batters who stepped up to take a turn at the bat, eighteen were thrown first pitch strikes. Four defensive errors led to two unearned runs. The final score was 10-3. Best of all, his pitching performance was mentioned the next day at school over the public address system during morning announcements.

For the year, the Norcross junior varsity team record was not a bad one. Hitting was a bit inconsistent, but the area most in need of improvement was fielding. Overall, the pitching was not bad either, relatively speaking. As difficult as it was to evaluate, Norcross pitchers were probably about as good as the pitchers from most of the other junior varsity teams around the county.

By any measure, Alec's season statistics were exceptionally good. He appeared in nine games, pitched thirty-one and two-thirds innings, faced one hundred and fifty-one batters, walked four, and struck out sixteen. He surrendered forty-two base hits of which there were thirty-three singles, six doubles, three triples, and no home runs even though the Norcross center field fence at the old school was only three hundred forty-two feet. When using metal bats, three hundred forty-two feet for high school athletes should be considered shallow center field. There were no wild pitches or hit batsmen, either. His ERA was a decent 3.76. Although Alec had the slowest fastball on the team, maybe even in the whole county, he managed to put up the best performance, earning for him the recognition he rightly deserved. Near the end of the season, Edwards called him up to the varsity team. With this promotion, he had accomplished a goal that seemed beyond the realm of possibility just fifteen months before when, as a complete unknown, he first showed up for freshman tryouts. Two varsity uniforms were retrieved from the storeroom, one each for home and away games, with the lowest player number in a size that would fit. Happily, it turned out to be the number "six," just like that of another left-hander from the glorious baseball past, Stan "The Man" Musial. The shared excitement continued at home all through the evening, as did an element of private grief, being mindful that his grandfather did not live to see this day.

At the point of his call-up, the varsity team found itself in a position where it had to win its last two games to be sure of going to the playoffs. A cluster of upperclassmen pitchers was ahead of him, but he was there, too, and, as usual, he was ready to pitch, if needed. If they had won the last game at Berkmar, they would have advanced to the tournament. Edwards told Alec before the game he would get the next start. The team lost its last two games, so Alec's only varsity pitching this season was done in the bull pen at Berkmar, getting warmed up even as the game ended. Had the team tied or taken the lead, the ball would have been his in the bottom of the seventh inning. They did not rally in the top half. He would have to wait for the summertime Connie Mack season to get underway before pitching his first game with the varsity squad.

Meanwhile, the boys did not sign up for the Dixie Youth team in Norcross. The recreational league went further into decline this year, largely due to the poorly maintained Wingo-Carlyle Field, but also due to alternate playing opportunities. One team did materialize. A group consisting of experienced varsity players was assembled for the sole purpose of going to the state tournament. This team was not assembled to play a regular schedule of recreational baseball. Had he been asked to join, Alec would have done so. Instead, he put his focus entirely on the high school summer team with enough work to be done there in trying to show he could hold his own when pitching at the varsity level.

The decline in the previously active Dixie Youth summer program for high school age boys in Norcross was, indeed, unfortunate. First, four teams were reduced to just two in the previous year. Within a couple more years, there would be just one team and then none. The one hundred and thirty year-old historic Norcross baseball field was still not being maintained. The Gwinnett County Parks & Recreation Department, while continuing to lease Wingo-Carlyle Field from the City of Norcross, had allowed it to deteriorate even more. The skinned infield suffered additional erosion every time it rained. Finally, it became so shabby hardly anyone wanted to use it anymore, even for practice, since it took a real effort to make it playable. The many local boys who did not play for the high school team had lost their best alternative to play baseball.

Edwards was the type of manager who relied heavily on his senior players because of the high value he attached to experience. Going into the summer of 1998, five senior pitchers and three juniors were coming up. The junior pitchers he used to fill in the gaps until they could prove themselves while the seniors, having been given the benefit of the doubt, were in the rotation until and unless they proved themselves utterly unfit. This plan did not make much sense because the senior pitchers had failed to prove themselves as juniors during the previous season.

Of the five rising senior pitchers, the two thought to be the best also played football. With priority given to football camps, it meant they would miss several of the summertime baseball games. Both were good athletes, no doubt, but did not devote enough time to pitching, as was shown by their failure to live up to expectations. Another senior pitcher who probably would have been the best of the bunch was Jeff Hunt. However, Jeff suffered an arm injury from which he was not yet fully recovered, at least not well enough to pitch. He could play first base and he could hit, but would not be available to pitch for at least several months. The last two seniors, while promising at one time, never saw much varsity action. Edwards, hoping to rely upon the experience and leadership of his senior pitchers, gave the four of them ample opportunity to prove themselves. They failed to do so. Even after they fell short in both effort and execution during the summer, it was mostly expected that the two best would come through in the spring. By some new-math calculation, their pitching was expected to improve by playing football throughout the fall months. It did not.

The problem was a typical one and simple to identify, yet unsolvable. The four available senior pitchers never put enough effort into pitching, not this year and not any year before. They never had to. Being good natural athletes as little leaguers and pony leaguers, they were automatically on all of the youth league all-star teams. Not until they played high school varsity baseball did their lack of skill become evident. By this time, it was almost too late to do anything about it even if they had been inclined to try. They were not so inclined, yet only two of the four were penalized for this lack of ability.

Alec did pitch twenty-seven innings for the varsity team during the summer. The results were mediocre, but thanks to the overall low quality of the entire staff, it is doubtful anyone took particular notice. He had a respectable 3.15 ERA, achieved only because a lot of runs scored after errors were made making most of the runs he surrendered officially unearned. He gave up forty-two hits, including two home runs, and though there were more unearned runs than earned, all the runs count the same on the scoreboard. On the bright side was his strike to ball ratio, a respectable sixty-four percent. Additionally, he only issued five walks out of one hundred and thirty-six batters faced. There was not much joy to be found within these numbers, but, as a rising junior, Alec had been given a good taste of what to expect the next year. Since he had until February to get ready, he was hopeful of picking up a little more velocity, too.

The most satisfying game while pitching that summer was against Duluth, their perennial rival. They had the McCann brothers, Brian and Brad, both of whom were recruited by colleges in addition to being drafted by major league teams out of high school; Brian by the Braves and Brad by the Phillies. Brad chose to delay his professional career by going to college first. He played a year at Gulf Coast Community College in Panama City Beach, Florida before transferring to Clemson University. Brian entered the minor leagues right away where he spent a very short time before the call came to join the major league club in Atlanta.

Alec entered the game in relief with one out and two men on base in the second inning losing 5-0. The Norcross starting pitcher was already struggling in the first inning. After just a couple of batters in the second inning, Edwards called out for Alec to start warming up in the bull pen. He had just started playing catch, not yet throwing from the rubber, when the first Norcross hurler committed the one unforgivable deadly sin; he threw an 0-2 pitch in the strike zone that could be hit. Not only was the ball hit, the batter managed a solid RBI producing single. Now, in the first place, for most of the Norcross pitchers, an 0-2 count was an extremely rare occurrence. In the event it did happen, Edwards had made it clear that if any batter hit an 0-2 pitch, that pitcher would be taken out of the game at once. This may have been a bit harsh, but he was the skipper and he made his point well.

Edwards started out from the dugout and yelled for Alec to get out there, one of the most abrupt pitching changes I ever witnessed. He was just going to have to warm up while pitching. Fortunately, he threw a little during pre-game warm-ups, combined with it being a hot afternoon. He could handle it.

The first batter to be faced was Brad McCann, no stranger to anyone even back then. Brad took the first pitch, something that used to be common in the old days after a pitching change. The umpire called the strike as the pitch nipped the outside corner at the knees. The batter did swing at the 0-1 pitch resulting in a bloop-single that landed about ten feet onto the outfield grass right behind second base, while each middle infielder initially looked for the other one to go get it. The runner on second could not score as he waited to see the result of the play. In fact, there was an easy force out at second base if the ball had not been subsequently kicked around and bobbled. The runner from first, pausing between the bases, had to wait and see if it fell in.

The misplay caused no harm as the next batter hit a 1-2 pitch into a 4-6-3 double play to end the inning. The middle infielders had redeemed themselves. The third inning was interrupted by an unhelpful twenty-five minute rain delay. The next time McCann batted, he made the last out in the fourth inning by grounding to Chris Horwath, who was now playing first base, for the unassisted put out. The ball squibbed off the end of the bat due to an ill-timed swing. While the first baseman was stepping toward the bag and McCann was hustling down the line, Edwards sarcastically called out,

"They're hitting you hard, Alec!"

He continued to pitch tenaciously into to the sixth inning while holding Duluth scoreless. Meanwhile, Norcross managed to take a 6-5 lead by scoring two runs in the third inning and four runs in the fifth inning. The sixth inning started poorly when a Duluth player reached base due to an error by the first baseman. The following batter reached base on a 4-6 fielder's choice when Norcross failed to convert a relatively easy double play opportunity. Next, there came a double, a walk, and a single. The bases were loaded, one unearned run in, and Brad McCann coming up to bat again.

The score now tied at six apiece, Edwards decided to make a change. He strode out to the mound to get Alec. The kid looked a little tired to me and he was tired, even though he had only thrown fifty-three pitches during the four-plus innings he worked. The rain delay had taken a toll. More than two hours had passed since he first entered the game. Still he plainly wanted to stay in to face McCann one more time. Extremely disappointed though he was, he had to come out. Edwards did not want to let this game get away. Losing to neighboring Duluth was the worst thing imaginable except maybe losing to Meadowcreek. Confidently, he turned to the unassailable senior experience held in reserve and brought in the fresh arm of his number one pitcher and sometime star football player to face Duluth's most powerful batter. In a wildly imaginative sort of way, this face-off was vaguely reminiscent of the July 4, 1929 Ernie Nevers/Roy Carlyle mid-afternoon duel in San Francisco.

Remembering once again how things used to be, following a pitching change a batter would automatically take the first pitch, especially with the bases loaded during a tied game in the late innings. The Duluth manager was known to be an adherent of this strategy. An attentive pitcher, especially one with senior leadership abilities and experience, would have guessed correctly that McCann probably was going to take his first pitch. This reasonable assumption, in addition to the fact that here was not the time to fall behind in the count, made a first pitch strike highly desirable. Instead, the pitch was wild, very out of control, bouncing in the dirt wide of the plate, almost going by the catcher. It took a sensational block to save a run from scoring. McCann, to no one else's surprise, with his duty to his manager's directive being fulfilled, was not automatically taking on the second pitch. If the ball was in his zone, he was going to swing. It was and he did. He swung and hit the 1-0 pitch so hard it was still on its way up when it cleared the fence. It was a thunderbolt type of grand slam, would have been out of any park, Turner Field, Yankee Stadium, Wrigley, you name it, against a stiff breeze in the rain at Candlestick, any park. For his efforts, Alec was awarded three of the four earned runs and the loss. Not to be outdone, the other three able senior pitchers eventually brought their experience and leadership in to complete the final one and two-thirds innings of this seven-inning game before it finally ended with Duluth winning 21-9.

"Tough game, kid."

The importance of knowing how to pitch is a point that could not have been better illustrated on this afternoon. Two relief pitchers came into the same game at different times facing similar circumstances. Men were on base and the same dangerous batter was up. First, Alec knew to get ahead in the count. Then, thanks to Ro, he knew that after getting McCann to look outside, he should then move something back in to get a ball hit off the handle of the bat, one that could not leave the park, one that would be grounded weakly or popped up. It was popped up and even though it fell in for a base hit, no real damage was done. The ball probably should have been caught. Failing that, the force out at second base should have been secured. In spite of the mishaps, he did not lose control over the situation, maintained his composure, and thus gave his defense the opportunity to bring the inning to a quick end.

The senior ace pitcher, on the other hand, took the mound and instantly created a crippling 1-0 situation. With the bases loaded and the game on the line, his second pitch had to be a strike, which it was, neatly positioned right over middle-in section of the plate. In the first instance, Alec displayed a perfectly executed and thoughtful strategy; in the second, McCann was given extra batting practice. In the first instance, the pitcher relied on skill. In the second, he relied on bravado as if saying,

"Here's my heater; I dare you to beat me."

He should have said, "Where would you like the ball to be pitched today, Mr. McCann?"

The one great thing about competent, thoughtful baseball players is not that things go right for them all the time, because they do not, rather, it is that, after every game, they clearly understand what happened. Alec's analysis was always correct. If we ever argued about it, he would prove me wrong every time, this surely attributable to the advantage gained by being in the dugout. On this particular afternoon, he knew he was the only one of the six Norcross hurlers who even resembled a pitcher. It positively made the team's outlook very distressing. Though deeply disappointed that the team lost the game, he could always separate the winning/losing aspect from objectively analyzing performance. However, for this game analysis, as fifteen additional Duluth base runners crossed home plate while the four senior pitchers labored to get the final five outs, not much else occurred that one could call a performance.

Following this miserable loss to Duluth, there was still the last game of the summer to be played, the last chance for the team to show the level of pride remaining in the Norcross baseball program. They went to play Meadowcreek with Alec starting. The football players were long gone, off to some other football camp again. Barely enough players showed up, a mere ten, to field a team. The summer having been less productive for the Norcross squad than all had anticipated, now it was simply a matter of pitching this last game as well as he possibly could, letting it be the preview for next season. Going the distance, he threw ninety-seven pitches, sixty-eight strikes, four strikeouts, and no walks. The Meadowcreek batters managed ten singles and one double. Fortunately, they were scattered well enough, along with the four errors, to allow just six runs, only two of them earned, as the team's defense continued to be less than mediocre.

A few of the singles were of the infield variety for which better fielding could have produced outs. Such is life on the high school diamond. Often the duty of the pitcher is to pick up his mates when needed. He did the best he could. Norcross still should have won the game, but I sensed a general resignation on the part of the players in addition to a great deal of displeasure by the manager. Along with the poor fielding, the base running was awful, too, which led to several unnecessary outs, stifling otherwise good scoring opportunities. There were not many quality at bats, either. The only player who had a good day at the plate was Chris Horwath, but he usually did.

This game probably annoyed Edwards more for the poor and lackadaisical attitude on display than for the fact that they lost. He was not happy. Nor was anyone else. The most difficult thing to understand was how all of these young men were not totally thrilled every day that they got to put on their uniforms and go play baseball on a high school varsity baseball team. What could be better? Sometimes it seemed many of them did not even want to be there. What would happen the next season was anyone's guess. Who knew what kind of pitchers would show up? The lack of fielding, hitting, and base-running skills, combined with the overall poor effort during this summer of Norcross baseball, did not bode well.

Exactly one and one-half years had passed since Alec made it onto the high school team. To this point, he had pitched 103 innings in thirty-six games, thrown 1,535 pitches (sixty-eight percent strikes), and faced 506 batters, striking out forty-nine and walking twenty-three. His record was seven wins, eight losses, two saves, and an overall seven-inning ERA of 3.47, not great, but much better numbers than those of his team.

Examining these stats left me more than satisfied with what he had accomplished, especially at his height and weight. He had always pitched well, as the consistency of his delivery along with his ability to locate and change speeds was tremendous. While watching the films of the season just passed, it was easy to forget this was just a high school sophomore. He took on the appearance of a pitching machine. Ro had always had unwavering confidence in Alec, saying it was there for him if he wanted it, and Ro was talking about something beyond high school or college ball. We would see. He still needed about fifteen mph more on the fastball. He needed to get to the mid-eighties, at least, for the professional scouts to take notice.

Consistently and repeatedly, Alec displayed an ability to undo some of the better players in the county. He had something special. His mechanics were outstanding. He hid the ball well, delivering each pitch with the same motion and arm speed. It was not possible for a batter to tell what was coming. He had become so adept at his craft that if he detected a sign had been stolen or a tip given to the batter, he would change his grip during the windup and deliver a different pitch, though not one that would cross-up the catcher.

After facing the same batters several times, the batters usually did not fare any better against him, instead, they often did worse. Alec deciphered their weaknesses, using this knowledge to his advantage. His biggest problem, as he would often tell me while reviewing films, was not the batters so much as it was trying to pitch around his own team's defensive weaknesses, afraid that certain positions were undermanned leaving them prone to errors. Every time a certain pitch selection seemed questionable, he would point out some very good reason for it. Often he would say the best selection would likely have caused the ball to be hit to someone not able to handle the play, so he would take a chance with another pitch. These kinds of comments showed a depth of knowledge and understanding of the game of baseball that was a struggle for me to match. I do not rightly know exactly when he surpassed me in this regard. A good guess would be that it happened about the time he finished the eighth grade. This meant he was way ahead of his high school coaches, too, all of them except Ro, of course.

*Chapter Thirteen*

# Varsity

Except in a playoff or other equally important do-or-die type of game, is it better for a high school baseball team to play well and lose, or to play poorly and win? It may be a frivolous choice for a team, certainly not one offered beforehand, and entirely rhetorical, since neither supposition would be considered applicable. Yet, if a selection were made between just these two, something about the outlook of the team might be exposed. As a rule, high school baseball is played to win. In fact, the inclination of coaches and players is to win at any cost. The sad part is that, in reality, for most high school teams, "any cost" does not include a consistent and tireless effort at skill development and conditioning.

Varsity baseball seasons are short, somewhere around twenty to twenty-five games. Teams in Georgia compete in regions determined by their location. The competitive level to which a team is assigned is generally determined by the size of the student body. Win/lose records against teams of the same competitive level within the same region determine which teams qualify for the playoff tournament and where they are seeded. Non-regional games, mostly played during the first half of the season, are important only for team development and experience. They provide an opportunity for the manager to try different things and see how players respond to different situations. Then he can make his final decisions about which players to use when the region schedule starts. Once these personnel decisions are made they usually do not change very much for the remainder of the season. There simply is not enough time to keep making major adjustments.

During the first part of a season, the preferred state of affairs is for the players to play well and for the team to win games, very simple, keep it up. The second easiest situation with which to deal is one where the players play badly and the team loses games. Very simple again, an increased effort is the obvious solution. If the team is playing well and losing, the most likely culprit is the manager. Quite a delusional situation can arise if a team wins in spite of playing badly, and if the players do not recognize their poor play for what it is. The players on such a team should be told to give credit where credit is due: dumb luck. Then they should be instructed to increase their efforts. However, there is a deceptive tendency, natural though it may be, to equate winning with being good and losing to bad luck. Indeed, after a win, what players are amenable to being told they stink? Worse yet, after a win, what players want to admit they stink?

In reality, there are two different types of "stink." One type is a good player having a bad day. The other is a bad player having his usual day. The same can be said of teams. Good players (and teams) generally take care of themselves. Bad players need to face reality, try working harder, or, if that is not palatable, go on to play something else, maybe a game that uses fewer limbs and produces nebulous results.

Win or lose, a team's goal to succeed can be realistic only so long as it has good players to lead and less-than-good players who are trying hard to become good players. When a team is full of bad players who think they are good, or when a team is full of bad players who know they stink and do not care to do anything about it, very little will be accomplished besides causing the manager to become increasingly frustrated. If a team has only a few good players who continue to do their best, often they cannot overcome the slack left by the others. Their attempts to exhibit leadership may be ignored or even resented. Norcross was well on its way to becoming such a team as it exuded most of the common by-products of hopelessness.

When a team has a poor attitude, it is more than obvious to spectators. One thoughtful Norcross player's parent, while sitting in the stands one afternoon watching another feeble effort, offered a clever solution. He suggested sending the entire varsity team out to run laps around the ball field until they started dropping, until nine players were left running. Those nine would remain on the team, the others cut.

As soon as the summer season ended, the Dugout Club was busy putting together plans for a fall team. Joe Testa was going to be the manager. They decided to play again at the place called the "Field of Dreams" operated by the Renz Baseball Academy. Renz already operated a well-established baseball teaching facility in nearby Lilburn.

They had purchased this baseball complex located near the small town of Grayson on the other side of Gwinnett County about twenty-five miles away, and tried to make a go of it. The sellers were some former professional athletes who lost money on the investment and were very glad to dump this loser onto someone else. Norcross had played a game or two out there during the past two Connie Mack summer seasons so it was a familiar place. If there were to be a third kind of "stink," this field would qualify. Actually, it was two fields, neither one worth the powder to blow it up.

The two adjacent fields were so close that it made foul balls a frequent hazard to players on the other field. The backstop consisted of a cinder block wall about four feet high, not more than twenty-five feet behind home plate, with netting stretched upward. Wild pitches and foul tips rebounding off that wall could hit the umpire in the back or even reach the pitcher on the fly. The soil was bad, the infield grass thin, and the ground lumpy. Not a true bounce was to be found anywhere. The nearby dusty gravel parking lot was also a nuisance. Every time a car came or went a choking cloud of dust was raised. These were two of the worse baseball fields around, worse even than my little league field in Springfield Forest *before* it was converted from a pasture. The only comparably bad field in the area was Wingo-Carlyle Field in Norcross.

Fall games at the Field of Dreams were limited to one hour and forty-five minutes, which meant a team was fortunate to play five innings. Nothing worthwhile came of this place, just a complete waste of time and money. Complaints were ignored, as were alternative suggestions. The dugout club went ahead with their plans, so we declined to participate. We made our own baseball plans.

Soon the workouts became an enjoyable diversion, meeting in the late afternoon or early evening usually at the school field, or occasionally at home, to go through his daily throwing routine. The drills consisted of a lot of long-toss and throwing at the tire along with throwing to the bases from the stretch position, covering first base on balls hit to the right side, covering bunts, and fielding come-backers. For variety a couple of times each week, the long toss drill was combined with outfield practice. Tracking down fly balls and liners, followed by the long throw to home plate, does just as well for arm conditioning.

Practice in the field came in handy when the fall team played a couple of practice games at the home high school field and Joe Testa saw fit to use Alec as an outfielder. In one of those scrimmage games, after catching a liner, he made a terrific throw from right field to third base.

Testa remarked later that Alec could throw BB's from the outfield, but could not break a windshield with his fastball standing on the hood of a car. Had his pitching been done with the mechanics of an outfielder, perhaps glass would shatter. We both wished we had had a better answer.

The autumn quickly passed. Alec looked forward to the coming spring baseball season of his junior year with excitement and a spry anticipation born of his characteristic optimism. The dream of his life, the dream that was so unlikely as to be unspeakable just two years earlier, was about to unfold. Since pony league days, he had wondered what it would be like to pitch for the high school varsity team during its regular season, to be teammates with some of the best young players in town. Now it would happen, but only for this one year when most of them were seniors. After this group graduated, there was very little left of which to speak optimistically. The current senior cast included infielders Brett Moon, Brad Teaver, and Jesse Erickson; outfielder Troy Fallaw and catcher Tony DeMauro. From his own class were catcher Inman Dubberly, outfielder Kerry Gray, infielder Chris Horwath, and another left-handed pitcher, Andrew Dodson. Enough talent was there to have a good season, if only the four "healthy" senior right-handed pitchers would come through.

With true and unwavering optimism, Alec had no doubt these players would all have good years because surely they would see the great potential in themselves and each other. In his judgment, this was going to be the best year for Norcross High School baseball in more than a decade. If they all put forth the greatest effort of their baseball careers, if they all made the commitment to work harder than they ever had before, they would have a great season. Finally, Edwards was going to be the right man to manage this team.

Alec had high regard for Edwards for some specific reasons. As manager, he did not delegate very much, staying personally involved with every aspect of the program. Edwards also spent much time with the junior varsity and freshman teams. Whenever time allowed, he went to other high schools in the area to scout their games, or he would send an assistant. Extensive scouting is not customary in high school baseball. However, if playing well enough to make the playoffs is the goal, scouting is almost essential for success.

In spite of valiant managerial efforts, the usual discouraging signs persisted. Other than Alec, no other pitcher at the school even knew how to chart pitches. They did not know how to use, nor did they care to read, scouting reports. Alec routinely showed up early to games to review these reports, even when he was not scheduled to pitch. He assumed his teammates, especially the pitchers, would eagerly catch on to the advantages of being prepared and they would learn to use this information, too. They did not. The others would feign reading a scouting report until Edwards turned away. Then they would drop it on the bench saying something with an equivalent meaning to,

"I don't see a need to read this stuff."

To one so committed, this indifference was disconcerting, but, as he was told, it did not matter. In order to put a scouting report to good use a pitcher had to be able to make good pitches. Those other pitchers were just throwers who could not locate anything, for whom a change of speed meant slowing the speed of the arm, for whom curveballs more often than not bounced in front of the plate. So what good can a scouting report do? Not very much. This revelation came gradually, and to his increasing dismay. The intensity level of varsity high school baseball at Norcross was not what he expected it to be.

During games, Edwards liked to call the pitches from the dugout, that is, both the type of pitch and the location. The pitch sequences were usually very good when Alec was on the mound, with only a few exceptions. Every pitch was easily discernable just by watching what he threw. Not so for the other pitchers. Without seeing the signs, their pitches were usually difficult to distinguish.

The Norcross manager's largely unmet expectations were not unusual for high school baseball; the lack of effort was what probably riled him the most. All summer long he tried to impress the pitching staff with what he wanted them to do, to no avail. When the season got underway, his frustration erupted like so many volcanoes. Pitchers who could not execute were bad enough. When they shook off the signs sent in to the catcher . . . well, sometimes Edwards was fit to be tied, especially when the alternate pitch was an ineffective attempt at some made-up foolishness like a palm ball or a knuckle curve.

Since Joe Gullet graduated the previous year, Alec was the only pitcher left who could pitch with any consistency. Each one of the others lacked pitching skills, lacked the effort to learn those skills, and lacked the will to improve whatever limited skills they may have had. The expected consequence, a losing season, was sure to be realized. Edwards still tried. He had the catchers giving good targets, setting themselves inside or outside, framing the pitches well. It continued throughout when Alec was on the mound. For the other pitchers, the catcher would start out that way, but quickly had to abandon the effort. It made far more sense to stay behind the middle of the plate, moving just the glove to chase the ball one way or the other, because no one could know where it would actually go.

Another wasted effort was managing the team as if the position players understood the game and were capable of executing their assignments. Perhaps some might have said Edwards expected too much. I would say he expected the bare minimum. After all, the next level after high school is professional ball, the minor leagues. A high school manager has every right to expect his players to accomplish basic, simple tasks, along with understanding the reasons things are done. Was it too much to expect these players to pick up signs, execute the sacrifice bunt, hit a cut-off, or force a rundown to the previous base? How about expecting them to obey signs, improve their skills, and study the game? Almost no one practiced independently on a regular basis. No one, other than Alec, read scouting reports voluntarily. The only noticeable game plan amongst the players was when they were figuring out who on the team had the most expensive metal bat and how to borrow it.

When the effort to improve is minimal, errors and misplays are that much harder to tolerate. Edwards came from a different era. In his younger days, he played baseball at the University of Georgia. His son, Clint, was currently there doing likewise with the same kind of work ethic. Edwards certainly did have high expectations; they were influenced by his own experiences. His son had no trouble rising to this level so why not expect the same from these Norcross high school players. Even though few on the high school baseball team would be drafted, or be able to continue playing in college, so what? The question was not whether they could go to the next higher level; the question was whether they wanted to give it their best effort, just in case. If a high school ballplayer does not have this minimum desire, or have this dream, what is he doing on the team? A high school male athlete that aspires to nothing more than modeling a uniform and collecting another varsity letter is a sorry sight. Indeed, he is a wasted space in the dugout.

Clint Edwards was a very good player, very impressive, especially with the bat. Alec saw him several times and even pitched some batting practice to him. He told me that, in terms of bat control, this was the best hitter (to this point) he had ever seen, better than Steven Horwath, better than Jeff Keppinger, better than Jeff Francouer, and even better than the McCann's, all of whom were terrific high school hitters. Bat control is something many professional players do not have. So, what is bat control? When a player taking batting practice can consistently hit line drives to points starting at one foul line, working towards the other foul line sequentially at twenty to twenty-five foot intervals, and then work back again in reverse fashion, this player has bat control. If he can do it switch-hitting, well, it is a rarity. (Randy "Fico" Guzman, a Braves' minor leaguer and member of the Norcross Baseball Club, could do it.)

As a father, there did not seem to be a reason to go watch the Norcross baseball team practice after school. Some fathers occasionally did. I caught a few brief glimpses from atop the overlooking hill outside the gymnasium when picking up my daughter, Pam, after basketball practice, which was enough to discover Edwards was well organized. His practices were purposeful, extremely rigorous, and with maximum utilization of drills and stations. Alec had high praise for what Edwards was trying to do with the team. Going by the full reports at supper every evening, all indications were that the team was on the right track to have a good year. Knowing the players as I did produced some skepticism, but Alec had great hopes this manager would get through to them. The thought of too little, too late reoccurred, and if only they had practiced like this throughout the autumn, instead of wasting time traveling to Grayson.

Edwards found out from Alec about some of his training methods and tried to get the other pitchers to use them, too. Included were throwing at the tire, more consistent pitching mechanics, moderate throwing everyday, and wearing long sleeves. None of it was received well, nor did these things persuade them to do any work on their own. Instead, the other pitchers avoided working any harder than they had to, just enough to avoid reprimands. Even when it came to running poles, they cheated at every opportunity. In front of Edwards, they behaved well. When he turned his back or was not there, they promptly regressed.

Early in the season, it became apparent the team was not prepared, not physically, not mentally. The players designated as starters assumed they were going to remain starters no matter what happened because they were always a little bit better than the guys behind them were. It had been this way since little league. As far as the two designated starting senior pitchers were concerned, even if they had been aware of their inability to make quality pitches or hit their spots, it would not have caused concern because only one other pitcher could. They would have rightly figured his fastball was not fast enough for the manager to make him the premier starter. Even if it did, the team needed all the pitchers it had. There was little incentive to do more than show up.

The arrogance born of this collective attitude gradually incited a profound displeasure within Edwards as well as with his assistant coaches. Norcross had some very talented players, but their bad habits and lack of motivation were just about impossible to change. A very few saw the potential in these players, or even how this potential could be educed and made kinetic. One real vexing problem was that almost every other parent saw no potential talent at all; they falsely saw the talent as already being applied! The summer had been wasted by giving two football players, who never learned to pitch, most of the pitching assignments. The autumn was wasted traveling to Grayson to play in some short and pointless games when the team could have stayed close to home, playing intra-squad scrimmage games along with extra fielding and hitting drills. Finally, they found themselves in February with no preparation time remaining. Just before the 1999 season began, it was already too late to salvage anything.

Not knowing what is inside the mind and heart of others, one is left to guess by estimating actions and judging dispositions. From preseason conditioning all the way through the last at bat in the final game, the level of commitment displayed by most of the Norcross players made it plain they did not view this season as anything special. It was just like the previous one, and the one before that, and the one before that, etc. There were goals, but none for which these players were willing to increase their effort to achieve. They hoped to reach these goals some way, some how, just so long as it was any way that did not require much extra effort. For the few who may have held a vain hope for a winning season, it quickly evaporated. What should have been a memorable year in the history of Norcross baseball became a testament to indifference.

Given the talent available, a worse season than this one could not have been imagined: nine wins, fourteen losses, and one tie, yes, a tie in baseball, courtesy of time constraints. Most of the starts went to just two of the seniors. Alec pitched sporadically, only about fifteen innings during the entire season, appearing in just five games. His numbers were nothing to brag about, nine earned runs, thirteen hits, eleven strikeouts, and eleven walks. The only argument that could have been made for more innings to pitch was that the other pitchers pitched badly, too. He received starting assignments for a couple of games, and, although he was leading both times and pitching very well, he was pulled early, before earning a decision. The several relief appearances yielded no decisions, either. Sitting on the bench trying to stay ready to pitch is not an easy task. At least Alec got two starts. Five other varsity pitchers got one or none.

Somehow, even when there is limited playing time, baseball often turns out to be a lot of fun. Things may not go the way you want or expect, opportunities may be limited, but, invariably, some things will happen that are worth remembering. This season was no exception.

One of the starts was against Meadowcreek in which Alec gave up two earned runs. With one out in the fourth, the next two batters reached, one with a walk, the other with a single. Edwards pulled him fearing he was getting tired, or maybe wanting to let some other guys pitch that day. We lost the lead quickly; finally losing the game after a last inning comeback was quashed.

Alec's other starting assignment, the third game of the season, was much more memorable. Campbell High School, a school from Smyrna with a team destined to go to the state tournament, visited Norcross on February 27. Norcross was actually playing very well that day, almost looking like a good baseball team. The home faithful were still optimistic about the new season, still hopeful for a winning record, maybe even a trip to the playoffs. After three innings, the Norcross team was leading 5-3. One error led to an unearned run, the other two were earned. To this point, Alec had given up two singles, struck out two, and walked two. Not great, but noticeably better than others had done in the first two games against easier teams which Norcross lost 11-10 and 8-7. For a change, the home team had a lead and looked to keep it.

The fourth inning began most agreeably when the Norcross left-hander struck out the first batter and induced the second to hit a foul pop to the catcher. With two out, Alec walked the next two batters, his pitches not missing by very much. Edwards kept calling for curveballs, one after the other. Maybe the arm was a bit stiff in the cold air, maybe he could not get the right snap of his wrist, maybe the baseball was hard or slick, maybe he could not pull completely through in his motion, maybe the mound dirt was loose, maybe Mars was over Australia, who knows why. He kept missing the mark, usually a little high and away, very unlike him. If Edwards had not been calling the pitches, Alec would have shaken off any curveball signs, staying with what was working that day, the fastball and change-up. However, he did not want to disobey his skipper, in whom he usually had much faith, also thinking he was fortunate enough just to be in the game. This was his first regular season start as a varsity pitcher, after all. Instead of doing what he knew he should do, he kept trying to make the curveballs work.

Edwards should have accepted the fact that the breaking ball was not biting, but he did not. After the two walks, with men on first and second, rather than go back to a change-up and fastball sequence, and with the leadoff man coming up, he decided to go to the bull pen for one of his star seniors. A third loss was to be dreaded this early in the young season. He must keep this lead, and must win this game. Alec had struck out this same leadoff man on three pitches in the first inning. The next time he came up, he popped-up a 1-2 pitch to the shortstop to end the second inning. That Edwards decided to make a pitching change right then, under these circumstances, surprised me. Why had they been throwing breaking balls repeatedly, with two outs and the lead, to the number eight and nine batters?

The reliever, with the aid of his senior experience, threw his first pitch in the dirt bouncing past the catcher allowing both runners to advance. The second pitch was a two run double to the right center field alley, that is, two earned runs for Alec. Three more seniors and the other junior lefty also pitched during the remainder of this seven-inning affair, which Norcross finally lost 13-8.

This was precisely the point at which it became abundantly clear the season would be another bad one. Walking back to the car after the game one of the Campbell coaches came up asking if my son had been injured, assuming that was the reason for the pitching change in the fourth inning. When I told him there was no injury, he said,

"Good thing for us. I don't think we could've beaten him today."

Unquestionably, a nice gesture, but who knows what would have happened. One thing certainly would not have happened. If Alec had been left in the game, and shook off a few signs, Campbell would not have scored ten more runs during the last three innings. When a season is evaluated, especially a short season, very often one single game can be considered a turning point. For this season, the Campbell game was it. This one game could have turned the team and the season in another direction. If Norcross had held on to the lead with good pitching and fielding, much confidence, and increased optimism, would have ensued. Instead, the failure of those senior pitchers, deemed to be the best at Norcross, seemed to cause a deflation in the overall attitude of both the team and its supporters.

During the fourth inning, Alec recognized the trouble he was having with the curveball and should have changed the pitches being called. In this respect, it was his fault. Furthermore, it was a missed opportunity. Had he resisted, had he ended up winning the game, his entire season could well have gone differently. However, it was also true that the manager, by calling pitches from the dugout, assumed some of the responsibility for the results. A day like this one was not a day made for breaking balls. It was a good day for making batters hit off-speed pitches. A cold ball hit on the handle or the end of a cold metal bat gives the batter a high voltage sting that frays every nerve from the fingertips to the shoulders, a tingling feeling that usually remains long enough to affect the next at bat, too. There was no reason to risk walking batters with successive curveballs, especially when no one at the bottom of any high school batting order was going to hit a well-located change-up out of the park.

Nothing was going to go right, or so it seemed, as the season progressed. Finally, something unexpectedly did go right, in a way, but even a mark of success for this Norcross team could not be born without the stain of humiliation. On April 9, they played at home against the Brookwood High School team from Snellville, the third to the last game of the season. Overall, Norcross had eight wins, twelve losses, and one tie. In region play, where it counted, the team had compiled a record of five wins and ten losses. There was only a remote mathematical chance to make the playoffs at this point, so remote that no one even talked about it. Finally, what was already known, or suspected, about the future of the manager, was officially confirmed by an announcement before the game that Edwards was resigning after just two seasons. It did not seem to matter as most of the players were just going through the motions of finishing the season, anyway. This game against Brookwood would not be worth mentioning except for the fact that it was so peculiar.

The Norcross number one senior pitcher threw the complete seven-inning game during which he walked fourteen batters, in addition to giving up several hits and delivering numerous wild pitches. Every pitcher has bad days, no exceptions. This one was his worse ever and, for the good of the game, should have been pulled by the third inning. He was not. In spite of the pitching, Norcross experienced a day when every bounce went their way, no exceptions. Brookwood left so many runners on base during the game that the cumulative number, when stated, seemed incorrect, as if there were more runners left than bases available to be occupied. The Norcross team helped itself immensely by fielders throwing out three runners at home, probably setting a school record in this regard. Brookwood, for its part, repeatedly made base running blunders that lowered every standard imaginable, succumbing to pick-offs and run-downs, or reacting inappropriately for the number of outs. One runner returned to tag third base on a fly ball with two outs. Another kept running after a catch with less than two outs. The quality of play on both sides was, well, if stated diplomatically, it was not one iota short of breathtaking.

Norcross finally did win the game 4-3. Although they would have been hard pressed to beat an enthusiastic bunch of junior high school pony league all-stars that day, they managed to beat a good high school team, one that played pretty well on most days. However, if an unjust reward does more harm than good, the Norcross players would have been better off if they had lost. Be that as it may, the lack of an early pitching change was puzzling. Saying that this pitcher averaged two walks per inning makes it sound much better than it actually was. It is one thing for baseballs to be nearly missing the corners of the strike zone, quite another when they start finding the far corners of the backstop. Control is then no longer the issue. The opposing batters, always anxious to hit the ball, especially during a meaningless, end-of-the-season game, swung freely. Some balls were hit hard, but, on this day, nearly every ball hit by Brookwood went directly to a Norcross fielder.

The obvious question is why the manager left a pitcher in a game while he walked so many batters, had absolutely no control of the baseball, allowed the other team to threaten a lead every inning, and escaped trouble by sheer good fortune in every instance. Other pitchers were available. The fact that the game was won does not validate incorrect managerial decisions.

Perhaps this was just an overly frustrated manager who was at his wits end with his players. Maybe he thought leaving this pitcher in this kind of game would teach him a lesson. Maybe leaving him out there to get his brains beat out would embarrass him, a payback for not having worked harder, and for not living up to the expectations of a senior. Or, maybe, as the game proceeded, the entertainment became just too rich to let it end. With only a couple of games left in the season, and to a coach who was soon to leave, it could not have been for motivational purposes.

After the last out was made and the game was won, the boys were extremely jubilant. The pitcher was congratulated by his teammates for his outstanding performance! No one could ever accuse these Norcross players of knowing much about baseball as this dim celebratory display clearly demonstrated. They should have been happy, but out of a sense of relief rather than by the false belief that they had played a good game. During post game remarks, Edwards, mostly disinterested by this point, took the only reasoned course he could take and gave the pitcher some minimal praise for getting out of jams.

The rest of the season was brief, just a meaningless couple of games with no highlights as mesmerizing as a fourteen-walk, seven inning complete game. Only one more somewhat entertaining episode did occur. The other favorite of the senior pitchers started a game at home against their ever-faithful rival to the north, Duluth High School. This thrower had the fastest fastball combined with the worse control on the staff. Though it made an inelegant combination, it was not enough to instill even a modicum of humility in his young spirit. Overconfidence has a legitimate place in sports when descending from talent and skill, though not from an arrogant demeanor.

This day's performance was slightly worse than his usual with just about every other pitch bouncing in the dirt. The result was several bases-on-balls and runners advancing on wild pitches that could not be contained by the catcher. Norcross made some outs here and there because batters, especially in high school, especially near the end of the season, do not like to walk. Given any kind of a lead and an opponent they dislike, many will swing almost indiscriminately at just about any ball thrown close enough to reach. The game, looking more like a circus as it went, progressed badly for Norcross. An early pitching change was indicated once again. Instead of changing pitchers, however, Edwards started changing catchers!

Norcross went through three catchers. Before a substitution, each catcher was thoroughly rebuked for failing to block the wild pitches. Actually, only the first two were real catchers. The third one was Brett Moon, the third baseman. What a scene. Even before any bull pen activity started, Edwards was calling on position players to come in and catch. Sometimes in an unusually long extra inning game, position players are called on to catch, or even pitch, when everyone else has been used up. To see it happen in this game was just plain weird.

Finally, the bull pen activity started, though it came about not as the result of walks, wild pitches, and more runs scoring. It came about when the other team's players started some of the most outrageous vocal ridicule ever heard in these parts, outrageous even for Duluth, regarded by many as the unofficial champions of landfill-suitable oratory. The taunting got under the skin of the man on the mound to the point where his torment became quite visible; so much for the theoretically reliable, self-confident, experienced, mature, team-leading, football playing senior leadership. The Norcross pitcher became so flustered and angry that he should be so disrespected, he resolved to show them what for. He determined to hit one of their batters. However, when he threw the baseball intentionally at the batter, it went two feet behind him, eluded the catcher's reach, and skipped all the way to the backstop. Two runners advanced and one of them scored.

When something goes wrong on a baseball field, there is nowhere to hide. The ensuing catcalls from the other dugout were almost drowned out by those of the visiting spectators, as some of them (some moms) demanded the umpire do something before somebody got hurt, but to no avail. The umpire, not turning to acknowledge anyone's plea, was trying unsuccessfully to keep himself from laughing behind his mask. This was first-rate entertainment in that such a script could never have been written and performed so well.

So what can you say to your own kid after a game like this?

"Be glad you didn't pitch today, son."

In a game such as this one, a player is better off not having played because it allows him to go home comforted by the knowledge he had nothing at all to do with it.

We had discussed the topic of pitchers intentionally hitting batters before. No other topic about which a father lectures his son gives him a stronger feeling that he is addressing a brick wall. Nevertheless, after this game, we went over it again, not that Alec needed to hear it, but I felt a need to say it. In amateur youth baseball there is never an occasion when it is reasonable or desirable to hit a batter intentionally. Never. In adult amateur baseball, it should happen only in the most unusual circumstances. Even then, it is difficult to justify.

In professional baseball, the intentional hitting of a batter is a very important part of the game. When done, it should only be for a very specific reason. This reason, simply stated, is to define the tolerable limits of behavior during play. When done properly, i.e., when it is measured, equitable, and reasoned, it is universally understood to be a legitimate part of the game. A pitcher does not throw at a batter to inflict serious injury.

The man in the batter's box has a role to play as well. When the baseball's intended (or unintended) flight path intersects the space occupied by the batter, the batter is supposed to know how to get out of the way or how to allow himself to be hit by the ball. When it is intentional, the reasons legitimate, the batter should know beforehand that the occasion has arisen. He should not be surprised. If he is surprised then he is probably not paying attention. In that case, he needs to be hit by a pitch in order to wake him up and he should thank the pitcher for doing him the favor.

Most high school pitchers, sorry to say, do not have enough knowledge and understanding of the game even to begin to think about hitting batters. Most do not know the purpose of the act, nor do they recognize the conditions under which it is appropriate. Furthermore, when they try to hit a batter, it can be an extremely amusing spectacle because often the ball does not go where they intend. It is just plain humiliating for a pitcher to throw at a batter and miss him.

Youngsters, even though they are oblivious to the protocol of hitting batters, think they understand it, especially when they, or one of their teammates, is the one being hit. There is an immediate and uncompromising willingness by the hit batsmen to assume the pitcher did it on purpose regardless of the game situation and regardless of the kind of pitch thrown. At the same time, they seem to regard being hit by a pitcher as elevating their status, as if they are so feared and despised as batters, the opposing pitcher was compelled to throw at them. The immediate response, i.e., attention getting response, is usually feigned outrage with attendant stare-downs, verbal challenges, promised reprisals, hereditary insults, etc. Getting plunked is, for many a high school baseball player, a badge of honor, an event not to be wasted, milked for all it is worth.

Some high school pitchers seem to think that throwing at a batter is a good way to intimidate, as if it were a football game. They may even think it will make them look tough and gain for them the admiration of their teammates. In fact, to those who know baseball, they appear to be something less than venerable. A good, knowledgeable batter does not mind being hit by a pitch because he knows how to take the hit, and the base, and then steal second, and then start stealing signs. How tough does a pitcher look with a man in scoring position and nobody out?

Baseball is a game that cannot be won by egoistic intimidation. Kids should be taught to set vanity aside and focus on skills, good decisions, and execution. Brute strength has limited value, too. Home runs and well-thrown ninety-five mph fastballs are exciting and useful; however, they are only two of many important elements of the game. A sixty mph backdoor curveball that nicks the corner for strike three is also very useful. So is a sacrifice bunt and good slide. Emotion driven actions, rather than being intimidating, often have an opposite effect.

During one summertime varsity game out in Conyers, a powerful player came up to bat for the other team, a big kid, the size and shape of a defensive lineman. He was thrown a perfect pitch to hit and, with a mighty swing, he drilled a solid base hit to right field. Then he paused to beat the head of the bat into the ground in disgust while making oaths, I reckoned for not hitting a home run. Due to his delayed and unhurried trot down the baseline, and to the alertness of the right fielder, the ball was thrown to first base in time for the force out. At this juncture, the young man did not look very intimidating to me, even when he side-kicked his batting helmet into the dugout. In fact, he sort of looked like a silly soccer player.

The manager of the team would have been justified to ask a kid like this to turn in his uniform before leaving the dugout. However, many high school coaches love this kind of player. They regard this kind of behavior as showing toughness, intensity, and leadership. Where does the value of leadership appear amidst needless distractions during a game that requires concentration? Perhaps more thought should be given when defining terms like a take-charge attitude, a real competitor, or a gamer. Of all the qualities a manager needs to have contained within his roster of players, of all the various components needed for pitching, hitting, base running, and defense, the two components that, as always, do not appear as useful tools for devising a successful campaign are foul mouths and bad attitudes.

Alec was used sparingly on the varsity team during his junior year. I surmised that the coaching staff reached the unfortunate conclusion that his pitching was only good for one trip through the batting order based on a belief that the batters would then have figured him out, so to speak. They thought this for one and only one reason: his fastball was not very fast. When the meanings of words are understood though their application is not, it is difficult to construct a useful sentence. These coaches knew what it meant to locate and change speeds. They just had no concept of how it worked. The overpowering and intimidating fastball they understood in both meaning and application, therefore, for them it was an essential part of pitching. No matter where the ball went, as long as it was fast, it was good.

"Rock and fire, baby!"

The theory about one trip through the line-up was statistically not true, as well as illogical. Unfailingly, when a false premise is employed, there will be an unfortunate consequence. A higher cost is always associated with the inability to bridge knowledge and understanding. In this case, one might say, the plaintiff was convicted by the ignorance contained within his own testimony. Saying the batters could figure Alec out after one trip through the order was an admission that, indeed, there was something about his pitching that had to be figured out. This fact alone put him above the rest of the pitching staff because no one else could make quality pitches. There was nothing of the others to figure out.

Batters, when facing a pitcher unable to locate and change speed, and with no more than a low 80's mph fastball, adopt a very simple strategy: see the ball, hit the ball. Only a pitcher who has a variety of quality pitches is capable of giving a batter a different look every time up. If batters are successful in making crucial adjustments to these pitches, then the problem is not with the pitcher, it is with the pitch sequence. In the case where the manager insists on calling pitches from the dugout, the circumstances cannot be expected to improve by calling on a different arm to enter the game. The better result can be had by calling on a different thought process, or on a different brain, to decide which pitches to throw.

Very few men, even those who ardently follow baseball, including most youth coaches, truly understand pitching. The misunderstanding comes from not knowing what the roll of the pitcher is. First of all, pitchers do not win games with their pitching. A pitcher can only help his team to win games. A pitcher can strike out twenty-seven batters in a row, but that will not win the game. The one crucial question to ask about a pitcher is how well he does in giving his team a good chance to win within his limited sphere of influence. Even with a decent ERA, if two out of every four runs scored by opponents are unearned, what else can a pitcher do other than come to bat and hit a grand slam to make up the difference. Even then he needs teammates to get on base before him.

The reason there is a considerable prejudice against control pitchers and their style of pitching comes not only from a lack of understanding about the value of what they are trying to do. Sometimes it is due to the lack of good defensive players. Control pitchers such as Glavine, Maddux, and Moyer are not going to get many strikeouts. They do not usually look to strike out the batter. Instead, they look to keep the ball in the park thereby necessitating good defensive play. When a team does not have good defensive players, the obvious default position is to use pitchers who throw hard, those who look for strikeouts. These pitchers usually have a higher number of walks, too. Such a strategy can actually work, at least in theory, as long as the strikeouts and walks come in almost equal numbers. By alternating strikeouts and walks, three outs can be had before runs start walking in. Crucial to the success of this approach will always be the necessity to avoid contact, and that is its downfall. With two men on, two men out, if the opponents start hitting the baseball to a weak defense, the result is not going to be good.

Norcross lacked good defensive players and it became abundantly clear that the coaches loathed seeing the other team's batters make contact of any kind. Norcross chose not to work on defensive skills very much; rather they emphasized weight training, hoping to generate more offense. Their basic pitching strategy became thus: throw hard, forget about defense, and out-slug the other team. Metal bats play a large contributory role in this abysmal way of thinking. Predictably, it did not work very well because it precluded using all the talents that were available. Like an exhausted swimmer continuing to stroke against a rip current, this unfortunate course was pursued with fruitless vigor. For the coaches, so skewed was their thinking, even a well-hit foul ball caused them concern.

A well-hit foul ball is an indication that the batter's timing is off. It indicates nothing else. It is analogous to throwing a beautiful pass in football to a receiver who is out of bounds. Who cares? Instead of being alarmed by a solidly hit foul ball, credit should be given to the pitcher for giving a batter a ball to hit, but one that he could not time well enough to hit into fair territory. Moreover, when there is a well-hit foul ball, a knowledgeable control pitcher gains the upper hand because he has just crafted a very good set-up pitch. The batter is primed to swing at the next pitch if it looks the same, thus he can more easily be fooled by movement or speed change. Unfortunately, when a strategy is built on illogic, one mistaken conclusion follows another. When a pitcher allows a well-hit foul ball, what is the Norcross solution? I suppose it is to bring in another pitcher who can straighten it out.

For most of the 1999 season, starting even before the Campbell game, the performance on the field was pitiful. The attitude in the dugout was no better. As losing causes go, this one began tepidly, gradually becoming hopeless. About halfway through the season, after one particularly pathetic loss, Edwards' frustration showed through when he told the players something to the effect that they were a bunch of

Norcross losers and that was all they would ever be. What did the junior lefty pitcher think about the substance of these post game remarks?

"Edwards was right."

Without a doubt, he was right. Maybe he should not have said it quite this way. Maybe it would have been better to say something more constructive and reassuring, such as,

"You are all cut from the team. Leave your uniforms in the dugout. The freshmen and sophomores are going to finish out the varsity season."

When Edwards officially announced his intention to resign at the end of the season, the current varsity players knew they would soon have their third varsity manager, assuming that the school could find someone dumb enough to take the job. Who in the world would want to coach baseball at Norcross High School at this point? The answer was nobody very good. The athletic director, esteemed yet non-compliant, decided, over the strenuous objections of just about every parent, to give the job to the inexperienced junior varsity coach. The parents had no one to offer as an alternative. However, this was a case where no one may very well have been a better choice.

Pitching in five games with a couple of starts qualified Alec for a varsity letter. In spite of the team's terrible record, he was as proud of this letter as he was of anything else that had ever come his way. After putting aside thoughts of all the malarkey that went on this season, it made me proud, too. Very, very proud. Norcross High School baseball was heading for the dumpster, but my kid had earned his varsity letter. It was well earned, indeed, and just in time, too. Effectively dealing with many things in life often means having to separate the good from the bad, the useful from the useless, the meaningful from the insignificant. A job well done can be its own reward, made better when the effort is large and more satisfying when recognition follows.

Throughout the late spring of 1999, Alec played on a revived NDY team out of the deteriorating Wingo-Carlyle Field. By design, more than half their games were played away on better fields. Some of his high school teammates were also on that team including his favorite catcher, Dubberly, left-handed pitcher Dodson, and center fielder Gray. Once again, Alec was the most used and most durable of the four or five pitchers on the team. He pitched twenty-four innings, started in five games, and had a record of four wins and one loss. Best of all, they were having a real good time playing baseball again, something not happening at the high school. However, these good times abruptly ended, too.

When the manager picked his team to play in the state tournament he told Alec he would not be used as a starter and maybe not at all, only if needed as a last resort. Performance did not matter once again. They were going to use the harder throwing pitchers, in spite of their worse records. Once again, rather than waste the time and effort, he did not accompany the team down to Augusta. Once again, the team that did go embarrassed both themselves and the Norcross baseball community. The generation of "Norcross losers" had already begun to perpetuate itself.

The new varsity manager for Norcross High School was appointed just in time to take over the Connie Mack summer team. Disillusionment continued to reign among players and parents. It became evident that Alec would not get to pitch much when, as a rising senior, he was only used for three innings during the first seven games. The fact that he was this manager's best junior varsity pitcher as a sophomore did not matter. With Edwards gone, the program under new management, there was another new definition of what a high school pitcher should be. Created in his own image and likeness, the ideal for this manager's starting rotation was a position player with a good bat who could throw hard. Good control meant getting half the pitches somewhere inside the strike zone. There was no room for finesse. Location and speed change? What is that all about? Aim it down the middle and maybe hit a corner every once in a while. Just keep throwing the ball hard until too tired or too sore.

The three innings he did pitch, before he got around to quitting the team, were interesting, however. The first appearance was a mid-inning relief over at Parkview High School. Norcross was losing 8-3 in the bottom of the fifth inning with men on first and second bases, and no outs when Alec was summoned from the bull pen. His first pitch produced a very desirable easy-hop ground ball to third that should have been a double play if the turn had been handled cleanly by the second baseman. Instead, it yielded a 5-4 fielder's choice. With runners at first and third, the next batter grounded an 0-1 pitch to the first baseman for the unassisted out. This allowed the runner from third base to score. Now with two outs and a runner on second base, the batter was right-hander Jeff Francouer. The first pitch was up and in, a slider, which he fouled off. The next pitch was on the outside corner at the knees. He reached for it, tried to pull it, and chopped a grounder towards third.

Instead of stepping to his left to field the ball, the Norcross third baseman inexplicably darted to his right as if to cover his base, which allowed the ball to dribble into left field. It was the strangest reaction by an infielder one could imagine, almost as if he never saw the ball, or did not know the situation, or both.

The runner at second was not forced to run, nor was he attempting a steal. Parkview players know not to risk making the third out of an inning at third base. The left fielder charged the weakly hit grounder and the runner from second had to stop at third. He had every reason to expect the third baseman to field the ball and, not wanting to run into a tag, paused momentarily before advancing so that a presumed throw would have to be made to first base. Or maybe he paused in total bafflement, stunned by what he was seeing. When the count reached 2-1 on the next batter, Alec looked at Gray playing center field and indicated the ball was coming his way. He was not going to take another chance with these infielders! The batter swung at the next pitch, a change-up high in the strike zone, hitting a fly ball to straight away center, to the exact spot where Gray was standing, for the third out. Gray took two steps back, but then had to take two steps forward to make the catch. He could have just stood still.

"Good shot, kid."

Alec went out to start the sixth inning and struck out the first batter on three pitches. For him, this was an act of total contempt for his manager, the fact that he dared to throw an 0-2 strike. He was pulled from the game forthwith. Greg Hunt was called to finish up, concluding another loss. Greg, a sophomore, was Jeff's younger brother and the second of four Hunt boys, good baseball players all.

Eight days later Alec got to pitch his last inning for the Norcross High School baseball team. The new manager was busy trying to convert infielders with strong arms into pitchers. His brand of baseball, to put his hardest throwers on the mound and focus on out-slugging the other team, was on full display. On this day, they had a double header, six innings apiece, against a middling group from Dacula High School. Alec had the reasonable expectation that he would surely get to start one of the games. He did not. Instead of starting, he was put into the first game to pitch the last inning. Norcross was losing 5-3 after five innings. The first batter he faced laced a solid double to the gap in right center. Not a good way to begin as the pitch was up in the strike zone and caught too much of the plate.

Nevertheless, in his usual undaunted fashion that had become his trademark, he checked the miserable defense, adjusted his cap, spit on the ground, put his left foot on the rubber, looked in for the sign, and entered the stretch. His pitching was always done in the most serious manner and so it was here. There was no time to waste in thinking about how his status on the roster had been downgraded. The fact that his team was on the verge of oblivion could not be considered, either. The few good infielders had just graduated and, from what he knew of this group, including their play at Parkview the week before and since, he could not count on their ability to help him get outs, certainly not with infielders breaking away from ground balls and dropping the ball before making the turn at second. In this game, Norcross would have one more chance at the bat. Being down two runs, he knew he could not afford to give up any more.

Totally unappreciated by Norcross coaches and disregarded by most everyone else in his dugout, Alec knew he was universally respected by the teams and batters he faced. When parents of opposing players seek out the father of a pitcher after a game to pay compliments, it tends to assuage the disdain acquired for the home team manager. Nothing changes, but it tends to lift the spirits. The stark baseball reality of what was going on was easily understood, it was unalterable, and it was disgusting.

The situation in this Dacula game set a perfect stage for exiting the climactic tragedy of a once proud baseball heritage, now furiously sinking to a new and abysmal nadir. What I, and anyone who knew anything about baseball, saw standing on the mound was something rarely seen in the high school game. It was the personification of authentic senior leadership and experience. He was the exact kind of senior player that freshmen and sophomore players, especially pitchers, should be asked to emulate, for his skill, for his work ethic, for his knowledge and dedication to the game. He was precisely the kind of senior this Norcross team desperately needed at this time. He deserved to be honored by his coaches. Instead, he was being discarded. To his everlasting credit, none of this was allowed to influence the way he pitched. He stood there alone, looked in to get Dubberly's sign, and then efficiently retired the next three batters, striking out the side with twelve pitches, leaving the one base runner stranded on second base. Norcross did not score in the bottom half of the inning; consequently, the game was lost. I did not know if the manager would want to use him again in the second game, but, even if he did, I would never have allowed it. To risk his arm in such a way was unthinkable, certainly not for the sake of this manager's team.

Alec packed his equipment bag after the first game and left. After about an hour discussion, he decided to quit the team. The facts were simple and straightforward. He was not going to pitch much this summer if he stayed on the team. He was the best pitcher on the team, actually the only pitcher who could pitch in the true sense of the word. Staying aboard would be a frustrating waste of time. In addition to regular games nearby, a week-long trip was planned to a high school tournament in Carrollton, Georgia, a trip for which I was not about to pay unless there was some reason to expect that he would be used as a starter. This was not going to happen. Hence, it would have been ridiculously wasteful to contribute money and spend time for the benefit of lesser ballplayers on a poorly managed team. At the core of the situation lay this basic fact: without a pitcher, there was no baseball team. Without Alec, there was no pitcher.

Recognizing reality may have alleviated some of the built up angst, but still, when left with no choice other than to quit his summer high school baseball team, it was not a happy occasion. It probably meant the end of his high school baseball career, too. However, without a manager and with no pitching, Norcross baseball was essentially dead. What was the point in staying? Returning to the field after the second game was over, walking into the dugout amidst his teammates, quieted, heads hung low after losing another, all beginning to realize the rest of the summer would bring nothing but baseball misery, he told the manager he was quitting. The coach made no response at all. On the bright side, this lonely act of resolve offered a glimmer of hope to those remaining; there was, after all, a way to escape. My fees already paid to the dugout club for the summer season were refunded promptly.

"Thank you very much and here is his jersey back, barely used. It probably doesn't even need to be washed."

Growing up into a man has its challenges, no doubt, sometimes more than is necessary. First lesson is to recognize reality, to let go when there is nothing worthwhile to hold. Second lesson is to maintain a stance, to display resolve and leadership, even when others deem it to be unduly assertive. Alec somehow understood that being a willing hostage to cowardice is not a manly pursuit. The situation into which he and his team had plunged was simpler to understand than it was to accept, especially for a youngster. Here was a bunch of high school boys, hoping to participate on a sports team, victimized by an unqualified coach who was installed by a wayward athletic director and who plainly blamed the parents for the mess he helped to create. Whether the A.D. could have found a better manager was doubtful. In any case, his own termination was now justified. The athletic department needed new leadership. Not surprisingly, the principal did not agree when the suggestion was made.

This script read as if a first act for a horror movie except that its reality was less believable than most fiction. If someone had determined to ruin a high school baseball program, he could not have found a better way to go about it. Nothing could be done to change course, either. If an athletic director and baseball manager do not recognize their deficiencies by yielding to the suggestions of their betters, there is no rational alternative except to withdraw and move on. Certain men in certain positions, especially those in government or other public institutions, cannot be easily removed. Men such as these are best left to stew in their own juices. The least productive use of valuable time is to attempt to reason with them, to work with them, or to cooperate with them. Incompetence is just what it is, obdurately useless.

Being the first victim of these unfortunate circumstances could have caused a sense of martyrdom. Not here, though. As it turned out, the other players, the ones who chose to stay, continued to suffer. They became the real victims. Leaving ahead of the crowd actually had some advantages. During the months to come, several others made it to the exit. The ones who stayed were treated to needless humiliation and frustration beyond what any youngster should ever endure. The failures of a couple of men, the severe and widespread damage they inflicted, would eventually affect hundreds of boys. The destruction of the Norcross High School baseball program was not very pretty and it took many years to build it back.

*Chapter Fourteen*

# Major League Tryouts

As goes everything else in life, baseball has its ups and downs, too. The summer of 1999 appeared to be over, as far as playing opportunities were concerned, when it had only just begun. The junior year of high school was successfully completed. The next important task now appeared to be college applications, not summer or fall baseball. The young left-handed pitcher who loved the game faced a completely unanticipated situation. Without knowing the future, and the limitless possibilities now held there in abeyance, it would have been easy give it up. Frustration surmounts contentment with the greatest of ease. Happily, at times like this, with just a modest change in focus, anticipation can revive self-confidence just as quickly.

Alec had been throwing a baseball nearly every day for a decade. He had appeared in sixty-five official games, as a starter in twenty-six and a reliever in thirty-nine, compiling a record of twelve wins, twelve losses, and four saves. He had pitched 177 and 1/3 innings, faced 836 batters, and thrown 2,482 pitches of which 1,621 (sixty-five percent) were strikes. For the first time in a long time, he had to go look for a place to play. As a left-handed pitcher who could locate and change speeds, this was not going to be a problem. The questions of when and where to start looking had obvious answers, in his mind, anyway: right away and at the top.

Rising very early the next morning, following the Dacula doubleheader episode, he went to see the Atlanta Braves open tryout camp. The tryout was being held at the Georgia State University baseball field on Panthersville Road in south DeKalb County. A couple days earlier, an announcement appeared in the newspaper for the camp. Facts like this never escaped his attention or his memory. Besides, a desire to see a major league tryout seemed to be a very normal prod of curiosity for a high school baseball player, so normal as to make one wonder why such an event was not attended by many other high school players. Were they not at all curious about what went on in a professional tryout?

Scouting for professional baseball players must be the most thoroughly comprehensive enterprise in the free or oppressed world, including the Central Intelligence Agency's cataloging of this nation's enemies. If a player is good, he will be found. However, if a player thinks he has been overlooked, he does not have far to go to correct the omission. Major league teams hold tryouts all summer long. They begin immediately following the amateur draft in early June. These summertime camps are so numerous that a young player from a place like Georgia could attend a tryout nearly every day within the state of Georgia or one of the bordering states of Florida, Alabama, Tennessee, North Carolina, and South Carolina. By doing so, he would be seen by scouts from practically every major league team, the Major League Scouting Bureau, independent leagues, and many colleges, too. As might be imagined, such gatherings produce very interesting spectacles, both informative and entertaining. As one of baseball's truly unique traditions, the ubiquitous professional baseball tryout camp is a show that does not disappoint, one that every high school baseball player should witness.

Rarely did I allow work at the office to interfere with baseball though an important meeting happened to be scheduled later in the morning. Truthfully, not wanting to go along, it was best, under the circumstances, for Alec to go by himself. In light of the events of the previous evening, it would be a chance to figure out what next to do with baseball, perhaps an opportunity to forget the fact that he quit the one major achievement of his young life. Having reached the once seemingly unattainable goal of playing on the high school team, it was discarded like yesterday's newspaper. Besides, it looked like rain all day; the tryout would likely be cancelled.

Returning home in the afternoon came one excited former high school pitcher. What could be so good about a rainy day at the ballpark? The first thing to happen, Alec ran into some recently graduated seniors and a few college players he knew. While the rains came down they gathered in the dugouts, talking while waiting to see what the scouts decided. What else is there to do in a dugout full of baseball prospects? Maybe fill out a prospect card? Sure, why not?

It rained enough to postpone the fielding and batting parts of the scheduled workouts. While the mound and home plate areas were covered with tarps, the rest of the field was thoroughly soaked. Position players were invited to attend the tryout scheduled in Macon the next day. However, between the downpours, Braves' scouts Al Goetz and Rob English, managed to look at the pitchers. When his turn came, the rising high school senior, a mere twelve hours after being disregarded by his high school team, took the mound.

Incredible, how some young men have the capacity not to be deterred by anything. Daring to perform along with very talented, older players in front of professional scouts was difficult to imagine. Feeling not at all nervous or intimidated, for Alec, the experience seemed as pleasant as playing catch in the backyard. The way he related the story confirmed it. He thoroughly enjoyed himself, not feeling out of place the least bit. One player was made to feel a lot out of place when he made the mistake of pulling a metal bat out of his equipment bag in the presence of one of the scouts. The verbal harangue that followed was not likely ever to be forgotten by anyone present in the ballpark that day. The offending implement was removed to the parking lot to be locked in the trunk of a car. This tryout was for "real" baseball, not schoolboy baseball. Only wood was welcome.

Al Goetz, a well-known baseball instructor in the area, doubled as a Braves' scout and directed the tryout. Mr. Goetz was part owner of an indoor baseball training facility located in Duluth called, "The Ballpark." Alec recognized some of the players, those with whom he had played against in high school and recreational leagues. One was a former Parkview player who was currently playing shortstop for the University of Georgia, Jeff Keppinger. Jeff eventually made it to the major leagues with the Mets. The rain delay provided an opportunity to talk extensively with some of the other players, learning much about what was going on with their baseball careers, a good experience, to be sure. This part of Alec's narrative was all very interesting as background information. The main question was how he actually had the nerve to take the mound at a major league tryout with his mid-sixties mph fastball. Asking a question to which the answer is already known is done so mainly to hear the form and tenor of a reply, to better share in the experience.

After warming up, the lefty was called out to the mound. Goetz watched him throw for a while, about twenty to twenty-five pitches altogether. Goetz also asked questions regarding his age, where he had pitched, etc. Then he proposed trying a few pitches with different grips that made the ball do different things. The evaluation that followed contained much encouragement to keep pitching, to keep working out, and, most of all, to keep throwing long toss in order to build velocity. Finally, Goetz told him to come back next year after finishing high school because he had good stuff and wanted to see him again.

Then came a pitch-by-pitch account of what he did, followed by a meticulous analysis of what the other pitchers did, too. All the others were all harder throwers. Although they had much better location control than most high school pitchers, most could not hit spots consistently, even with their fastballs. Many of the curveballs were bouncing in the dirt. He was surprised that no one else had a good change-of-pace.

The catchers generally started out placing their mitts right over the middle of the plate and moved to catch the balls, which were often missing the target. Since Alec was accustomed to pitching at targets on the edges of the strike zone, he requested that the catcher move his mitt back and forth, which he did.

The mental image was easily created. Here he was, a still-growing high school rising senior who looked much younger than his years, amidst a group of college players and former minor leaguers, most of whom were into their twenties, taller, bigger, with much more experience, and, after just being practically dismissed by his own high school team the night before, was standing on a mound pitching for scouts from the best team in the National League, while giving the catcher instructions about where he wanted the mitt to be placed. There is nothing quite like a well-coached ball-playing kid. He was that, thanks to Ro Fitten.

Alec reported hitting his targets consistently, as well as he had ever done. The fastball velocity, as recorded by a Juggs radar gun, reached sixty-five mph, so they said, more of a vent fan than a heater. No doubt, he stood out as an oddity. For this kid at this moment, the experience had been great because not only was he treated with respect by Goetz, he listened to and conversed with the other pitchers discovering many things about their backgrounds in baseball.

There may be a curiosity about such a situation for those never having been in it. Once a group of baseball players is in the same dugout pursuing a similar purpose, they tend to become like teammates. Looking inside the dugouts at a major league all-star game confirms this phenomenon. A couple of days earlier, the same fellow one player would have happily spiked in a slide, or mowed down in front of home plate, or brushed back with chin music, is given hearty congratulations for his home run.

From this place, Alec came away with a feeling of having attained somewhat of a peerage among these ballplayers, not so much in skill level, but in purpose. Going down to this tryout allowed him to have an important, though brief, association with an unusual array of young men, all of whom loved to play baseball, all of whom played better than any of his former teammates could do. He gained from them a new and clear perspective from which came an interesting rhetorical question. What exactly did he leave behind the night before inside the dugout at Norcross High School and how much was it worth?

These fellows at the tryout had a totally different outlook on the game. They thought about baseball more the way he did, with a seriousness of purpose, accompanied by a greater respect for both the game and for each other. The contrast was enormous and it was impressive. His high school team, on the one hand, was void of any semblance of real baseball commitment, but in this Georgia State University dugout, there was a full complement of accomplished and knowledgeable young baseball players, committed to improving their skills, to playing the game well.

The time and the effort taken to go see something better in baseball paid immediate dividends. This personal glimpse into the world of advanced baseball, one that had only existed in his imagination up to this point, relieved him of all the indignity imparted by the Norcross baseball coaches. How ironic that this single enriching experience, unlikely and unplanned, all occurred before noon, before most of his former teammates were even out of bed. His previous position on the varsity baseball team, hard won and once highly valued, regrettably left behind the night before, now seemed like nothing at all.

The best baseball players in Norcross played on Sundays at Wingo-Carlyle Field in the Liga de Beisbol Hispanos Unidos, commonly referred to as the Hispanic League. The players were mostly Spanish speaking adult men from all parts of Latin America. Spanish was the language spoken on the field by the players, the umpires, and most of the spectators. They played nine-inning games except that double headers were sometimes seven-innings apiece depending largely on the terms they could cajole the umpires to accept. The most unfortunate aspect of this league, besides the poor condition of the field, was they normally used metal bats. The league's six teams contained players matching all levels of baseball skills. The best nine would have made up an excellent semi-professional team. The current Norcross High School team would have struggled if it played in this league, without doubt they would have compiled a losing record. When the unemployed left-hander went there looking for a pitching job, the Hispanic League was about halfway through their season.

On a Sunday morning in early July, watching the first game of a double header between the Yankees and the Framers, it appeared the Yankees were more short-handed and more in need of another pitcher. Only eleven players were visible in their dugout while the other team had about eighteen. Near the end of the first game, it seemed to be a good time to visit the Yankees' dugout. The manager was called Luis Alfonzo Garcia. When told a pitcher wanted to play on his team he looked puzzled, almost annoyed at the interruption. They were losing in the late innings of the first game and had another one to go. Baseball managers do not like to be bothered at such times.

Before he could think of a good excuse to reject the notion of looking at a very young kid, well, why not watch him throw a few in the bull pen. Mr. Garcia went back into the dugout to take care of the last half inning of the game while Alec started to warm up. Garcia came back out after about five minutes as the whole team gathered around him to watch. Fastball on the outside corner, fastball on the inside corner, curveball down and away. What else would you like to see?

"How about the curveball again?"

Garcia turned to go into the dugout and came back right away holding a league registration form and a liability release, written in Spanish. He pointed to the commissioner over in the scorer booth, the same one where Hankins and I had watched "The Game" between the Norcross Red and Blue teams two years before. We were to turn in the signed documents with sixty-five dollars and, oh, by the way, can the kid start the next game?

"What'd you say your name was?"

"Alejandro."

He pitched six innings to earn the win giving up six hits, all singles, with only one earned run. He also struck out five and walked two. The rest of the summer and early fall was spent playing with the Hispanic Yankees, a great playing opportunity, much better than would have been the case with his old team. The Norcross High School team finished their summer season around July 1. The Hispanic League season went on into the autumn, which meant much more baseball as well as a much more convenient location. The style of play was very different, too. Here the game was played by men with an adolescent affinity for the game, but whose baseball skills were mature. Thus, the quality of play was far better than anything the school team had to offer, and getting better all the time.

Nonetheless, rejoining his former teammates continued to be an enticement, regardless of the type or level of baseball. The high school manager could be ignored, too, since he was irrelevant. When school started in August, Alec decided he would show up for the January tryouts and try to play his senior year, while ignoring the fact that the team's outlook was dismal. Alec wanted to play for his school and with his friends. That part made sense.

Joe Testa managed a fall team, again, and they were planning another season at the "Field of Dreams" in Grayson, one destined to turn into a nightmare. I expressed my reservations, again, and suggested my perennial alternative: get the boys together every day after school and run practices, along with two or three intra-squad scrimmage games each weekend with umpires, or even invite other teams to come over. It would have been a much more prudent use of money and time. Most of all, it would have emphasized the need to improve playing skills that were seriously lacking. No one cared for the idea.

"What lack of skills? They need to play games."

The prime objective was to play games against other teams from other schools. They wanted to go to Grayson because other teams in the county were going to play there, too.

"Everybody was going to go there."

Another forceful part of the argument was that those fields had lights so they could play evening games during the week, whereas our school field had no lights. Wingo-Carlyle Field had lights, but making this point caused no reaction whatsoever. The Norcross town field was, truthfully, in extremely poor condition, worse than the fields at Grayson, though not by much.

To say I was totally disgusted with Norcross High School baseball would be delicately gracious. No reason existed to participate in or contribute to the dugout club this year until, and unless, Alec was given a prominent position on the spring team. Meanwhile, word had it that Renz was losing so much money on their "Field of Dreams," they sold it, or abandoned it, or gave it away to someone else to manage. A few stories emerged that partially explained the situation although it was never made entirely clear what actually happened. Apparently, the new proprietors, who ever they were, took money from the teams and failed to pay their electric bill so, without lights, weekday evening games were not possible. An attempt was made to start earlier and shorten the games, but logistics roundly foiled this alternative. Finally, even the Saturday games had to be cancelled because they did not have umpires, concessions, bathroom facilities, or running water. Baseball is a game, but it is also a business. Money is essential, even if brains are not. When you run out of both, though, it is a dismal sight to behold.

Alec and I started to meet at the ball field almost every day late in the afternoon, whenever I could get away from the office. I had a key to the gate, as did some of the other fathers who had volunteered their time to keep the field maintained. The day after the Labor Day weekend, we were confronted with "No Trespassing" signs and new locks on the gates, courtesy of the athletic director and probably at the suggestion of the varsity manager. This ill-mannered dictate was definitely directed at us since we were the only ones who ever used the field. Nevertheless, baseball demands perseverance. The posted warnings were duly ignored as we adroitly and unabashedly climbed over the fence. Our trespasses continued until early in January when the manager either decided on his own (unlikely), or was told by the A.D. (likely), to deal with our flagrantly criminal behavior. A minimal confrontation ensued. He spouted some drivel about insurance and I wondered why they were never concerned about insurance when we dads came to shovel dirt and repair fences on workdays. As there was no one present with which a worthy argument could be made, we left and went over to Wingo-Carlyle Field to work out. It was about a half-mile closer to home, anyway.

The late January tryouts finally came. Alec went fully expecting to be on the team, especially since they badly needed pitching. On the last day, the manager called each of the players into his office to individually hand out uniforms. When Alec went in, he was told the team had all the pitching it needed. Since he was a senior, it did not make sense carrying a pitcher on the roster who would sit on the bench all season being only seldom used, if at all. Arriving home, entering the kitchen, mostly looking stunned, he simply said,

"I got cut."

I thought to myself, "Thank God for small favors!"

During the previous summer, after Alec quit, the Norcross team proved a disaster, unmitigated and abject. They played so badly that the last few games were cancelled due to lack of interest, imagine that! The continuation of the program was even in jeopardy. Morale became so low that the players did not even want to go to games, forget about practices. Since the few decent players had graduated the previous spring, those who remained were in great need of training. Above all else, they needed pitching.

The manager must have realized he was in trouble right away evidenced by the way he scheduled games for the coming regular season. Norcross was in the highest of the five classifications of schools in Georgia, which was determined by student body size. The lowest classification was occupied mostly by small private schools with just a few hundred students. Many of those had to use just about every boy in the school to fill up the rosters of their football, basketball, and baseball teams. Sometimes they only had enough for a varsity and junior varsity team, omitting the freshman team altogether.

Every school belonging to the Georgia High School Association was required to play a certain number of games within their own region and within their own classification to be eligible for post-season tournaments. The rest of the schedule for baseball, usually between one-third and one-half of all the games to be played, was discretionary. The Norcross manager succeeded in scheduling discretionary games against schools mostly in the lowest two classifications and the very weakest teams he could find.

This took care of their win/lose record, but not their pitching. The plan for pitching remained approximately the same, use a few infielders and outfielders who had high velocity arms, then rely mostly on hitting to outscore the opponent. In terms of baseball logic, this kind of thinking had limited utility besides being rather idiotic, though it fit this situation as well as anything could. With limited talent, very inadequate defensive skills, no inclination to work on improvement, and a lack of manly resolve, the manager, with the concurrence of the athletic director, chose to play easier teams, the easiest ones they could find.

Enough small schools were available to give the team a .500 season. One might think it would be difficult to get smaller schools to schedule a game with a larger school. Not so. Utilizing a concept foreign to Norcross High School baseball at that time, many small schools welcomed the greater challenge of playing a larger school. A tried and true way to improve is to play better teams, even though the challenge of playing the Norcross team for these other schools may not have turned out to be as great as they had expected. However, they cannot be faulted for being unaware of how meager Norcross baseball had become.

The season slogged on. Fortunately or not, for Norcross, in this one year the playoffs were expanded to include more teams. Within their own region, Norcross managed to secure the eighth and last playoff spot out of eleven teams, barely edging out three other very weak teams. For a team that needed no more pitching, and played the easiest schedule possible, they still gave up an average of more than one run per inning during the season. Rather than being a season ending honor, making the high school playoffs for Norcross only meant becoming first round cannon fodder for one of the legitimate playoff caliber teams. Predictably, the enfilade of shot and canister was brief, and each report perfectly clear.

The culmination of their campaign came without more ado in the Region Eight playoffs which took place at South Gwinnett High School in Snellville. Each region playoff round was a three-game series, two wins needed to advance to the next round. The first day featured a double-header with a third game, if needed, on the following day. Norcross lost the first two games by something called the "slaughter rule." Some call it the "mercy rule." It could just as well be called the "self-esteem rule" because, when employed, it stanches the continuing loss thereof in the event any of this substance remains. Whatever this rule is called, it causes a game to be ended after five innings if one team is ahead by ten runs or after three innings if the lead is fifteen runs. In the later case, the losing school is assured at least one complete trip through their batting lineup. If the home team is the one performing the slaughter, the last half-inning is not played. Even so, they would have sent a minimum of twenty-one batters to the plate during their two turns at the bat.

In the first game, South Gwinnett, as the home team, took the win without having to bat in the third inning. Another way to describe the Norcross playoff pitching performance, South Gwinnett batted around three times in two innings. In the second game, the Norcross nine played much better, treading water until the middle of the fifth inning. If this was not humiliating enough, disrespect for an opponent reached a new level in the history of Gwinnett County high school sports as reported in the Gwinnett Daily Post the next day. In a post-game interview, the South Gwinnett manager praised his players for their efforts in the first game. However, he personally and emphatically took *the blame* for the second game saying he had made an incorrect pitching decision that allowed the game to last four and a half innings before winning by the slaughter rule again. To put this debacle in a broader perspective, South Gwinnett proceeded to win Region Eight, but did not advance in the District rounds. Their team was good when compared to other teams in the region, a very weak region this particular year, but not so good when compared to other region winners around the state. As for the playoff team with "all the pitching we need," the Norcross pitching aces gave up an average of five runs per inning that day.

Thanks to the combined efforts of the athletic director, the varsity manager, and the dugout club, what should have been a memorable and rewarding experience for young baseball players became an unmitigated disaster. There is no other nice way to put it. Norcross High School had now reached the lowest point in its baseball history, as low as anyone alive could recall. Alec was very fortunate not to have been a part of it. If the manager thought having accomplished a .500 season would justify his continuation in this job, a group of incensed parents, perpetually looking for someone else to blame for the inadequacies of their own sons, did not. Before the A.D. could use this win/lose record as a defense, he heard an earful. Therefore, rather than try to defend his head varsity baseball manager, he changed tack and insisted that it was his policy to give every coach a minimum three years before reevaluating his status. This was something he would not change.

How brilliantly detached a man may imagine himself to be when he relies upon an institutionalized policy, a policy of which he is the author, no less, instead of an exercised judgment commensurate with his position. Actually, this three-year rule is a very useful bureaucratic device in a clever sort of way. It corresponds with the natural turnover rate of parents as their kids graduate. Most of the parents are gone after two years of varsity. After three years, everyone is gone, and a whole new batch has arrived. As a ruse, it should have worked, but in circumstances so dire, it failed. Following the 2000 season (the next year), the baseball parents would not back down. They kept up the pressure and after this manager's second season, a new manager was hired. The change coincided with a move to a brand new high school building on Spalding Drive, a move that some others viewed as an opportunity for everyone to start anew, that is, everyone except those recently graduated student baseball players who could never go back and relive their high school years.

Time proved that not playing baseball for Norcross in his senior year was, indeed, the best thing that could have happened. Soon after being cut from the team, Alec, following my suggestion, looked into playing with a team in the Atlanta Men's Adult Baseball League. The MABL was the league for men age eighteen and over within the Men's

Senior Baseball League (MSBL), a national organization of local amateur and semi-professional baseball leagues. The older age groups of the MSBL were somewhat competitive, but the participants played mostly for recreation. The younger players of the MABL, on the other hand, could sometimes be very serious, with a brand of baseball that was fairly decent, typically better than high school, though usually not quite as good as college.

The league held a tryout at Chamblee High School in early February. Alec was the only high school senior there. The players were mostly in their twenties. Most all had high school experience with many having played in college. Some had played semi-pro ball and a few had even been in the minor leagues. For the young lefty, it was another good experience to be on the field with grown-ups. They were there to play some grown-up recreational baseball, quite a different situation than playing ball with school kids. Alec tried out as an outfielder and as a pitcher. The outcome was grand as he joined in forming a new team to be called the Orioles. The manager was Greg Willis.

Being on a new team had both good and bad points. It was good in that there was no established order for positions. Everyone was starting fresh. In all likelihood, Alec would have many opportunities to pitch. A bad part was that nearly none of their players, being new to the league, had played recently. It would take some time for them to get back in shape, maybe the whole summer. Meanwhile, they would be playing against established teams. Steve Rosenberg, the commissioner of the Atlanta MSBL, met with the team briefly at the start of the season and frankly told them that most first year teams win few, if any, games. To a competitor like Alec, such words sounded like a welcome challenge, most welcome as long as he got to pitch.

The best player on the team was Shane Schofield, an engineer who had graduated from Georgia Tech having played baseball there as a walk-on. Though his tenure on the college team was brief, it nonetheless required a substantial skill level to be considered worthy of inclusion by one of the best college programs in the country. Schofield was instrumental in helping Willis get the team organized from a managerial and coaching standpoint. He could also play well at just about every position, but it was decided he would help the team most as catcher. His favorite pitcher was Alec. During the season, Alec pitched in twelve games and started eight, more than any other pitcher on the team.

For a young pitcher, the importance of working alongside an experienced baseball player like Schofield cannot be overestimated. This was the first time Alec had a regular catcher with advanced baseball knowledge backed up with experience. Schofield, as a Georgia Tech player, had been teammates of players like Garciaparra, Veritek, Payton, and Bonifay, players who made up a NCAA championship caliber team. Therefore, conversations between the two before and during games were at a completely different level than he had ever experienced before.

After the first few games, I asked him if playing for the Orioles in the MABL was better than playing for Norcross High School. The answer to that question was emphatically yes, but came after he took a few seconds to remind himself about the relative value of the Norcross team, so easy was it to forget. Between the two situations, the differences were so great that mentioning both in the same sentence created an incongruity. The only similarity between the two was they also played a game called by the same name. In every other respect, the Orioles team was much better than the Norcross High School team. The Orioles may have struggled in their league, a more competitive league to be sure, but Norcross floundered.

The Orioles improved every week trying to overcome numerous fielding and throwing errors, which were lamentable, but not unexpected, as the players slowly regained their form. Schofield and Alec, meanwhile, functioned more or less in a world of their own. The game that Schofield called and Alec threw was an intelligent inside game of baseball. Both knew how to analyze batters and discover their weaknesses. With Alec's ability to locate and change speeds, they had very good success.

Unlike the high school seven-inning games, MABL games went nine innings. The starter was expected to go as long as he could. Pitch counts in excess of one hundred were routine. On three occasions, Alec went over one hundred thirty, once a complete game. High school pitchers rarely get this kind of work. The other benefit came in terms of pitching maturity. He grew up as a pitcher this summer, something that would have otherwise been delayed.

Rather than going winless, Alec's first win was also the team's first win, coming in the sixth game of the season. He pitched eight complete innings in an effort that allowed just one earned run with eight strikeouts and one walk. Overall, for the season, he recorded two wins and six losses though he contributed to four of the Orioles' five wins.

Other season statistics included seventy-five innings pitched with an ERA of 4.40. The number of unearned runs was about twice as many as earned runs, so there were many extended innings. He faced 410 batters, striking out fifty-eight, and walking twenty-nine. Total number of pitches thrown was 1,335 of which 838 (sixty-three percent) were strikes.

As they entered into the heart of the MABL season, playing late-spring baseball became fun again. For his former senior teammates, with whom he was graduating, baseball was already over. The underclassmen were inheriting a decimated program, for which there was absolutely no prospect of improving in the near future. Being outside the program did allow for a more circumspect view of the situation. He would have preferred to play his senior year with his high school friends, but, in reality, Norcross had no team on which to play. The MABL, on the other hand, gave this one Norcross kid who loved and respected the game the means to continue a little farther on the road towards the still faraway big leagues of baseball.

During the college application period of his senior year, Alec applied to just one college in Georgia, Valdosta State University. A college education was first on his priority list, but he also intended to try out for the baseball team as a walk-on when he enrolled. He knew it would be a long shot, but the kid never was shy about aiming high nor was he ever slow to lock and reload, even after the most distressing of disappointments.

Upon being accepted for admission, a visit to the school was in order and made on a Saturday near the end of April. Naturally, it just happened to be the last weekend of the 2000 VSU baseball regular home season featuring a double-header against the University of North Alabama. Our arrival time allowed about an hour or so for looking around the grounds before getting to the baseball park for the first pitch at 1:00 p.m. A perfect day for baseball, a beautiful ballpark, a very good baseball team, after a couple of innings it seemed appropriate for the same old question:

"Do you think you can play with these guys?"

Same old answer, "Sure."

So goes the confidence of youth.

Well, he needed more strength, I thought. Their number one starter, right-hander Andy Boutwell, pitched the first game and looked good to me. He also looked good to the Cincinnati Reds who drafted him a month later. Alec had the stuff and he had good knowledge and experience, but he still lacked the velocity on his fastball. The question was whether he would get strong enough in time for the tryout.

Along with the assumption that he would naturally get stronger over time, the workouts continued, in addition to pitching one MABL game each week. The day before a game was a day of rest, but the other five days were normally covered with throwing drills that included long toss and throwing at the tire. The few exceptions he made to his usual baseball routine where to accommodate visits to major league tryout camps, including the Braves again. Although good for experience, the results were always the same; they wanted more velocity. The magic number seemed to be eighty-five mph. Scouts were not hesitant to tell him this was his ticket to the Gulf Coast Rookie League in Florida.

One of the first available tryouts of the summer, for the Major League Scouting Bureau, came a week after winning the MABL Orioles' first game. These tryouts are open to all players. Several are held at different locations around the country. The closest and most convenient one this year happened to be on June 14 at Francis Marion University in Florence, South Carolina. Making the 9:00 a.m. camp required leaving Norcross about 3:30 a.m. For such an out-of-the-way place, we were surprised to see that over two hundred players showed up. The tryout took most of the day but still was an enjoyable spectacle.

When a player goes to a professional tryout, he needs to come equipped with more than a glove, a wood bat, and cleats. It sounds almost too obvious to mention, however, it bears saying he should also bring something that would indicate he has more than just a very good high school game. Most of the participants do not. A player should approach the tryout as if he is there to apply for a job. In order to go to work in this business, a player needs to have the right tools. As it should be viewed from the other side of the backstop, consider that the scouts have job openings or they would not be there. Also, consider if a player's tools are better than what a scout knows his team already has, the player can create his own job opening. Before making a job offer, there are specific capabilities a scout wants to see in an applicant.

Every position player is checked for five basic tools. To be considered a true prospect he must possess at least three of them at a competitive level. These tools are arm strength (Roberto Clemente), running speed (Ricky Henderson), fielding ability (Ozzie Smith), hitting ability (Tony Gwynn), and hitting with power (Mickey Mantle). These parenthetical hall-of-fame examples are meant to illustrate the standards by which professional ballplayers are measured. By showing up at a professional tryout, one should expect to be measured against professional skills.  When comparisons are to be made, they will be made against the very best.  Why should it be otherwise?  The major leagues are for the excellent, not the adequate.

Each tool has specific parameters.  Therefore, analyses and judgments of performance based on these tools are far more objective than most like to admit.  A prospect cannot just look good; he has to put up some good numbers, too.  The following describes what the scout has in mind while looking at prospects during these tryout exercises.

Arm Strength.  The ball should be thrown with a straight-line trajectory, very little arc.  An infielder should be able to throw at least eighty mph so the ball makes a hissing noise and a loud smack in the first baseman's mitt.  An outfielder should make a strong overhand throw with a low, straight-line trajectory, through the cut-off man, with a long, one-skip bounce to third base or home.

Running Speed.  As they say, speed is the one skill that does not go into a slump.  The brain can go into a slump thus negating the advantage of speed, but that is another matter.  The standard measure in baseball is the sixty-yard dash.  The cut-off time is seven seconds.  While seven seconds by itself will not earn any meal money, it may prevent immediate disqualification.  To time the run, the runner begins in a position as if he were leading off from first base, i.e., turned sideways to the sprint line.  On a signal, he does his crossover step and then sprints.  This run, it should be remembered, is set up on the outfield grass while wearing baseball cleats.  It is not done on a sprinter's track with track shoes and starting blocks.  To be well considered as an infielder or outfielder, an impressive time would be under 6.9 seconds.  A catcher should aim for less than 7.2, unless he can hit like Brian McCann.  Pitchers are not asked to participate, but sometimes the scouts indulge them if they want to run and there are not too many players at the tryout.

Fielding Ability.  Scouts look for quickness of movement to the ball and for proper positioning of the hands and feet.  They measure range by the ability to move laterally.  They note how quickly the player gets rid of the ball.  For instance, the length of time it takes a major league shortstop to backhand a ball, to transfer the ball to his throwing hand, and to release a throw to first base is seemingly instantaneous.  The entire sequence is accomplished so quickly that it is almost impossible for an untrained eye to perceive the separate actions as they occur.  The player must also be able to charge the ball and to go back on the ball with ease.  Posture and feet position are critical during these drills.

Hitting Ability. This is the most difficult tool to evaluate at a tryout camp. There are too many players and being able to hit batting practice pitches is nothing special, although a surprising number cannot do it. Predicting accurately how a prospect will hit as a professional ballplayer is extremely difficult, but it is the scouts' job to try. When it comes to hitting, scouts look for bat speed, consistent contact with the ball, good timing, knowledge of the strike zone (without being too particular), the ability to hit to the opposite field, and the ability to make adjustments to various pitches. The problem is that there are no professional pitchers brought in to pitch to these guys. Either a batting practice pitcher does it, or sometimes they use the pitchers who are themselves trying out.

Hitting With Power. This category is just simply good hitting ability combined with strength. A player needs to be able to drive the ball in batting practice four hundred feet with a wood bat. If the player can normally hit a baseball over four hundred and seventy-five feet with a metal bat, he has this tool. It is extremely rare to see a player able to hit with power at a tryout. High school players who hit metal-bat homers that barely clear a three hundred fifty foot center field fence and think they are real sluggers, find out that with a wood bat they are hitting pop-ups that can be caught by either a charging outfielder or a back-peddling infielder.

The tryout routine for infielders is generally four or five grounders taken from either the shortstop or third base position. A typical sequence is one ball hit straight at the fielder, one to his left, one to his right on the backhand, and one slow roller to charge accompanied by a bare-hand catch and throw. Every element, the position of the feet, the release, and the throw, is important. Doing the "hand pump" before the throw may look stylish, but so do clean socks. Get rid of the ball; let them see some quickness.

The outfielders take a couple of fly balls and a couple of one-bounce or two-bounce liners off the ground, and then throw through the cut-off to third base first and then to home. The mechanics of the throw, the position of the body and feet, the accuracy of the throw, and the flight of the ball are all important. No less important is the time taken to complete the mechanics of the throw. While an outfielder is crow-hopping and wind-milling to the beat of a symphony orchestra playing Bach's Brandenburg Concerto No. 5, the base runners are making their strides around the bases. Get it in, quickly.

First basemen at a tryout are critical because someone needs to catch the throws from across the diamond. They show their ability to pick the throws from the infielders and then they get to field a few grounders themselves, followed by throws to third base. Those slow runners who tryout as first basemen better know how to hit.

Catchers are measured by the throw down to second base. The interval begins when the pitched ball hits the catcher's mitt and it ends when a very accurately thrown ball reaches the middle-infielder's glove down at second base. The standard for this maneuver is two seconds. Anything under two seconds gets a gold star along with a remark such as,

"Can you hang around? I want to talk to you."

The catchers' technique, especially hands and feet, are closely watched. The total body motion from catch to release should be a smooth, quick, and graceful blur, the separate parts of which are visible only to a trained eye. His ability to block pitches in the dirt is evaluated while catching for pitcher prospects. No catcher at a tryout ever experiences a dearth of opportunities to demonstrate this skill.

Finally, there are the pitchers. While all the other players are running the sixty-yarder, fielding grounders, and tracking fly balls, the pitchers are sitting over in the other dugout. When they finally get on the mound to throw, the scouts check velocity first. They want to see at least an eighty-five mph fastball for left-handers and a little more for right-handers. The thinking in baseball is that the pitcher must have at least this much velocity to be effective in the professional ranks.

Next, they evaluate individual pitches. They look for location and movement. In fact, they usually tell the pitchers beforehand that they are not looking for velocity; they want to see control, they want to see quality pitches. This may be so, but every scout has his own Juggs gun, and every one is turned on for every pitch. As a practical matter, pitcher evaluation initially is a speed check. A pitcher may as well go ahead and throw the ball as hard as possible. It is best to keep it high in the strike zone where it registers a little bit higher speed, too. If the speed requirement is met, then the quality of each pitch becomes important.

Occasionally, a pitcher shows up at one of these tryouts who can throw in the mid-nineties mph and the first question everyone asks is,

"What is he doing at a tryout?"

The answer usually is that he cannot get anybody out! The reason is always the same. He lacks control. Sometimes the scouts will send him down to instructional ball, anyway. Most fellows who throw this hard and have any potential are already playing somewhere, or they have already been released. Everyone who throws this hard is known by the scouts, all of the scouts.

Most of those pitchers at tryouts who have the upper eighties to lower nineties velocity cannot control their location and often lack ball movement. The few who have good control and movement are usually the ones who have to wait for the wind to pick up behind them before they wind up and throw.

The breakdown for hurlers goes this way. All pitchers have a fastball. The second pitch is usually a good breaking ball. Highly desirable, but very rare, is a workable change-of-pace. The most problematical hindrance for most of these pitchers is the delivery. Typically, young pitchers coming out of high school have poor to horrible mechanics. Why this happens is mostly due to improper or no instruction from an early age. Perhaps one reason pitching mechanics are not corrected along the way is the fear of making things worse. The correction of mechanical flaws is a tedious and time-consuming venture. Every high school in the history of baseball (except the 1999-2000 Norcross team, of course) has been short on good pitching so the thought of shutting down a pitcher for several months to give him instructional drills that will yield an uncertain outcome is never very appealing. The evidence of this omission can be seen at these tryout camps, many hard throwers who simply cannot hit the catcher's mitt.

Scouts hope to see deliveries that are smooth, almost effortless, without mechanical problems such as throwing across the body, landing on a heel, a stiff front leg, over-striding, or having an arm lagging behind the body. Mechanical problems mean one of two things nearly all of the time with very few exceptions. Either they are indicative of a current arm injury problem or they are predictive of an arm injury problem to come.

During this day of tryouts in Florence, the pitchers worked in the bull pen, two at a time. The scouts set up a portable screen for a backstop behind the catchers and then took seats with their clipboards and radar guns. There were thirty-five or forty pitchers, about a dozen of whom were left-handers. If they had been divided into pitchers and throwers, most of them would have been called throwers.

One tall right-hander with a fastball measuring in the low to midnineties attracted a great deal of interest. His biggest problem, besides having horrible mechanics, was running out of baseballs. Half of his pitches were going over or outside of the portable backstop, which meant he could not throw a baseball much over sixty feet and hit a target that was about eight feet high and six feet wide. The other half of his pitches were in the dirt, ricocheting wildly. Forget about hitting a catcher's mitt or even keeping it within the catcher's reach. He could not deliver a baseball to any intended location smaller than the broadside of a large barn. One of the scouts walked up to the mound attempting to give some instruction. They longed to see something, anything, that would justify sending this strong arm down to rookie ball. Finally, they gave up.

Alec got his turn to pitch. He went through his routine of telling the catcher to give him spots, which he consistently hit. He and one other left-hander had the best mechanics of the entire group. Both had several good quality pitches in their repertoire and both lacked velocity. There would be no contract offers to either of them even though they were the only two who looked like real pitchers.

Tryout camps can be gratifying to watch for someone who likes baseball so much he can never seem to get enough of it. When the camp in Florence got under way at 9:00 a.m., the temperature was already eighty-five degrees heading for the high nineties. Humidity was not a problem, either. There is always plenty of atmospheric moisture hovering near the Low Country coastal plains of South Carolina. Had I known it would be so hot I might have brought my surfboard, continued on to Myrtle Beach, and spent a few hours in the ocean. On second thought, this was better. Baseball brings its own unique fulfillment, a sort of spiritual contentment, with every crack of the bat, every caught ball, every accurate throw, even when it is only a workout, as long as there are plenty of cold drinks and sunscreen.

In addition to representatives from the Scouting Bureau, the Mets, Astros, and Blue Jays had scouts present, too. A few others were hanging around; maybe college coaches, maybe just interested spectators. Curiosity led me to meander over near where some loquacious scouts were standing, anything to be amused. The comparative viewpoints, as they talked about what they saw, were very entertaining, as always. Moreover, one had to be amazed by the extent to which they got around to watch high school and college games, and how they had seen many of these players before. Information about baseball players travels very quickly, another reason, in addition to the pervasive and thorough scouting, that no one who can play is overlooked.

Through casual observations at many camps over the years, my very unscientific estimate is that about one out of ten players who attend these tryouts look like they can play a good game. Recently graduated high school varsity players comprise the least experienced group. Next are the ones currently playing in college. The most serious of the attendees are those who already finished college, but were not drafted. Finally, a few guys who were in the minor leagues before, now having been released, usually for injury, come around looking to get another chance. The players in this last category are more likely to go to a tryout at a spring training camp in early February since they have contacts to accompany their professional ball playing credentials. In summation, many different players come sharing the one hope that somehow, some way, another playing opportunity will materialize. It usually does not.

Baseball talent is a relative thing. The more levels of baseball one sees, the more accurate an evaluation one can make. Attending high school baseball games, especially in one of the top Georgia regions like Gwinnett County, one sees some very good ballplayers. In fact, the State of Georgia ranks fourth in the production of professional baseball players, right behind California, Florida, and Texas. Even though they were not drafted, most all of the players who show up at these tryouts were considered excellent players back home. A reasonable expectation would be that they would look good here, too, as they perform for the scouts. A few do. Most do not. Somewhat surprising is to see that most of them are not very good at all. The reason is that, at a professional tryout, there are different circumstances; consequently, perceptions are quickly altered.

How did these top-notch high school players appear back in their high school games? They looked mature, almost like men, displaying confidence, and even swagger. They were the starters, the big men on campus, and the local heroes. When playing in a high school game, these top-level players set the standard by which others were measured, so they looked a cut above the rest. Not so at a professional tryout. On these occasions, as is always the case, it is the best of the best that sets the standard. Under these circumstances, most of the attendees look to be a bit timid, lacking confidence. Many appear physically immature. The higher standards set by the excellent few reveal that the very good others are lacking in proficiency of even the most fundamental skills.

Consider that there are about a dozen schools in Gwinnett County playing in the top region, including Norcross, where, in most years, some of the best high school baseball is played anywhere. On all of these rosters, there may be a couple of hundred players. First, take the five or six who are drafted into the minor leagues or who are offered a Division

I or II college scholarship. Add to those the next five or six best players to make about a dozen. These players set the playing standards in high school. This also means that, on average, there is only one superior varsity player per school, one who may be ready to play at the next higher level. When this particular player is seen playing his position during a high school game, he will look great. However, at a professional tryout, all it takes is for one real good college player or a recently released minor leaguer to show up for there to be a change in everyone's perspective. Then it becomes apparent why the handful of boys in the second tier of excellent high school players were not drafted or offered scholarships. In baseball, excellence makes the above average look very mediocre.

The same theme can be tested and verified for any level of baseball. For instance, observe closely the players in a minor league game. After a short while, it becomes apparent why they are in the minor leagues. Watch a while longer and it becomes apparent why they are in the minor leagues. First, one sees the skills needed to reach this level; then, one does not see the skills needed to escape this level.

During the preceding four or five years at Norcross High School, there were about seventy-five different varsity players. None was drafted. None went to play at a Division I school. A subjective estimate, one with a limited view, determined that the only ones who had skills that would have placed them in the top ten percent at a professional tryout would have been Steve Horwath, Brett Moon, Josh Turner, and Patrick Turner. Several others were excellent high school players, maybe good enough to play for a small college, but just were not yet prepared for the minor leagues. Could they have been? Perhaps, with much more work. How many were willing to put in the extra hours of work every day with the knowledge that, if they do, the odds were still against them? Apparently, no one, and so it goes. Talent without desire equals no talent at all.

Finally, this tryout concluded, or fizzled, or died out, as the last two pitchers finished throwing. The walk from the baseball field at Francis Marion University to the parking lot was a meandering promenade along a beautifully landscaped pathway through the shade of the woods. The few minutes it took to traverse was enough time to begin to ponder the events of the day, a day spent driving a long distance for most, then much standing around for over six hours in oppressive heat and humidity. Was it worth it? A lot of effort was expensed for the chance to field a few balls, make a few throws, and take a few swings, just to be told,

"Thanks for coming out, fellows."

One way to describe this desultory parade of aspiring professional baseball players is to call it a gut-check, an appropriate slang, not to measure the horsepower of the engine, rather to determine the level of fuel in the tank. These players should be admired for their fortitude in showing up, to give it a try in the face of near certain rejection. While walking to the parking lot, what do any of these players say to each other, to themselves, to anyone who will listen?

"Is this it? Is it time to give up on baseball?"

"Maybe not."

"Maybe there's still a way."

"I know what I have to work on. I'm better than they think. What can they tell from this little bit of playing?"

What many of these young men do not understand is that one does not have to listen to an entire sonata to learn much about the skill of a pianist; a few measures will do.

No player was signed that day. Most of the cards and comments were destined for oblivion, to be filed away, somewhere, though likely never to be seen again. One player offered this interesting comment,

"This was a waste of time. All they're looking for is pitchers."

No pitchers were signed, either.

The fact that so many young men come to display their skills in front of major league scouts is a very good thing. It is good for them personally. It is good for the game as well. At most, only a precious few of these prospects will ever play professionally, so the value of this experience is to be found in knowing exactly why they did not make it, if they paid heed: lack of speed, lack of coordination, lack of skills, lack of commitment, lack of desire, lack of luck, lack of something. Take a pick, but be honest. The truth of the matter is that it is almost never just one thing. Whatever way the result can be viewed, there is no denying it is a difficult verdict to accept. Still, it is an important lesson to be learned as most real life lessons tend to be.

Coincidentally, whether they realized it right then or not, these baseball players did acquire some valuable first hand knowledge about the professional game. At least they learned how difficult it is to play professionally, evidenced by how few players get signed. Maybe the best comfort to be had was in the fact that nearly every one of them saw other better players get rejected, too.

There may be some valuable information here for average baseball fans, elements of the game about which they are unaware, namely the ones that lead to errant critiques of players. Accompanying a favorite local prospect to one of these camps should forever cure any propensity to call even the least major leaguer a "no-good bum," especially when one considers that, of all the players who manage to enter into the minor leagues, of all those who actually sign a professional contract, not quite two percent will ever reach the major leagues. Relatively speaking, minor leaguers are not bums, either. Some appreciation for the largely underpaid talents of the majority of professional ballplayers is in order.

Finally, these young men acquire one very important lasting bit of baseball wisdom at a professional tryout that will make them better equipped to coach youngsters when they have their own sons in the not too distant future. Attending a professional baseball tryout is not a waste of time, not a quixotic adventure born of delusional immaturity. After all, this is baseball, the national pastime, the greatest game ever. Seeing hundreds of young American men on a hot summer day stepping up to the plate, taking a couple of cuts, hoping that someone else will think they might be good, is every bit as heartwarming as fireworks on the Fourth of July.

A very sad thing to see is a young man who is too timid to follow a dream. What is infinitely worse is when such a young man is deemed by others to be wise, or rational, or circumspect, or erudite because of his caution in not trying. It is easy to rationalize that a difficult task is futile, beyond one's grasp, the odds of success just too high to beat. How tempting it is for one to claim sagacity right away rather than admit foolhardiness later. No one wants to be just another baseball player who spent years trying to make it, but was never signed. Or if he was signed, to have spent years in the minors, never making it to triple-A or even to double-A. It is a shame that such opinions persist, that so many believe unless a ballplayer actually gets to the major leagues, the farther he goes, the worse he looks; if he does not ever get to the big show, as some call it, the time must have been wasted.

"Look, kid, you don't want to spend years riding in smelly old busses between hick towns, going nowhere."

"Only a few ever make it. You've got to be lucky as much as good."

"Do you want to be thirty years old with no education, no family, no job with benefits, no nothing?"

"Baseball is for kids. You gotta grow up."

"You think you can make it to the majors? Fuhgedduhboutit!"

Who is not aware of this sort of chronic wisdom, and not just about baseball. There is a simple comeback.

"To lose heart requires no courage and very little intelligence."

On the brighter side, boys who do not pursue challenging dreams when they are still young are destined to become good, ordinary adults. The good news is that by being ordinary, they will fit right in all the time, that is, fit into whatever else is considered normal. Since normal is what is defined by their very ordinary nature, they establish what is normal by simply being what they are. The "fitting in" comes about mindlessly. They will be acceptable to and indistinguishable from the vast majority of other men that make up the real world. Fortunately, the real world can be easily distinguished from the un-real world. Take a risk? That's not smart. Quit a hated job and lose that medical insurance? Can't do that; it would be ill-advised. Be a leader and speak my mind? Always, when everyone else agrees. Otherwise, it is better to say nothing.

We have a culture that lionizes professional athletes as much as it disapproves most of those who aspire to become one. If a kid is drafted high and signed for a large bonus, well, it is fine for him to try. But for the others who want to make it through perseverance, well, it is plain stupid. The fact is if it were not for those stupid, hard-working, persevering baseball players, there would not be thirty major league teams. There may not be even two. Many of those originally signed with big bonuses fail to make it through the minor leagues. We all want our boys to become grown-ups, mature adults, but the best men among us never exhaust the possibilities discovered during the stages of childhood and adolescence. If the desires of the heart are not discovered by the mind, what good is either organ? Playing baseball is always a good thing, even when not being paid.

It would be a sinful omission not to give plaudits to the baseball scouts. These men are simply magnificent. They go to tryout camps with the almost certain knowledge that they will not find even one player they can sign. In truth, the scouts at these camps are looking mostly for pitchers. They do take notes and they do file the rating cards if they see someone with any potential. Above all, they are very congenial. They are also scrupulous in making sure every player is given a fair chance to display his skills, even when it is painfully obvious that no skills could possibly exist. Their viewpoint must be that if any kid loves baseball enough to show up, they will at least let him field a few grounders and take a couple of swings. It makes perfect sense, too. If scouts did not think this way, they would not be able to do the job all of them do so well.

Any gathering of so many young men is going to have some rambunctious moments with wisecracks and showing off, but the scouts take it all with surprisingly good humor. One of the best is an old trick that some outfielders will use to show off an exceptionally strong arm and it was put on display this day in Florence. The outfielder purposely fails to catch a liner so that the ball rolls all the way back to the fence. He then hurries back to retrieve it. In the interest of saving time, the man who hit the ball calls out,

"Let it go, take another one."

The fielder does not respond to the call, as if he does not hear, hustles back to the fence, grabs the ball, and fires a strike all the way to home plate, well over three hundred feet away. Very impressive. No need for a cut-off man, either.

The comments from the scouts are best left unquoted. The gist is always that they were aware of his arm strength; let's keep things moving along without such delays. Any baseball player with an arm like that cannot be hidden for long. The scouts already know who he is.

Sometimes at the conclusion of these camps, the scouts make themselves available to answer questions and to make comments to players individually. After this camp, the man from the Scouting Bureau remained for about an hour to talk individually to anyone who wanted to hear about his evaluation. Alec thought I would be anxious to leave after being there all day so he started to leave. I told him to stay if he wanted to. Though apprehensive, he got in line to wait his turn. The scout told him two things. First, he had great stuff. Second, they got his fastball just over seventy mph. He added the comment to keep working on velocity because if the fastball were anywhere near eighty-five he would definitely have had a place for him down in Florida.

The five-hour drive home seemed like about thirty minutes, talking baseball all the way while listening to the Braves' game on the radio. There were a few more tryouts during this summer held by the Braves, Orioles, and Expos, all of which were held close to Atlanta. The

Phillies' tryout in Gainesville, Florida was just too far out of the way so I called Marlin Jones, their scout down there. After telling him what we had, left-hander, good stuff, no velocity, he still wanted to see a game tape. So I sent one. To my surprise he viewed the tape the day he received it and called immediately afterwards, in the middle of dinner. He wanted to know how fast the fastball was. I told him probably just low seventy's at best. He said he was afraid of that. But he liked what he saw and told me if he ever got near eighty-five to give him a call first. After the Orioles tryout at the Perimeter College field in Clarkston one of the scouts went over to Alec in the dugout while he was removing his cleats to tell him the same thing, great stuff, eighty-five mph would buy a ticket to the rookie league in Florida.

"I don't know. Say a Rosary. Maybe that'll help."

## Chapter Fifteen
# Valdosta State University

The town of Valdosta was founded in 1860 by residents from a nearby farming community called Troupville, now situated near the Highway 94 & North St. Augustine Road exit on Interstate 75. The name is an adaptation from that of the old George Troup plantation, Val d'Osta. Another geographic name contributed by George Troup went to Troup County in West Georgia for which the town of LaGrange serves as the county seat.

Owning a population of about forty-five thousand souls, Valdosta is a magnificent South Georgia town, magnificent in the sense that it dares to exist. Well mannered and fetching, this seat of government for Lowndes County progresses at an easy-going plantation pace, imparting a friendly demeanor while providing homes for meaningful business enterprises, a university, and a military base. Upon first glance, its past, its purpose, its history, most of all the reason it came to be, is not immediately apparent. Yet, it is an attractively unique hamlet in the middle of what geographically could be considered nowhere, unless one considers an area adjacent to a vast, formidable swamp as being somewhere. Unlikely as it may have been, Valdosta became itself, a place somewhere, a distinguished town. Hahira, Quitman, Lake Park, and Naylor did not. For any high school student, the decision to pick Valdosta as the place to receive a college education is mostly uncomplicated.

Valdosta State University, a very fine four-year school, is part of the University System of Georgia. As the University of Georgia in Athens is prominent in the northern part of the state, VSU is busily constructing a similar stature in the southern part. The university grounds are beautifully landscaped with much shrubbery and palm trees, and with a great deal of open space complimentary of the predominant Spanish colonial style architecture. If the Flagler County, Florida courthouse were placed in the middle of this campus, it would not be the least bit conspicuous. Oak trees adjoin the walkways, their boughs plentifully adorned with Spanish moss, forming canopies that provide a welcome shade from the sun. The various creeks teem with reptiles.

During the extended months of summer, the air is hot and moist though not suffocating, as it seems to be in many coastal northeastern cities such as Washington, D.C., Philadelphia, and New York. Perhaps this is due to Valdosta's comparatively minimal amount of air pollution. Perhaps the relative humidity is not quite so high, either. This is a semi-tropical, inland region where frost seldom occurs. The Atlantic Ocean lies one hundred ten miles to the east; the Gulf of Mexico is nearly seventy miles to the southwest. The Florida state line is a mere fifteen miles away as a crow could fly in a straight path southward along Interstate 75. Besides the university, Moody Air Force Base is the most prominent public facility in the area. The premier business establishment is the Langdale Forest Products Company.

Valdosta and Lowndes County High Schools have been known for sports, especially football, for as long as anyone can remember. On November 1, 2002, Valdosta High School became the first high school in the nation to have won eight hundred football games. Over the course of eighty-eight seasons, their football team compiled a record of eight hundred wins, one hundred and sixty-three losses, and thirty-four ties while capturing twenty-three state championships. On six different occasions, it was named the number one high school team nationally. Lowndes County High School has been a powerhouse in sports as well, winning its third state football championship in 2004.

These two schools are also perennial baseball powers in the state. Being nowhere near any professional sports franchises, the local sports talk on television and radio is devoted mostly to high school sports, about ninety percent of it focused on football. The games are always sold out. Even after half a century and counting, scores of local residents have not missed a Valdosta High School home football game since World War II, a tale with shades worthy of Green Bay Packers' lore.

Valdosta State University is no slouch, either, when it comes to quality athletics, or for having an abundance of dedicated fans. Their NCAA Division II football and baseball programs are normally ranked near the top of the national polls. Contending for conference and national championships is customary. Alec knew how difficult it would be to walk-on to his college baseball team. So why try? Why not attend a smaller school in a less-competitive environment? Suggestions to attend a smaller school with a baseball program on which he would have a greater chance to play were dutifully ignored. He would not be swayed. He said he would rather be rejected by a very good team than to make a lesser team at, say, a school belonging to the National Association of Intercollegiate Athletics (NAIA) or Division III college.

The main thrust of his thinking came from a strong desire to earn his college degree from a larger school. VSU was a well-established four-year university, offering a good academic experience in an environment that seemed to suit him well. If he made the baseball team, fine; however, the education came first. Business administration with a major in accounting was his goal. VSU, thanks to the good graces generously bestowed by the local Langdale Family business in the form of financial support, boasted an excellent business school. Not surprising, it bears the name of its primary benefactor, Harley Langdale, Jr., who at the time was Chairman of the Board of the Langdale Forest Products Co.

The Langdales originally came to Georgia from Virginia in the early part of the Nineteenth Century. Their business legacy began somewhat later. The founder of the forest products company, John Wesley "J.W." Langdale, was born in 1860 and became orphaned in early childhood. Both his father and grandfather left home to fight for The Cause during the Rebellion, never to return. In 1894, at age thirty-four, J.W. leased some turpentine timber, which formed the basis of a new enterprise. His three sons carried on the business with Judge Harley Langdale, Sr. being the first to grasp the potential they had before them. He continued to expand their enterprise by buying up land and timber leases, having reached the conclusion that the most important crop in South Georgia was not cotton, peanuts, or tobacco; it was pine trees.

The Valdosta State University business school has been the recipient of this most notable, so typically American, entrepreneurial heritage. The Langdale story fits accurately this sentiment expressed in the Wall Street Journal Thanksgiving editorial:

". . . the richness of this country was not born in the resources of the earth, though they be plentiful, but in the men who took its measure."

Therefore, to give credit where due, a business education at Valdosta State is largely provided as a courtesy of South Georgia and Okefenokee Swamp pine trees. The good fortune, along with the good example of the Langdale legacy, augments VSU's business school experience. Unfortunately, there is no evidence that a Langdale ever played professional baseball. Yet, the men who created the greatest nation in world history out of a "desolate wilderness," men like J. W. Langdale and his heirs, were necessary to the creation of the game of baseball. Ample evidence exists that one came with the other.

In college baseball, Division II is not at all the large step down from Division I as is the case in football and basketball. Whichever level of baseball college players have experienced, after four years they are generally considered about one year ahead of high school drafted players, at most. The best football and basketball players coming out of college go directly to play in the National Football League and the National Basketball Association. The best baseball players coming out of college go directly to the minor leagues. In fact, most of the college baseball draftees start their professional careers alongside high school draftees in rookie ball. A few top college picks may start a bit higher by going directly to advanced rookie ball or maybe single-A. Rarely do they start at a higher level. One of the rarest occurrences in all of sports is for a first-round college baseball draftee to go straight to the major leagues. Even after a full summer of professional ball, a college player drafted in June would be among a select few if chosen in the September call-ups. To appear in a major league game so soon would also be very unusual. In recent times, we have seen many more high school basketball players go directly into the NBA than college baseball players go directly to the major leagues.

Skills are not the issue among drafted players in baseball. All of them have skills. The minor leagues exist to teach these schoolboys how to use their skills in the professional game. The amount of time they spend in the minor leagues has more to do with learning the game than with skill development, although both are important. One could easily illustrate the need for much minor league instruction by placing the team that wins the college World Series into a low Class-A professional summer league. Such a team would end up in last place every time. Of this, there is no doubt.

The major leagues of baseball are not a place for on-the-job training as is the case in the NFL and NBA. Free substitution exists in football and basketball, not so in baseball. Moreover, a larger issue comes into play, namely the integrity of the game. Baseball is just very different. There is much more for the baseball player to learn before he is ready for the majors. To say that football and basketball teams are run by head coaches while baseball teams are run by managers is not a verbal miscue. The nature of baseball is such that it requires more individual decision-making of a higher order. A baseball player is not sent in for a couple of plays or a couple of minutes, taken out, and then reinserted when propitious. In baseball, the normal course of the game does not require that the player learn plays, per se. He executes his duties only in reaction to situations. Once the ball is in play, he must know how to use his skills while making judgments on his own.

College baseball has continued to be well represented in NCAA athletics even though it takes a back seat to the so called "money sports" of football and basketball. As a summertime game, baseball is hindered by the weather in many parts of the country for much of the school year. Therefore, independent summer leagues for college baseball players are very important. The Cape Cod League is one renowned organization, as is the Stan Musial League in Georgia.

Major League Baseball and colleges could work together more closely, or so it would seem. If they did, college players would graduate at a more advanced level. Before this can happen, though, colleges would have to remove a couple of pointless barriers, namely, the metal bat and the raised seam baseball. If schools would go back to playing genuine baseball, they might be surprised to find their efforts better supported by the professional game. Traditionally, though, college has not been considered a worthy substitute for the baseball minor leagues, not in the same way it is for football and basketball. To alter the relationship between professional and scholastic baseball, to make the two separate entities more compatible, a complete change in the way high schools and colleges think about the game is necessary.

The end of this summer of the year 2000 approached. Following a week at Wrightsville Beach, the lefty pitcher, the first-born grandchild, left for college, leading off for his generation's pursuit of higher education, now the fourth generation to do so. It was the middle of August, still the dog days in Dixieland. Arriving early in the morning on move-in day had the obvious advantages of beating the crowd. Soon the campus population could be seen swelling by the minute. Knowing in advance the importance of securing a good parking space, such as one marked "no parking/tow away zone" so that unloading the car could be done in the most expeditious manner, was a consequence of experience. Patterson dormitory had only a few of these convenient spaces. Next, we visited the bookstore, which gave the credit card a good workout. Quite noticeable was the fact that the price of college textbooks had increased more than a little in thirty years. Fortunately, class registration had been accomplished during orientation earlier in the summer so all that remained was to make the rounds to see where those classes would be held, a good excuse for taking a tour of classroom buildings. Many other new students and their parents had the same idea. The professors, several of them, were easily met in the hallways. Conversations between parents and teachers were running rampant, a good time being had by all, except the kids. For some reason they seemed anxious for us to leave.

The parents seemed to be in no hurry to go. At orientation earlier in the summer, we had been treated very well, an unexpected pleasure to be so warmly greeted. The faculty and staff, from President Bailey on down, seemed genuinely happy to see us all there. On this day, the day before classes started, we found that Valdosta State's persistently gracious southern hospitality continued. Rarely does one experience an institution with as affable an atmosphere. Whether it was Alec's first year math professor, Mrs. Bezona, whom we met outside the mathematics laboratory, or the athletic director, Mr. Reinhart, sitting nearby at a baseball game, or the young lady at the housing office, cordiality was a constant. This continued throughout, whether in person or on the telephone. Engaging employees of VSU always meant being greeted by people who were glad anyone called, glad they stopped by, and happy to join in idle chitchat. This was what Valdosta State University was like, all of the time.

The final official stop was the baseball office. We met Shannon Jernigan, the assistant coach, and found out the team would have an open tryout the next week. Finally, it was time to return to the dorm. Before leaving, what is there to say?

"Do you want to play catch?"

We threw the ball for about ten minutes out in the big open field in front of the administration building. There is nothing like watching the flight of a baseball back and forth during a catch, each throw ending with the distinctive sound of the ball hitting the well-formed pocket of a well-conditioned leather baseball glove. I noticed other students arriving, some walking around with their proud parents. The start of a new college career is a time of great hope, pride, and anticipation. After returning home to Norcross, there would not be anyone with whom I could play catch everyday. Most of the neighbor kids played football or basketball. Of a sudden, the years had passed. The eagerly anticipated moment was at hand, the one where satisfaction and rectitude intersect. Whence the dread? Nothing was left except to try to be a bit philosophical, a bit circumspect.

It is fair to assume universal affirmation to the proposition that a father playing catch with his son is a normal and acceptable endeavor, always and anywhere. Yet, in reality, it is a very uncommon activity. Granted that upon a college green on the day one leaves his son to begin his university career there may not occur the most likely confluence of circumstances to cause the play of catch. How many fathers thought to bring a ball glove? Indeed, how many fathers could throw a baseball anymore? We were the only ones out there tossing the ball. Not everyone realizes, or remembers, playing catch is, among many things, an exquisite form of communication. I did not wonder if we were unusual or abnormal though we could have been considered one, the other, or both. Such a wonderfully warm, sunny August day in Valdosta it was, perfect for anything, conducive for everything, whether to start a college career or to play catch. I was proud he made it here, that he was intent on getting an education, and that he was ready to give his college baseball team a try. A pleasant feeling came from being enveloped by the hot, not-too-humid air, a bead of sweat forming under the brim of the cap, catching the ball each time, snapping a throw back on a line as best I could, clean and accurate, back and forth, with no more need to stop than there was to start, until the kid said,

"I'm good."

Just a passing thought, a few seconds.

"Yea. Me, too."

To the list of prominent places in our family's history that included Erie, Springfield, Charlottesville, LaGrange, Atlanta, and Norcross, we now could add the very innocuous South Georgia town called Valdosta. Here we were, having come to this place to part ways, after a catch and a handshake, because of a series of very unlikely events, the kind of unlikely events that do the most to depict life's remarkable journey. It did not have to take fifty years to get to South Georgia from Western Pennsylvania. The journey could have been done in a day, maybe two days back in 1959, but then the better part of a good life would have been missed.

This catch was otherwise no different from the other three thousand or so. No reason for it was required. Being the last one for a while made it a bit more special, easier to recall. As the journey can mean everything to one who is traveling, what does it mean to the one who has already arrived? For us, something so ordinary as throwing a baseball could satisfy the need to mark an end and a beginning. In playing catch with my son, I may have fashioned together some vaguely related thematic coincidences as a way to transform the mundane into the magnificent. It would also serve as mental sustenance for the drive back to an emptying house. Speaking of coincidences, the year also marked the end of a millennium, one that was arguably no better than the previous one. Also marked was the end of a century, the first to be blessed by the game of baseball throughout.

This moment was significant. There are many significant moments in a lifetime, which should all be recognized and appreciated, even preserved for a while, but not to be preferred for too long. The time spent reflecting upon any of them may be better spent creating new ones. Pausing briefly to mark these occasions is fine, but better still to get on with living another adventure. When a game is over, it is time to prepare for the next one. Could throwing the baseball back and forth have been for us the best way we had to mark the significance of this moment? Maybe it was a way to divert attention from it.

I assumed Alec would probably not make the baseball team for several reasons. Since Valdosta State was nationally ranked nearly every year, it recruited well. They had a full complement of ballplayers arriving each August many of whom came from junior colleges with advanced playing skills. Under these circumstances, it was unusual for any freshman to make the team. Then there was the issue of his fastball velocity. The minimum fastball speed college coaches expect from a left-hander is at least low eighties. In his favor were great mechanics along with an ability to control a wide assortment of quality pitches. There was a small but realistic chance the manager, Tommy Thomas, would place him on the fall roster of about forty players because he was a left-hander with good stuff. Even if Mr. Thomas did not expect to include him on the final spring roster of twenty-five players, his presence on the fall team would give their batters a good look at this style of left-handed pitching during intra-squad scrimmage games. Perhaps the following year he might come back a bit stronger.

Tommy Thomas had managed VSU since before the time I was a college student, 1968 to be exact. No doubt, he had seen about everything imaginable when it came to college baseball. Not only did he win the most games in Division II history, he was also quite a gentleman. When Alec stopped by the baseball office to learn he did not make the fall roster, Thomas took some time to encourage him with an assurance, come back next year at eighty-five mph, he would make the team. It was another validation of the quality of his pitching. This year no walk-on's were taken, not even two right-handed pitchers who threw ninety mph. In their case, velocity was not the issue; it was a lack of pitching skill.

Not being on the team simplified the plan for school, so in a way, it was a relief. He would be free to focus on doing well in his studies, which he did, completing the first year of college with a good academic standing. After taking a full load of classes that were more difficult than necessary, he came through his first semester with a very respectable solid B average. Still there was time to devote to baseball, throwing the ball everyday, building strength, while trying to gain weight. He was barely one hundred twenty pounds. Playing on a team again was going to wait until he returned home after spring semester, perhaps in the MABL. Meanwhile, over the Christmas holidays, the subject of possibly taking in some spring training was discussed.

Major league teams hold different kinds of tryouts at their spring training facilities every year. The players who show up for these camps are mostly older fellows in their mid-to-late-twenties. Many have previously played professional ball. Most have been released, some for performance reasons, some because of injury. Some are playing in independent leagues and trying to advance. Some are former college players who were not drafted the previous June. Whatever the reason for coming, these young men can all play baseball well, each one desperately wanting a job within a major league organization. Nearly all of them know it is a race against the clock. For a youngster like Alec who loves baseball, to see this side of the game is an eye-opener. The spring training tryout camp is quite different from the summer version.

The Tampa Bay Devil Rays were conducting a spring training tryout camp at their Raymond J. Naimoli Complex, previously called the Busch Complex, in St. Petersburg, Florida on Saturday and Sunday, February 3 and 4, 2001. The timing was perfect, too, being at the start of the semester and over a weekend. No classes would be missed.

The trip from Norcross to Valdosta was two hundred fifty miles, exactly the same distance as it was from Valdosta to St. Petersburg, Florida. The camp was scheduled to start at 9:00 a.m. with sign-in at 8:30 a.m. Since the drive was almost entirely on Interstate highways, no traffic problems were anticipated. By leaving Valdosta no later than 5:00 a.m., we would be sure to arrive on time. To be safe, we planned to meet in front of Patterson dormitory at 4:30 a.m. Leaving Norcross at a few minutes before 1:00 a.m. proved sufficient as our appointment outside his dorm was kept at precisely 4:30 a.m. Waiting near the door, dressed in baseball workout clothes, holding his baseball equipment bag, was the left-handed business student, looking a bit groggy, but ready to travel south.

Even though I had not been in the Tampa/St. Petersburg area for about twenty-five years, it did not look entirely unfamiliar. We pulled into the parking lot of the Naimoli Complex at a few minutes past 8:00 a.m., ahead of most of the other players. One of the great images of baseball spring training in Florida is of the mild breezes that blow in the middle of winter while much of the rest of the country is snowed in and shivering. Most of the time Florida during February is this way, but not on this particular day.

This day was overcast. A very chilly morning breeze was blowing in from over the Northern Gulf of Mexico. Rain was expected while the temperature hovered in the upper forties. A similar forecast was issued for Philadelphia minus the Gulf of Mexico breeze. Only the presence of palm trees indicated the more southerly latitude. Despite the Pennsylvania-like weather, Florida was where we were. Trying to imagine it was much colder in North Dakota helped to make it feel marginally warmer.

Arriving early allowed some time for a grand walking tour of the place. Spring training complexes are located throughout Florida, mostly in the central and southern parts of the state. The typical layout has four full-size baseball fields symmetrically aimed away from a central area as if they were four opposing quadrants of a compass. The central area covers perhaps half-an-acre of land with a few buildings that house meeting rooms, locker rooms, equipment, concessions, and various other accommodations. Between and around these structures a generous amount of space is available for pedestrian spectators to mosey about. Between the northeast and northwest fields in the Naimoli Complex sits a large bull pen with about a dozen mounds. South and east of the ball field area is parking, offices, and an indoor workout facility with several batting cages. The complex is surrounded by a residential area of modest one-story homes, very similar to those in Springfield Estates, and probably built just before or just after World War II.

Beginning around the first of February every year since long ago, a mobile army of hopeful baseball players arrives from all possible places east of the Mississippi River, along with a few from the west side, as their license plates will attest. Some players travel alone, some are in pairs or more. A few of them bring their wives and babies. A few more bring girlfriends, some of those with babies, too. Some have their fathers or brothers tagging along. None of these players brings an agent.

The typical motor carriage boasts features such as faded paint with rusted out panels and dented fenders. Those from north of the Mason-Dixon Line have more holes where once there was rust. Few are less than ten years old. Most seem to be in need of repair or of an engine tune-up made evident by clanking noises, clouds of bluish exhaust smoke, and long-cranking, laborious engine starts. Fortunately, the air pollution disappears quickly, abducted by the prevailing gulf breezes, carried away to dissipate over the brackish waters of Tampa Bay. These young men look weary when they arrive. They also look lean and hungry. The two main differences between these players and typical high school baseball players are immediately apparent. First, these fellows can play baseball very well, and, second, they are not arrogant.

Meeting many hopeful young ballplayers over the years, chatting with many of them at many different camps, always leaves one with a new perspective on the virtue of humility. There is much to say about how they think, what they are all about, and what motivates them. Plainly and succinctly, it can be wrapped up by quoting their most frequently uttered remark,

"I'm just looking for a chance. That's all I'm asking for."

Sometimes for a listener, if feeling talkative, a good response would be,

"Good luck. You'll get your chance. Just be ready."

Most times, an unadorned nod suffices.

The players all wandered over to the offices where the tryout cards were distributed. Those without their own writing instrument, with meandering glances, sought to borrow one. Filling out the card did not take very long, maybe a few minutes. The multitude had grown to a few hundred by 9:00 a.m., at which time all players and coaches convened in the central area taking seats on some bleachers. They were assured by someone from the Devil Rays' staff that each of them would be evaluated fairly. No one would go away thinking he had not been given a chance to show what he could do. At the end of the Saturday session, the coaches would post a list of players who were invited to return the next morning on Sunday to participate in scrimmage games for further evaluation. This part was critically important because those asked to stay overnight might get some meal money, or possibly a motel room, not for sure, but maybe.

The first part of the workout was stretching and running for about thirty minutes. Then the pitchers and catchers were told to report to the bull pen while the outfielders and infielders went to adjacent fields. The players were put through their paces as in any other tryout camp though this one was run more efficiently than most. These players were, as expected, much more skillful than those who attend the summer camps. All except a few of them had already played in the minors or in college.

So what was Alec doing here? He filled out a card and was hanging around with the other pitchers. He was also learning something about the business of baseball, seeing what goes on during the first days of spring training, finding out first hand that there is no shortage of very good players who just are not quite good enough. The lesson also included something about the relative importance of organizational needs. In other words, this assembly could have been the introductory lecture of a business school class called, *Business of Baseball 101*. Here was the first step, the screening of applicants for full-time and part-time positions. He was getting a different perspective, a first-hand view of the real thing. He was also there to spend a Saturday having some fun with his old man. Nothing unusual, surely most American fathers do this sort of thing with their baseball-playing sons, do they not?

The coaches were taking long, hard looks at everybody, especially the pitchers. Overheard conversations indicated that they already knew many of the players, which only made sense. Most of them had been around before. They had a history. Much could be learned watching each of them throw, their mechanics, assortment and quality of pitches, ability to locate their pitches and adjust to the requests of the coaches, and, finally, why each of them had not yet been signed by any team. Some of them showed ability that would definitely qualify them for a more complete workout. The coaches' dilemma was to determine which ones had a reasonable possibility of helping the organization in the next couple of years. The younger guys could possibly get a trip to rookie ball or low single A, but those over twenty-three or twenty-four had to be just a step or two away from being ready for the majors. Within this situation was created a scramble.

Rain had been falling lightly and intermittently since we arrived. By 10:30 a.m., it was coming down more steadily. Presently, as the mounds began to get a bit slippery, the correct decision was made to end the outdoor session. Moments later the steady rain quickened to a downpour. Alec was scheduled for his session soon after they reconvened near the indoor mounds. Now the kid would get to participate in his first spring training chance, throwing to a professional catcher, and being looked at by real big league coaches, not just big league scouts.

His performance was the usual with great looking mechanics, excellent control, but not much more than mid-seventies on the fastball. The pitchers had been told not to throw their hardest because they did not want anyone getting hurt, or worn out, on this chilly day. This made Alec's fastball appear not too slow, because he was throwing as hard as he could while most of the others eased up a bit. The coaches here were intently focused on the quality of pitches, more so than in the summer tryouts run by scouts. They wanted to see movement and location. However, they also knew who the best prospects were beforehand. They seemed to wonder who this left-handed kid was. He looked awfully young. The evaluation continued and everything went as expected.

I knew there was no chance of being signed out of this camp, to continue with some spring training instructional team. There was, however, a very slight possibility that they might want him to come back in the summer for a stint on the rookie league team. He did his best, while the coaches looked at him like all the others. We waited around for the retention list to be posted. At about 3:30 it was ready. Alec was not one of the approximately twenty-five or thirty names. He actually expected to be invited back for Sunday, conforming to his normally optimistic outlook. Those sentiments along with the feelings of disappointment he shared with a couple hundred other guys. One small difference, though. The others were heading down another alligator alley searching for the next spring training complex, hoping to find a job, a place to sleep, and a meal ticket. Alec was heading back to school where his meal ticket and room were already paid in full.

If Alec had had the chance to pitch in a scrimmage game the next day he would have done all right, of that there is no doubt. The reason is simple. He would have had a professional catcher and very good defensive players allowing him great latitude in pitch selection. By making good his pitches, the batters would have had trouble hitting safely. Baseball works this way.

We had an interesting time that Saturday, a good time, even with the lousy weather. Much was learned. After a stop to eat, we headed back to Valdosta. The drive passed quickly while engaged with mostly baseball talk. This excursion was something done out of a sense of adventure for me. For Alec, to display his pitching ability in front of major league coaches took more than average daring. He had done it well. In fact, the way he delivered the baseball, his throwing mechanics, were as good as anyone else present was. He looked as confident, as accomplished, as polished, as able as the other pitchers, just not as fast. The quality of his performance was noticeable because at this sort of tryout, the very highest standards are set. If a pitcher can fit in here, he can fit in anywhere. In this type of setting among professional caliber players like this, any hint of immaturity or lack of form screams of incompetence. Not so for the kid: he looked good.

At 7:30 p.m., I dropped him off and immediately left to continue my trip home, arriving in Norcross shortly after 11:00 p.m. Quite a twenty-two hour escapade it was, covering a full one thousand miles, including eight superb hours of spring training baseball courtesy of the Tampa Bay Devil Rays, every minute of it thoroughly enjoyed. Nothing was missed by being gone, either, since not much happens on Saturdays in early February. The day probably would have been spent at the office out of sheer boredom. Instead, while all of my work stayed put until Monday, we did something very special, something that we most likely would never have the opportunity to do together again.

*Chapter Sixteen*

# Major League Fields

The MABL started its spring training in March. Greg Willis was going to manage the Orioles team again with some changes. The first unfortunate change was that Shane Schofield had moved to Columbus, Georgia. He would be too far away to play for the team. The reason Alec had pitched so much the previous season was mainly because Schofield insisted on it. Willis preferred to use a couple of other pitchers who threw harder. More to the point, he also wanted to pitch himself. After catching wind of that, Alec was informed of the situation by an e-mail. There was no point to stay on this team. With Schofield gone, the entire character of the team would change. They had no other competent catcher, either, and the prospect of finding a suitable replacement was low because good catchers were hard to come by.

For the Orioles to progress very much in other departments was doubtful, too. Fielding, which was sorely lacking, could only be improved marginally because the good gloves would be taken by the better teams, unless Willis had contacts to locate and recruit good players not already in the league. Maybe, with a little luck, the Orioles would find a couple good defensive players. Probably not. Such is the world of semi-professional and recreational baseball. Building a good team takes time.

Thus, the search for another team began. Next step was to stop by the league's open workout held for new and unassigned players one Saturday morning. Besides adding Alec to the availability list, with the proviso that he would be back from college in early May, it was a chance to see what new players showed up. Sure enough, it was a pleasant surprise. Many familiar faces appeared including some former Norcross players, Tommy Dillingham, Patrick Turner, Bernardo Fulleda, and Ryan Williams. Three had played all the way through in the Norcross youth leagues and two of them, Dillingham and Turner, played varsity for

Norcross High School. They were seniors when he was a sophomore. Dillingham determined to assemble a team with the intent to manage it. The core of his new team was going to be these Norcross players. They took the name, cap, and uniform of the Chicago Cubs. Alec joined when he finished the semester.

After successfully completing his first year of college he was back to playing summer baseball with some old teammates. It seemed no matter what happened, even the bitterest of disappointments, things usually turned out better than what would have been. Baseball can be this way as long as one does not lose heart.

The MABL Cubs was probably the most interesting of all the teams for which Alec had played to this point. Early on there were seven members who said they could pitch. In the end, only three, Alec, Brent Harlan, and Justin Hesenius, proved to be actual pitchers. Harlan, a college pitcher, frequently failed to show up for games. However, when he was there, he pitched very well. He was a good fastball/curveball thrower, getting the ball past many of the batters in the league. Hesenius was the best overall player. He had much advanced playing experience, a playing career cut short by an arm injury. Now he was coaching a high school baseball team, while starting a family. The arm still caused him some trouble and it was difficult for him to pitch more than a couple of innings at a time. Due to these circumstances, Alec received more than his share of the pitching duties.

Hesenius became the primary catcher. As Schofield did the previous year with the Orioles, he called an intelligent, thoughtful game. His extensive baseball experience was apparent. When he and Alec got together, they had little trouble keeping the batters off their balance. When Hesenius could not make a game because of other commitments, Bernardo Fulleda came in from the outfield to take over behind the plate. Bernardo and Alec knew each other well after being teammates through the years in Norcross Dixie Youth. Both having being instructed by Ro Fitten, they worked well together.

The best team in this league was the Rangers. The Cubs lost to them early in the season in a frustratingly close game by the score of 3-2. A rematch occurred on July 7. The Cubs came in with a record of 5-3 while the Rangers were undefeated. Alec got the start and Hesenius caught. Going to the ninth inning the Cubs were ahead 10-3. Alec was tiring and should have been replaced, but Dillingham figured that with the big lead he would let him try to finish the game. The inning started roughly with a double, a hit batsman, an E6, and a single. With one run in, nobody out, and the bases loaded, Hesenius came out from behind the plate to try and close the game. He brought about a rather quick end to the contest with the Cubs winning 10-7. Alec pitched eight-plus innings, seventy-two percent strikes, with five strikeouts, one walk, nine singles, and two doubles while being charged with four earned runs.

The important thing was the Rangers finally were beaten. This game became the talk of the league for the following week. Near the end of the season, the Cubs met the Rangers again with Fulleda catching. Alec pitched the complete nine-inning game giving up seven earned runs. Except for a break or two, the Cubs would have won this one as well. Three unearned runs in the ninth by the Rangers sealed it and a Cubs' comeback fell short. They lost by the metal-bat score of 12-10 which was his one and only pitching loss all summer.

Playing on a good Cub's team with an agreeable group of guys made for a most enjoyable summer of baseball. Alec worked sixty-seven innings in twelve games. He started eight times, relieved in four, and finished with a record of 6-1. His earned run average was a respectable 3.39. The number of batters faced was 301, of whom forty-eight struck out and ten walked. From year to year, his statistics varied little. The numbers were never spectacular, never causing one to stand up and take notice. They just showed remarkable similarities, even as the level of competition increased. He was very consistent. When Alec took the mound, there was no doubt what kind of game it was going to be. The other team would have to hit the ball, while his team would have to make plays. Such are the kinds of games thrown by control pitchers who do not walk batters and keep the ball in the park, using location, movement, and speed change.

Between Cubs' games, he attended a few tryouts held by the Cincinnati Reds, the Baltimore Orioles, and the MLB Scouting Bureau. This time his fastball was being clocked as high as seventy-six mph. It was increasing though progress was agonizingly slow. The opinion of his trainer, along with our family physician, Dr. Hugh DeJarnette, was about the same. He had to gain some weight. At the end of the summer, he left for his sophomore year of college five feet, ten inches tall, weighing one hundred twenty-nine pounds. The medical experts confidently predicted that his fastball would pass eighty mph when he weighed one hundred fifty pounds. He was advised to eat more. Anything in particular, doctor?

"Whatever doesn't eat him first."

Alec's practice regimen this summer continued at a pace that few non-professional pitchers would be able to stand. Some new drills were adopted, a new workout including a form of long toss similar to the one being used by John Burkett. Burkett, who had been released by Tampa Bay, then signed by the Braves, had to increase his strength and endurance if he hoped to prolong his already long, successful pitching career in the major leagues. When Alec heard of the conditioning he was doing for Leo Mazzone, he decided to try it out, with only slight modifications.

The drill requires a bag of thirty-five baseballs along with the old tire hanging on the backstop as in our "throw-at-the-tire" drill. First is the usual warm-up that includes a good stretch before playing catch for about fifty to seventy-five easy throws, until the arm feels loose. Then the entire bag of thirty-five balls is thrown three times, once each from sixty and a half, one hundred and thirty, and one hundred and seventy-five feet, with intervening ten minute breaks to pick up the baseballs. These lengths of throws equal the distances to home plate from the pitching mound, from just behind second base, and from shallow center field. All throwing is done on a flat surface and out of a complete windup as if pitching to a target.

Finally, there is a session of pitching from rubber to plate with a catcher, still from a flat surface, not a mound. During this segment, the full assortment of pitches is thrown until good location and movement is achieved. This brings the total number of throws to about two hundred and fifty. After the throwing session, cleats are replaced with sneakers for the one-mile run back home to complete the workout. When done in the middle of the summer afternoon, a water jug and sunscreen come in handy. He did this drill four or five afternoons a week during the entire summer.

The first of the three professional tryouts Alec attended during the summer of 2001 was on Monday, June 11 held by the MLB Scouting Bureau in Columbus, Georgia, about two hours away by car from Norcross. The venue was the Golden Park stadium, at that time the home of the Columbus Red Stixx, the single-A minor league affiliate of the Cleveland Indians in the South Atlantic League, also called the Sally League. We arrived at about 8:00 a.m. The stadium is built on a bluff along the Chattahoochee River between the Columbus riverfront area and Fort Benning. Across the river lies a former part of Georgia now called Alabama. This tryout attracted one of the larger crowds we had seen at any camp outside of Florida. Not only were there many players, an unusually large number of spectators were also present. Most were friends and family of the ballplayers; however, I suspected a good number of folks just wandered in from 4$^{th}$ Street to see what was going on or, maybe, were not in a hurry to go to work on this particular Monday morning preferring to see some baseball, instead.

A large plaque was prominently displayed near the entrance of the ballpark just past the turnstiles so that it was not possible for any visitor to miss seeing it. It bore the heading, "WELCOME TO GOLDEN PARK," followed by a list of some of the major league players who had played some of their minor league ball in Columbus, Georgia since 1909:

| | | |
|---|---|---|
| Wee Willie Keeler | Ty Cobb | Shoeless Joe Jackson |
| Rabbit Maranville | Babe Ruth | Walter Alston |
| Dizzy Dean | Al Lopez | Mel Ott |
| Ray Sanders | Johnny Mize | Monte Irvin |
| Bob Lemon | Enos Slaughter | Ray Jablonski |
| Gil Hodges | Stan Musial | Red Shoendienst |
| Whitey Ford | Lenny Green | Mickey Mantle |
| Willie Mays | Bob Gibson | Harmon Killebrew |
| Roy White | J.R. Richard | Ferguson Jenkins |
| Greg Gross | Johnny Ray | Bill Doran |
| Glenn Davis | Ken Caminiti | Eddie Murray |
| Don Mattingly | Jose Canseco | Randy Johnson |
| David Justice | Steve Avery | Marquis Grissom |
| Fred McGriff | Harry Heilmann | Jim Bottomly |
| Frankie Frisch | Terry Moore | Arky Vaughn |
| Jackie Robinson | Roy Campanella | Rip Repulski |
| Luis Arroyo | Satchel Page | Jackie Brandt |
| Ernie Banks | Hoyt Wilhelm | Hank Aaron |
| Frank Robinson | Rick Monday | Ken Forsch |
| Dale Murphy | Dave Smith | Frank Thomas |
| Cal Ripkin, Jr. | Cecil Fielder | Tom Glavine |
| Grover C. Alexander | | |

Besides the great fun of watching youngsters display their baseball skills at these tryouts there is always an opportunity to meet and converse with some interesting people. A comfortable comradeship forms quickly amongst those who would rather linger around a baseball field than go to work. One such person was an older gentleman who turned out to be one of the most fascinating baseball men I have ever met, a long-time vendor at Golden Park. His name was Willie Bowman, though he was known to many as "The Goody-Goody Peanut Man."

Mr. Bowman, then in his retirement, worked as a peanut vendor during games. However, he sold not just regular peanuts; he sold wholesome, "goody-goody" Georgia peanuts, the best peanuts in the world, he would be sure to inform. Since the crowd was large this day, Mr. Bowman decided to sell concessions. He brought out the carts with drinks and snacks, including those famous peanuts that everybody loved. When he sang out his offerings, it reminded me very much of the animated characters who entertained up and down the isles of Griffith Stadium long ago during Senators' games.

Arriving early afforded an opportunity to have an extended conversation with Mr. Bowman. As the morning wore on and the players went through their exercises, he told me about his baseball playing days as a young man, how he tried to make it as a baseball player. He recalled the time when he played for a local minor league team, working all day in the mill, playing baseball in the evenings and on weekends. Like many other very good ballplayers that were not quite good enough, the years passed while the need for steady employment income precluded further attempts to fulfill fading baseball dreams. The responsibilities Mr. Bowman had to fulfill as a young man, along with the sacrifices he had to make for his family, would not be understood by many kids today. Few, if any, of the players on the field in front of us, or even the players on the Red Stixx team, ever had such burdens. During Mr. Bowman's early days in West Georgia, adulthood came at a very young age.

His comments concerning baseball constituted a genuine treasure-trove of ruminations, including a complete review of the current Columbus team and its players. He told some fine stories about past players who had gone on to the majors. All levels of baseball, from the local high school team to the Atlanta Braves, scrutinized. It was like listening to a local baseball encyclopedia recorded on tape. Mr. Bowman was an amazingly knowledgeable man probably capable of managing a professional baseball team if given the chance. He was never offered the chance.

When he asked about my son, he listened to a brief outline. He nodded as he listened in a way that gave the idea he knew precisely what the situation was. When I finished he said quite emphatically,

"Don't never let him quit baseball."

He said he was sure the day would come when Alec would get that velocity; it may even be that very day.

"The body is a funny thing," he continued, "and one day he'll go out there and have what he needs."

Then he asked me, which one was my son. I pointed him out down below getting warmed up on the side of the field. He said,

"He looks like a ballplayer. You did a good job with him. Remember what I said."

I had not noticed it before, probably because I saw my kid every day. Now, suddenly, after meeting Mr. Bowman my perspective seemed to have been changed. It felt a little bit like owning a new pair of eyes able to detect altogether new visions, or maybe a more efficient optic nerve capable of reporting to the brain newfound information. Down on the field I saw someone new to me, someone who, indeed, looked like a baseball player, a real baseball player, especially as compared to many of the others. Someone who strangely resembled someone I thought I knew very well, treading the playing surface of a minor league baseball stadium, warming up as if he belonged here, as if he did this every day.

The tryout went as usual for the fielders. The pitchers were evaluated in the bull pen by what amounted to a speed check. Alec fell short again. Nevertheless, the scouts had a time with him. Before he threw a pitch, not wanting underage players (under seventeen) trying out, they asked him his age. He looked very much younger than his twenty years. Taking their eyes away from their clipboards and Juggs guns, the scouts looked at each other, smiling in disbelief. They thought he was about sixteen, at most. Then one of them said,

"O.K., lefty, let's see what you can do."

He put on his usual excellent display of control, which drew some praising comments, something you very seldom hear on these occasions. They did ask him to throw harder, as hard as he could. The problem was he was already doing that. After he exited the bull pen they called him over to give compliments even as the next two throwers were working, something else you seldom see. Velocity again was the issue. Putting my new eyes to work, I did notice something while I watched all of the pitchers work out. He was the only one that looked like a professional with a dazzling combination of demeanor and mechanics. After his session, those scouts knew he probably was as old as he said he was while they expressed regret that he could not get that fastball over eighty mph. Another disappointing tryout, yes, though it was not a waste. Meeting Willie Bowman was worth the drive from anywhere.

The Baltimore Orioles and the Cincinnati Reds held their tryouts later in June. These camps were a bit different in that all the pitchers faced batters in simulated game situations. The Orioles formed squads that played each other for three outs, and then changed the side, continuing in this manner until everyone had a good look batting. Each pitcher remained on the mound until he got six outs, unless his pitching was ineffective. If a pitcher experienced too many difficulties, if he could not get batters out, he was tactfully relieved.

"Is your arm getting tired?"

"No, sir. I'm all right."

"I don't want you to hurt yourself, son. Next pitcher!"

Alec faced the minimum, six batters. He struck out four, got one to pop up to the second baseman and got the other one to pop up to the first baseman in foul territory. With eight or ten more miles an hour on his fastball, he would have been on the way to Sarasota before suppertime. A week later at the Reds camp the hurlers faced live hitting again except that each of the pitchers received only three outs worth of indulgences, or in some cases, penance. Once more, he faced the minimum, once more doing it with an inadequate mid-seventies mph fastball.

Getting all these batters out so easily was producing a great deal of satisfaction, enough so that a reality check was in order. He needed to be reminded that this was a tryout. If any of these guys could hit they would probably not be here, rather they would already be playing somewhere. Therefore, it was not all that newsworthy when he got them all out so easily. His ready comeback was to point out that no other pitcher did as well.

True. Very true.

Classes at Valdosta State began during the second full week of August. Soon thereafter, the baseball tryouts for walk-ons afforded a second opportunity for would-be ballplayers to make the fall roster. The fastball that Coach Thomas wanted to see was not there. Undaunted, he was going to show up, say hello, and throw as hard as he could. Made stronger by the summer workouts, there was some evidence of a gain in velocity, just enough to make the frustration continue. Perhaps in time, the fastball would get above eighty mph. Whether it would ever get to eighty-five or more, there was no way to know. At least pitching ability was there, easily good enough for professional baseball. The work ethic was there, too, along with remarkable endurance. Knowledge of the game was not lacking, either. If there was anything else that could be done to solve the velocity problem, anything we had not already tried, it was not apparent.

Reports of the baseball tryouts at VSU came via e-mail:

Date: Tue, 28 Aug 2001 18:20:50 (EDT)
Hey Dad,
I tried out for the baseball team and I was the only left-hander (pitcher). I did not check my speed on the gun. Coach Thomas was recording the speed. He was standing behind the screen and did not tell anybody what it was. He did not talk with any of the players and Coach Jernigan ran the whole practice . . . Thomas stood in the stands with a notepad . . . The catcher I had was really good . . . he moved around the plate . . . Also, Coach Thomas kept making me throw a lot of breaking balls and change ups. I felt like I threw the ball hard and I felt pretty good.

Date: Wed, 29 Aug 2001 12:15:05 (EDT)
Hey Dad,
Well, I did not make the team and the (baseball) office was closed today.

He tried. There was always next year. He was a good student, doing very well in school, a reminder of the relative importance of things. Baseball was a side dish, not the main course. Was it time to admit that the limit of his physical capabilities had been reached? It would not have been a surprise had he reached this conclusion back in high school, or in pony league, or in little league. But he did not. Rather he kept on pitching wherever he could, still hopeful, but also for the love of the game. Pitching must have always been some kind of an unusually joyful enterprise. Every occurrence of playing the game must have brought new cherished memories. If this was the case, why quit until pitching became more trouble than it was worth?

Memories built over the years had much to do with furthering the urge to pitch again. His most treasured success to date was earning a high school varsity letter. Just being given the opportunity to pitch on the varsity team fulfilled his wildest little league dreams. How many boys from his little league got that far? Very few, to be sure. He had nothing to prove to anyone, not now, not after holding his own against all kinds of players, adolescent to adult, many with advanced skills. He knew how to pitch as anyone who ever had to bat against him would attest. With all he accomplished he could conclude, without regret or shame, it was not within the realm of possibility that his fastball could ever reach the mid-eighties no matter how hard he worked, no matter how many baseballs he threw at a tire, no matter how much spaghetti he consumed. On the other hand, perhaps there was a little more potential left in his arm. The question for which there was no definitive answer was whether the time had come to hang them up. Perhaps some day soon, just not today.

Since before starting high school, it was made clear to him that, as far as his father was concerned, he could give up baseball anytime. The effort began as just a two-year or three-year plan for little league. He was the one who took it farther. Even before joining his very first team at Murphey-Candler, the mere prospect of playing baseball drew from his core a sensation of having purpose. Baseball was an adventure, an avocation, a challenge, not merely another activity.

For some boys like Alec, baseball becomes a life within a life, the importance of which becomes apparent only when the game is being played. When the field is made ready; when the teams arrive and the players warm-up; when the umpires walk out to home plate and the line-up cards are exchanged; when every position is manned; the exhilarating effect of that singular dramatic moment, when the pitcher goes into his wind-up to deliver the first pitch at the start of a new baseball game, is almost indescribable. Then, somehow, the game itself becomes a vessel containing the essence of another being, the being of a baseball player.

Alec kept playing because he wanted to; the excitement of being a baseball player grew over time, right along with his skills. But he was not a young boy any longer. If he was going to keep playing at this age, he ought to be dead serious about it, working hard towards a higher goal even while enjoying the challenge. Satisfaction and austerity were not mutually exclusive conditions, certainly not in the advanced world of sports. Besides, if baseball was not enjoyable while giving a maximum effort, how could it be more enjoyable when malingering?

Never was he lazy about it. His fanatical work ethic was imprinted at a young age. From the very beginning of playing baseball, way back in little league, he was disabused of any notion he may ever have had of making an excuse for not pitching well. No mercy was to be had from his coaches because, as it was explained, mercy would never be shown him by an opposing batter. While crouched behind the plate catching his offerings during practice, if there was ever an utterance, and they were rare, that could be mistaken for something like, "I can't," or "I'm tired," I would quickly interrupt with a forceful and angry retort,

"What was that?"

It always turned out to be "nothing." I must have misunderstood what I thought he said.

However, after catching him most every day for twelve years it was not often I misunderstood what I saw. If something was not right, it was obvious. I could tell if he was tired or stiff or whatever. If he needed to stop throwing, no one had to tell me. Never was a workout stopped for my benefit, only for his, even though catching is not the easiest thing to do, especially as you get older. Thankfully, my knees withstood the crouching, also figuring that if Bobby Dews could still catch in the Braves' bull pen at his age, I should be able to do it, too.

Occasionally he would get annoyed with me and we would argue over some minuscule element of pitching. For instance, once we had a serious confrontation over the position of the thumb under the ball on the two-seam fastball. Another time it was the right foot landing one-half of an inch off the mark leading to an examination of cleat marks while we continued shouting at each other. There were arm angles, leg angles, length of stride, and finger pressure. Add to that release points, head movements, and a dozen elements of the follow-through. He was a machine and someone had to squirt oil and tighten bolts, whether he needed it or not. We were able to carry on like this because we had a way to settle things if the need arose. No matter how big the quarrel no impasse ever lasted long, as we would just call Ro to meet us at the field. Whatever Ro said was final. As we went along, sometimes I wondered why Alec put up with all these demands. Perhaps it was because during the ninety-nine percent of the time when he was performing his pitching drills perfectly, we got along quite well.

A throwing session on a side mound should be more than just a warm-up exercise. It is an opportunity to evaluate mechanics, breakdown components, upgrade skills, and then reassemble all these elements of pitching into a final product. When completed, the pitcher should be ready for his next start. Our side mound was not a mound at all. The throwing area containing the pitcher's stride was essentially flat. The rest of the surface from rubber to plate was a gently inclined segment near the edge of the front yard at home, declining about fourteen inches, maybe slightly more, similar to that of a regulation baseball field. The setup was simple, requiring nothing other than a regulation pitcher's plate and home plate, both anchored into the ground with steel spikes, situated sixty feet and six inches away as measured from the front of the pitching rubber to the back point of the plate. Having such a throwing area near at hand all year long was very convenient for us.

A pitcher working in the off-season should do all his workouts on a level surface instead of pitching from an elevated mound. The reason to avoid pitching from an elevated mound in practice is that it tends to break down a pitcher's physical strength. Throwing on a flat surface builds up a pitcher's strength, which is vitally important during the off-season. There is no need to be concerned that a pitcher will not be ready to pitch in a game because he has not thrown regularly from a mound. Any necessary adjustments can be made easily with a ten to fifteen minute warm-up session in a bull pen.

The ability to mix pitches effectively requires constant practice, as is needed to maintain any other baseball skill. Pitching exercises should be designed to develop and maintain command of each type of pitch while throwing these pitches sequentially. For instance, if a pitcher is only having trouble locating his curveball he will want to focus on this one pitch during a session between starts, throwing it repeatedly. However, working on only one pitch may result in going to his next game with a great command of the breaking curveball while finding he is unable to control his change-up. Such a practice session may accomplish the initial goal; however, he has not gained much ground if another skill is depleted. The simple fact to remember always is that a pitcher does not normally throw the same pitch repeatedly in a game. He throws sequences of pitches. Therefore, the challenge is in figuring out how to upgrade one particular pitch without losing or downgrading another. The best way to accomplish this is by focusing on mechanics and repetition.

Obviously, any mechanical flaw should be corrected first before repetition is used to establish muscle memory. Since the wind-up for every pitch should be identical up to the release point, it should not matter which pitch is thrown, although the fastball is generally used since it is thrown the most. Once the mechanics are correct, the quality of each pitch, including location delivery, can be perfected.

Consistency sometimes seems to be an elusive goal, near impossible to reach, and very difficult to maintain. It is not. The key is to exert a constant effort. Through trial and error, our best consistency building routine was to throw the entire sequence of pitches at about half-speed, or fifty percent effort, concentrating on the wind-up and delivery. The order of pitches used was fastball, change-up, curveball, and slider. Once the mechanics of delivery was acceptable, focus shifted briefly to the offending pitch, throwing it repeatedly until it, too, was acceptable. Because of having thrown in sequences at the start of the workout, the offending pitch never took more than five or ten throws to be corrected.

As soon as the offending pitch was thrown correctly three consecutive times, the drill returned to throwing a slightly modified sequence of pitches cleverly called "the sequence." It went thusly: fastball, change-up, fastball, curveball, fastball, slider, and fastball. The slider was always thrown up-and-in to an imaginary right-handed batter because it was the only place this lefty would throw a slider in a game. The other pitches were mostly down-and-away with occasional shots at an inside corner. The sequence would begin with about a sixty percent effort, gradually increasing to an eighty percent effort.

Throwing at full effort is not very useful or productive, but may be done if the point of near perfection is reached at eighty percent effort. Even then, "airing-it-out" with a few fastballs and change-ups, mixed in with a curveball or two, is quite enough. Not much can be gained by throwing a full-force slider other than a damaged elbow. Pre-adult youngsters should never try to pitch at one hundred percent effort. For an experienced adult pitcher, some benefit may be had while trying to reach maximum effort, or "maxing out," as it is commonly called. When done, it should only be under very controlled circumstances. One useful purpose of such an exercise is that it serves as a test of ability per strength, indicating how hard the pitcher can throw the ball while still maintaining control over it. As the effort is increased, one can identify where a pitcher's timing breaks down, as control is lost. Knowing the point of maximum useful effort helps the pitcher to avoid overthrowing, i.e., surpassing the limits of his abilities. Past this point, the maximum useful effort turns into just plain too much useless effort.

A pitcher should remember that without certain precautions during a "max out" session, there is a serious risk of tearing up an arm. For this reason, a youngster should never be told to "reach back for little more," either in practice or in a game. This phrase is spoken occasionally during broadcasts of major league games, for instance when a closer tops his normal fastball by a couple of miles per hour. No matter, such an effort should never be imitated by kids. Youth coaches should remember that major leaguers are men, they are professionals, and they are paid a lot of money. No player wants to be injured, but when a professional risks crippling his arm, it is a calculated risk, an economic decision as much as anything else is. If an unexpected disaster occurs, he is covered by insurance, both medical and disability. A kid who cripples his arm will probably never be able to pitch again. Ever.

Following normal workouts for young pitchers, the pitching arm should not require the application of ice. If so, the workouts are too severe. For instance, thirty minutes of throwing at seventy percent effort should not create the need for ice. However, five minutes of "airing-it-out" probably will. In reality, high school pitchers ice their arms frequently so it is important to do it correctly by consulting a family physician and a good athletic trainer. Finding your fifteen-year-old son asleep at night with his throwing arm wrapped in ice packs should be enough to make a father pause and consider.

Along with nearly every sporting activity, indeed, with most every activity in life comes some risk of injury. One very necessary pitching workout that contains no possibility of arm damage is the one that involves working on the mental aspects of pitching. Brain damage is unlikely as well, even when reaching back inside the skull for a little bit more. Unfortunately, mental preparation is the most neglected training activity for youngsters, sad to say, since there is no substitute for thinking in baseball. Charting pitches, watching game films, analyzing situations, measuring batters, anticipating the approach the next opponent might use at the bat; all thoughtful elements of preparation are essential to successful pitching. If the pitcher does not prepare mentally he can do little more than throw his stuff while hoping the batters do not beat him. Being nothing but hopeful is always and everywhere a fool's trap. The ditches alongside the road to the big leagues are clogged with talented arms, arms full of hope, arms that never became attached to a brain.

Such a problem did not exist with Alec. Beginning in his junior varsity season, almost nothing existed in my store of baseball knowledge that could add to what he already knew. Any suggestion or comment offered for elucidation seemed to be something he had already heard or read before, or thought of by himself. Mental deficiencies notwithstanding, my penchant to instruct was not diminished, though instructions gradually took on the form of observations while bearing in mind that the kid was a very knowledgeable baseball man, young though he was, who knew more than most coaches.

Knowledge of baseball, like most things, is cumulative, gained by continual watching, playing, and reading. When baseball becomes a young man's vocation at a very early age, persisting through adolescence and the teen years, it should not be a surprise when he turns out to be an expert. During the evenings, when most kids his age watched television or played electronic games, this one lefty spent hours thumbing through the baseball encyclopedias. He read and re-read books by great players, most notably Tom Seaver. Baseball was what he did, what he was, and what was important to him, to the point where it carried over to the rest of his life. He came to value his high school baseball friends according to their level of understanding of the game, their attitude in playing the game, and, perhaps most importantly, their respect for the game. He loathed the ones on his team who, as ballplayers, though not necessarily as buddies, seemed mostly interested in modeling a uniform. To them, collecting a letter at season's end was important because it would look good on a jacket or on a college application. Likewise, he did not care for or understand those who never tried to improve their skills, never practiced on their own, the ones whose highest aspiration was to achieve the minimum needed to get by. Needless to say, his coaches were not exempted from an even more severe scrutiny. There was nothing elitist in his way of thinking; he simply had standards. Above all else, he had respect for the game.

As it was in his freshman year at college, the second year contained the same good news-bad news; failed to make the team, succeeded in making good academic progress. He continued enjoying a student's life in the business school. On balance, college was going very well. However, just when there was a chance to put baseball aside for a little while, allowing more focus on the increasingly difficult business school courses, his pitching arm was summoned to duty. A couple of weeks into the semester, Dillingham called asking him to accompany a team from the Atlanta MABL to play in a tournament down in the Clearwater/St. Petersburg area during the first week of November. No arm-twisting was required.

These particular baseball tournaments draw teams from all over the Eastern United States. Games are played on beautiful, well-kept major league spring training fields. Players who attend pay their own way unless the team acquires sponsors. Since several games are played in a relatively short time period, teams use up their pitchers very quickly. Due to roster limitations and the format of these tournaments, pitchers generally have to play positions when not pitching. This is fine as far as it goes except that in order to maintain good fielding and hitting, there is a tendency to fill out the roster with position players who can also pitch rather than with pitchers who can also play positions. Most players going to a four-game weekend tournament, after all, would like to do more than just pitch in one game. The player who only wants to pitch is an unusual exception. For the unusual exception on the Atlanta team, Valdosta was conveniently located halfway to Clearwater. The first part of the tournament was to be played between Friday evening and Sunday morning. If the Atlanta team advanced to the final rounds on Monday, some classes would be missed.

Team manager, Martin De Leon, pulled together a good group of players, not a superior team, but a very good team that was expected to hold its own. The team, called the Atlanta MABL Stars, contained several players from the Cubs. Their uniform cap was the Houston Astros' batting practice cap made of a knit or mesh-type material with the usual Astros' star on the front. The reason they chose this particular cap was not clear, nor did it seem worthwhile to seek an explanation.

The first two games were scheduled as a day/night double-header on Friday in the Carpenter Complex in Clearwater, then the spring training home of the Philadelphia Phillies, with the first game at 3:00 and the nightcap at 7:00. Game three was set for Saturday afternoon at 4:30 in famous Al Lang Stadium in St. Petersburg. For the fourth and last regular tournament game, the fellows would return to the Carpenter Complex Sunday morning at 9:00. Alec's last class ended at 11:30 a.m. on Friday. I was waiting outside the business school on the North Campus as class was dismissed. We drove directly to his dormitory where he changed clothes, grabbed his bags, and we were on Interstate 75 heading south by noon.

De Leon knew that we would arrive during the early innings of the first game. This was not a problem because Alec was slated to start the game at Al Lang Stadium on Saturday evening. He would only be used, if needed, as a reliever on Friday night.

The drive went smoothly until running into a little Tampa traffic on the expressways, especially south of the airport while trying to get on Florida Route 60, the Gulf to Bay Boulevard. Even so, it was nowhere near as bad as Atlanta traffic. Once across the upper end of the bay entering Clearwater, we made the turn north onto U.S. Highway 19. The Carpenter Complex fields were located near the intersection of Highway 19 and Drew Street. Arrival time was 4:00 p.m., in the middle of the third inning.

The Carpenter Complex layout is the same as the Devil Ray's Naimoli Complex over in nearby St. Petersburg. Four fields, symmetrically aligned, point outwardly. The backstops delineate the borders of a substantial central quadrangle. Within this area are buildings, viewing stands, and concessions.

Each field here was named in honor of a former well-known Phillies player. The Atlanta Stars double header was to be played on the Robin Roberts field that faced northeast from the center area. One small problem had to be solved before the lefty could play; he needed a uniform cap. An exhaustive search of Atlanta area sports stores for this particular Astros batting practice cap turned up nothing, not even one in the wrong size. I figured he could use another cap of a similar color or just a regular Astros cap. The MABL in Atlanta enforces a uniform code, sort of. After more than ten years of being associated with the league, never was a player refused entry into a game for not being in uniform as long as the other manager did not object, which he would not do so as long as the outfit was not confusing to team identity.

Well, apparently they were being very strict about uniforms in this tournament. De Leon said he had to have a uniform cap or he could not play. Splendid, it was 4:30 on a Friday afternoon in Clearwater, Florida and the kid needs a baseball cap. Nothing unusual, just an official, fitted, mesh, Houston Astros' home field, batting practice baseball cap. Where within driving distance could one be found? De Leon suggested a sports store up Highway 19 a mile or two away in a shopping mall on the right. He heard they had lots of baseball caps. It sounded like a hopeless quest. As no other options were available, a run to the mall was in order. Fortunately, the store was easy to locate taking a mere ten minutes through light traffic. Upon entering, I inquired of the baggy-panted, ear-ringed, pony-tailed, presumably male clerk, did they carry the Houston Astros fitted mesh home field batting practice baseball cap? He seemed surprised that someone thought to ask such a question, probably assuming it came from an out-of-towner. The immediate reply,

"Sure, man, there over on that table."

Towards the back of the store was an enormously wide selection of baseball caps, thousands actually, including at least thirty of the style we sought. As luck would have it, they were placed on the clearance table, marked to fifty percent of their regular price, along with an adjacent sign on the table indicating another fifty percent discount. We could not find one in his exact size; however, one slightly large fit could be worn without falling off the head. Under the circumstances, it was good enough.

At the cash register, the price came out as one-half of the already marked down price. Seeming to be an overly generous discount, and not wanting to gain from a possible pricing error, we asked the clerk if these signs were correct and not redundant. They were correct. The final cost was about seven dollars including tax.

I hate malls. I never go there except for emergencies, even then making great haste while diverting all glances away from any displays in any store windows lest it slow the pace. Perhaps it is a fear of having the mind tainted with vagrant mercantile whims. Be that as it may, seven bucks for a baseball cap is quite a deal, enough to relieve the consternation of being in such a discomfiting environment. Admittedly, the thought of buying more did occur, a thought decisively allayed upon realizing the need to exit. A slight thirty-minute departure from a baseball game is quite enough, would that every shopping adventure be this efficient.

The still inexplicable mystery was why did a sports store in a Clearwater, Florida shopping mall stock up on Houston Astros fitted mesh home field batting practice baseball caps. The obvious way to find out was to ask the manager. On the other hand, the idea of conversing with a store manager who employed baggy-panted, ear-ringed, ponytailed, presumably male clerks was not very enticing. Besides, this clerk may have been the manager of the store. One never knows what to expect, anymore. Whatever the case, there was no burning desire to know the answer to this mystery, or to the mystery of why the team picked this unusual uniform cap in the first place. Who needs to know everything?

The last few innings of the first game were equally as brief and efficient as our shopping spree, though the outcome was not as providential. The Stars lost a close one to the Charleston Reds. To advance to the playoff championship round on Monday the team rightly assumed it was almost necessary to win three out of four games. Having lost the first, everyone knew it essential to win all three remaining games. Two wins out of four would probably not be enough.

The second game Friday evening was against the Orlando Twins. By the time they reached the middle innings of this game, the Atlanta team was already on its fourth pitcher. De Leon did not want to use Alec, but he was running out of options. In the home half of the seventh inning the game turned as the Twins took a 7-4 lead even as Alec was warming up in the bull pen. Going in to pitch the bottom of the eighth inning, still losing, the only thought could be about the necessity to hold them right there if the team was to have a decent chance of winning the game. With Tommy Dillingham doing the catching, the first batter grounded out to the shortstop, Jason Waddell. The next batter hit a solid double, advancing to third on a throwing error. Losing by three with a man on third and only one out was not what the Atlanta team needed. To add some spice to the stew, Alec proceeded to walk the next batter on five pitches. Phantoms from earlier panics were settling in as everything bad that could be visualized flashed through the synapses, mainly the ones that tend to trigger irrationality. Was this long day, full of classes and travel, manifesting itself in depleted pitching skills?

The situation was becoming somewhat desperate. Hints of both resignation and panic seemed to have crept into the dugout afflicting various members of the Atlanta team because there was no one else to pitch except more non-pitcher position players. Alec had to get the job done, and then the team had only more chance to score some runs. Ever since his junior high years pitching at the old field in Norcross, Alec had considered any unoccupied base under all circumstances to be an open base. It did not have to be first base. If a runner occupied first base with no one out, he considered second and third to be "open." Most normal people in baseball consider a base open when, upon intentionally filling it, there is created an increased likelihood of ending the inning without another run scoring because of the additional force out opportunity. To compliment Alec's rather peculiar outlook, though, was another ever-present aspect; the assumption that he could pitch out of all situations. Therefore, he never fretted over filling any bases as long as runs were not scoring. I do not think De Leon knew this. Some of his longer-term teammates may have known this and, though it usually worked, they probably did not like it or agree with it. Rather, I am sure it tended to make them nervous. Nerves aside, first and second were the open bases here.

While a batter is easy to figure out, it is difficult to know what goes on inside the head of a pitcher. The perspective held by the one man who holds the baseball while standing on the mound is very complex, not easily simulated. At this point in the game, this pitcher was doing two things. First, he was trying to figure out and maybe expand the strike zone. Not starting the game created a disadvantage for a control type of pitcher. Pitching effectively depends on knowing the absolute edges of the strike zone. With the game at stake and only two bases to fill, finding the corners had to be done in a hurry. Pitching just off the corners resulted in a walk, a bad thing that could produce some good if it prompted the umpire to expand his field of vision even if it was ever so slightly. Second, since his pitches were just missing the edges of the plate, the batter on-deck plainly saw that he was not a wild pitcher. This might induce him to look for a fastball strike on the first pitch, rather than to think of taking pitches until he was thrown a strike. It was a late inning. The batter, with his team enjoying a nice lead, had an RBI opportunity. He did not come all the way to a tournament in Clearwater just to collect bases-on-balls; he wanted base hits. Assuming fastball, the batter was probably prepared to swing at the first pitch if it appeared to be in the strike zone. It may be, after all, the best pitch he would see.

The first pitch was a change-up, not a fastball. Who would have expected a change-up in a situation like this? When a batter is out in front of a change-up and makes contact, he will most likely hit a pop-up pulled to the left side. If he is able to wait on it, being unbalanced, the result will most likely be a grounder to a middle infielder and result in a double play.

This batter was out on his front foot swinging. He hit the ball a high, lazy foul down the left field line. The runner on third base watched it going foul, apparently not thinking the charging left fielder was going to make the catch. By the time it became evident a catch would be made, he was tardy getting back to tag the base, thereby losing the chance to score. He may have been able to score, indeed, with more alert base running. The ball was not hit very deep and the runner was not fast, but the left fielder was running away towards the fence when he caught it, not immediately set to throw the ball home. We will never know. As it stood, the Stars were left with a brighter outlook now that there were two outs with runners still on first and third. Suddenly, after a very clever choice of what to throw, Alec was completely in command of the situation. The odds were in his favor because the next batter, without realizing anything, had to overcome a pitcher who had reached an agreement with the umpire on the definition of the strike zone. Few batters in this kind of tournament would have any idea what was about to happen. Alec struck him out on three pitches.

Having seen him pitch out of situations like this one so many times before, I wondered why I still became so concerned. I, above all people, should have assumed that he knew the best way to get through anything. The good news was the team still had a chance. Three runs were not that many with metal bats and designated hitters. While batting in the top of the ninth, the Atlanta team managed to get a couple of base runners. Alas, it came to naught. The first two games of the tournament were lost. The possibility of advancing to the second round was all but gone.

A trip to Florida would not be complete without a visit to the shore. The next morning we spent a couple of hours touring some of the Clearwater and St. Petersburg beaches, viewing the tranquil waters of the Gulf of Mexico. The coastline of the United States being the more dominant one, a better name for this adjunct of the Caribbean Sea would seem to be the Gulf of America. Perhaps at one time, much of the American coastline belonged to Mexico, but this fact does not validate the current name any more than if it were to be called the Gulf of the Confederacy or the Gulf of Spain. Packed in our wagon were a couple of surfboards just in case of waves. There was none, barely a ripple, only good for a refreshing swim.

Returning to the hotel after lunch, we split up. Alec stayed to do some homework while I toured the area looking for a Catholic Church with an early Sunday Mass. Attending a Saturday evening Mass was not possible because we had to be at Al Lang Stadium before 3:30 p.m. The Sunday morning game was scheduled for 9:00. The only possibility was to go early. The best deal I could find, or so I calculated, was the 6:45 a.m. Mass at St. Catherine of Siena Church on South Belcher Road in Clearwater, about three miles from the Carpenter fields. With my Sunday obligation done, I would have the rest of the day to watch baseball followed by the drive back home to Norcross.

A 6:45 a.m. Mass was what would have been called the fisherman's Mass in the old days back in Erie, except back then the early Mass was at 6:00 a.m., following confessions at 5:45 a.m., and said in Latin. Attended by a mere handful of faithful men, it was brief, a sermon being unwarranted at that hour of the day. A man could be out on the water with a baited hook by 6:45 a.m. lighting up a Camel while popping the top off of that first bottle of Kohler beer. Alec planned to go to the Sunday evening Mass at the Newman Center back in Valdosta. Sleeping in was his best plan in order to get some extra rest before the last game.

Later in the afternoon, the players had a team meeting at the hotel. The middle of a tournament is a good time to get organized, as good as any other, I suppose. We then got something to eat before heading downtown to the famous Al Lang Stadium in St. Petersburg, site of the spring training home games of the Tampa Bay Devil Rays. A long time desire to see this place was presently to be fulfilled.

Al Lang, a one-time mayor of St. Petersburg, became known as that city's "father of baseball," a moniker well-earned by the heroic efforts he undertook in bringing major league spring training baseball to the Florida West Coast. Although this dignified baseball park had been known for a long time as "Al Lang Stadium," the new, official, awkward-sounding, store-bought kind of name was *Florida Power Park, Home of Al Lang Field*. Since 1916, Al Lang Stadium served as the winter home for several major league teams including the Braves (1922-24), Yankees

(1925-37), and Cardinals (1938-97). The Devil Rays took it over in 1998. It was also used by the Class-A St. Petersburg Devil Rays in the summer.

The ballpark is situated on First Street South in the downtown area right at the edge of Tampa Bay, only a few blocks from the Devil Ray's major league park, Tropicana Field. Al Lang's capacity is a friendly and comfortable seven thousand. The view from the grandstand seats, while looking out beyond the outfield wall, is quintessentially Florida, a vista filled by palm trees, a boat marina, and the expanse of the bay. Perhaps it is possible to hit a baseball into Tampa Bay over the left field fence, but it would take an awfully mighty blow.

Al Lang is a special place with a baseball heritage almost too pleasant to contemplate. One could safely assume that nearly every major league ballplayer attending spring training in Florida since 1916 played in this ballpark: Murderer's Row, the Gashouse Gang, the Miracle Mets, almost the entire century of the baseball encyclopedia, almost every member of the hall of fame, left cleat marks in this imported dirt. (Florida dirt alone is too sandy for baseball fields.)

Occasionally, amidst the routines of everyday life, special moments occur that are remembered because they exude an unusually high level of comfort. Within surroundings pleasant and hospitable, the mind released of anxiety, the body freed of aches and pains, temporal worries forgotten, absolutely nothing but the good, the decent, and the optimistic exist. This was Al Lang Stadium, picture-perfect and balmy on a Florida autumn evening as a very slight variable breeze made shirtsleeves feel a tad cool though donning a jacket retained more warmth than desired, until the later innings. For the moment, it was most comfortable being seated right behind home plate, puffing on a very fine cigar, reflecting about this place and its past, about the game of baseball in general, and about the game soon to be played. My son was scheduled to be the starting pitcher in Al Lang Stadium this night, playing for an Atlanta team against the St. Petersburg Red Tide. None of the many other all-star players from his past youth leagues was asked to pitch for this team on this night, but he was.

Thoughts turned to Mickey Mantle playing here back in 1959, 1960, and 1961, before heading north for the regular season, and all the other Yankees, Roger Maris, too. Then I would go see them play at Griffith Stadium. More thoughts about my father's favorite ballplayer and my own hero, Stan Musial, who spent every spring of his career with the Cardinals while Al Lang was their spring home for Grapefruit League games. If only the clock could be turned back, just for an hour or two, maybe for just a few innings, perhaps to 1948 or 1949. I thought of all the pitchers who had pitched here, especially left-handers, like Koufax, Ford, and Spahn. Now I was about to watch my favorite pitcher of all time. There was no other place in the world I would rather have been. There was no other life I would rather have lived. This was perfect.

The reminiscences would not stop, some of them about an opening day at Murphey-Candler Little League ten years earlier where all of this began. Could this be where it ends? There was no reason to think it would, yet the thought materialized. Our baseball memories made so far could last several lifetimes already, yet they kept coming. This game to be played in this stadium would be a brilliant final deposit to our bank of baseball recollections. What could have been more unlikely for my young lefty than to end up here, in this historic place, to pitch a ballgame? Was it ten years since he was first signed up for the little league? Already ten years. Why did they go by so fast?

The baseball playing men from Atlanta experienced enjoyment from the first moment they entered the stadium. Having been designated the home team they dutifully occupied the first base dugout. Instead of going to work, everyone participated in a thorough exploration of the facilities, beginning with the back door leading out of the dugout, a privy immediately on the right, down the tunnel leading under the grandstands. While taking turns playing with the telephone to the bull pen, someone remembered, there was another reason for being here, to play a baseball game. Perhaps it was time to warm up.

Martin De Leon inserted himself as starting catcher so he went with Alec down to the bull pen to start throwing. What a pleasing thought it was that these guys had the opportunity to play here, especially the three from Norcross, Tommy Dillingham, Patrick Turner, and Alec. They were now grown-ups, already men, while still evincing a demeanor reminiscent of boyhood. Retained in their faces, enunciated in their discourse, was that unmistakable enthusiasm for the game carried over throughout all the years they had played it. This was baseball in one of its finest forms. As they prepared to play in this legendary baseball venue, the realization intensified among them that this was indeed a special occasion, a special place, a special game, even though absolutely nothing except pride and self-respect was at stake in the outcome. It was merely another opportunity for them to express the pure, unadulterated, never-to-be-defiled love of this game.

Somewhat surprising was the appearance of a few people coming into the ballpark not connected to the two teams, just some passersby who noticed there was going to be a ballgame. In they came for some free baseball. Game time was approaching as the Atlanta team took the field for their final warm-up tosses. When the announcer turned on the public address system to announce the starting line-ups, I was ready for the moment of truth, the one long anticipated since way back on Holy Thursday, 1981. Here it was, a major league ballpark, Alec warming up on the mound, player introductions being made, the sound of the announcer's voice echoing down from the public address system speakers hanging from mounts underneath the roof above the grandstands. Then, suddenly, after a dramatic two or three second pause, loud, clear, authoritative, distinctive,

"On the mound for Atlanta, Alec Barnes."

How about that! His name, I would humbly say, sounded poignant, unambiguous, engaging, magnificent. It worked. It was a perfect-sounding name for a public address system in a baseball stadium. The announcer should have added,

"Good job, Dad!"

Ah, well, fathers often must labor in anonymity; a job well done had to be, once again, its own reward. I had done my part, the hard part I should think. Indeed, I had done it well. Now, all the kid had to do was pitch.

The first inning went nicely. The leadoff man hit a pop-up on a 1-2 pitch to Turner at second base. The second batter did likewise to the shortstop, Waddell. The change-up was moving. The next batter took a 3-2 pitch for ball four. Again, he was taking advantage of two outs, bases empty, early in the game, trying to define the strike zone, possibly getting it stretched out a bit. Good idea except the cleanup batter was the designated hitter, a big guy who looked a lot like Ted Kluszewski, the former Cincinnati first baseman who three times (1953, 1954, and 1955) hit forty or more home runs, while striking out forty or fewer times. This could have been Teddy K., Jr., from the striking resemblance.

Fortunately, this turned out to be someone other than Kluszewski, or his son. Although he swung mightily with his metal bat at a 2-0 pitch, and sent the ball rocketing skyward, it settled directly into the center fielder's glove, as he barely moved from his medium depth position. It was a very good start: no runs, no hits, no errors, one walk, and one man stranded.

The second inning was a nightmare. There were six hits, five singles and a double, a walk, and an error. Seven runs scored, five of them earned. He was making good pitches because not one ball was hit particularly well. At least everything stayed in the park. Still it resulted in a cascade of seeing-eye grounders and one hundred fifty foot bloopers that fell between the fielders. I could not remember an inning this horrible in all of the three hundred fifty innings he had pitched up to this time. The next three innings went more like the first. This outing for the left-handed Valdosta State accounting major concluded after five complete innings with a strike out of the last batter he faced. Not too bad, could have been better.

The other pitchers understandably wanted a chance to pitch in Al Lang Stadium, too, so a rotation took place for the remainder of the game. The Atlanta team's bats finally did get going in the late innings as they mounted a valiant comeback, almost enough to win the game. In fact, the run that would have tied the game was in scoring position during the bottom of the ninth inning with the heart of the order coming up. It was not to be. The game ended without another run crossing the plate. The Atlanta team lost 12-10.

A unique opportunity presented itself after Alec came out of the game, which was to go down into the dugout under the pretext of bringing some ice for his arm, and, afterwards, finding there was no apparent reason to leave, find a seat on the bench. Actually, the temptation of watching the rest of the ballgame from inside the dugout was irresistible. Such a good vantage point can rarely be had. Looking over at him during a lull it seemed fitting to remark that he pitched pretty well for four innings. He already knew that. So I said,

"Do you remember Glavine in the '92 All Star game?"

He turned and looked at me, saying with a sigh, "Yea, I know."

Glavine was pulled from that game before completing the second inning after giving up five earned runs on nine singles. Within the art of pitching is contained an aptitude for averting disaster. The greatest of the great major league pitchers can do it most of the time. No one can do it all of the time. If a horrible inning can happen to Glavine, it will happen to everyone else, too. Thankfully, these occasions have been few and far between. Besides, he got to stay in the game for three additional innings and show he could do better against this line-up.

Playing in this ballpark was an experience to be long remembered. Many pictures were taken before, after, and during the game. As in other games, it was filmed with a camcorder. Losing was a big disappointment; there was no doubt about that. However, in the larger scheme of things, winning would have just been a bonus. The experience alone was extraordinary.

Going to any ballpark to see a baseball game is special. When going to play the game, it is a hundred times better. When going to a ballpark like Al Lang Stadium, well, maybe it is not Yankee Stadium or Turner Field, but it comes close, especially for these ballplayers. Just as the greater part of playing baseball is between the ears, the greater part of baseball memories is pieced together by the imagination.

There was nothing cheap about this experience. On such a beautiful night for baseball as this one was, maybe they should have played two, though one was special enough. Were they appreciative of the opportunity to play here? Yes, it would be very safe to assume so. They loved the game of baseball and loved playing it. They had traveled a long way for this. By the time they left the stadium, each one had acquired for it a special affection, now that each added his cleat marks to those of the great ones. Win or lose, it was well worth the effort.

De Leon did not say much after the game, nor did anyone else. No one knew what to say. The usual chatter that follows most games was not heard, no talk about how the game was played, about this hit or that play, how someone should have cut a throw or should not have swung at a particular pitch. Losing a third close game guaranteed a dismal tournament outcome. There was not silence, either. Talk could be heard if an effort to hear was made, a quiet sort of talking, subdued, even-paced to slow, not boisterous. Perhaps no one knew how to express this unusual combination of grief and delight constructed of both the disappointment for losing another game and the satisfaction for having played in a great ballpark. Twenty-four hours earlier an easy atmosphere of hopefulness prevailed. Now, an effort was required to fend off despondency.

If they had won this game at Al Lang, combined with a win of one game of the previous evening's double-header, there would have been a lot more chatter. One more well timed hit and one more strikeout in place of an RBI single would have done it. Then the Sunday morning game would have been very important, the outcome of which would have determined if the Atlanta Stars would go home a loser or stay over into Monday as one of the elite teams of the tournament. As it was, one more game, inconsequential and compulsory, remained to be played.

The trip back to reality, to the world which all of us belonged, was as long as the stadium's small parking lot. First order of business was to stop for some hamburgers on the way back to the hotel. Nothing else brings one back to being ordinary again as emphatically as standing in line inside a fast food joint. Even with the kid wearing a baseball uniform, in this part of Florida baseball uniforms were not considered unusual attire. In fact, as casual as society had become, it was much more common down there to see a man wearing a baseball uniform than a jacket and a necktie. Lost in some incongruous thoughts came this musing: if an announcement had been made to everyone in the place that this very kid just pitched a baseball game in Al Lang Stadium, the response surely would have been a mostly underwhelming,

"Big deal. You and how many thousands of others?"

Some of the fellows on the team decided to take in a little nightlife while checking out the local saloons and some other premier establishments. Some did not and turned in early. They had no chance of advancing, but it only made sense to try to play the last game as well as possible, to enjoy it for what it was. This cannot be done by staying out late engaging in various sorts of deviltries and excess. Besides, what did Clearwater offer that was not available in Atlanta? The answer: baseball on major league fields. Plenty of nighttime entertainment awaited them back home. In spite of the call to duty, some of the fellows could not wait that long.

Alec did not think he would be able to pitch the next morning since he reached ninety-nine pitches in the five innings worked that evening, including thirty-two pitches in the second inning alone. He had also pitched an inning late Friday evening to close the second game of the double-header. The starters in the two Friday games would likely have to split the effort Sunday morning then, maybe, he could come in to relieve an inning or two, if needed. This was his expectation.

Awaking at the usual weekday time of 5:30 a.m. came without the need for an alarm clock even though it was the weekend. The days of sleeping in on Saturdays and Sundays were long gone. First chore of the day was normally to look for a newspaper. Reaching the lobby at about 6:00 a.m., a ritual had to be performed including the grab for a cup of coffee and a glance at the morning paper before taking off for St. Catherine's. The stale jellyrolls were not yet out.

The situation was strange from the start. Many cars were in the parking lot, surprising for such an early Mass, more so because hardly a soul was inside the church. This changed quickly. As if by design, people started pouring in, a rather large crowd it was. It appeared as if they came together, as a group. Did a Bingo game from the night before just let out? Whatever was going on, these folks did not look much like fishermen.

The Mass, instead of being brief, turned out to be as long as one would expect an Easter Vigil at an archdiocesan cathedral to be. By 7:45, they had just started the Canon. An hour and fifteen minutes into this Mass, before Communion had started, I bolted for the door. The St. Michael's 7:00 a.m. Mass in Clearwater probably would have been out by that time. How frustrating it can be when a man finds himself inconvenienced by the oblivious intentions of others?

The Atlanta team's fourth and final game was scheduled to be played on the Mike Schmidt field, the one that faced towards the southeast from the center area of the complex. The opposing team was called the Long Island Storm. Word had it they were very good after having easily won their first three games. Arriving at 8:30 with fistfuls of whatever looked edible from the breakfast buffet, along with several cups of coffee, we would have been half-an-hour late for warm-ups at a normal game. Not surprisingly, almost no one else was there. Alec did not even care to try loosening up because the arm was very stiff. I badgered him until he made a few throws. After about ten easy tosses, he said he could do no more and sat down. By 8:55, only eight players were present meaning everyone had better get loose. Sore arm or not, the previous night starter was going to have to play an outfield position if no one else showed up right away. At exactly 9:00, with the umpires taking their positions, a few of the other players arrived looking rather haggard and pale. A few more straggled in during the first half inning. Eventually everyone got there. Fortunately, two of the first late comers had thought to put on their uniforms back at the hotel so there were ten Atlantans dressed to play. Alec sat back down. It was also fortunate that the Stars was designated the visiting team because nine were not present to take the field at game time, but only after they started their at bat. Thank God for small favors.

Small favors, indeed! Luck ran out quickly when the Atlanta starting pitcher got into trouble during the bottom of the first inning, promptly giving up five runs. De Leon, portraying a melancholic alarm, searched throughout the dugout for help, almost pleading for someone else to pitch. A man reduced to begging is never a pretty sight.

It had been in Alec's nature to want to pitch all the time. One would think, perhaps, there must be a limit for everything. Well, even under these circumstances, he said he would pitch when no one else volunteered. He started to warm up very slowly, continuing to do so all the way through the top of the second inning, until it was time to go out to the mound in the bottom half. Perhaps he could last an inning. After that, they could use the infielders, then outfielders, then old men from the stands. Were my cleats in the car?

He survived the second inning in decent shape, giving up two singles along with one run scored, which was unearned due to an error. The inning ended with a double play. Surprisingly, he walked out to the mound for the third inning. No one else wanted to pitch this day, including position players. It brought back memories of the little league Blue Jays when the question was asked who wanted to pitch, almost every hand went up. What changed during the past ten years?

For the lefty, apparently, nothing had changed when it came to desire. He continued to pitch the rest of the game. The Stars lost 15-8. He yielded but five earned runs. Although the Stars had some very good baseball players, there were seven errors committed behind him, which gave incontrovertible proof that not one of these guys was as good a man as Mickey Mantle or Billy Martin. The entertainment of the previous night had taken its toll, and it showed.

Alec threw one hundred thirty-four pitches of which sixty-nine percent were strikes. There were many deep counts and two-strike foul balls. He struck out four and walked none. One home run, a solo shot, hooked just inside the left field foul pole. With the metal bats, this contest looked like a typical mediocre small college baseball game. There was some consolation to be had in that this Long Island Storm team went on to win the whole tournament. If that was the whole story, well, not a terribly bad effort under the circumstances.

However, there was a bit more to the story. There always is. A few months later, an article appeared in *Hardball* magazine, the official magazine of the Men's Senior Baseball League, which reported the Long Island Storm had been disqualified, their championship win in the tournament taken away. Apparently, they had several current professional players on the team who were not eligible to play at the time under the league's eligibility rules. Some of the Storm's players were filling in a playing gap between the end of their minor league season and the next spring training. Some others may have been released from their minor league teams for injuries or performance reasons. Playing on this team in the interim was an opportunity to stay in game shape while they hoped to get a real playing job back. No doubt, several of them planned to show up at the nearby spring training sites in a couple of months after this MABL tournament. Whatever the case may have been, reading this story I said to myself,

"I thought they looked pretty good."

No kidding. The pitching performance, with a tired arm, good hitters, and metal bats, was not too shabby.

What a weekend, so full of activity, yet passing by so quickly, it was over in a flash, or so it seemed. Beginning on a typical Friday morning with classes in Valdosta, ending on Sunday afternoon after gathering a whirlwind of baseball memories in Clearwater and St. Petersburg, made one think, just how does one manage to acquire such wonderful experiences with such ease? The answer is simple. This is baseball; anything can happen.

Between 9:00 pm Friday and 12:00 noon Sunday the kid pitched fourteen complete innings, faced seventy-eight batters, and threw two hundred forty-seven pitches, a good combination of capability and endurance. The first inning at Al Lang was the good one, the most memorable. The last inning against the Storm facing erstwhile minor leaguers was three up and three down. In between, all kinds of things happened, good and bad.

Here it was, midday Sunday, the fourth game over, and seeming as if almost no time had passed since we arrived. Good-byes with plenty of hearty and sincere handshakes marked an end to this very unusual, somewhat satisfying experience. There was no getting around the fact that the Atlanta Stars lost all four games, yet it was not necessary to discuss this at any length. The outcome could have been entirely different if they had had just a little more pitching, maybe just a little more hitting, and perhaps a little bit better fielding. A little more speed running the bases may have helped in a couple of key situations, too. Yes, if only a few things had been slightly better they could have been contenders. Yes, if . . . as Ernie Johnson used to say,

"If your Aunt Minnie had a beard, she'd be your Uncle Fred!"

De Leon had done a magnificent job pulling the team together, while making all the arrangements. Until someone has successfully completed the logistics for such an event, he cannot fully appreciate the effort involved. The team was managed very well, too, regardless of the outcome. Everyone got to play, everyone had a good time, and no one was injured. As weekends go, when playing baseball in Florida on major league fields, this one turned out just fine. Some of the fellows stayed over to spend Sunday afternoon at the beach and then to watch some of the Monday games. We grabbed a bag of ice from the concession area, threw the equipment bag in the back of the Volvo wagon, and began the drive back to Valdosta. The kid had school the next day and my neglected office needed some attention.

    The trip back was just long enough to recap the four games. It went quickly. He was back at his dormitory at 4:00 p.m. with plenty of time to shower, change clothes, drop by the Newman Center for Mass, and then get ready for Monday classes. Thinking that it might be nice to do something involving baseball for a change during the three-and-a-half hour drive back to Norcross, I listened to a tape recording of the radio broadcast of game six of the 1995 World Series between the Braves and the Indians. Center fielder Grissom caught the ball for the final out on the ramp to Interstate 285, the perimeter highway surrounding Atlanta. Those three and a half hours went by fast, too. All Glavine needed for his win was a poke from Justice. Now that was a good baseball game.

## Chapter Seventeen
# Summer Baseball and Surfing

Quite a year had just passed. The first year of the new millennium, 2001 A.D., had been a very good one, notwithstanding the September 11 dastardly attacks on America by some of the most errant dregs of humanity, cowardly males who probably grew up playing soccer and never learned the game of baseball. In spite of the widespread sorrow and a righteous retaliatory resolve, life in America continued in earnest because life in America was well worth living.

For the lefty, baseball in 2001 began during the first weekend of February at the Devil Rays' spring training in St. Petersburg and ended a few miles away during the first weekend of November at the Phillies' spring training site in Clearwater. The full-time business student pitched seventy-nine and one-third innings, while facing three hundred and seventy-nine batters. The line read fifty-five strikeouts, fourteen walks, ninety-six hits, and an ERA of 4.08. The hits broke down to seventy-nine singles, twelve doubles, and five home runs. In addition to these official game numbers, he pitched in a few practice games and at several tryouts.

On the "off" days, he completed the usual rigorous throwing drills accompanied by much running. Anyone might have wondered when his arm was going to fall off. It never did. If it could withstand the MABL tournament in St. Petersburg and Clearwater, without injury, after throwing two hundred forty-seven pitches in three different games on three successive days during a period of thirty-nine hours, his arm could withstand just about anything.

Baseball was important, but school remained a priority. The spring would come along with another opportunity to play, if he chose to do so. Meanwhile, his attention returned to classroom work. As far as baseball was concerned, maybe one more summer of pitching and workouts would bring enough added velocity to get a shot at rookie ball or the Valdosta State fall roster. Maybe it would take two or three more years of work along with further weight gain. Possibly, it would never happen. For the time being, there was no indication he was thinking about giving it up.

At the start of the summer, actually in early May, after returning from college, Alec had not yet sought out a spot on any team. The Cubs' team from the previous summer had dissolved, and then it was partially resuscitated by some others. The players he knew scattered to different teams, one of which was the MABL Angels. He joined, but it proved to be a mistake as the team turned out to be a disjointed, poorly managed one. Dillingham was not the manager, unfortunately. After just a few weeks, Alec left the Angels and became a free agent. This meant he was available for any of the other managers to pick up. When his name went through e-mail to all the MABL managers, calls came the very next day from the Indians, the Cherokees, and the Swamp Dragons. He joined the Swamp Dragons.

Alec took the time to attend only one professional tryout during the summer of 2002, a camp conducted by the Baltimore Orioles at Lassiter High School, about ten miles from Norcross. According to my count, approximately seventy-five players attended. The tryout began with the fifty or so non-pitchers going through the usual regimen of the sixty-yard run, infield drills, outfield drills, and catchers throwing to second base. The pitching was evaluated during live at bats with each pitcher allowed three outs as long as it did not take too long.

This time, not everyone was allowed to bat. About twenty were selected from the group of position players according to their running and fielding abilities. By making the batting exercise selective, the aura of the tryout changed drastically. Those few who remained had the greater baseball skills so the pitchers would face only the best of the group. Out came the wood bats. Pitchers started warming as the scouts chatted with each other, clipboards handy, occasionally jotting a note or a number. They took seats behind the backstop, pulled Juggs guns out of their cases, and started to call out the details needed to proceed.

Alec pitched near the middle of the pack of hurlers. This time it took four batters to get three outs. The second batter managed a base hit single. He struck out the other three. As always, many other pitchers threw harder, none of them had better results. Without exception, all of the eighty-five to ninety mph fastballs thrown by others inside the strike zone were being severely lined to points all over the outfield. Alec's catcher was good, gave good targets, and thoughtfully mixed up the pitches. Not one of the other pitchers this day had such good mechanics, either. As usual, none of the pitchers was signed out of this camp.

Two position players who had already played in the minors, now having recovered from the injuries that had caused their release, stood out so much it made most of the others look very mediocre. One of them, a middle infielder, ran the sixty-yard dash in an almost unbelievable 6.4 seconds. He was also the one who reached base with the hit off of Alec. The other batters were sitting on the fastball, making them easy strikeout victims. Not so for the former minor leaguer who immediately saw what Alec was doing and went with an off-speed pitch away, hitting the ball to the opposite field. It was a fine piece of hitting by the professional player, totally unexpected by the lefty in this setting. The scouts had a follow-up chat with both former minor leaguers and, most likely, they managed to find a playing job for the remainder of the summer.

The rest of the group was typical. Only a few other fielders had even above average high school skills. The same went for the pitchers, most of whom were wild throwers employing peculiar methods of delivering the baseball. A few threw hard enough to draw some attention. One kid still in high school, a right-hander, already known by the scouts, threw about ninety mph. They were very interested in him even though he would not be eligible for the draft until June of the following year. Only one catcher consistently threw the ball down to second base in less than 2.0 seconds, as he was the only one with good footwork and throwing mechanics. The scouts spent some time talking with this young man, too.

A constant source of dismay at these tryouts is the prevalent lack of proper technique at every defensive station. For some reason, though, most of the players look good swinging the bat, as long as they are swinging at good hard fastballs. Could it be that most of the practice time and lesson money for youngsters is spent with hitting instructors rather than fielding and pitching instructors? Even so, when the pitches are something other than fastballs, most of the hitting ceases to be very graceful. Major weaknesses appear when adjustments cannot be made to baseballs thrown to different locations and traveling at different speeds. A knowledgeable pitcher knows right away these are the easiest outs to get, as he will eagerly explain, because the batters who have no trouble clobbering fastballs, and nothing else, are mostly "cage hitters."

A cage hitter is a batter who takes most, or all, of his batting practice in a batting cage, usually hitting balls delivered by a machine. Employing a batting practice pitcher who throws a consistent sixty mph straight pitch from forty-five feet does not help matters, either. Sessions in a cage help batters develop a consistent stroke, not an ability to make adjustments. Even with wood bats, the hard throwing pitchers get hammered when they throw fastballs because they are throwing the ball like the machine. When the ball is completely in the strike zone, especially middle-in and up a bit, it gets smacked every time. If a pitcher delivers the ball varying the velocity with good location on the edges of the strike zone along with some movement, the best that most of these batters can manage to do is a foul ball, or maybe a weak ground ball, or a pop-up on the infield.

For Alec to strike out the side at a major league tryout camp is not that noteworthy, except to say again that usually no one else manages to do it. The paradox is that he is not a strikeout pitcher. So, how does it happen? It is really very simple, no more complicated than understanding how one player tries to take advantage of the other. Given batters not able to understand pitching, combined with the pressure of the situation, their desire to impress the scouts by hitting the ball hard, and finally, the most important element, a skilled pitcher who knows how to read a batter, this result of mostly strikeouts or a few weakly hit balls can be predicted. Another fact worth mentioning is that the batters know the pitchers want to put a large number on the radar gun, so they look for the fastball mistake up in the strike zone, and they usually get one.

Well, it was an enjoyable way to spend a weekday morning, even though nothing came of it. When I arrived back at the office after lunch, my work was still there, as always. I did not miss a thing.

The Swamp Dragons were made up of current and former college players and a couple of former minor league players. To date, this was by far the very best team on which Alec had ever played. Some of the players also played on another team in the Stan Musial league during the week, as many college players do during the summer. The Swamp Dragons played what could be characterized as decent college level baseball. They were in the top division of the MABL, so their competition was the best in this league. The Angels team played in a lower division, as did the Cubs. Within their division, the Swamp Dragons were a middle-level team trying to improve. The main thing holding them back when Alec joined in late June was their hitting. This aspect most definitely improved by the time of the playoffs in which they finished strong.

During the previous season with the Cubs, Alec pitched in twelve games, including eight starts. His record of six wins and one loss with one save and one complete nine-inning game was satisfactory. His other stats were also good, including a 3.39 ERA. In this upper division, it would be different. The caliber of play was much better. His pitching ability would be put to a much more severe test, much more than just an entertaining diversion from the daily throwing drills. He would definitely be challenged, but it would be a legitimately good challenge because there would be a decent defensive team behind him. So much for the good part, the bad part was that he would not get to pitch as much since the Swamp Dragons had a few other very talented pitchers ahead of him.

When Alec joined the team, only a few weeks remained until the end of his summer break. He was left with enough time to play in just a few more games. We were going to take our usual late summer trip, this year to Wrightsville Beach, North Carolina, during the first week of August. Immediately afterwards, he had to go back to Valdosta to begin his junior year.

In the first game with his new team, the Swamp Dragons played the Cardinals on a field behind Shamrock Middle School (previously a high school) in DeKalb County. The starting pitcher was Bryan Seals, about whom we knew nothing at all. To see him for the first time, even during just the first inning of the game, it was obvious that he knew how to pitch very well. His velocity was not that high with the fastball maybe reaching eighty mph or so. Perhaps he had suffered an injury. He had excellent mechanics, very good control, and good quality pitches, the kind of pitcher that is a joy to watch. A pitcher this polished, this skillful, I thought, must have played in college or the minor leagues. Bryan Seals had pitched advanced-level baseball somewhere, no doubt about it.

The game was going along well for the home team. After six innings, the Swamp Dragons held a 5-4 lead. Seals reached the point where he had pitched all he wanted to, or was able to. He had pitched a very good game so far, but it was one of those contests where the other team was able to manufacture a run here and a run there until they had accumulated four runs. With metal bats, it is much easier to neutralize even good pitching. Besides, the Cardinals had some good hitters, in addition to being an exceptionally good base running team with speed they did not hesitate to use.

Alec had been warming up in the bull pen during the sixth inning in order to enter the game in relief. He strolled out to the mound to start the top of the seventh, a long save type of situation. The quality of the Cardinals team was similar to that of the teams he had faced in the MABL tournament in Clearwater and St. Petersburg the previous November. This made the situation problematical. It was July 7 and he had not pitched in a game since June 8 for the Angels. He lost that game 8-7 in a five and two-third inning start during which he gave up five earned runs. Since he had thrown every day all summer, he was, like always, in great physical condition. If pitching in practice were as good as pitching in a game there would have been no need to worry. Practice helps to prepare, but is never a total substitute for facing live batters. Luckily, this Swamp Dragons team had a superb catcher, Chris Salmon. Salmon had caught Seals perfectly with good pitch calling, framing the delivery, trying to take advantage of each batter's weaknesses. The Cardinals, for their part, did not mind seeing a new pitcher coming into the game.

Their sanguinity soon turned to despair as the battery performance for the Swamp Dragons continued strong. The lefty reliever faced the minimum for the final three innings, striking out four of the nine batters. In the ninth inning, after striking out the leadoff man, he surrendered a single. The next batter bounced an 0-1 pitch to the third baseman for a 5-4-3 double play. The Swamp Dragons won the game 7-4 in spite of needless worry, mostly due to a magnificent display of pitching by two accomplished lefties.

There was more to the story about Salmon and Seals. Salmon had played some minor league ball, which explained the level of his abilities. His catching in this game made a perfect demonstration of how true it is that a pitcher can only pitch his best with a very good catcher. Confirmation of this adage came when Alec remarked afterwards that the two of them were immediately "on the same page." Youngsters would do well to understand that whenever a pitcher and catcher are "on the same page," a sturdy combination forms, one that is very tough to beat at every level of the game.

Seals was a highly recruited high school pitcher who played Division I baseball at Georgia Southern University in Statesboro. One of the other schools that sought his services was Valdosta State. Coincidentally, Seals had played on summer teams with VSU's assistant baseball coach, Shannon Jernigan, so he was well acquainted with the Valdosta State baseball staff. Seals, having shown real promise as a pitcher, would undoubtedly have been drafted. The opportunity to play professional ball was within his grasp. Unfortunately, while in college, he injured his arm in a way that made further advancement next to impossible.

Seals undoubtedly enjoyed watching from the dugout as Alec saved his win. However, the performance probably surprised him as much, or more than, the results. He was very impressed with the pitching ability, that is, the manner in which the result was accomplished. So much so, that after the game and after hearing he attended VSU, Seals explained about his relationship with Valdosta State and with Jernigan. He was surprised when told that Alec had not yet been able to get on the team down there. This caused Seals to make an offer; he would gladly call the VSU coaches on Alec's behalf. So again, another unlikely circumstance, a product of an earlier disappointment, was turning into a favorable consequence of perseverance. The Angels did not want to use him very much so he looked for another team, which led to something better, a better team, better teammates, better competition, and even a recommendation that just might tip the balance in giving him a chance to play on a very good college baseball team, or at least get him a better look.

These three innings showed more than just a good pitching effort. They showed how a knowledgeable and skillful pitcher could work well with a new catcher on a new team against batters he never saw before. For a pitcher to keep advancing to higher levels, the skill of being able to work with catchers is just about as important as any other pitching skill. In this game, every pitch Salmon called was the pitch delivered. The intended spots were accurately hit while he was deceptively changing speed. At times, it seemed the batters would have done just as well had they been swinging at ghosts. The five pitches that the Cardinal batters put in play were hit more with permission than with authority. They included two medium fly balls to left field, a squibber off the end of the bat for an unassisted out at first base, a ground ball single up the middle into center field and, lastly, the double play grounder to third. He had a good day.

The team treated him with enthusiastic praise. Why not? This new kid shows up out of nowhere with his mid-seventies mph fastball amidst all these good players on an established team and immediately goes about his business making a significant contribution the very first time out. Furthermore, here was a pitcher with textbook mechanics and a confident demeanor, a perfect compliment to Bryan Seals. These two fellows were what control pitchers ought to be. Both could have served as models, as textbook examples, to show to every youngster who wants to become a real baseball pitcher, the right way to do it.

Naturally, Alec took Seals up on the offer to call Jernigan on his behalf giving him the telephone number of the baseball office. He took it as a superb compliment, not just a mere overreaction to the elation of the moment when winning an important baseball game. Not intending to be a spoiler, still the question of whether Seals would actually follow through and make the call was posed. Alec thought so. I was a bit skeptical. People say things on the spur of the moment with perfectly sincere intentions; however, often is the case that a sudden impetus can diminish with time. Seals barely knew Alec. Such a telephone call on his behalf would be strictly a magnanimous gesture. Would he even remember to make the call? What if he did call and Jernigan was out? Would he remember to call back? Call it a realistic opinion of a grown-up. Pessimism aside, the important point was that even if he did not do as he said he would, the reaction Seals and the others had to his pitching was not any less meaningful. These were good baseball players who knew about good pitching. They thought he was good. This alone mattered a lot. Too bad one of these fellows could not have been his high school coach.

He pitched a couple more times for the Swamp Dragons. Then we took our beach trip to wrap up the summer before school started. The entire extended family had grown to be partial to Wrightsville Beach over the years, preferring it to the Outer Banks and most of the other beautiful spits of sand up and down the Southeast Coast. Wrightsville is the barrier island immediately east of the historic town of Wilmington. The entire beach area is well maintained making it one of the best places to vacation with the whole family.

The surfing is generally good here, though not the best on the East Coast. That honor has to go to Cocoa Beach, Florida. Within Cocoa Beach and a bit southward, there are many good surfing spots. In particular, the beaches across Highway A1A from Patrick Air Base, called "Second Light," are just superb. About fifteen minutes farther south is another excellent spot called Sebastian Inlet, but it gets a little crowded with incommodious attitudes. Cocoa Beach itself around the pier and down towards Ron Jon's Surf Shop represents what many consider to be the headquarters of East Coast surfing. This section of the Florida coast has miles of good breaks with room-a-plenty to accommodate all the surfers who congregate by the thousands when well-mannered groundswells roll in. We do not go there nearly as often as we would like because, from Atlanta, Cocoa Beach is a good eight hours drive time.

The usual destination for our short excursions is another very good surf spot called Folly Beach in South Carolina, only about five hours away. The best thing about Folly is just about everything. As an older beach town, much of its character derives from an intriguing history. Long ago, Folly offered a cooler summer respite for the residents of Charleston in the era before air conditioning. However, even before the time when city-dwelling plantation owners took over the island, occupiers of less permanence prevailed. Legends tell of pirates and runaways roving between Folly's dunes and hiding in the marshes trying to elude their pursuers.

Folly's next greatest attraction for many is that it lacks the attractions found within the more popular beach resorts today: not many eating-places; no movies, arcades, or carnivals; only a few shops. Minor league baseball can be found nearby, though, as the Charleston River Dogs play in a ballpark only about ten miles away. There is no golf course very near Folly Beach unlike Kiawah Island next door or Isle of Palms, Sullivan's Island, and Mount Pleasant north of the harbor. For the real South Carolina golf vacation, Myrtle Beach is the place to go. That resort town up the coast seemingly has more golf holes than hotel rooms.

Finally, Folly has good surf. Better said, if the surf is up anywhere else in South Carolina, the break will be bigger and longer at Folly. The island seems to pick up both the northeast swell and the south-southeast swell better than all the other Carolina beaches. The swells produced over the open ocean by tropical storms travel unimpeded towards both Cocoa Beach and Folly Island. The shape of the continental shelf and the curvature of the coast from Cape Canaveral to Vero Beach, create a compressing effect that magnifies the swell along that stretch of coastline. Folly Island, though it does not have this particular advantage, just seems to be aimed in the right direction. Both beaches are usually best during the incoming and high tide though anytime that the waves are breaking, even if they are small, good rides can be had.

Wrightsville Beach is a little less than seven hours away from Atlanta. The surfing there becomes not good when there is a north to northeast wind blowing at ten knots or more. Then the sea turns into a choppy mess, usually accompanied by a strong drift. A drift is a lateral current created by wind and swell direction, mostly wind. It becomes very evident when sitting still on a surfboard waiting for a wave and the beach goes drifting by. On one particularly breezy day, the drift was calculated to be about two hundred fifty feet per minute, which meant that by just sitting still on a surfboard at Wrightsville, one could be surfing in Cocoa Beach by the end of the week. A similar drift from the south would have delivered the Hamptons in about the same amount of time. Usually under these conditions of crosswinds and crosscurrents, the sea becomes very choppy, too choppy to surf, as there can be no decently formed waves to ride. Fortunately, on days like this, Wrightsville offers a spectacular alternative.

Just south of the Wrightsville Beach Island is a place called Masonboro. The inlet between the two islands is appropriately called Masonboro Inlet. Masonboro Island faces more south-southeast with the north end marked by a long protective jetty fortified with large boulders. Because of the positioning of this island, wind from the north or northeast is mostly offshore, maybe slightly quartering, while the jetty cuts down the current drift. Therefore, the same conditions that make Wrightsville Island totally unsurfable cause Masonboro Island to become an exceptionally fine surfing spot. Because of the bottom contour and the offshore shoals, it is best there at the high end of the tide cycle for about two or three hours before until two hours after the high water mark.

On previous trips, we had never visited Masonboro. My awareness came by hearing the locals talk about it when out surfing and while loitering in the local surf shops. One day, the wind conditions were hopeless at the pier, so the time had come to visit this ostensibly famous surfers' paradise.

Access to the island is limited to seafaring conveyances. No bridges have been built over to the island, nor are there any roads on the island itself. For a surfer without a boat, there is no alternative except to paddle over on his surfboard. The passage can be enjoyable as if sightseeing, perhaps catching glimpses of various sea creatures. With a little luck, maybe a tiger shark heading inland with the tide will cruise by, much better than visiting an aquarium.

Masonboro Inlet is only about a half-mile or so across. On the first attempt through the channel, an improper accounting for the currents resulted in a landing amidst the algae covered and extremely slippery rocks of the jetty. The alternatives were to continue paddling another half hour past this barrier, or stay right there and attempt to scale it with bare feet while trying to avoid dinging the board. The propriety of the decision to assault the rocks became increasingly questionable as the water ebbed and flowed with each passing swell, causing several slips and falls. With persistence, finally, this barrier was conquered.

Upon reaching the other side of the rocks and jetty, the ocean was a mere couple of hundred yards over and around sand dunes covered with sea oats and grasses. In minutes, a totally startling sight appeared. In fact, it was astounding. This place, only a couple miles away from the Mercer Pier where the seas were choppy and disorderly, here the ocean was perfectly glassy with beautifully formed swells breaking top-to-bottom upon a shallow reef, with an occasional head-high face set standing up against the offshore breeze forming remarkably smooth-breaking waves. The water was unusually clear for an Atlantic Ocean beach, looking almost like crystal clear Caribbean waters. Any surfer would have been totally stoked. What a shame that none of the other surfers in the family came along. After a memorable surf session lasting about three or four hours, the tide had finally ebbed too much. Gradually the loss of water caused the break to close itself out marking the time for the surfers to come in, which we all did. By chance, an acquaintance with a boat offered a ride back across the inlet, for which I was very grateful.

Not more than a few miles away from the beach is located the campus of the University of North Carolina at Wilmington. Dawdling on the beach is a major intramural sport at UNCW, just as it is at most other coastal area schools such as the College of Charleston and the Space Coast Community College in Cocoa. Many of the students visit the shore to relax, visit with friends, have at least a few beers, and smoke some richly flavored, fresh-from-the-factory cigarettes produced nearby with fine Eastern North Carolina grown tobacco. Some of the students, however, eschew such sedentary pursuits when good waves are breaking. On those days, they come down to surf, assuming it is allowed. Unfortunately, during the summer, by law, surfing is not permitted all the time in most places.

When it comes to surfing, city councils in beach towns bend to the whims of the uninformed populace, just as politicians do everywhere. Some visitors to beach resorts become irate at the presence of surfers, insisting the activity is dangerous to swimmers. This is rubbish. The ocean itself represents the greatest threat to swimmers, while surfers offer the greatest protection. In fact, the safest beach for swimmers is a beach where surfers are present. Surfers occupy the most useful and effective life guarding position, that being just past the reef break.

Most vacationers understand the sport of surfing about as much as they understand the ocean. Whenever an overweight, out-of-shape, blubber capsule gets caught in a rip current, about ten seconds of panic is all it takes for him to be a goner. Then it is usually left to the local rescue squad to retrieve the body. Surfers are very alert and savvy ocean experts. They can, and often do, rescue swimmers, before situations turn critical. Such rescues, though frequent, are never reported because no one drowns. In beach towns, not drowning is normally not a newsworthy event.

If coastal area city councils wanted to enact intelligent safety regulations, assuming they have the constitutional authority to legislate ocean usage in the first place, they would allow swimming under moderate to high surf conditions only if surfers are present. Better yet, surfing should be allowed at all times in all places by surfers who register as lifeguards. This will probably never happen. Contained in the DNA of government, whether in Wrightsville Beach, the City of Norcross, or anywhere else, is a genetic marker discovered by Thomas Jefferson, and alluded to in his *Notes on Virginia* (1782): "It is error alone which needs the support of government. Truth can stand by itself."

At Wrightsville Beach, the municipal summertime surfing restrictions are in force between 11:00 a.m. and 4:00 p.m. except in a couple of very small, inconvenient, and isolated places. What else can surfers do when they are not allowed to surf? We went to play baseball. Rather than relax on the beach or take an air-conditioned nap inside the cottage, playing baseball at mid-day takes full advantage of the warmest part of the day. As luck would have it, adjacent to the beautiful UNCW baseball stadium are spacious practice fields, seemingly available to anyone who happens along. We happened along everyday after lunch. Six of us came to play including my nephew Nick, brother Don, and brothers-in-law Mark Ross and Mike Kurowski. Nick was going into his senior year at Paul VI High School in Fairfax, Virginia. He was a member of the baseball team, a second baseman.

The name Kurowski should sound familiar to baseball fans. Whitey Kurowski was the well-known St. Louis Cardinal third baseman who came up to the majors in 1941, the same year as Musial. He went on to compile a solid nine-year major league career. Mike contacted Whitey years before and began a correspondence with him attempting to learn if they were related. While a worthwhile acquaintance was created, evidence of family ties has not yet been found.

Our baseball sessions consisted of the four washed-up adults trying to relive moments from their glory days, as they were imagined, plus the two kids. At least the workouts were productive and physically exhausting, lasting nearly two hours. We did combination drills for throwing and fielding followed by batting practice. Nick did some hitting with Alec pitching from the mound. This made the situation more interesting as the two cousins tried to best each other.

For the benefit of the youngsters, some game situation instruction was also included. Most young baseball players these days do not play too few games, they just practice too little. It is not uncommon for elementary and junior high kids to play three games during a week while practicing for only one hour. With that schedule, it is no wonder why so many kids fail to learn basic fundamental skills. We did not want that to be the case in our family.

Beginning in junior high school, an aspiring infielder should be taking at least fifty ground balls every day, perhaps a few less on game days. An outfielder should be throwing to each cut-off position at least a dozen times. Catchers should be blocking dirt balls, covering bunts, and throwing to bases. Pitchers should be fielding come-backers and bunts, covering first base, and going through back-up procedures. Batting practice needs to be much more than just hitting BP fastballs. Batters should practice bunting, hitting to opposite fields, and contact hitting, not just swinging away all of the time. Whenever possible, there should be base runners. If these drills were done every day, along with personal fitness training, many more youngsters would be ready to play by the time they reached high school.

*Chapter Eighteen*

# College Baseball

Summertime in Georgia ends the second week of August, nowadays; at least it does for those who have school kids, because, at this time, classes resume at most schools. The time is long past when summer vacations occupied an uninterrupted expanse of the calendar from Memorial Day to Labor Day. The major concern of teachers' unions and frazzled parents seem to be that no child should be left behind to have fun.

Valdosta State baseball tryouts for walk-ons this year were going to be delayed for about a month due to some reason or other that had something to do with NCAA rules, as it was unclearly explained. The eyes glazed over before comprehending the details. Anyway, when Alec stopped by the baseball office upon returning to school it became apparent that Mr. Seals was a man of his word. Indubitably, a fine gentleman, he had indeed made the telephone call on Alec's behalf. Coach Thomas, noticing the arrival of his latest prospect, came out of his office to say he had heard about the lefty's pitching over the summer. The team started practice the next day and Alec was told to be there at 2:00 p.m. A workout schedule would be posted on his locker. Thomas already knew he had good stuff. Now, with a useful scouting report from someone he could trust, he wanted to see about building some velocity. Just like that, the door to college baseball was open. He was not on the team yet, nor was he on the outside looking in.

Only one afternoon class had to be altered to accommodate the team's workout and practice schedule. Other adjustments had to do with life style. The life of a college student athlete is busy, very busy, especially when trying to win a spot on the roster. An eighteen-hour class load for the first semester of his junior year, along with the pursuit of an accounting major, rigorous afternoon workouts, and weight training twice a week at 7:00 a.m., left little free time. Finally, after almost two weeks he managed to find time to send a few e-mails:

Date: Mon, 26 Aug, 2002
Hey Dad,
The Newman Center is going on a retreat Labor Day weekend to St. Augustine, Florida. My roommate is going to bring his surfboard so I can use it. We are going to be right near the ocean and the surf is supposed to be good. The Newman Center is in charge of all the meals and hotel costs. They are also renting vans so I do not have to drive my own car. We will go to Mass in the Cathedral down there as well. I am planning to go, but, first, I have to see if the baseball team is having practice.
Coach Thomas has been working with the pitchers for the last couple of weeks and there are a lot of guys with real strong arms.

Date: Tue, 27 Aug 2002
Hey Dad,
Coach Thomas is having all the pitchers doing throwing drills such as throwing to the hat. We are throwing on the mound at about 60 to 70 percent effort, for about 25-35 pitches. The coach was filming us until the camera broke and he only got two people on it. Also, I developed a blister on my index and middle fingers that has been getting progressively worse. The baseballs have a raised seam and I have to apply a lot of pressure on my fingers in order to get my change-up to move. We are also doing a lot of long toss and I am working out with weights twice a week. I am the only pitcher out there trying to make the team as a walk-on. All the players that I have seen are returning players. We had a short practice yesterday because it started to rain.

Date: Wed, 28 Aug 2002
Hey Dad,
There was a player from a Detroit Tigers farm team at our practice today. His name is Mike Smith and he played for VSU. He was drafted last June. He has a fastball over 90 and an 85 mph breaking ball. He is about 6' 6" and left handed. I watched him throw from behind the plate and he is pretty impressive. Talk to you later.

Date: Fri, 30 Aug 2002
Hey Dad,
I am leaving to go to the beach this afternoon. The team is off for Labor Day. I heard that the players and owners of MLB have

reached a deal and they are not going to strike. They have also made an agreement not to contract teams until 2006.

Date: Sat, 7 Sep 2002
Hey Dad,
I went to a tailgate party before the VSU football game. We beat Fort Valley State 32-6. It was not a very close game. My classes are going well. They are tough so I am spending a lot of time studying and practicing with the team. The beach was great. I went down there and stayed with some friends. I went to Mass at the Cathedral and it was where the first Mass was said in America. UVA beat South Carolina.

Then, not a word came for ten more days, until the final verdict.

Date: Tues, 17 Sep 2002 14:07:47 (PDT)
Hey Dad,
I did not make the fall roster, but I had a lot of fun and I met a lot of guys on the team. The baseball team looks very good and they have a lot of good pitching. They have three left-handers that have very good control and throw real hard. It is tough to make the team because the talent is so good. Several of the players on the roster are capable of playing in the minor leagues if they want to. About 40 guys are on the fall team and they will cut that down to 25 for the season.
The electrical cord on my laptop broke and it needs to be replaced. I just noticed it yesterday and I want to send the cord back to Dell. I was wondering if I could send it back during Thanksgiving break. Do you know if my warranty will last that long? Talk to you later.

Earlier in the year during their spring campaign, the 2002 Valdosta State baseball team compiled a record of forty-one wins and twenty losses, won the Gulf South Conference, and were ranked fifteenth nationally in the final NCAA-Division II poll. Michael Smith was drafted in the sixteenth round by Detroit. He was a six-foot, six-inch tall, two hundred pound left-handed pitcher. Another pitcher, Corey Wachman, a six foot tall, one hundred and eighty pound right-hander, was drafted by Cincinnati in the seventh round. The good news for VSU was that finding replacements for those drafted was a routine venture. In addition to a solid group of returning players, they had a few new recruits, mostly from junior colleges. The fact that they even spent time with Alec was amazing. Thomas must have thought his abilities as a pitcher warranted an effort to try to upgrade his fastball.

Alec's effort was not a waste, either. One surefire way for a player to develop a better game is by spending a month working out with a successful, well-managed college baseball team. College teams do not find themselves nationally ranked, as Valdosta State is year after year, by accident. The formula for this achievement is simply stated, good recruiting, a well-structured training program, a manager who knows how to use his talent, and some money from corporate sponsors. Winning games then becomes fuel for a self-perpetuating cycle, or one hopes it will. A little bit of luck is useful now and again, too. As simple as it might sound, though, continued athletic success is extremely difficult to achieve in a highly competitive environment.

Once the recruiting is done, the focus turns to training. This is where Alec entered the scene. The pitchers did a lot of running. The usual route through the campus covered over three miles. They ran from the ballpark in North Campus to the University Center in South Campus and back, about a mile and a half each way over flat ground, as there are no hills in Valdosta.

The new lefty prospect reported not being surprised by anything he experienced here during the month-long tryout. These college ballplayers were what he expected, very different from his high school teammates. They were, in his estimation, what baseball players at this level should be. They were all good. Most of all, they wanted to play. By understanding the game very well, these college players could also understand their own place in the scheme of things. Self-confidence was an abundant commodity though it was accompanied by a healthy dose of realism, in most cases. By and large, they were diligent, completing workouts willingly and faithfully. The principal difference between high school and college athletes, Alec discovered without surprise, was the number of slackers. In high school there were many, in college almost none. Although his definition of "slacker" would probably have become a bone of contention with many from his high school past, it was correct.

Camaraderie was high, complete with a healthy bit of boasting, along with friendly challenges. One attention-grabbing example was the story of a player who claimed he could throw the ball on a line from behind home plate down the foul line and over the fence three hundred thirty-five feet away while keeping the ball less than twenty feet off the ground. Then he did it. The Valdosta State baseball players turned out to be on the same level as the best of the best of all Alec's teammates from the past. They were like Schofield, Hesenius, and Seals. For any young baseball player, this was a wonderful environment in which to be, even for a brief while.

Alec was not a scholarship player, not a returning player, and not widely known from playing in high school or in other leagues. He did not even grow up in this part of the state. He was also not recruited, not by anyone. He just showed up, basically, out of nowhere. Nevertheless, he passed the test of fitting in with the other ballplayers, both on and off the field, something akin to a successful peer review, something from which good life lessons could be learned.

The inter-personal dynamics of a baseball team are no different from any other skill-defined work group. Baseball players accept or reject first on the basis of baseball skills. Later on, knowledge of the game, application of skills, and personality factors come into play. The initial verdict of his mates came quickly when he found himself welcomed to go for pizza and beer, etc., with them on the weekends. They judged him a competent pitcher and, very possibly, a future teammate. Even though it did not turn out that way, while there, he was accepted. This was not always the case for others.

Sometimes players just showed up randomly before a practice session looking to finagle their way onto the team. One afternoon a couple of students decided to go to the baseball field to show Coach Thomas they could pitch. They claimed to have pitched successfully in high school, and probably did. Gentleman that he was, Thomas agreed to give them a quick look. It turned out to be a very brief one. About one wind-up and one pitch was all he needed to see. They were politely dismissed.

Instead of leaving the field directly, the two passed by the dugout in which several team members were milling about. Perhaps these low-skilled aspirants were looking to intermingle with the real players. They paused, but, the absence of pleasantries, or even eye contact, suggested they were welcome to keep moving along. The hint was enough. These two erstwhile prospects finally ambled away probably convinced they were almost good enough, but not quite. At least it was a conclusion that could protect their self-esteem, and one they could embellish for their dining room and dormitory friends later on.

Coach Thomas could not be fooled easily, if at all. He had been the manager of Valdosta State baseball for over thirty years, accumulating more wins than anyone else had. He understood what he saw and he knew what he wanted. He wanted a pitcher like Alec who had more speed on the fastball. He had several pitchers who could throw a baseball in the mid-eighties and higher, even left-handers, but not all of them could throw with quite as much consistency. Like every other baseball manager, he wanted pitchers with velocity along with good mechanics, pitchers who could locate and change speeds. He wanted pitchers who knew how to play the game, how to read batters and situations, how to apply their skills, pitchers who could get every kind of batter out. He wanted the kind of accomplished pitcher the pros draft before college eligibility is used up. He wanted the likes of Tom Glavine and Greg Maddux. Since those two were not available, he had to keep looking.

College athletes are challenged in many ways. They have their own pressures and predicaments with which to deal. One of those is fitting in socially with fellow students while their status as athletes tends to set them apart. By necessity, they have both athletic friends and non-athletic friends, sort of like living in two separate worlds at the same time. Although their sport is a major part of their everyday lives, they usually have a strong preference not to discuss it in any depth with non-athletes. Even when it comes to their old high school teammates, a gulf of understanding has undoubtedly formed, spawning conversations more superficial than fruitful. The high school game bears little resemblance to the game beyond, that played in college or, especially, in the minor leagues, the differences being far greater than most non-participants can grasp. The more advanced these players become, the more reticent their public demeanor tends to be. In talking about their sport, instead of being substantive, they typically succumb to the use of jargon.

It is not that accomplished athletes dislike discussing their game; rather they discover that conversations with just anyone can become very tedious and unproductive. Imagine if Tom Glavine had a next-door neighbor who may have pitched a little in high school. Surely, he would be glad to chat over the fence about all kinds of things, like the kids, the neighborhood pool, the new church down the road, the new golf pro at the clubhouse, anything other than his latest game. Imagine if this neighbor audaciously asked why he threw a 3-2 change-up to Juan Pierre with two on, one out, and the score tied in the eighth inning.

"What in the world are you asking that for!" might be the unembellished thought that would cross his mind.

Even if coming from a high school varsity pitcher who is a big baseball fan, who reads the sports page every day, and watches *SportsCenter* every morning, how could anyone realistically think Mr. Glavine would care to talk to him about his selection of pitches? He might if it were Leo Mazzone, Greg Maddux, or Chipper Jones. Maybe he would if it was with a former minor league pitcher. To think he would care to discuss the inside game of professional baseball with the former little league all-star across the yard is not being realistic.

For a culture so saturated with sports, a working knowledge of the professional game by most people is woefully inadequate. Some of the most ardent life-long fans, including many who may have played high school varsity sports, possess an entirely superficial concept of the world of professional sports. It mostly occurs when one projects himself into the place of the accomplished professional athlete without benefit of the perseverance, skills, knowledge, and courage requisite to become one. Proof of this can be found by listening to any sports radio call-in talk show. The show hosts themselves do little to elevate the content beyond continually offering repetitious and moronic aphorisms. The worst of the lot are the local daytime radio talkers, followed by the networks, with the local evening radio call-in programs slightly less worthless. For these hosts, suffering sports-addicted fools is a job requirement, conducted for one main purpose, the selling of advertisements. They are paid to do it. Maybe the listeners think they are getting the scoop on the inside game from all the pap. They are not. Sports talk is just another form of mindless entertainment masquerading as intelligent analysis, another form of junk food for the brain. At least it will not clog the arteries, though it may cause indigestion while eating.

One evening around suppertime a caller on a Braves pre-game call-in show had this comment:

"We need to get more pop in the middle of the line-up. We need somebody like Bonds, Sosa, or A-Rod. How about we trade X, Y and/or Z (here named a few of the worst pine-riders) and a couple of minor-leaguers?"

Is it any wonder why Skip Caray gets exasperated sometimes? The stupidity can be so profound that it is difficult not to imagine that at least some of these calls must be staged, and may even be the principal part of the evening's entertainment for some socially inept Georgia Tech engineering students. Then, after hearing the call that simply cannot be beat, the next caller comes up with something like this:

"Why doesn't Bobby Cox have Smoltz bat eighth? He has a better batting average than so-and-so who is in the eighth spot now."

What's next? Left-handers can play shortstop? It is a wonder anyone listens to these shows. Imagine the callers sitting on hold waiting to participate. Some of them are on cell phones while driving cars, too.

Here is a better idea. For the sake of public safety, and for better quality entertainment that informs the listener, radio sports call-in shows should be replaced with live broadcasts of Kangaroo Courts. If the public craves jargon, let it be based upon genuine humor.

Athletes are a separate bunch. As in any other field of endeavor, their advancement can be measured in terms of a declining number of peers. They could be just like regular guys, except for two things: everybody knows who they are and everybody gets to watch them work. By necessity, they have to be careful what they do in public, shielding their personal lives as much as possible. Top corporate executives also belong to a select group; however, most people do not recognize them and their offices are not open to spectators, nor are their meetings broadcast on television.

The extra public exposure given to athletes leads many fans to think of professional athletes as acquaintances, or even friends, as if it were appropriate to address them informally without ever being properly introduced, as if their personal time, under any circumstances, belonged to whoever watches their games. Some audacious fans think it proper to approach a professional athlete in any public place, to request favors, to give unsolicited advice, even to offer instruction on how to play a position better. Maybe this is a good thing. A fan can pour all of his emotion into a team, or a game, and suffer no lasting consequences from the outcome. For the non-athlete, sport exists in a fantasyland and probably better that it remains so. Perhaps it is better for fans to be entertained in ignorance, than to be jaded with understanding. As for the general lack of etiquette, though inexcusable, most of today's athletes are paid enough to endure that, too.

Aside from games, the sports interview can be greatly entertaining, mostly for misstatements, miscues, slip-ups, etc. Even lacking any verbal gaffes, it is another great source for misinformation. When coaches and athletes are interviewed, they are careful to say only what they want the public to hear. Whether or not it coincides with what they are thinking is of no matter to any situation. It would be a fascinating exercise for a group of fans to parse the live half-time television comments of a football coach heading to the locker room. Then afterwards, allow those same people to see a video recording of what that same coach actually said privately when addressing his assistant coaches and players as they prepared for the second half. The same could be done by comparing a manager's comments at a team meeting to his public comments on a radio interview show. The discrepancies are often astounding.

By being a part of the college team, even for a brief period, Alec gained much more insight to the game, as well as a greater appreciation for those who play it. That they gave him a substantial look for more than a month testified to his skills as a baseball pitcher, as well as to his attitude and work ethic. Unfortunately, even the craftiest of left-handers needed to top the velocity hurdle before gaining a spot on most college rosters. Nothing was lacking in his effort or in his training regimen. The velocity just did not happen. By way of an honest evaluation, one had to recognize that there was this distinct possibility his baseball career had reached its zenith. Even the greatest antipathy towards resignation would not change the facts.

Fortunately, he remained a good student in the business school and baseball was not the only thing he had in life. He had given the game everything he could. Indeed, he had a love for the game that surpassed the knowledge and understanding of most men. He had enjoyed every minute spent on the field, including those under very trying circumstances. He had played the game with intensity and skill. He played with a passion. At times, he had outdone many very fine batters, some of whom even then were playing in college and the minor leagues. Certainly, the time working with the college team was time well spent. Could it be that it was time to move on? If he would devote the same level of commitment and energy to his business after finishing school, assuredly it would render a fruitful career.

Even as the final destination on the road to the big leagues seems far away, the Slough of Despond looms near at hand, always to be studiously avoided.

*Chapter Nineteen*

# It Takes Heart

Oh, but if life was that easy . . . Back in August of 2002, just before Alec began working out with the VSU baseball team, I had the occasion to meet a man who was among the most adept at using some relatively new methods for training athletes, and it came about in a rather unlikely manner. His name was Chip Smith, the athletic director at the nearby Atlanta Athletic Club. Mr. Smith had extensive experience training collegiate and professional athletes, though mostly for football and basketball. He had previously guided the workouts of some members of the U.S. Olympic team. At the time we spoke, he was working with a couple of younger boys in the neighborhood who were still in junior high school, one for basketball, and the other for football. Their fathers, who had been accomplished professional athletes themselves, sought out Chip Smith to help prepare their sons for their high school sports.

Mr. Smith's training regimen made extensive use of elastic bands to increase resistance on specific muscles. Apparently, there was much scientific support for his methods since trainers everywhere have adopted them. Moreover, his successful record of application was the proof of the pudding. Many athletes who used these techniques in their training showed impressive results.

Resistance training exercises cause muscles to "fire" quicker. If the arm can be made to move faster, the baseball should also move faster. Although this fact may lead one to focus on building the throwing arm, the primary place to attend is in the core muscles, those contained in the thighs and lower back. This makes sense because, as every pitcher knows, the strength needed in pitching comes mostly from the legs.

Mr. Smith had worked some with baseball players before, including pitchers, although his focus was training football players, more specifically to prepare them for the combines. Years before he did some work with one of the Braves' pitchers, Greg McMichael. Now Mr. McMichael was himself working with other pitchers using these same muscle-fire resistance techniques. After an extremely informative, hour-long three-way conversation, including Alec, Chip said he wanted to talk to Greg about Alec's particular situation. This led us to develop a useful work out plan for the next spring.

The prescription focused on the left hip. Alec was directed to attach an elastic band to a hip belt so there was tension on that hip when he threw the ball. Overcoming the tension is supposed to cause the core muscles to "burn." By this simple application of force, quickness should be increased.

The physiological basis for this exercise is the supposition that quickness is a learned response. Though it may be contrary to much popular opinion, the assumption that professional athletes are born with all the tools they need to perform at the highest level of their sport is false. Certain physical characteristics, along with some natural abilities, are made available by genetics. Genes, however, only create a potential. Physical effort is the essential ingredient that converts potential into something useful.

How many times in history has someone declared that a certain barrier of height, speed, quickness, agility, or accomplishment in a given sport would never be broken? Then someone comes along and surpasses it. If athletes as a group cannot be subjected to arbitrary limits, then athletes individually cannot be, either.

As many professional athletes will say, success in sports comes more from desire, or heart, than most people are willing to believe. Desire creates the willingness to work hard, obsessively hard. Many frustrated athletes, and non-athletes, do not want to believe this is true for a very good reason. If it were true that only certain men are born to be professional athletes, one has established a ready-made excuse for failure. One can simply blame God, the Creator of the non-athlete. If one chooses to believe that Michael Jordan was born to be the greatest basketball player, it must mean that no one else could have been.

"Well, maybe not exactly. He probably had to work at it a little bit. But, let's face it, he was born with the right height and the right size and the right quickness and the right everything. And that's why there is only one Michael Jordan. Right?"

Wrong. Such an epilogue is preposterous. There are and have been thousands of others who could have been like Mike. Something was lacking other than favorable genetics. Maybe it was the opportunity for proper instruction. Maybe it was desire. Maybe it was heart. Maybe they chose another sport or another vocation. Maybe the negative influence of others convinced them as youngsters that athletes like Michael Jordan are born this way and if one is not the best eighth grade basketball player in the county, he better forget about the NBA.

Just as bad, or maybe even worse, is to insist that a youngster keep playing because he is destined for future stardom. The numbers do not justify it. How many "can't miss" prospects and "real deals" never get to play for money or end up uneducated and physically broken? A life plan, one based on a premise that will almost certainly end in failure, can turn corrosive when taken to an extreme. However, being extreme does not mean giving one hundred percent effort to a sport; it means simultaneously giving zero percent to every other worthwhile pursuit. The best way is to steer clear of any mutually exclusive extremes. One can play ball and finish school, too. How about this idea,

"Give a sport your best shot while maintaining a realistic plan B."

At some point early on in the athletic career of a kid, he can become infatuated with his sport. If this happens, he has a chance. If it does not, he has virtually no chance. If the youngster loves to play the game, if it becomes a healthy passion, part of a purposeful life, his sport is a great thing. Passion can motivate a man to do extraordinary things; to sacrifice for his family's welfare, to charge a hill under a hail of bullets for the sake of his country, to suffer martyrdom for a true faith. If a youngster loves his sport enough, he will be willing to work hard, make almost any sacrifice for it, without the need for much cajoling. He will refuse to give it up until the time is right no matter what evidence is presented to discourage him, as long as it is not from those whom he respects the most. Does he need some encouragement? Yes, everyone does, occasionally. However, not all the encouragement in the world will create a love for the game or a desire to play with the best. Encouragement can only help to maintain such motivations.

Chip Smith's final conditioning instructions were relayed to Alec at the end of September, just after he was not included on the team's fall roster. One of his apartment mates, Daniel Hinely, was studying to be an athletic trainer. In fact, he worked with the Valdosta State baseball team. When the elastic bands arrived, he conveniently had some help nearby in utilizing them. Even so, it was difficult at this point for him to continue working on baseball. He thought that maybe he had reached the peak of his physical abilities. He also had a tough academic schedule and had to devote much effort to his studies. By Christmas, his conclusion was that going any further in baseball was probably not a viable prospect.

Again, like many times in the past, I told him that quitting baseball would be entirely his decision, meaning that no one would be disappointed. He did not even know if he was quitting for good or merely taking a break. What was certain was that he had to focus on school if he wanted to complete his major courses and graduate on time. Maybe it was the end; maybe it was a break. We would see.

The psychology of quitting must be an interesting subject for one to study. The relevant factors alone could totally baffle even a well-ordered brain. What of talent, ability, achievement, and desire? What of failures, denials, rejections, and ridicule? What of age, stature, economics, and social values? Then the endless number of other choices and non-choices, where do they begin, where do they end? When is the best time to sell a stock, trade a car, change careers, or take up golf? A man has to pose these questions, evaluate the alternatives, and carefully decide, by himself, for himself. Then he must live with the consequences. These decisions do not have to be made quickly, not necessarily. Yet, many times, once made, they become final.

Exactly how hard had he worked on his baseball? The answer: Much harder than anyone else from his high school team ever did. Was it enough? He left for Valdosta in August throwing about seventy-five mph. We checked it on Ro's Juggs gun. Coach Thomas put him on the most rigorous workout program he had ever had for more than a solid month. At the end, the best fastball he could throw was just triggering eighty mph. He reached the tentative conclusion that this was probably all he could ever do. I wondered. How does one determine where and when the physical limits have been reached assuming there are no injuries?

He now weighed about one hundred thirty-five pounds and was about five feet, eleven inches tall in his cleats, Jamie Moyer size less ten large bowls of pasta, or Whitey Ford size less a couple cases of beer. What would happen if he continued the same workout during spring semester? Would he pick up any more speed? He could spend an hour or two each day in the workout room at the gym, and it should not interfere with school. I pointed out that if in May he was still not over eighty mph then we would know he had done all he could short of an arm transplant.

Coach Thomas thought he had the potential to pitch in college. Otherwise, he would not have wasted a minute of time with him. Not because he was not a nice guy, but because he did not have the time to waste on every kid who came by the ballpark thinking he knew how to throw a baseball. Being a successful college baseball coach for over thirty years was not an accident. You can take what Tommy Thomas says about baseball to the bank. Alec was told by the man himself that a little more velocity on the fastball was all he needed to be on the team, the same thing he heard from many professional scouts, too. These people did not tell lies just to make kids feel good, nor did they hand out trophies just for showing up. They had mastered the art of being brutally honest in a polite kind of way.

Another reminder offered in conclusion was something Ro had told him years ago, in case he had forgotten, that it was there if he wanted it. Still he needed a break. He knew there was a chance the end had not quite arrived. He just needed a little more gas in the tank to get back on the highway.

Visiting family in Virginia at Christmas, his Uncle Mike suggested that he ought to watch the movie, *Rudy*, for some inspiration. Not a bad idea. Obviously, the point of the Rudy story was not so much one of opportunity, as opportunities abound. The point was perseverance, a lesson in life that can be applied everywhere, not just in baseball.

Father Cavanah had spent a lifetime learning two incontrovertible theological truths, as he put it, which he shared with the young aspiring Notre Dame football player:

1. There is a God.
2. I am not Him (sic).

As bits of wisdom go, these two can easily lead to the formation of trite clichés with indeterminate meanings, the kind used in profusion by motivational speakers and authors of self-help books, designed to reveal their profane secrets to success. Theologically speaking, there is only one real and lasting success: eternal salvation. Worldly success, if done within the bounds of the Ten Commandments, i.e., for the love of God and Man, may be considered practice for the real thing. The Giver of Life yearns for every man to use his gift of life to attain this one ultimate goal. The most direct way, though not necessarily the easiest, is for a man to do his moral and unselfish best every day of his life at whatever worthy task confronts him, making good use of the gifts bestowed upon him.

Regrettably, behavioral observations suggest that the overwhelming preference of men is to spend a lifetime modifying goals rather than increasing efforts, that is, to redefine success continually by lowering standards. Thus, success in the noble pursuit of excellence comes to mean the avoidance of failure and disappointment. Tragically, fathers often pass this pessimistic example on to their sons. If a boy does not run the race fast enough to win it, rather than suggest more effort, the meaning of "fast enough" is redefined.

"Everybody who finishes the race is a winner, so, Johnny, you're a winner, too. Besides, winning isn't everything!"

This is supposed to build self-esteem, and an optimistic outlook? Is disappointment such a difficult emotion with which to deal that satisfaction achieved through goal modification can balance the equation of self-actualization? Or is this just a kind of philosophical trickery that can be justified with bogus statistics masquerading as logic? Is Johnny expected now to grow up into a man by thinking it is okay to be a loser just so long as he thinks he is a winner? Very well. If this is to be his source of inspiration, better to sign him up for co-ed soccer or environmental hiking camps. Keep him away from baseball, and, more especially, from baseball players, if he is to remain confident in his delusions.

Perhaps the stickiest trap created from all the ill-conceived notions degrading to human nature is the use of another man's failure to justify abandoning the pursuit of excellence. The amount of time man has to live is finite. As time is used up it becomes more and more apparent just how limited it truly is. When is the pursuit of an unlikely dream, even a noble one, a waste of precious time? The prudent investment of money is usually determined by measuring risk and return. Is it the same with time? How can one ever be confident that there would or would not be a better use of time? If Mr. Ruettiger had not played in even one football game at Notre Dame, if he had failed to graduate because of a learning disability, would his time spent in college have been better spent working in the blast furnace, in a good union job with benefits? The answer is so elemental it should be obvious, yet, apparently, to many, it is not.

If beforehand, a man considers another man's improbable effort foolhardy, he definitively misunderstands the matter. If afterwards, a man considers another man's improbable success to be a one-in-a-million fluke, he misunderstands again. How valid is the notion that the greater the goal and the higher the risk, then the greater the foolishness of the effort? Well, actually, to all non-participants, judgment is customarily reserved pending the outcome. After the fact, while acknowledging another's success, most are quick to congratulate, though not for being an achiever. The congratulations are given for beating the odds!

"Way to go. It's better to be lucky than good (or smart)."

In the case of another's failure, the refrain can be anything from condescending affronts to insincere patronage.

"Don't feel bad. Nobody could have succeeded doing that," or

"We all could have told you it wouldn't work. Next time, ask. That's what we're here for."

In evaluating the pursuit of true excellence, because of the assumed improbabilities, different outcomes are evaluated differently, but the effort is judged the same, no matter what, to have been foolish. Virtually no one provided Mr. Ruettiger the impetus for his "one-in-a-million" journey. He found it within himself. He had to. It could be found nowhere else. Which brings up another question: what does it mean to be one-in-a-million? Perhaps it means that although it worked out in this one, unusual case, anyone who tries to emulate Rudy must be out of his mind. Logic dictates that a one-in-a-million risk is imprudent and will lead to almost certain failure. This viewpoint also has merit, but only perversely, in that if it were not for people who value security above all else, life would be humorless, i.e., there would be no one for the imaginative to ridicule. However, a preponderance of risk-averse adherents would also pose a threat to liberty. Any society in which they might prevail would necessarily tend towards lethargy and totalitarianism.

Not to be outwitted, though, Mr. Ruettiger was not a one-in-a-million. He was closer to a one-in-a-one. There were not 999,999 other young men competing with him for his dream. By getting into Notre Dame and onto the prep squad as a blocking dummy, he achieved complete personal success. The final goal he sought was not even for his own benefit. He wanted to dress out for a real game to show his father and everyone else back home that he actually was a part of the team. They would not believe him otherwise. Finally, he did get into a game against Georgia Tech, participated in a couple of plays, made a tackle, and was triumphantly carried off the field on the shoulders of his teammates, held high so that his parents and everyone could see. This made him known to the rest of us. Rudy had already found out who he was before the game.

Great accomplishments come from perseverance. Yet, of the many who have celebrated Rudy's success, how many would have been there to encourage him during his journey? Yes, he took it upon himself to live a dream, a decidedly improbable dream. Through nothing but faith and resolve, the single-minded pursuance of the one goal afforded attainment of two unlikely objectives; he made that one tackle and he graduated from college. He accomplished something so unbelievable, so special, and so unusual, that no regular thinking man on earth would have thought it was possible.

To reconcile that which we may have thought with what we should have known, the examination of one more justification is necessary, the justification that comes with the clearness of hindsight. The cognoscenti would want to propose that what Rudy did was not at all unlikely, that no one else was so dumb to pursue such a nonsensical dream. Therefore, since it was uncontested, it was actually easy to achieve. Besides, what is so remarkable about graduating from college? So he made a tackle in a college football game, that and a token will buy a ride on the Number Seven train out to Shea Stadium. Besides, success does not always justify an effort. If everybody did what Rudy did, nothing would ever get done in this world because everybody would just be chasing outlandish dreams. What would the world be like then? Well, perhaps the world would be much more competitive, much more efficient, much more rewarding, and have much less self-induced mental illness.

It is a scientific and metaphysical certainty that not everyone can be above average. Genetics see to it that dreams, desires, needs, talents, abilities, etc., are sufficiently dispersed so as not to allow the situation where one million young men from around the world show up in South Bend to try out for the Notre Dame football team every year. Then there are opportunities that vary greatly due to environment and social conditions. Qualifications and possibilities arise from altogether separate realms. When they combine, an almost infinite number of variations are formed, making every man unique in some way.

From where do dreams come? They seem to arrive everywhere. Even Rudy's father understood that dreams made life tolerable. Coming from a man who worked in the blast furnace all his adult life, this wisdom was unusually profound. Admittedly, Rudy's father offered counsel against pursuing this Notre Dame dream. He suggested it would likely result in heartbreak. Presumably, he thought heartbreak was not a good thing. Rudy was left with the difficult task of sifting through all these contradicting indicators, while trying to keep the passion inside unrepressed as he followed his heart.

Everyone, I suppose, is born with heart. Most keep it through childhood. Then it usually goes away, not to be employed again, except maybe when called upon to compose a eulogy or a commencement address. Very few allow it to control their ambitions to the same extent as Rudy did, even in their youth, and especially not into their twenties. However, since few, if any, adult ambitions require heart, it does not matter very much. At least everyone should recognize that when it is appropriate to exceed the bounds of normalcy, there exists this phenomenal source of energy and inspiration that should not be underestimated.

Father Cavanah said that we pray in our time, but God's answer comes in His time. Ostensibly, Rudy perceived that the solution to this problem was to pray all of the time so as not to miss the parcel of time immediately prior to the moment when God tuned in to listen and give His answer. This, he knew, was impossible, so he lit every candle in the church so the praying would continue when he had to study, practice, or sleep. To anyone who might otherwise smirk at this behavior, Rudi revealed by his action an intellectual and sophisticated form of theology, one that combined a mature understanding with childlike devotion. He found the stuff that can give a man unshakable faith, the stuff that can open the mind and fill the heart. He found the "right stuff" that, if properly applied, can get a man into Heaven, and accomplish many other things before he gets there.

Alec was not Rudy. Alec was Alec. What was Alec going to do? The Rudy analogy could be made to apply or it could not. The Rudy story, while very compelling and inspiring, as motivating as any could be, does not necessarily mean that everyone should beat their heads against locked doors until they open or until a fatal concussion is achieved. He had nothing to prove anymore in baseball, but he did have to finish college. Except for a measly five or six mph on the fastball, he would have been on the roster of a nationally ranked team, or maybe in the minor leagues. This had to give him a bit of personal satisfaction. It did not qualify as a laurel, true enough. In fact, it sounded more like an epitaph to his baseball career than a preamble. No matter what the point of view, it was still a good thing.

Watching the movie about Rudy, though, convinced him that if someone with little more than heart and determination can play football for Notre Dame, then his very good pitching skills might get him a little farther in baseball. He was persuaded enough to carry on, or at least to consider not quitting quite yet. The physical training would continue during the spring semester and the throwing would begin again in earnest during May. By early July, we would know if there was any more velocity in that magnificent left arm of his.

*Chapter Twenty*

# The Big Leagues of Life

The 2003 season turned out to be another rewarding summer of baseball for us and for Norcross. The Norcross Baseball Club semi-professional town team was formed to draw attention to this town's great baseball heritage. A special game on the Fourth of July brought together all the good baseball forces in the community. As in times past, young and talented baseball-playing gentlemen took to the field for the love of the game, the way it ought to be. The spectators were many, and they went home satisfied. Unfortunately, the mayor would not budge in her opposition to renovating the field. Within the margins of good, honest government, it made no sense, especially since she had had the field named after herself years before.

The Norcross Baseball Club finally decided to make "official" the name, *Wingo-Carlyle Field* in hopes the more dignified name would do better in convincing the public of its value. Therefore, a press release was issued the following spring and appeared in the Gwinnett Daily Post:

> Webb Field to get New Name:
> NORCROSS — The city of Norcross produced many professional baseball players over the past 100 years, four of whom made it to the Major Leagues. They are brothers Ivey and Red Wingo, and Roy and Cleo Carlyle. Beginning July 4, what is now known as Webb Field, will become Wingo-Carlyle Field, according to the Norcross Baseball Club.

The date picked for the renaming of the field, July 4, 2004, coincided with the seventy-fifth anniversary of Roy Carlyle hitting the longest home run in professional baseball history. The local sports writers, along with those truly interested in local baseball, eagerly adopted the new name. As expected, the mayor was said to be not at all flattered. She should have been, though, since not anyone with an ounce of self-respect would have wanted his name associated with such a dilapidated, run down, ballpark. Even though she should have appreciated the gesture, the town team expected the negative reaction that followed, judging it as characteristic of her public-life persona. The interest of a community is better served in the long run by those who respect it. The new name envisaged cultural progress; the old name conserved a community eyesore. A well-maintained, useful ballpark would very appropriately bear the right honorable names of Wingo and Carlyle. The dispiriting name of Lillian Webb would only be appropriate if the field remained in its current neglected condition. Battle lines could not have been drawn more clearly.

On the home front, frustration continued as Alec did not add much, if any, velocity to his fastball after a full summer of pitching in 2003. The fastball still was not consistently topping eighty mph. He had not gained much weight, either. Upon returning to school for a fourth and final tryout with the baseball team, Coach Thomas again did not see what he wanted. Good try, as were the others, but still no cigar.

When the end of anything approaches, there is a tendency to reminisce, to look back, to remember. How many good and wonderful baseball experiences had there been? Many times more than could have been imagined just a dozen or so years before. Actually, it had been thirteen years already. They passed by in a flash. He only pitched during ten of those years. Could it be, truly, ten years of pitching? Yes, it was true. Not only was it true, but the accumulation of statistics gave convincing testimony. To date, he had appeared in one hundred and four games, fifty-two starts and fifty-two in relief. The record for starts was twenty-one wins and twenty losses, not bad when considering the quality of the teams for which he had played, teams altogether that had well below .500 winning records.

During the previous four years, his games were normally nine-innings long. During those seasons, he started in twenty-five games, compiling a record of ten wins and eleven losses. Three were complete games. In fifteen of the twenty-five games, he threw more than one hundred pitches. The highest number of pitches he ever threw in a single game was one hundred seventy-five.

Some of the accumulated numbers posted through the years from all of his official games were also notable: 382 and 2/3 innings pitched, 1,887 batters faced, and 5,949 pitches thrown. Along with 267 strikeouts, less notable were the 190 earned runs, 482 hits, 129 walks, and 13 hit batsmen. Of the 482 hits, there were 362 singles, 82 doubles, 11 triples, and 18 home runs.

Statistics can be read all kinds of ways. The scorebooks and films can be reviewed until every pitch has been scrutinized, along with every strikeout, walk, hit, throw, catch, sign, call, decoy, run, slide, tag, error, steal, spit, and scratch. Endless speculation about what should have been, what could have been, what was, and what was not, is all rather pointless in the final analysis. None of this will lead to the correct interpretation of these numbers. These numbers contain only one notable truth: the kid must have really loved to play baseball to have played this much.

After a summer of pitching for the town team, he was back at college that fall of 2003, studying accounting, determined to graduate in 2004. Back in Norcross there was much to be done in promoting the cause of preserving and repairing Wingo-Carlyle Field. Even after the name-change, widespread public support, and the continued existence of a town team, the city council remained taciturn. They disregarded all pleas as if ignoring them would make them go away. It did not. The tremendous goodwill of many people around town had been tapped. The idea of combining history and tradition along with current community needs captured many imaginations. Favorable press attention added impetus, too. Several supportive opinion editorials appeared in just about every local publication. It is hard to resist an idea that is built around the most basic theme of good civics, namely pride of ownership. Nevertheless, the elected mayor and some city councilmen still refused to grasp the concept.

For determined citizens faced with incorrigible elected officials, the only intelligent alternative that remained was to make sure continued criticism was relentlessly heaped upon them. There must be a price paid for ignoring a worthwhile civic proposal. Repeated abuse in the press was one such tactic. Amusing though it was at times, press attention would never transform ne'er-do-well politicians into prominent statesmen. Rather, it provided a larger audience for any nefarious actions they may wish to take. The publicity created just enough apprehension to prevent any action at all, buying time until some future election installed men of quality and conscience. Ultimately, every important issue is resolved by elections, as it should be.

Meanwhile, during the following summer of 2004, the Norcross Baseball Club team played about a dozen games, only a couple of them in Norcross, since the condition of the field was just too poor for regularly scheduled games. This summer of pitching for the left-hander was merely, solely, completely for the love of the game. During the fall, the Norcross team played a schedule against teams from the MABL. In addition, there were some extra games, not scheduled, usually against a team from the local Hispanic League, usually in Norcross on Sunday afternoons.

During the previous couple of years, even though it remained no better than a sandlot, Wingo-Carlyle Field had gradually become sort of a hangout for some professional baseball players between the end of the minor league and major league seasons and Christmastime. It offered a semi-secluded place to throw the ball around and take some batting practice. More recently, scrimmage type pick-up games were not unusual, either, as the professionals mixed it up with some of our regular locals. In order to prepare the field for a game, extra effort was required. Aside from dealing with broken base anchors, deteriorating plates, breaks in the backstop, and mud holes around the bases, someone had to drive a car out to drag the entire infield, and then it was watered while others lined it with powdered white lime. The pitching mound and batter's boxes were never right. When an umpire or two was found, a game began. Amazingly, word about these get-togethers did not spread much outside the local inside-baseball community, that is, the players and their immediate families and friends.

Alec remained on the town team roster even though he was in Valdosta. He came up a couple of times when the team was short a pitcher. The week of Thanksgiving was different since there were no classes scheduled, yielding two free weekends in a row to spend at home. On the Sunday before Thanksgiving, he pitched in the fall league game, but no game was scheduled for the Sunday after Thanksgiving, November 28. The Norcross Baseball Club tried unsuccessfully to get a game in Norcross. No one seemed able to commit to anything because of the holiday. Moreover, there was no telling what the weather would be like. At this time of year, it could be sunny and sixty-five degrees or it could be thirty-five degrees with rain.

Without a game to play that day, Alec decided to leave for school early, anxious to get some studying done since exams were the following week. He would have graduated on time the previous June except there was one accounting class that could not be scheduled the previous year.

Although only this one additional class was needed to graduate, he had signed up for a full load of worthwhile courses, mostly in the business school. Graduation was scheduled for December 11 just two weeks away, at which time he would receive his well-earned bachelor's degree in accounting.

The car was packed and ready to go, yet another familiar idea prevailed: that of stopping by Wingo-Carlyle Field for a short while to do a little throwing, play some catch, maybe throw from the mound a bit, loosen up the arm. By taking two cars over, when finished, each of us could go his separate way. No one else was at the field when we arrived about 10:00 a.m. Then, by the time he got warm and started throwing off the mound, the president of the Hispanic League showed up carrying his equipment bag. It turned out that they called together a pickup game that morning since the weather was going to be warm and sunny. Several players were available, several good players, among them some of our usual professional ballplayers. Marco Rodriguez walked over and asked Alec if he was able to pitch for his team. They were in need of a good starting pitcher.

Alec was not immediately sure he wanted to hang around and pitch a ballgame that day. Besides, he was in casual street clothes, not baseball clothes suitable for pitching. Thinking this was going to be just another pick-up game, he was inclined to take a rain check. With exams looming, he was anxious to get back to school. Since he had only a vague awareness of the kind of Sunday afternoon games we had had there recently, I started to remind him of who was likely to show up. He listened more attentively. After making a strong suggestion that, perhaps, he did not want to miss this game, he dutifully returned home right away to change into baseball clothes.

There was no way to tell for sure who would show up, not with this crowd, until they began to arrive. Soon it became apparent that this would be a good day for playing a baseball game. When Alec returned, after about twenty minutes, most of the players had started to warm up and the teams were formed. He knew most of the players on both teams, either personally or by reputation. To the few that he did not know personally, he was introduced.

Fatherhood has had many chores, some enjoyable, some not. Introducing a son to some major league ballplayers was decidedly an enjoyable one. Alec was to pitch for the team that included infielder Jesse Garcia and pitcher Odalis Perez. Jesse played with the Atlanta Braves the previous season though he had just signed a new contract earlier in the week with the San Diego Padres. Odalis was currently a free agent after having played for the Dodgers the previous season. He eventually signed with Los Angeles again for the 2005 season. There were no fewer than eighteen teams interested in him at this time, not surprising since he was one of the more experienced left-handed pitchers available in the major leagues. Odalis declined to pitch this day saying he was giving his arm a rest until January. He would play center field.

The other team had Rico Carty, Jr., Lorenzo Furcal, and the Atlanta Braves' Rafael Furcal. Carty played for the Mariners in the minor leagues and was the son of the former Atlanta Brave of the same name. Lorenzo Furcal was another terrific Dominican baseball player, having played in the Oakland A's organization. Like so many others, he had the misfortune of an injury, which prevented him from ever advancing to the majors. Included in our regular crowd were several top-notch players with advanced minor league playing experience, some played on our town team, including Odalis's brother Carlos, Randy (Fico) Guzman, Juan James, Algurys Lopez, and Aneury Abreu. A player who came for the first time this day was a tall, hard-throwing high school pitcher visiting from the Dominican Republic in whom scouts were very interested. He started for the other team. As they said of him before the game, he could bring it. Without a Juggs gun, the best guess had his fastball velocity at least upper eighties to maybe the low nineties mph along with surprisingly good control. He was a very good-looking young prospect.

The day started innocuously enough. Father and son on the Sunday after Thanksgiving; son driving back to college to study for exams; father and son decide to play catch first; other people show up at the baseball field; father introduces son to his new major league teammates; son decides to stay and play a baseball game; father watches. Pretty normal stuff, is it not? Father, son, and baseball? Most American fathers and sons do this sort of thing, do they not?

Alec's team was the home team, though they occupied the third base dugout. The players exited the dugout looking like a bunch of overgrown sandlot kids dressed in every conceivable color and style of baseball clothing, uniform, workout, warm-up, cool off, and whatever else came out of equipment bags. They did manage to find an umpire. I wondered who would end up paying for him, again. The kid strode to the mound to start the game just as he had done many, many times before. This time things were slightly different. His shortstop was Jesse Garcia and his center fielder was Odalis Perez. Everywhere else around the diamond, in each position, stood a very good baseball player, most with professional credentials. The only one he cared about right then, however, was his catcher, Marco Rodriguez. The father of the pitcher, also not seated, stood frozen in time; consciousness narrowed, a straight-line anxiety slightly elevated, strategically positioned behind the backstop wondering what it was that was happening.

Finally back from school on a good late fall weekend, Alec was about to play with this recently gathering crowd. It looked like any of the other pick-up games on the historic Norcross baseball diamond on a Sunday afternoon except there were more professional ballplayers out than we ever had before. The players were all familiar as were the surroundings. Yet, somehow else, it was not the same. I guess it is never the same when your own kid is pitching.

The chatter was the normal baseball chatter, the warm-ups were the same, outfielders playing long toss, infielders taking grounders thrown to them by the first baseman, the pitcher making his tosses to get the feel of the mound. In and around the on-deck circle were the one, two, and three batters loosening up by swinging their bats as they watched the pitcher and exchanged comments. A casual passerby could not have detected even one shred of evidence beforehand that major league and minor league baseball players were here to mix it up with some of the best amateur players in town. This event may have been considered very unusual by some. For Wingo-Carlyle Field, it was not, not since 1874. Perhaps unlikely events here had become all too frequent by this time. Unlikely or not, this one was terribly real, very exciting. The year was 2004, in the present; however, this scene, as it unfolded, just as easily could have been one hundred thirty years before if it were not for the cell phones, now busily sending out notification to family and friends about what was going on at the Norcross ball field.

"*Everyone* is here today. Come now!"

Should I call the mayor and councilmen? Nah, they would not be interested. This kind of a special game just happens. Those who show up get to participate. Others need to have friends, the right kind of friends, who might call to alert them. The elected officials in Norcross kept friends of a different stripe, less substantial sorts of friends, friends who did not appreciate baseball, or the town's glorious baseball history, nor did they understand the virtue associated with pride of ownership. They did not care about this famous baseball park so why would they care about a game played upon it, or about the men who came to play?

Alec appeared to warm up just as he did for every other start, about six or seven throws at about three-fourths effort; not much need to adjust to a mound he had thrown from so many times before. It had the same incorrect slope across the stride. Planting the left foot against the disintegrating rubber plate was as comfortable as sliding a dry foot into an old leather shoe. Familiar, too, was the texture of the dirt, though it was the wrong kind of dirt for a mound, too loose, too powdery, too dry. One could always rely upon the Gwinnett County Parks Department to maintain this baseball field with the fullness of bureaucratic ineptitude.

The young lefty knew this imperfect pitching mound very well. He had played in scores of games here. It was from this mound that he had thrown his first pitches on a full, regulation-size baseball field, as a relief pitcher, just a few months after the cast came off his throwing arm. That was back in 1995. This mound was his again in 1997 when he pitched for the Norcross Red team against the Norcross Blue team, a game that occupied the town's baseball conscience for weeks beforehand and had yet to be forgotten. When Norcross celebrated the Fourth of July in 2003, he took this mound to start for the town's brand new semi-pro team in a special game against Rick Stockfield's Georgia Cherokees, in the presence of all of the old guard of Norcross baseball, reunited for the first time, and given long-overdue recognition for their baseball achievements. If this mound belonged to any one current local player, it belonged to this left-handed pitcher.

The catcher's throw went down to second base; Garcia turned it over to the third baseman, who tossed it to the pitcher. There was no detectable difference in his demeanor as he tucked his ball glove under the left armpit leaving both hands free and bare to rub the baseball. His normal level of focus was intact this afternoon, made obvious when he followed the usual routine, a purposeful climb up the back of the hill, spitting to the right, adjusting the cap, stepping tall onto the rubber with both feet, and looking in for the sign. He was ready to pitch to any batter who cared to dig in beside the plate. It did not matter who he was or where he was employed. One batter or the other, they were all just like any other baseball players. They each held a bat; he held the ball. Nervousness did not exist in him, not even a little bit. It never did before, why should it be so now? Who's leading off?

A couple of weeks after the game I queried him on this very same subject, supposing it a bit strange that he seemed to be more excited and apprehensive about meeting major league ballplayers than about pitching to them. Most people would have been filled with angst if faced with a similar situation. He was not concerned about it at all, offering some very good reasons not to be, reasons sensible to him. First, as he pointed out, he had faced good hitters before, guys like the McCann brothers, Brian and Brad, Jeff Francouer, and several others who went on to play professionally. He knew he could keep the ball inside the park, especially with wood bats, and probably not give up anything more than singles, maybe a double at worst, but not home runs, not if he kept it off-speed and away most of the time and stayed ahead in the count. In addition, he had good defensive players up the middle, as well as a very good catcher. He was a bit cocky, to be sure, or maybe overly confident, depending on the point of view. One thing was sure, the way he assessed the situation betrayed no self-doubt whatsoever.

He had fashioned a quite valid second point within this analytical mind, too. Professional ballplayers were supposed to be better than he was. Based on expected outcomes, he could not lose; therefore, they could not win. Their best outcome was akin to a tie. If they killed his stuff, well, this is what they are supposed to do. Some of them were paid a lot of money to hit baseballs. They were some of the best men in the world at playing this game. He was cut from his high school team, passed over by scouts and college coaches, and was never paid a nickel to pitch a baseball, not that this mattered even a whit. He would beat them. He knew what he was doing.

Rafael Furcal must have made him a little bit nervous, did he not? No. He did not feel intimidated by anyone based on who the player was or what his playing credentials were. Any man's level of baseball was of concern only so far as it could be used against him. They were just batters, like any other batters. A thought from the past came to mind from which he claimed to have been more nervous pitching in his first high school game. Why was that? Because he wanted to impress his coach. All his teammates and friends were there watching, too. Here, no such matters persisted. This was just business, another day at the office.

Finally, through purposeful training and substantive understanding of the fundamentals of the game, he knew, he believed, that a batter does not hit a pitcher; he hits a baseball. All a pitcher can ever do is put the ball in a place where it is more difficult to hit and, therefore, let the game be played.

The first two pitches to the leadoff man were balls. A minor leaguer, yes, but it was not going to get easier. Could we do something other than dig a hole? Watching two feeble pitches to start this game, of all games, began to induce those familiar heart-stopping palpitations.

Once again, there was no need to worry, as some people never seem quite able to learn. A called strike followed. The man at the bat grounded out to the third baseman on the fourth pitch.

Batting second was Lorenzo Furcal. He had seen plenty, seen Alec before, knew him very well, did not need to take one, and the first pitch was sent a high fly ball that settled into the glove of Odalis Perez, who hardly had to move from his spot in medium center field. Straight away, the center field fence was only three hundred fifty feet. Down the lines, it was a more standard three hundred thirty feet in left and a bit more challenging three hundred forty-five feet in right. The power alleys were shallow in the three hundred thirty-five to three hundred forty foot range so routine medium-range fly balls to the power alleys in a major league ballpark would be home runs here.

With two outs and no one on base the next batter up was Rafael Furcal, just another batter, just another baseball player, just the leadoff man for the best team in the National League, the team that had won thirteen division titles in a row at this point. No need existed to ponder the fact that Furcal compared favorably to the other major league leadoff men. He was a switch-hitting speed demon who knew how to handle a bat, one who could knock it out of the park if a pitcher missed inside, and one who could hit almost anything he could reach to almost any part of the field he wanted to go. This man had good bat control. He dug in, batting right-handed against the left-handed pitcher.

When standing down on the field close up, watching any major leaguer swing a baseball bat, the quickness of the hands is absolutely striking at first. Add to this the level of coordination and the knowledge these men must have to play at the major league level; it is no wonder that pitchers are always in short supply. Even a very skillful pitcher has little chance unless he can focus. If ever there was a time to use Ro Fitten's four "C's," this was it. Let's see, they were concentration, confidence, consistency, and control.

Normally a pitcher wants to get ahead of a batter, but Furcal, even when he is batting in the leadoff position, is sometimes anxious to demonstrate his power if presented with a first pitch mistake. Alec had seen him do it before in major league games. Now was the time to hit some corners.

Given these particular circumstances, Alec did not consider himself to be at a disadvantage at all. Instead, he thought himself to be at an advantage because he had seen Furcal bat hundreds of times. Furcal had never seen him pitch until today, though Lorenzo knew him well and, surely, information was exchanged. Alec stood on the mound thinking two things. First, do not throw a fastball near the strike zone and, second, he cannot hit a down and inside curveball. The dad is thinking; please do not throw the curveball because if it hangs over the middle of the plate, the ball is going back right where it came from. Off the bat of a major leaguer, it may not be easy to get out of the way. He needed to go back to school that day, not to a hospital emergency room. Thank God, they were using wood bats.

The biggest difference between this inning and the very first inning he pitched as a little leaguer for the Norcross Dixie Youth Blue Jays on April 21, 1993, a mere eleven years, seven months, and seven days previous, was that this time his father was not worried about coverages. The kid knew how to play his position, cover bases, and back up plays. Other than that, just about everything else was the same including my position behind the backstop, charting pitches, while wishing I had a video camera. Who knew this was going to happen? The kid was calm as could be as the ball came back into the infield from Odalis along with some quick encouragements from around the diamond. Situational awareness had set in, everywhere. He gloved the toss from third, spit to the right, adjusted the cap, stood tall on the rubber, and looked in for the sign.

The first pitch was a straight change-up on the outside corner at the knees; swing, a miss, strike one. I could imagine Furcal thinking something like this:

"What the heck is this kid doing throwing me that change-up on the first pitch? Doesn't he know who I am! He must think he's Glavine or something. Yea, let's see that change-up again."

Next came the breaking ball, big and wide, starting way outside, batter gives up, and in it comes, nipping the outside corner at the knees once again.

"Steee-rike two!"

My goodness, the dream situation cannot be unfolding as it seems to be. He has Furcal 0-2. The brain cannot race fast enough to accommodate the accelerating flow of information, as it were, being more like the telemetry during the launch of a Saturn V rocket.

Rodriguez calls for another breaking ball, motioning with the mitt to keep it down, down, down. Please, keep it down. The batter looks long, he takes, ball one in the dirt. Furcal is probably thinking,

"I don't swing at that stuff no matter what the count is. You got to throw the fastball sometime."

Thus, the set-up is done. Yes, indeed, he has set-up Rafael Furcal. Now he has to go get him. He has to finish what he started. Two strikes really amount to nothing unless the job is completed, until this at bat and the inning is over.

For the next pitch, with a 1-2 count, every option was available. Waste another hook in the dirt; change-up away; fastball up. Almost anything was good, anything except a curveball starting belt-high, middle-in, and breaking down-and-in. Remembering this was not some Sunday afternoon beer-leaguer, the curve would be a great choice only if perfectly thrown. However, it did not have to happen on this pitch. Perhaps some discretion was in order? Not a good time to be greedy when another one can be thrown away, maybe hit the corner, maybe get a weakly hit grounder off the end of the bat from an ill-timed swing.

Alec knew there was no way anyone could throw a fastball strike by Furcal in this situation, not Randy Johnson, not Dontrell Willis, and certainly not Alec Barnes. He had seen the change and the curve, got the spin and the speed. Whatever the pitch, he would pick it up. A strikeout was nearly impossible. This was not Andruw Jones, who came by earlier, but could not stay to play, where a good screwball could get him chasing away. He assumed that the ball would be hit if it were anywhere close to the strike zone. To avoid the extra base hit, no, to avoid the ball landing five hundred feet away down on Buford Highway, he had to forget the fastball. The best chance for an out was to get him to chase something down, away, and off-speed. This would probably make him pound it into the dirt, a grounder that would most likely go to either the second baseman or third baseman, depending on the swing, hands leading or following.

With only a few seconds to think about it he spits to the right, adjusts the cap, looks in for the sign, and starts the windup as Rodriguez moves inside. Why is he going over there? The right foot falls back taking weight allowing the left foot to lift a little and fall again to tap the rubber lightly as a trigger before it settles into the dirt hole carved out by steel cleats in front of the rubber. Right leg up, drop, turn, square, drive, stride, pull, release. Oh, no. It cannot be. He is not trying for contact. He is going for the strikeout. This is not at all the smart thing to do. This is Rafael Furcal. It is the curveball, again, though this time starting middle-in and belt high. For a split second, it looks like a hanging breaking ball, like a repeat of the ball he threw to Scott Neilsen that was hit back at him during the Red/Blue game. The bat was coming around, swung by great experience and awesome skill, inflicting panic to my whole being as there could be only one of a few outcomes, the worst being the most likely. The split second between the time the event began and would presently end afforded barely enough time to twitch and none to react except to think, "No!" as in, why did he throw that pitch? Why a curveball in? To Furcal. It was not moving. The worst thing was about to happen.

The worst thing did not happen. It takes a seventy mph curve ball about one-half second to travel from the pitcher's hand to the front edge of home plate. The split second of horror passed, nightmare averted. The baseball bit tightly in the late autumn air, it broke after all, wickedly late, and traveled unmolested into the catcher's mitt six inches inside at the height of an ankle; swing, a miss, strike three, the bat discarded in disgust, the eruption of chatter from everywhere expressing a collective disbelief as the sides began to change. It was a perfectly thrown baseball. Three up, three down. No runs, no hits, no errors, nobody left.

Marco Rodriguez was a baseball genius. He proved it every time he played. He and Alec had known each other for several years, ever since he first played in the Hispanic League. They had played against each other and they had been teammates so he had caught Alec in the past. Before taking the field for this game, they discussed strategy. Marco was a little more familiar with most of these batters so he had much input in deciding what to throw. Before the game started the two of them were on the same page, as Alec testified afterwards, agreeing what they should do. Once the game started, Marco put down the signs and Alec threw the baseball. Their success was determined by the level of their thought processes and cooperation, most of that occurring before the game. Execution was, as it needs to be in baseball, assumed. Getting good batters out is definitely a two-man job.

The batter he just faced was Rafael Furcal of the Atlanta Braves. Did he forget who the batter was while he was pitching? No. He did not forget who the batter was; he forgot who the pitcher was. Actually, there was no need to remember who the pitcher was just as there was no need to remember how to throw the baseball. He just knew how to do it. Amazingly, the situation did not interrupt his thinking while pitching, nor did it alter his mechanics. They figured out what they wanted to throw, and then he threw it. Simple. This was just another batter except that he knew this batter very well, having seen him many times on television and at Turner Field. He and Marco simply used what they knew to get Furcal out.

The result of the last pitch for the strikeout, though, surprised him, actually shocked him, because that 1-2 pitch was designed to induce a grounder to third base if he timed his swing, or to second base if he did not. For some reason the pitch broke more than either Alec, Rodriguez, or Furcal expected. It fooled the dad, as well. The timing of the swing appeared to be just a little bit off, too. Without showing this batter a fastball, Alec struck out one of baseball's premier leadoff men with just movement and location. There was a lesson in there somewhere, taught to him long before this day, on this very same field, by Ro Fitten, a lesson that the kid had learned for keeps.

Jesse Garcia was the first to dart over and slap gloves with him. He exclaimed,

"You just struck out Furcal!"

Odalis Perez, who had the very best view up the middle, hurried in from center field with his congratulations,

"Do you know you just struck out Furcal?"

Jesse and Odalis behaved as if they were otherwise teammates of Furcal, which, of course, they had been for years with the Braves. Therefore, this occasion contained its own separate significance for them. I wandered over, stuck my head inside the dugout for no longer than two seconds, and saw him chatting with Rodriguez, Garcia, and Perez and said,

"I guess you realize what you just did."

He nodded with a constricted smile. Realizing this was a conversation in which I had no business taking part, an immediate pull back was in order. Only real baseball players needed to participate here. Marco could be consulted later to verify the pitch calling, to find out exactly what they were thinking. I then returned to the backstop, in front of the scoring box, exactly where I sat with Hankins during the Red/Blue game years before, to watch this other pitcher about whom everyone was so enthusiastic. He was still in high school, very young and very good, though he needed a little more work to make his skill match his considerable ability. Even so, not much can exceed the satisfaction gained from watching another youngster in the process of learning how to play this magnificent game.

Alec was truly not in perfect form that day, but he was not off by very much. Though he had thrown the baseball nearly every day all year, he had pitched only about ten innings since summer, about half of those the week before. Most of the time he was in school trying to finish his course work so he could graduate in good shape. During the next two innings he gave up one run on a homer to Carty, on an 0-2 pitch no less, that should not have been anywhere close to the strike zone, just a big mistake, a lapse in concentration that was not missed.

"Are you forgetting some of these guys are professional ballplayers? Didn't you know that was Rico Carty?"

"Oh, is that who it was? Why didn't you tell me?"

The rest of the batters made outs; fly balls to center and left, a grounder to second and to third, and two to the shortstop. Garcia made a throwing error on his first chance allowing the runner to reach base. That generated some entertaining multi-lingual chatter, too. No problem, Alec picked the runner off when he leaned a bit too far in the wrong direction. Good thing, too, since it was immediately before Carty smacked that 0-2 pitch. Maybe the pick-off, along with all of the other successes, had created some hubris. I knew there was something in his training we had not covered. Greek Tragedy! How in the world was that overlooked?

Batting ninth in the pitcher's spot, the lefty's turn came up in the bottom of the second inning. Their pitcher was being knocked around a bit as soon as the home team's batters had timed his fastball, which did not take very long. Alec swung way late on the first pitch, a good heater, up and in. It takes a pass or two to adjust to ninety-plus mph. The second pitch was the same and so was the result, although he was not quite as late on the swing. This young right-hander, now somewhat perturbed, wanted to finish off Alec quickly. The third pitch came, another fastball though more toward the outer half of the plate that could have been expected to be strike three. It was not. Alec had this one timed, leveling the bat while lining it hard, a very well hit ball, although directly at the right fielder, caught for the third out before he had made three steps out of the batter's box. Even so, the kid was on his game this day.

Pitching in the fourth inning, with a good lead and everything going well, he was looking forward to facing Furcal again. So was everyone else in the ballpark, which contained an ever-increasing crowd by this time. He knew Furcal was anxious to make some big corrections to his first plate appearance. It may have been the same Rafael Furcal the second time around, but he stepped up to the plate with a different attitude, a new determination, having been fortified by all the taunting remarks mercilessly thrown around by several of the players, especially by shortstop Garcia and center fielder Perez. Carty mostly just smiled, but added a jibe every once in a while. The stands had been filling up all the while with spectators, but, in truth, everyone in the dugout was a spectator, too. Not so for the dad, he was involved. By this time, even the late arrivals knew about the last at bat and they were anxious to see what would happen the next time around. Nearly everyone at the ballpark knew both men.

"Hey, I know that pitcher. He struck out Furcal?"

Recalling the first time these two faced each other, it was at the beginning of a friendly pick-up game. They were all there to have some fun on a warm, late fall Georgia afternoon. Now it was no more a friendly pick-up game. It was not any kind of a game. Both men knew this was a duel, a personal one, at that. Alec assumed correctly that Furcal would be determined to hit the ball and to hit it very hard. He would deposit any pitching mistake on the other side of *Plaza Latina* into the traffic on Buford Highway. Did this worry the left-handed pitcher? Nope, a batter with such an attitude will find it used against him. There would be no fastballs thrown that Furcal could reach without a ten-foot pole and a footstool. None. Not a chance. The sequence had to change from the first time, but one thing would be the same, he would not allow himself even to think about a strikeout. Once again, he wanted ill-timed contact.

First pitch here was a change-up in the dirt, taken for a ball, and the advantage went quickly to Furcal, or so it would seem. Actually, being ahead in the count allowed Furcal to think he had the advantage, that it was more likely he would see a fastball strike, and that he could afford to swing from the heels, really launch one. The next pitch came; another change-up starting and staying low, over the outer edge of the plate. It had just enough fade that the murderous swing produced only a foul tip off the end of the bat. In my mind, this brought the question of throwing a fastball to the forefront. At some point, the batter's timing would correct if more speed change were not utilized.

The absolute speed of a fastball is only relevant at the very top of the range, say ninety-five mph or higher. Less than that, whether it is Odalis Perez throwing at ninety-one mph, Tom Glavine at eighty-five mph, or Alec Barnes at eighty mph, only the relative speed has importance. The difference in speed from one pitch to the other is what contributes most to the effectiveness of all the pitches. A pitcher must remember at all times, hitting is timing. Speed change upsets timing.

The upcoming 1-1 pitch was now purely academic. Furcal must have figured that if this pitcher was ever going to throw his fastball, this was the time. Alec and Marco figured differently. They figured it best to take a chance right then, not to get a strike necessarily, but to get a grounder. To get this at bat over with right then was very desirable. The batter must be looking for the fastball and the fastball would not be thrown. Instead, they decided to give him the same pitch with which they collected strike three the first time around, the curveball going down and in. Once again, it yielded the exact same result, a swing, a miss, and just as ugly. Furcal was missing this pitch by a foot or more. I could not believe it, not twice in a row. His timing was off, too, a result of being overanxious, I would guess. Once again, the chatter, full of good-humored, but less than well-intentioned, remarks emanated from the dugouts and from around the diamond. Could this local pitcher possibly strike out Furcal again? It seemed to me to be nearly impossible, though what I thought did not matter. What did the pitcher think?

Anything can happen in baseball. Every incremental occurrence creates a new situation, each one presenting a different challenge. Furcal thrust his wood bat at the fence behind the on-deck area in disgust, strode over, and grabbed a metal bat. Oh, my God! The situation had escalated beyond what could be considered casual or friendly. The puck had hit the ice, one might say, and the gloves were coming off. Pick-up game or not, these were not only accomplished baseball players, these were men with enough pride to build cathedrals. What began as a simple, casual, pick-up, sand-lot, baseball game on a Sunday afternoon took on the intensity of a World Series game for the stakes could not be higher, not when egos were involved.

A substantial crowd had gathered, increasingly engaged, nervous and attentive, wondering, estimating, predicting, hoping, what should happen, what could happen, what will happen. Talk about this game would continue for a long time in this community, where every intricate detail would be recalled and repeated, like a form of entertainment, as a movie played over and over again. The point was now passed where the outcome could only be incidental to the situation. Baseball was providing the circumstance to switch-hitting batter Furcal and to lefty pitcher Barnes one more infrequent opportunity to discover the substance of which one is made. This was a test of character.

Returning to the batter's box, Furcal said loudly and clearly,

"You struck me out last time. You're not going to strike me out again."

Words spoken without a smile do seem to be more direct. While making this utterance, Furcal did not smile. Alec never heard him speak, as he was a master of ignoring extraneous remarks while pitching. His focus was on his catcher and the situation; that was all. The major league batter, having determined that it was necessary to grab a metal bat, was reloaded against the lefty. If that ball gets hit back at Alec, he is a goner. Nothing could be done about it, though. These were two grown men. This was their duel. Dads were not allowed to participate except to hope he keeps the ball down and away, or maybe even throw the fastball in a bit and let him turn on it. Who cares? Let him yank one over the left fielder's head. Let him hit the ball over Buford Highway. It would be something to talk about for many years, another good reason to stay alive. Besides, there was another whole box of baseballs left; they could afford to lose one. Just do not throw the curve up there again. Next time it may not break so well. But the way the dad was hoping was not the way the dad had taught the kid to think.

The choice for the next pitch was made in complete deference to the situation, considering what happened in the first at bat, as well as anticipating the next time he might have to face Rafael Furcal. It may be once again this day or it may be in some other game on some other day. A pitcher like Alec remains mindful of everything. If they ever face each other again, whether on another sand lot or at Turner Field, the duel would continue where it left off today at Wingo-Carlyle Field.

The next pitch was the same one he threw for a called strike two during the first at bat, a curveball, breaking down to the outside corner at the knees. If Furcal recognized it, he would definitely reach for it and not let it go by, especially if it might catch some of the plate. He would not mind fouling it off, either, just to buy another chance to see "his pitch." In that case, Alec would have a good set-up to go inside, or to stay away again. No matter what, Furcal could not afford to take this pitch with two strikes if it was anywhere close to the strike zone, and risk a called third strike.

Throwing this same outside curveball was a safe pitch in that, other than fouling it off, there was not much productive use Furcal could make of it, unless he was already leaning in. Following the last one inside, he should not be leaning at all, being left to guard against another pitch in the same location. Alec had made the point rather emphatically, he would come inside at will. Staying away, if Furcal swung, most likely he would do one of two things: punch it to the right side, maybe dropping it in for a base hit, or try to pull it. Hitting it to Garcia playing shortstop would be a certain out. The outside curveball was not a pitch he could normally drive with too much authority. Realistically, Rafael Furcal was not Kirk Gibson, just as Alec Barnes was not Dennis Eckersley.

It would have been nice if the situation remained solely between the pitcher and batter. However, this day, during this friendly pick-up game, there was much verbal interplay going on between the players, especially the pros. It was all done in good humor and there was not a hint of animosity anywhere. However, even within a light-hearted environment among friends, when pride and subterfuge help define the duel between men, something has to give. The honest application of skill and cunning just could not be left alone to decide the outcome. After all, this was baseball, the best game ever devised by man.

Furcal was in the unenviable position of being set up in a way that he could not succeed no matter what he did. He had to depend on this little-known, local left-handed pitcher to help him a little bit. Alec set the table, got the count to 1-2 on this increasingly frustrated batter, and was in the middle of completing the task when, of all things, Garcia intervened. First, the usual routine: the spit, the cap, the look in. Rodriguez gives the sign. Suddenly, as Alec went into his windup, the catcher moving right, the unusual occurred. Garcia called out the pitch to Furcal. The ball was released; the little white dot verified the spin of a breaking ball, outside, Furcal probably thinking,

"I've got it this time!"

The notification got him looking and leaning. Recognizing the pitch right away and reaching, he snapped the light-weight metal bat around sending a very high fly ball towards a point to the left of straight away center field, but he did not get it all.

"He skied it!"

Alec thought at first it would be caught for an out. So did Furcal. So did everyone else. On second thought, this was a metal bat and a short fence, the ball having been hit with major league wrists; suddenly, topping the arc, it looked like it had a chance. It did. He turned to watch as it cleared the fence in left-center by about ten or fifteen feet, about three hundred sixty feet away from home. Before Furcal realized it was going to be a home run, he threw his bat down in disgust on the way to first base, thinking he had missed it. As it cleared the fence, he took on a more triumphant demeanor, head held higher, a stern glare, and tightened jaw, as if he knew all along that it would get out, and just in time as all eyes present returned their focus on the base runner. All eyes, that is, except of the dad whose managerial glances shifted back and forth throughout.

Alec smiled because he knew he did not get beat, not in truth. He also knew that he and Rafael had sort of evened the score, which was fine with him. At least Furcal had saved face publicly, so they could still leave as friends. Furcal hit a home run over a not very deep fence. With a wood bat, he would have been out, even at Wingo-Carlyle Field. By rights, this major leaguer swinging a metal bat should have parked the ball way down the hill into traffic over five hundred feet away from home. That would have made a statement, one that would have greatly pleased the assembled and genuinely corrected the humiliation of the earlier strikeout. However, he was not given the chance. This pitcher was not about to throw a pitch that would have allowed Furcal to hit the ball in that manner.

Back on the field, the hoots and the howls continued from shortstop, center field, the dugouts, and elsewhere, as Garcia's purpose was now apparent. I was relieved that my kid was still alive, glad to see him smiling about the fact that this very good major leaguer did no better than a routine fly ball with a metal bat and a tip on the last pitch. The final and most important point of pride not to be overlooked, though it be subtle, was that Alec never gave in to Furcal. No matter what else happened in this game or in any other game, this fact alone put this young man into the big leagues of life.

It was the fourth inning, time for player rotations as some other players had shown up by that time, all wanting to pitch or play with the special participants. Alec did have to get back to Valdosta with exams looming and the day getting long. When the inning ended, he walked off the mound with the lead, packed his stuff, and said his good byes to his newest major league teammates first, followed by a visit to the other dugout where pitcher greeted batters all, politely making new acquaintances. Then he got into the Volvo wagon and left, I am sure smiling and smirking all the way back to school while replaying in his mind every pitch of the day.

I stayed and watched the rest of the game, actually chatting more than watching. It was unlikely there would be another pick-up game here before a lot of these fellows had to report for spring training. The kid who started for the other team left after fourth innings, too. From this point on, the quality of the game deteriorated noticeably, becoming more like an after-church Sunday softball game. Without good pitchers, baseball is not an interesting game at all. Those who think that more offense is what makes baseball more interesting are wrong. Good pitching, backed by a solid defense, is what makes this game the greatest game of all.

By staying, I was afforded another opportunity to speak with all the fellows more at length between innings. The best time to catch professional ballplayers is during the off-season when there is no playing pressure, at least there is not supposed to be. These fellows, in spite of all their fame, stayed around, too, as if they were part of our usual pick-up crowd, which they were. Good sports, all of them. The ease with which they demonstrated their major league skills was always fascinating to see from field level. However, much more than that, the comfortable way in which they demonstrated their love and respect for the game of baseball was even more inspiring. A pick-up game on a crummy field with anyone who shows up keeps everyone, even major leaguers, in touch with the simple joys of playing the great game of baseball.

The best way to summarize this day's events it is to say that the only significant difference between this pick-up game and the pick-up games we had as kids growing up in Springfield Forest in the early 1960's was that we were merely young kids back then; this game had older kids. Everything else was just about the same. Well, maybe these guys had somewhat better skills, too.

After returning from his exams, there was almost no talk about that game. All that Alec wanted to talk about was what he had planned for Furcal the next time he faced him. First pitch would be the old curveball, outside at the knees. Whether a ball or a strike, the next pitch would be the fastball, also down and away. He had to show him the fastball next time, to let him know he was not afraid to throw it.

"Then it gets a little complicated," depending upon the count:

2-0: Look at the batter's stance. If he is leaning, pound him inside up on his hands. Hit him if necessary. No leaning allowed, *never again*.

1-1: Stay away. If he swung at the first fastball and his timing was off, stay with the fastball away. If his timing was on, go to the curve or a change-up away.

0-2: do not waste a pitch. If he fouled off the fastball, give him the same thing a few inches outside the zone. If he missed the fastball, throw the curve down, even in the dirt if there are no base runners.

If the situation is reached that calls for an out pitch, not necessarily a strikeout pitch, just any out pitch, there are two possibilities: get him to pull an outside change-up or outside curve; or get him to pound out the down-and-in curve. Under no circumstances would he throw a second fastball inside the strike zone.

While on the subject, what about the rest of the Braves line-up? He said he wished Andruw Jones had been able to stay, would have been "no problem."

"How about Chipper Jones?"

"That's a tough out!"

Am I hearing this? No longer in a position to doubt, there remained only the pride associated with discovering the student had acquired sufficient wisdom to instruct his teacher. Was I qualified to be in the same dugout with him anymore? Or even in the same league? No. Not any longer.

# Epilogue

A man seeks to become President of the United States for one of two reasons. Either he wants to be something or he wants to do something. The nature of any young man's dream, the motivation to attain a certain goal, can take on either one of these two forms. The little leaguer dreaming of making it to the big leagues is no exception. In the first instance, he can dream of crossing the white chalk line onto the surface of a diamond in a major league ballpark; standing there in all that glory, in front of a large crowd; knowing that after one pitch is thrown his name will be in the major league baseball encyclopedia forever, just like Archibald Graham.

In the second instance, he dreams of standing in the batters' box and staring down a major league pitcher, or conversely, standing on the mound and staring down a major league batter.

In one, he seeks the glory of being on the stage; in the second, he seeks the satisfaction that comes from the performance. Nearly all major league ballplayers have experienced both.

Doc Graham, who played just half an inning of a major league game, but never touched a ball or bat, realized the first dream, but not the second. Given the choice, he would rather have had the second one. Just once, he said, he would have liked to stand in the batters' box and face a major league pitcher.

Alec realized the second dream, not the first. He had no choice in the matter since this decision seems to have been made by the Almighty, not due to any lack of effort. There would be no line in any book of baseball players, no public media mention, no long-term contract for big bucks, just a job well done with its concurrent intangible reward. It was meant to be this way.

A young baseball player keeps playing with the hope that someday he will make it to the big leagues. Very, very few get there, and fewer still stay there very long. So many unlikely events have to occur it is almost ridiculous to expect that it will happen. Even so, a conscientious attempt to prepare for this possibility is never ridiculous. Any endeavor a man may choose, any goal for which a man may strive, if an opportunity is offered while he is yet unprepared, lifelong regrets will ensue. Far better is it to be well prepared, thus avoiding the haunting nightmares of grief.

Baseball may be a kids' game, but it requires a man-size resolve to play it well. Baseball playing men want to be recognized; they are dying to be called upon to perform; all they want is a chance. Wherever a player happens to be on the road to the big leagues, whether in the little league, on the school team, in the minor leagues, or on some local sandlot, he never knows when the call may come, or even if it will come. However, one thing is certain: there will be no time to get ready after the call comes.

"Hey, kid. You feel like pitching in the major leagues today? Here's the ball. You warm?"